Human J[illegible]

The eye of the beholder

Human Judgment

The eye of the beholder

Donald Laming
University of Cambridge

THOMSON™
Australia • Canada • Mexico • Singapore • Spain • United Kingdom • United States

THOMSON

Human Judgment

For more information, contact Thomson Learning, High Holborn House, 50–51 Bedford Row, London, WC1R 4LR or visit us on the World Wide Web at: http://www.thomsonlearning.co.uk

---

British Library Cataloguing-in-Publication Data
A catalogue record for this book is available from the British Library

---

ISBN 1-86152-777-2

First edition 2004

Typeset by Photoprint, Torquay, Devon

Printed in Hong Kong by C & C Offset Printing Co., Ltd

Beauty is in the eye of the beholder.

(Proverb, mid-18th century. Oxford Dictionary of Quotations, p. 595)

Contents

List of figures

List of tables

Preface

This book has grown out of a course of seventeen lectures that I used to give each year to students at the University of Cambridge under the title *Human Judgment*. The *raison d'être* of these lectures is roughly this.

A hundred and forty years of studying judgments in the psychological laboratory has provided two broad conclusions. First, people are generally poor at judgments of single stimuli by themselves; relationships between stimuli are much more accurately discerned. Indeed, the assessment of the magnitude of a single stimulus by itself, without any measuring instrument like a scale pan or a ruler, is much poorer than is generally supposed. At very best no more than five categories can be distinguished without error. This means that the subjects in laboratory experiments are often unsure of what the correct judgment is – and this leads to the second broad conclusion. In such an uncertain state of mind people are unable to resist extraneous suggestion. Most of the time people are unaware that they have been influenced; that just makes the influence all the more pervasive.

Now, the people who volunteer to serve in psychological experiments are some of the same people who populate the world outside; and if they are unable to make accurate judgments in the laboratory, when they know that their responses are to be analysed, they will not be able to do any better in the course of their everyday lives. So, those experiments that tell us about the limits to the accuracy of human judgment and the vulnerability of people to outside influence provide a basis for understanding a wide variety of events in the world outside. They provide an insight into art and literature, into advertising and religion, into child protection and the marking of examinations, into identification by eyewitnesses. These are all topics that capture the national newspaper headlines from time to time, topics about which people ask questions. *Human Judgment* provides some answers.

Colloquially, *Human Judgment* is about how people make up their minds. It presents a scientific study of social behaviour, even if an unconventional one. It is not an alternative to conventional social psychology, but a complement, because the domains of behaviour that this book opens up to examination are those which social psychology has usually found it difficult to study. To put the issue succinctly, the idea that the nature of our society is constrained by what its members can, and cannot, do leads to a whole new line of enquiry.

Human Judgment is an easy-to-read introduction to this new line of enquiry. Some technicalities, especially the correlation of successive judgments in

Chapter 5, cannot be avoided. That pattern of correlation tells us so much, and so powerfully, about the limitations of human judgment, that it cannot be omitted. But, I hasten to point out, the treatment here is still very much simpler than the account I have previously given in Chapter 10 of *The Measurement of Sensation*. If this new line of enquiry be pursued far enough, further, more complex questions arise from the manner in which sequences of judgments – successive diagnoses by a doctor would be one example – link together in a chain. But this introductory book deliberately stops short of that point.

In the course of preparing both my lectures and this book I have been assisted in many ways by many different people, who have drawn my attention to this story or suggested I look at that source. It is impracticable to name them all and invidious to name only some, but their help is gratefully acknowledged. At a more practical level, I thank the staff of the Cambridge Public Reference Library for their assistance over many years in looking up many minor details in newspapers, encyclopaedias and other sources. I would also like to thank Gemma Jackman and Helen and John Patrick for their meticulous reading of my draft manuscript, and the editorial team at Thomson Learning – Anna Faherty, Fiona Freel, Geraldine Lyons, Andrew McAleer and Melody Woollard – for their encouragement and support. Finally, my thanks are due to Angela Cole for preparing the transcripts of the television documentaries and to Ian Cannell for the photographs in Figures 11.5 and 16.5.

Donald Laming
Cambridge 2003

1 The eye of the beholder

Some problems for the eye of the beholder

This book is about how people make up their minds. That is something we all of us do, many times, every day.

Suppose you are going out for the evening: what are you going to wear?

You first go to a bar: what are you going to drink?

You then go on to a theatre: why this theatre, this show?

Ordinarily, I cannot tell why you choose as you do. I cannot read your innermost thoughts. No one can know what you are thinking, unless you tell them. So, how can there be a book about how people make up their minds? This is how –.

There is a picture for sale at auction. The painter is unknown, but is thought to be Italian, nineteenth century. The picture is knocked down for £170. Six months later the picture is auctioned again and this time it fetches £380 000! What is the difference? The difference is that in the intervening six months it has been identified as the work of a Renaissance master. This is an episode of a kind that happens from time to time in the art world and it tells us that the market price of a fine painting depends chiefly on who is thought to have painted it, not on how much anyone likes the picture.

It happens with books as well. A best-selling novelist publishes a book under a pseudonym. It doesn't sell. It is ignored by the critics. The author even has trouble finding a publisher! People choose their books according to the name on the dust jacket. They choose their wines according to the recommendations of the wine writers, and their plays and shows according to the reviews of the theatre critics. That is how people make up their minds or, perhaps I should say, have their minds made up for them.

Portrait of a gentleman in a red hat

But let us look at that picture; it is reproduced on the front cover. It shows an old gentleman in a red hat. It was put up for auction by Sotheby's at their Chester auction house on 11 June 1987. It is painted on slate, it measures $41^{1}/_{2}$" × $34^{1}/_{2}$" and, at that time, was unframed. It was described as 'Italian School, nineteenth century, estimate £200 to £300'. That was a little hopeful for so dull and lacklustre a picture; it fetched only £170 net of buyer's premium (Checkland, 1987a).

Nevertheless, this portrait is of some interest to us because the purchaser, a dealer named Buffy Parker, took it to Christie's in London for valuation. After some study, Christie's identified the sitter as Pope Clement VII who reigned from 1523 to 1534. This was the Pope who refused to annul the marriage of Henry VIII to Catherine of Aragon and thereby provided political motivation for the Reformation in England. Clement VII was a patron of the arts and commissioned work from Michelangelo and Rafael; he was the patron especially of Sebastiano del Piombo (1485–1547), whom he appointed to the office of the Piombo (Keeper of the leaden seals). Sebastiano worked at the papal court under Michelangelo and became famous for his portraits in oils. He painted this portrait about 1532 and it was sold by Christie's on 11 December 1987 for £380 000 (£418 000 including buyer's premium; Checkland, 1987a).

Some painters display much greater skill and artistry than others and accordingly their work costs much more. Some painters' work is rare or old and that also matters. So it is widely accepted that the work of some painters systematically fetches much higher prices.

But, wait a minute! There is something wrong with that argument. It was a *completed picture* that was for sale, not the services of the painter; and the picture is what it is, whoever is presumed to have painted it. And it was the same picture, the *very same* objet d'art, in the same physical condition, that had been auctioned six months previously at Chester. It was not that in the course of cleaning a restorer had discovered a Renaissance masterpiece underneath a nineteenth-century nonentity. The painting had not been touched. Let us do a little arithmetic.

Price of the painting attributed to Sebastiano del Piombo	£380 000
Price of the painting unattributed	£170
Value of the attribution to Sebastiano, in the abstract	£379 830

Why should the value of the attribution be worth more than 2200 times the painting itself? Does it not matter what a painting looks like? – merely who is presumed to have painted it? Suppose the painting had been a uniform blue all over? Who is going to pay £380 000 for a canvas painted a uniform ultramarine? In fact, if the ultramarine had been sprayed on the canvas by Yves Klein, the painting would cost rather more than £380 000. One of Yves Klein's blue monochrome paintings was auctioned by Sotheby's in July 1987 for £638 000 (Norman, 1987). So what is going on? There is a problem here of which we must not lose sight.

Suppose you are on vacation in Paris; you go to the Louvre and look at Leonardo da Vinci's *Mona Lisa*. You know what kind of comments other people have poured on this famous painting. You know what you should say yourself, if you wish to appear to have some artistic appreciation; in particular, you know what not to say, if you do not want to appear a Philistine. So, if I am listening to what you are saying about the *Mona Lisa* (that is, if you comment at all), I am unable to tell whether you are saying what you do say from a genuine aesthetic appreciation of Leonardo's painting, or whether you are simply reiterating comments that you have heard from others. By the same token, neither you nor

I are able to tell whether the art expert has a genuine aesthetic appreciation or is likewise borrowing his or her comments – until, that is, a picture becomes separated from its provenance. Then we can see how much of an expert's comment reflects the aesthetics of the picture and how much is borrowed from the reputation of the painter. What the story of Sebastiano del Piombo's portrait and other similar episodes tell us is that the expert's valuation is mostly borrowed. In that case, how can we have a science of aesthetics? And if there is no science of aesthetics, how can a painter acquire a reputation for expert appraisal to borrow from? That is the real problem.

The painting was bought at Christie's auction by Agnew's, a London art dealer, in partnership with Newhouse, art dealers in New York. They had the painting cleaned. Adam Williams, of Newhouse, said 'It was pitch black in 1987. We took a huge risk. If it cleaned like a dog, you'd be dead.' (Norman, 1991) They then sold it to the Getty Museum for more than £4m. Now, looking back at the front cover, you can see what a fine portrait it is.

'Diary of a Good Neighbour' by Jane Somers

This sort of thing happens with books as well. Doris Lessing has been described as one of the world's great living writers. Her books often sell 500 000 copies. In the spring of 1983 she published *Diary of a Good Neighbour*, not under her own name, but under a pseudonym, Jane Somers. Jane Somers, 'Janna', is the narrator of the story. She is a journalist in her late forties working on a glossy magazine for women. One day she strikes up an improbable relationship with a poor and very old woman and somehow comes to feel responsible for her. So here is a novel about the plight of the very old urban poor.

Doris Lessing had personal reasons at that time for not publishing under her own name. In a television interview she explained:

> I'd wanted for a long time to write a book under another name, and I couldn't write this book under my own name because there were people – various old people then alive who are now dead – I couldn't at that time write under my own name. (Eichler, 1984)

Doris Lessing was concerned about the difficulties which new authors have in getting their first novel published:

> I sent from Rhodesia short stories that were rejected. When I came here the same short stories, after I'd had a novel accepted, were accepted. They were the same short stories; and in America the *New Yorker* turned down with ordinary rejection slips two of my short stories, and somebody else wrote to me and said she had recommended – it was Nadine Gordimer [winner of a recent Nobel prize for literature] actually – that the *New Yorker* should look at my short stories. I sent the two short stories back and they accepted one. (Eichler, 1984)

Doris Lessing agreed with her agent that the manuscript of *Diary of a Good Neighbour*, about 120 000 words, should be sent out to her usual publishers

(Jonathan Cape and Granada) as a first novel by 'a well-known woman journalist writing under a pseudonym'. Both publishers turned the book down. But it was eventually accepted by Michael Joseph where a senior editor commented, 'This reminds me of the young Doris Lessing'. Early in 1983 nineteen proof copies were sent to literary people – regular reviewers, BBC producers, editors – hoping that some at least would be impressed. Only two responded enthusiastically. After publication most reviewers ignored the book. It was offered to eight paperback houses, but none would take it. As of 23 September 1984, when the true authorship of the book was revealed, it had sold only 2000 hardback copies (Tomalin and Witherow, 1984).

We accept that some people can write very well indeed, and others less well, and that the very good writers enjoy much larger sales because of the quality of their writing. But, wait another minute! That cannot be correct. If professionals – publishers, their readers, book reviewers and critics – are unable to recognise good writing when it is put before them, then neither can you or I. And if neither you nor I can recognise good writing when we see it, how can the books we buy depend on the quality of the writing? Quality of writing cannot be the reason for Doris Lessing's sales, nor for those of any other writer. So what makes a book sell? The author's reputation, obviously. Indeed, when the story broke, Penguin, one of the eight paperback houses who had previously rejected the book, quickly snapped up the rights (PHS, 1984). But how does an author acquire that kind of reputation? That is another problem of which we must not lose sight, and the next story – about wine – suggests the beginning of an explanation.

Robert Parker and 'The Wine Advocate'

There are a small number of people, the wine writers, who earn their living from writing about wine and, especially, from recommending wines to drink. Robert Parker publishes a newsletter, *The Wine Advocate*, every two months in which he evaluates as many as 600 wines, giving each a tasting note and a score from 50 to 100. He tastes his wines 'blind', comparing wines of a similar type against each other, without knowing either the price or the name of the producer or grower. The most repugnant of all wines scores 50, and the most glorious, perfect gustatory experience 100. (This is the grading system used in American schools.) This is an exemplary way to compare them, and Robert Parker's ratings reflect an independent critical look at the wines (Parker, 1987, pp. 11–12).

The selling power of Parker's points system is phenomenal. Eloi Dürrbach, of the previously unknown Provence estate, Domaine de Trévallon, found that a score of 92 brought with it 3 am phone calls from antipodean wine agents anxious to import the latest Parker discovery. And Charles de Nonancourt, of the little-known champagne house of Delamotte, found his sudden surge of American imports inexplicable – until he saw the August 1987 *Advocate*. 'If it scores 90 plus you can't buy it, and if it scores below 85 you can't sell it.' (MacQuitty, 1987).

Steven Spurrier, proprietor of the Caves de la Madeleine in Paris, said: 'He's so powerful, he can make or break a market for a vintage, and a producer. It's dangerous. There should be room for another opinion.' (Robinson, 1986). In France they refer to him as the Pope of the wine industry, while his book, the *Wine Buyer's Guide*, is known as 'the Bible'. The motto on a cushion given to him by his agent reads 'When Parker spits, the world listens'. He inspires such fear that his name has even spawned a new adjective in the French viticultural vocabulary: *parkérisation* (Lang, 1998).

In the first two stories, about Sebastiano del Piombo's portrait of Pope Clement VII and Doris Lessing's *Diary of a Good Neighbour* (and there are many others similar), experts appeared unable to assess the value of the painting or the literary merit of the writing without knowing who had painted it or who had written the book. It is as though they were borrowing their opinions from the reputation of the artist and the writer. Ordinary people do just the same with wine. But how is it that one man can come to exercise such influence over the preferences of people who have never so much as met him? Why do people not try the wines for themselves and make up their own minds what they like? That is another problem we must think about, though this one is relatively easy and will be answered in the very next chapter.

Clive Barnes, theatre critic for the New York Times

It is not only preferences for wine that are borrowed in this way. The theatre-going public in New York borrow their preferences too, which shows to go and see and which to pass by. From 1965 to 1977 the 'expert' was Clive Barnes, theatre and ballet critic for the *New York Times*, who is English by birth. It was said of him that he 'could make or break a Broadway show' (Mercer, 1978). In the title of a television documentary he was described as *The Most Powerful Briton in America* (Segrave, 1971).

There were other theatre critics in New York, but, in those days, Clive Barnes was 'the big one'. At that time New York was reduced to just three morning papers, the *New York Times*, the *Daily News*, and the *Wall Street Journal*. Most theatre-goers in New York read the *Times* and what its theatre critic said had immense influence. 'Directors make a point of taking his likes and dislikes into account, and have even been known to calculate where he will be sitting on the opening night, so that he can see things at their best.' (Strafford, 1976).

> His word is more or less law as far as we are concerned. The *Times* is the best read paper, it's the most respected paper, and usually what he says goes.
>
> Without the affirmation of the *New York Times*, you know, you are not going to get your money back on the production – that's about what it amounts to.
>
> It's always up to the critics in the end, and I am very wary of them constantly. (Neil Simon, playwright, in Segrave, 1971)

> On a straight play, a serious drama – sadly enough, Mr. Barnes is the last word. (David Merrick, producer, in Segrave, 1971)

> If you get panned by him I think you would think he was a Nazi. If you get a good review from him you just think he's God with an English accent. (Mart Crowley, playwright, in Segrave, 1971)

On 14 April 1968 Mart Crowley's first play, *The Boys in the Band*, opened in New York. Clive Barnes praised it. It ran for 1002 performances in New York and then transferred to London. It earned its author over $500 000 in royalties.

> Barnes was a monstrous disaster on the part of the *New York Times*, but I feel it's – it's an inconceivable mistake which the *Times* being a very arrogant paper is happy to continue with. (William Goldman, author and playwright, in Segrave, 1971)

At the time of the television broadcast (Segrave, 1971) Stuart Duncan had recently produced Eugene O'Neill's *A Long Day's Journey into Night*.

> This particular kind of a play, of course, appeals to the kind of audience that reads the *New York Times*. It's as simple as that. And Mr Barnes obviously writes for that paper, and what he says is read by the million people that will go to see this show. What the other critics say – well, sure it's always nice to have everybody love you. But the fact of the matter is that the people who come to this kind of show are the people who read Mr Barnes. No, it's not terribly important. It's just that if he doesn't say the right kind of things, we're dead. (Segrave, 1971)

The television programme attempted to portray the anxieties, the tensions and the tenterhooks of the cast of *Long Day's Journey into Night* as they waited after their first performance to discover what Clive Barnes would say. 'Come on Clive, for Christ's sake.' 'He's a little late.' 'No he's not.' Someone, quite illegally, telephones with the review before it goes to press.

> Three column head. . . . A rousing *Long Day's Journey*. . . . A great play, a superlative performance – this is an evening that should most certainly be experienced. It is no ordinary theatrical occasion but one to shout about. [*Applause from the cast.*] You can't have him back, English. (Stuart Duncan, producer, in Segrave, 1971. This and the preceding quotations reproduced with permission from *The Most Powerful Briton in America*, producer B. Segrave. ATV, 25 May 1971. © 1971 Carlton International Media Ltd.)

Why should one man so dominate the New York theatre world? In this instance, we know that Clive Barnes exercised his influence, not because of any personal reputation as a guru of the theatre, but solely because he was theatre critic for the *New York Times*. In 1977 he left the *New York Times* for the *New York Post* and his place at the *New York Times* was taken by Frank Rich. That changeover sets the scene for the comparison of two very different reviews of Rowan Atkinson's one-man show at the Brooks Atkinson Theatre in October 1986. First, Clive Barnes in the *New York Post*:

> The man is funny. Very funny. Hilarious. Side-splitting. Not that I actually saw any sides split, but anyone fearing a certain weakness at the seams should perhaps think twice before going to see 'Rowan Atkinson at the Atkinson.'
>
> . . . to voice my soundest suspicions, he [Rowan Atkinson] is actually an alien from outer space without a green card, and is posing as a British character actor pretending to be a comedian.
>
> He is no stand-up comic – for one thing, he slouches as if his rib-cage had deflated and his pelvis capitulated, and for another he is partial to lying down or simply falling over.
>
> His face is as mobile as an Alexander Calder sculpted in plasticine, and he makes faces with the diligent dexterity of Marcel Marceau. (Barnes, 1986)

And now Frank Rich's remarks in the *New York Times*.

> 'Rowan Atkinson at the Atkinson' – as the show is titled – is the interminable proof that the melding of American and English cultures is not yet complete. As long as the British public maintains its fondness for toilet humor, there will always be an England. Mr. Atkinson is very big on toilet jokes, and he is very big in England. He has starred on the BBC's 'Not the Nine O'Clock News', performed successfully in the West End, and earned the plaudits of highbrow critics. It's not inconceivable that this comic's biggest fans at home are products of an upbringing that encourages boys to tame their nasty bowel habits at an early age, with the consequence that their obsession with alimentary byproducts persists right through Oxford and Cambridge. (Rich, 1986)

'Rowan Atkinson at the Atkinson' was taken off after eight previews and six public performances.

Influence as a critic in the New York theatre world goes with the position of theatre critic of the *New York Times*; it is not personal to the occupant of that post. It is not that either Clive Barnes or Frank Rich were clearly 'right' in their judgments; simply that each in turn occupied the seat of influence. The *New York Times* is the paper that middle-class New York theatre-goers read; that is why that paper's theatre critic is influential. But why should that influence be so overwhelming? There are other theatre critics in New York; why do New York theatre-goers not find some other critic who reflects their own personal preferences? That is another problem we must think about.

Outline of this book

These are four stories that challenge our understanding of how people decide, judge and make up their minds. It is the purpose of this book to provide answers to the problems these stories pose – I shall come back to each of them in its proper place – and other problems beside. I sketch here how I am going to proceed.

In the first place, we need some basic principles, not so much about how people decide, but about limits to the precision of people's judgments. The next chapter begins with a 'Relativity Theory' for people's minds: all judgments are comparisons of one thing with another. There is a similar principle that operates at the level of our perceptions – in the way we see the world. Even worse, we shall see that the comparison of one thing with another in people's judgments is scarcely better than ordinal. We can say that this sound is louder, or softer, or about the same as that one, but that is all. An examination of each of these principles in turn will take us to Chapter 5.

Next comes the 'washing powder' problem. There are, perhaps, a dozen washing powders on the market and a housewife has no opportunity at all to compare any of them against another. So how does she choose which powder to buy? If asked, a housewife might say that she chooses a certain brand because it 'washes whiter', but that is just an advertising slogan. In Chapter 6 we shall examine the psychological basis of the practical knowledge which advertising agencies have built up. That basis will help us to understand why art experts need to know who painted the picture and book reviewers who wrote the book. To put the matter succinctly, the painter's and the writer's names serve as advertisements.

Most decisions that people make are not blind choices like selecting a brand of washing powder. There is some material basis for decision, but not so clear a basis that the judgment is obvious. Weather forecasting, specifically the failure to forecast the wind speed on the night of the great storm in the UK, 15 October 1987, provides a good example. In Chapter 11 I shall examine how these two strands, the comparison with some previous observation and the suggestion put about by advertisement, combine. This combination is important to the social worker worrying about the possibility of child abuse or to the police trying to get an eyewitness to identify a suspect.

Finally, the limited reliability of peoples' judgments and the possibility of errors accumulating from one judgment to another pose the question of how far we can predict the future of human society. The motion of the planets in our solar system can be calculated and predicted with great accuracy; but the vagaries of peoples' judgments mean that the society of tomorrow is forever beyond our purview.

2 Relativity

Let me be up-front and state a basic principle.

There is no absolute judgment. All judgments are comparisons of one thing with another.

In this chapter I look at some experiments and examples which show that the judgment depends on what comparator is available.

In Chapter 1 I introduced Robert Parker, author of *The Wine Advocate*. Because he tastes so many wines and because his scores are so influential, it is widely supposed that he is making absolute assessments of the wines he tastes. Now, many people are diffident about wine and, if you are unsure of your judgment, quoting a recognised authority is safe and comforting. But let us see, first, why people are so diffident about wine and about other things as well. There is an experiment that tells us why.

Absolute judgment of auditory frequency

A pure tone is sounded for 2.5 seconds. It is selected at random from various frequencies, from 2–14 different frequencies in different blocks of trials, arranged geometrically within the range 100–8000 Hz. (This takes us from the G that lies $1\frac{1}{2}$ octaves below middle C on the piano to about an octave above the top end of the keyboard.) The subjects in this experiment were asked to identify the frequency by giving a number between 1 for the lowest frequency and variously 2–14 for the highest, whatever number of different frequencies were being used. The subject was then told the correct answer. Some 25 s later another tone was sounded, and the same question asked again. This scheme of things is set out in Diagram (a).

(a)

The purpose of this experiment was to discover how accurately ordinary people (not musicians with perfect pitch) can identify single tones. With only two or three different frequencies, identification was easy; one does not need perfect pitch to be able to separate 'high' from 'low'. But as soon as the number of different tones that might be sounded reached five, mistakes began to appear.

Imagine that you hear a tone. You know that it is one of five (or 6 or 7 or 8 or 10 or 14) different frequencies. You are asked to say which of those frequencies you are listening to. The experimenter then tells you what the correct answer is and you wait for the next tone. Mistakes appeared as soon as the number of different frequencies reached five; there were even more mistakes when there were 6, 7, 8, 10, or, ultimately, 14 different frequencies to be distinguished (Pollack, 1952).

At the time when this experiment was published, it was fashionable to summarise a subject's performance in terms of the *information transmitted*, where a choice between n categories equates to $\log_2 n$ *bits* of information. When there are mistakes, the subject's response provides less information about the frequency of the tone that was presented than it might otherwise do. The accuracy of judgment can alternatively be expressed as an equivalent number of categories used without error, and the results presented in Figure 2.1 have been converted back to an 'equivalent number of categories' (which need not be a whole number).

Figure 2.1 Accuracy of identification of auditory frequency in the range 100–8000 Hz.

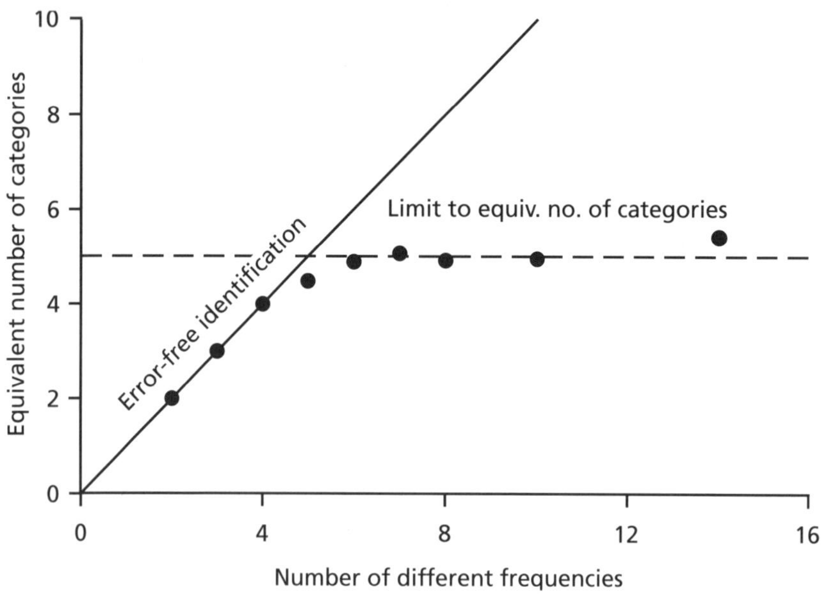

Data from Pollack, 1952.

The striking and unexpected result was that the accuracy achieved never exceeded a level equivalent to the identification of just five tones without error. While one might reasonably expect more errors when there are fourteen different tones to be distinguished, one might also expect people to say more precisely where each individual tone came on the musical scale. Not so. The number of errors increases so rapidly in relation to the number of different tones that division into at most five categories is a pragmatic limit. This result is even more striking when compared with human ability to discriminate auditory frequency, which is ordinarily very fine. Play two tones of 1000 Hz and 1001 Hz in quick succession – this new scheme is set out in Diagram (b) – and someone with acute hearing will be able to tell which is which with no more than about 70 per cent errors. There are about 1000 such '70 per cent' differences between 100 and 8000 Hz (Wier *et al.*, 1977); yet, separate the successive tones by 25 seconds, and only five can be distinguished.

(b)

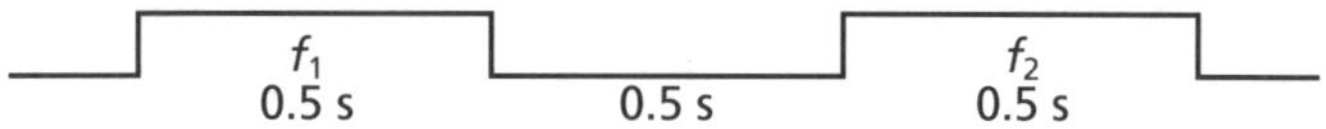

In a series of subsidiary experiments Pollack (1952) varied the range of the frequencies to be identified and their spacing within that range, but always with the same result. The limit to not more than five categories without error is not due to any sensory confusion between the different frequencies. Indeed, the only experimental manipulation that improved identification was the provision of a reference tone preceding the tone to be identified (Pollack, 1953). The scheme in this second experiment is set out in Diagram (c). There were 9 different frequencies. Before each tone to be identified there was a reference tone: 'This is tone no. 3'. The improvement that resulted from this reference tone will be examined in more detail in Chapter 5. For the present it is sufficient to note that the only way to improve the accuracy of identification is to provide an explicit standard for comparison. That is how auditory discrimination of frequency (Diagram b) can be so very fine. The much poorer accuracy of identification in Pollack's experiment results from the absence of any tone to make comparison with.

(c)

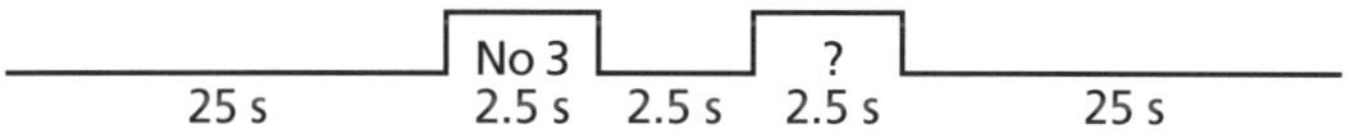

Other sensory attributes

If the tones vary in loudness as well as frequency, subjects can identify more than five distinct categories, though not so many as 25 (that is, not so many as five categories of frequency combined with five categories of sound level; Pollack, 1953). So the limit to 'not more than five categories without error' is specific to ordered categories and to single stimulus attributes. On the other hand, this limit applies generally to all kinds of stimulus attribute, with only a few exceptions. It has been established with the amplitude of a pure tone (Garner, 1953); the area of a square (Eriksen and Hake, 1955a) and of a complex figure (Baird, Romer, and Stein, 1970); with electric current (Hawkes and Warm, 1960); with length of line (Baird *et al.*, 1970); with luminance (Eriksen and Hake, 1955b); with smell (Engen and Pfaffmann, 1959); and with taste (Beebe-Center, Rogers and O'Connell, 1955). Unless there is some physical reference like a ruler or a scale pan against which comparison can be made, five categories of judgment is the pragmatic limit. The exceptions (angle of inclination, colour, visual position) arise when there is (arguably) a natural point of reference for the judgment, as in Diagram (c) above.

The quality of wine

One interpretation of Pollack's finding is that any and every judgment has to be expressed with respect to some frame of reference. Identification benefits from the provision of a reference tone because it anchors the frame of reference which otherwise slips and slides about from one judgment to the next. That internal frame of reference slides about in just the same way when people taste wine. In a laboratory experiment we use simple stimuli like tones, brightness, colour, taste, length, loudness and smell, which can be measured precisely. That precise measurement provides a framework for analysing the data and also a way of telling the subject what the correct answer is. With wine there cannot be feedback like that; there is no 'ruler' for measuring quality, and one cannot easily calculate how accurate a wine-taster's judgments are. But those judgments will not be any the more accurate on that account. At best, people can grade wine into only five categories of quality, and even then they feel uncertain about it. So it is comforting to quote an expert who can assess wine on a 51-point scale!

Robert Parker, as explained in Chapter 1, tastes his wines with a greater care and objectivity than ordinarily obtains at wine tastings (Parker, 1987, pp. 11–12), though not more rigorously than is usual in a laboratory experiment. So the limit to not more than five categories without error must apply to Robert Parker's judgments as well. Wine drinkers know about their own difficulties in judging wine, but do not realise that experts face the same problem. So they buy their wine according to Robert Parker's numbers.

Escape from East Berlin

The principle of the relativity of judgment was applied in one daring escape from East Berlin in the days of the communist regime in East Germany. At that time West Berlin was surrounded by a wall. Facing the West there was a smooth-faced concrete wall with a rounded top; behind, up to 100 metres in the rear in some places, was another concrete wall. The area in between was levelled with yet another barrier of barbed wire, guards, watch towers, dogs, trip wires and booby traps. Floodlights illuminated the wall at night (Gelb, 1986, Ch. 1). It was like the wall round a concentration camp, except that West Berlin, although enclosed by the wall, was technically on the outside.

After it was erected in 1961 many people attempted to cross the wall, and not a few were shot dead whilst so doing. There was, however, a much easier way to the West – through Checkpoint Charlie, which was the principal access by road. A permit would be required, of course, for each person passing through from East Berlin. But if you were in the boot of a car, the East German border guards would not see you. Of course, that possibility was well-known to the border guards and they used to examine the boots of cars precisely to make sure there was no one inside, trying to escape. However, at certain times of day the volume of traffic passing through Checkpoint Charlie was so great that it was not practicable to examine the boot of every car. That did not, by itself, provide a means of escape because an adult man in the boot of a car would weigh it down. It was sufficient to examine just those cars which appeared heavily laden. But that economy of inspection made the following, subtle, method of escape feasible.

There were three cars. The person escaping was placed in the boot of the middle car, which had its rear springs stuffed with hard rubber balls. This gave the car a rough ride, but it did reduce the depression of the rear end. In addition – and this is the special subtlety of this method of escape – it was arranged that the cars immediately behind and in front should be heavily laden with goods covered by valid permits. The scene at the border crossing was something like this.

The guards examine the papers of the first car and then go behind to inspect its load; all is in order. They then examine the papers of the middle car and wave it through without any more ado because it appears unladen in relation to the first and the third cars.

Until the fall of the Berlin wall, the last house in West Berlin, on the right-hand side of the street leading to Checkpoint Charlie, used to be a museum, the *Haus am Checkpoint Charlie*, dedicated to escapes from the East. This particular escape was represented there by a rusty rear car spring filled with hard rubber balls, about six of them. The escape itself was organised in 1968 by Albert Schütz, a professional organiser of escapes from East to West and a friend of the museum director Rainer Hildebrandt (Schütz died in 1987; obituary Hildebrandt, 1987). It depended almost entirely on the border guards judging the loading of the middle car in relation to the vehicles in front and behind it. Indeed, the illusion is preserved in Diagram (d). The middle car looks level, but is in fact tilted, relative to its wheels, by about half the tilt applied to the two trucks.

Judgments of 'half-loudness'

The identification of the frequency of a tone and of the loading of cars at Checkpoint Charlie both show that our judgment is relative to whatever basis for comparison there happens to be. But maybe there is some capacity for absolute judgment as well. That possibility has been tested in an elegant experiment. But, as a preliminary, I need to explain first how the intensity of a sound is measured.

All the sounds that we hear are due to the action on the eardrum of very tiny fluctuations in air pressure about the atmospheric mean (14.72 lbs/sq. in.). At its most sensitive the ear can detect a variation as small as 0.00000002 per cent of that atmospheric mean. On the other hand, some of the sounds in our environment amount to a fluctuation one million times larger than this. This very wide range in the physical level of sounds to be measured poses a problem for finding a suitable scale of intensity, analogous to the marks on a ruler or the weights on a scale pan – a problem that has been resolved in the following manner (the decibel scale).

The softest sound that anyone can hear scores 0. A pressure fluctuation ten times as large (e.g., open country at night) scores 20. A pressure fluctuation greater again by ten times (e.g., a very quiet living room) scores a further 20, making a total of 40; and the scale value is increased by a further 20 for each additional multiplication by ten. Table 2.1 lists some common environmental sounds with their typical ratings on this scale.

Table 2.1 Decibel levels of some common environmental sounds.

Sound	*Sound level in dB*
Softest audible sound	0
Normal breathing	10
Open country at night	20
Soft whisper	30
Very quiet living room	40
Quiet conversation (e.g. library)	50
Average speaking voice at 5 ft	60
Television, typical sound level	70
Motor car at 65 mph, from 25 ft	80
Motor cycle 25 ft away	90
Underground train entering a station	100
Chainsaw (unprotected operator)	110
Loud rock group	120
Machine-gun fire at close range	130
Jet engine at take-off, from 100 ft	140

This decibel scale is widely used and works well in physical applications, but it poses problems for the acoustic engineer who needs to explain to his client how loud 90 dB, say, would, in fact, sound. The nature of these problems can be illustrated by the observation that a decibel level of 100 ought, at first glance, to sound twice as loud as a level of 50; but most people would say that an underground train coming into a station (100 dB) sounds much more than twice as loud as the ambient background of quiet conversation in a library (50 dB). So, a second scale – the *sone* scale – was devised to represent how loud different sounds appeared to the listener.

The sone scale is related to the decibel scale as follows:

40 dB ≡ 1 sone
50 dB ≡ 2 sones

60 dB $\equiv$ 4 sones
70 dB $\equiv$ 8 sones, etc.

Continuing upwards, 80 dB (16 sones) should sound exactly half as loud as 90 dB (32 sones). This is the specific relation which the following experiment (Garner, 1954) set out to test.

The subjects listened to a 1000 Hz tone (two octaves above middle C) at a level of 90 dB for one second followed, after a silent interval, by the same tone for a further one second, but at some lesser (comparison) level. The subjects were then asked whether the second, comparison, tone sounded more or less than 'half as loud' as the first (90 dB) tone. (This schedule is set out in Diagram (d)). There were six different levels of comparison tone covering a 10 dB range in 2 dB steps; each was presented 100 times in random order. The probability of judging the comparison tone to be 'more than half as loud' increased, of course, with its level, and this made it possible to estimate a level of the comparison tone which would have been judged 'more than half as loud' exactly 50 per cent of the time. This 'half as loud as 90 dB' level was estimated for each individual subject.

(d)

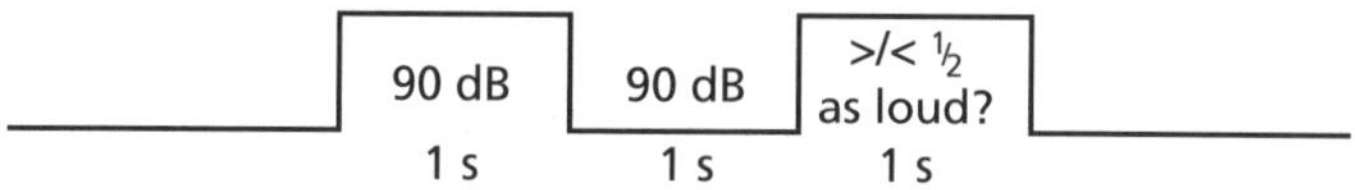

Now for the ingenious twist in this experiment. There were three groups of 10 subjects assigned at random to different ranges of comparison levels: (a) 55–65 dB, (b) 65–75 dB, and (c) 75–85 dB. Their respective half-loudness values are plotted in Figure 2.2 in the form of cumulative distributions, so that each data point records the number of subjects within the group whose half-loudness levels were equal to, or less than, that value. The half-loudness levels for the 75–85 dB group all fall neatly into the range 75 to 85 dB. But this is what one should expect, since the sound which is supposed to sound half as loud as 90 dB is 80 dB, exactly in the middle of this group's comparison range. But the 'half as loud as 90 dB' levels of the other two groups also fall neatly within *their* ranges of comparison levels, and this is contrary to received wisdom. All the subjects in these two groups ought to have complained that the range of comparison sounds did not cover the level that was half as loud as 90 dB. Only one subject did in fact complain. She said that all the tones she heard (in the range 65–75 dB) sounded *more than half as loud* as 90 dB – quite the wrong judgment. This subject was happily reassigned to the 55–65 dB group.

To summarise, for every subject that level of tone which was estimated to sound half as loud as 90 dB fell neatly within the range of comparison tones presented for judgment, whatever that range happened to be. That is to say, the subjects (students in America) had virtually no idea how loud a tone, half as loud as 90 dB, would in fact sound, and so judged the different comparison tones in relation to each other. Their judgments depended on a kind of self-context, which has been found to build up rather quickly. In a more detailed

Figure 2.2 'Half as loud as 90 dB' levels for three groups of subjects with comparison ranges (a) 55–65 dB, (b) 65–75 dB, and (c) 75–85 dB.

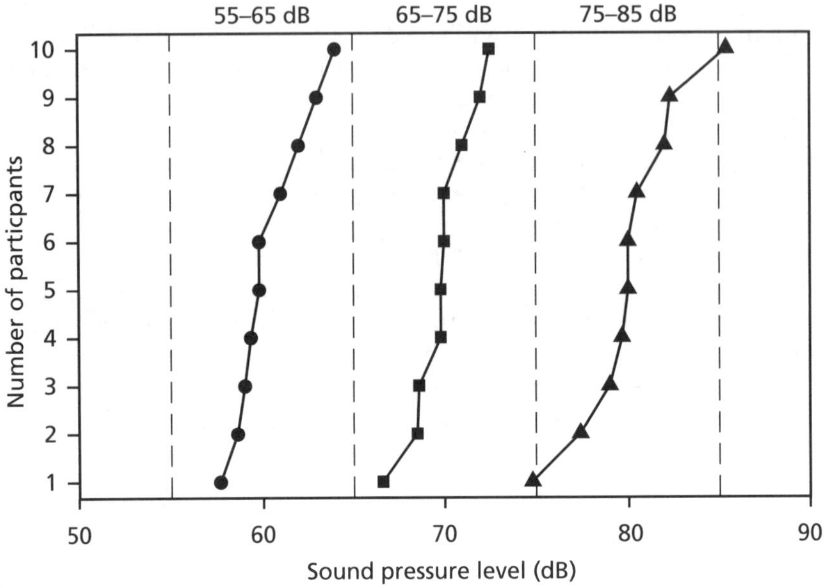

Data from Garner, 1954.

replication of this experiment (Garner, 1959) the self-context was found to be fully developed by the time subjects had each made 20 judgments.

Removing enlarged tonsils

Garner's (1954) laboratory experiment has its parallel in the world outside. In the 1930s it was fashionable to remove children's tonsils if they appeared in any way enlarged. This was thought be desirable in treating recurrent colds, bronchitis, bronchial asthma and acute rheumatism (Maitland-Jones, 1934). Indeed, so fashionable was tonsillectomy that 'It was stated . . . that 75 per cent. of the new boys entering Eton have had their tonsils removed and that this percentage is materially increased during the years of their school life' (Carr, 1933). The following story, which Poulton (1989) had from a surgical registrar while completing his medical training in 1941, explains how this came about.

> Before World War II it used to be fashionable to remove the enlarged tonsils of schoolchildren. It is said that a school medical officer would inspect the tonsils of all the children at a school. He or she would recommend that the 5% or 10% of children with the largest tonsils should have them removed. Later, the remainder of the children are examined by another school medical officer. He or she recommends that the 5% or 10% of children with the largest remaining tonsils should have them removed, and so on. . . . Each medical officer recommends removal of the largest tonsils at the top end of the range, whatever their actual sizes. (Poulton, 1989, p. 117).

So, a recommendation for tonsillectomy did not depend on the absolute size of a child's tonsils (which would, in any case, have been very difficult to measure) but on their size relative to the tonsils of the other children inspected, just as, in the experiment above, judging a comparison tone to be 'more than half as loud' as 90 dB did not depend on its absolute level, but on its level relative to the other comparison tones presented for judgment.

The use of words

This relative nature of the way we judge is apparent also in the way we use words. This was remarked three hundred years ago by the philosopher John Locke.

> There are yet besides those, other Words of time, that ordinarily are thought to stand for positive Ideas, which yet will, when considered, be found to be relative, such are Young, Old, etc. which include, and intimate the Relation any thing has, to a certain length of Duration, whereof we have the Idea in our Minds. Thus having settled in our Thoughts the Idea of the ordinary Duration of a Man to be seventy years, when we say a Man is Young, we mean, that his Age is yet but a small part of that which usually Men attain to: And when we denominate him Old, we mean, that his Duration is run out almost to the end of that which Men do not usually exceed. And so 'tis but comparing the particular Age, or Duration of this or that Man, to the Idea of that Duration which we have in our Minds, as ordinarily belonging to that sort of Animals: Which is plain, in the application of these Names to other Things; for a Man is called Young at Twenty years, and very Young at Seven years old; But yet a Horse we call Old at Twenty, and a Dog at Seven years; because in each of these, we compare their Age to different Ideas of Duration which are settled in our Minds, as belonging to these several sorts of Animals, in the ordinary course of Nature. But the Sun and Stars, though they have outlasted several Generations of Men, we call not old, because we do not know what period GOD hath set to that sort of Beings. (Locke, 1690, Bk II, Ch. XXVI, § 4)

Summary – the principle of relativity

Experiment shows that, unaided, people can distinguish only five categories on any continuum. That limit can be exceeded only by providing some physical standard of reference like a ruler or a scale pan; and if that matter of a physical reference is cunningly ordered, there appears to be no capability for absolute judgment at all.

If this is the best that volunteer subjects can achieve in the laboratory when they know that their judgments are to be analysed as experimental data, they will not achieve anything more accurate in the course of their everyday lives outside. Herein lies the reason why people are so uncertain about wine, how the

East Berlin border guards were deceived, and why the excision of children's tonsils became increasingly frequent in the days before the Second World War.

When someone comes to make a judgment in the everyday world, the point of reference is most often taken from past experience. Different people have different accumulations of past experience and for that reason make *different* judgments about the *same* issue. We call that difference a 'point of view' and to that I turn next.

3 Points of view

Until now I have been concerned with the effect of context on what people say, looking at the same people saying different things about the same issue in different contexts. But the principle of relativity also explains how different people can pronounce different verdicts about the same issue. This happens because different people implicitly bring different contexts and different prior experiences to that issue, looking at it from different points of view.

This difference is brought out in a simple experiment by Tresselt (1948). Thirty-six weightlifters and 36 watchmakers were asked to grade a series of twelve weights. 'You are to tell me whether the weight feels to you heavy, medium, or light.' The weights were between 11 and 560 gm and were contained in twelve otherwise identical cardboard cylinders. The weights were lifted blindfold to preclude the subjects forming any extraneous idea of how heavy they really were, and the orders of lifting, different for different subjects, were so arranged that each weight was lifted equally often in each serial position. The heights of the bars in Figure 3.1 show the means of the weights judged 'medium' by weightlifters and by watchmakers respectively for each successive judgment. A weightlifter's idea of a 'medium' weight is, as one would expect, heavier than a watchmaker's. There is just one inversion of the relationship (the third judgment in the series) associated with very small numbers of 'medium' judgments (4 and 3 respectively).

Piaget's 'three mountains' task

The notion of a 'point of view' is admirably illustrated by one of the tasks Jean Piaget devised to monitor the intellectual development of children. The apparatus is shown in Figure 3.2.

> A pasteboard model, one metre square and from twelve to thirty centimetres high, was made to represent three mountains. From his initial position in front of the model (A) the child sees a green mountain occupying the foreground a little to his right. The summit of this mountain is topped by a little house. To his left he sees a brown mountain, higher than the green one and slightly to its rear. This mountain is distinguished not only by its colour but also by having a red

Figure 3.1 Means of weights judged 'medium' by weightlifters and by watchmakers respectively.

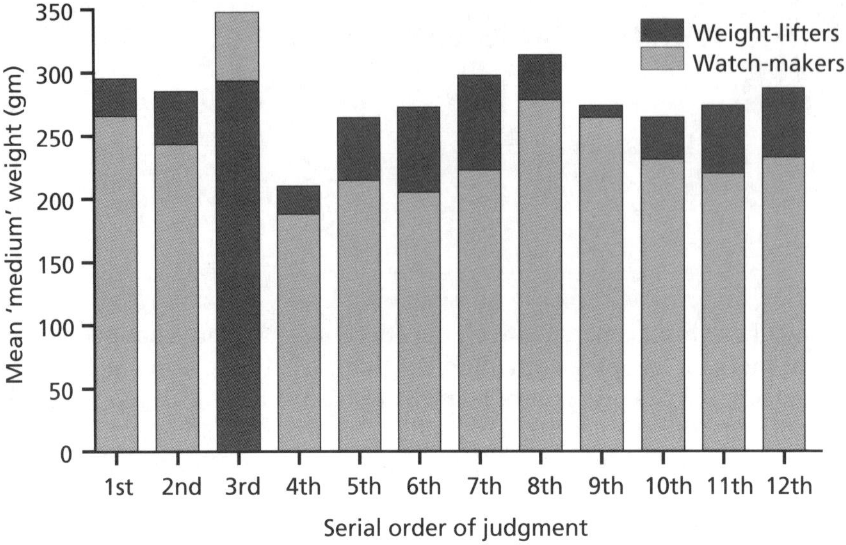

Data from Tresselt, 1948.

Figure 3.2 Piaget's 'three mountains' model.

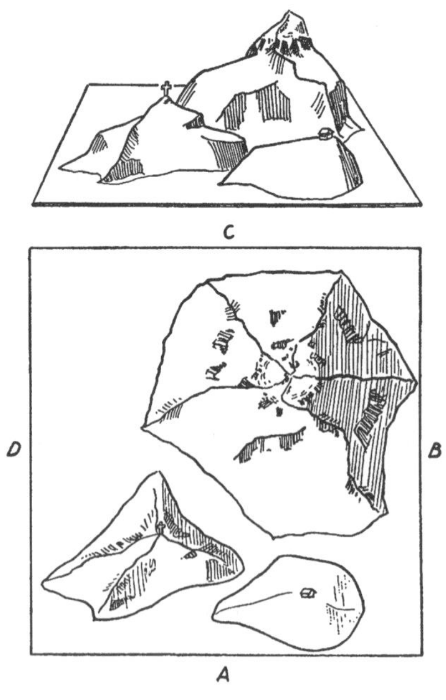

Reproduced with permission from J. Piaget and B. Inhelder, *The Child's Conception of Space*, p. 211. © 1956 Routledge & Kegan Paul.

cross at the summit. In the background stands the highest of the three mountains, a grey pyramid whose peak is covered in snow. From position C (opposite position A) a zigzag path can be seen running down the side of the green mountain, while from position B (to the right of the model, relative to position A) a little rivulet is seen to descend the brown mountain. Each mountain is painted in a single colour, except for the snow cap of the grey mountain, and the only reference points are those described.

The children are also shown a collection of ten pictures, measuring 20 × 28 cm. These represent the mountains seen from different viewpoints and are painted in the same colours as the model. They are clearly distinguishable and are large enough for particular features such as the cross, the house and the snow-capped peak to be easily visible. The children are also given three pieces of cardboard, shaped and coloured the same as each of the mountains, and these may be arranged to represent the mountains as seen in a given perspective.

Finally, the apparatus includes a wooden doll 2 or 3 cm. in height. The head of the doll is a plain wooden ball with no face painted on it so that the child can ignore the doll's line of sight and need only consider its position. This doll is put in a number of different places and the child's task is to discover what perspective the doll will 'see' in each of the different positions. It is not the child who moves around the group of mountains – except to check his answers – but the doll which is supposed to be doing the travelling. The child has the problem of trying to imagine, and to reconstruct by a process of inference, the changes in perspective that will accompany the doll's movements, or the different positions which the doll must occupy to suit the various perspectives.

(Reprinted with permission from J. Piaget and B. Inhelder, *The Child's Conception of Space*, pp. 210–12. © 1956 Routledge & Kegan Paul.)

Piaget's apparatus enables a child's grasp of perspective to be tested in a variety of ways. Up to the age of six, children typically fail to understand what is required. Thereafter, up to perhaps age eight, children realise that they have to rearrange the pieces of cardboard representing the mountains, but their rearrangements always reflect the view from their own position, not from that of the doll. From the age of seven onwards, however, children are increasingly able to realise that what the doll sees will be different from what they see, and to select a picture from among the ten offered that is appropriate from the doll's point of view.

Young children's imaginations are restricted to what they can see from their particular point of view – a defect of understanding that Piaget called 'egocentrism'. Older children, however, realise that the doll has a different vantage point, sees things differently, and are able to estimate, very roughly, what the doll should be seeing. But that is not to say that older children are able to see the scene from the doll's perspective. The scene can be seen from the doll's perspective only by moving around the model to where the doll is situated, and that is possible only because there is a physical model to move around.

Operation Granby

But the phrase 'point of view' is also used in abstract situations where there can be no physical model to support mental calculations of 'perspective'. In such a case, everyone is egocentric. This was amusingly illustrated in a report to the House of Commons Defence Committee on Operation Granby, the transporting of supplies to the theatre of operations for the war in the Persian Gulf in 1991.

First of all, I must explain that any ship entering harbour anywhere east of the Suez Canal, be it a passenger liner, warship or merchantman, is greeted by a shoal of traders in small boats seeking to do business, seeking to sell anything to anyone. Trade with passing ships is an important part of the local economy and a war simply increases the opportunities for trade. So, when the Chairman of the Defence Committee enquired 'Were there any problems with the crews of chartered ships entering the war zone?' Colonel Cubitt, giving evidence, replied:

> We had no problems with crews at all. They were all very co-operative . . . We had one ship's master who was very worried at one stage about being attacked by terrorists with a rocket launcher in a small boat, but it turned out to be an Arab trying to sell him a carpet. (Mates, 1991, p. 44)

Kate Moss modelling lingerie in Vogue

Another, more public, example of different points of view emerged when Kate Moss modelled some teenage lingerie in *Vogue* (Kasterine, 1993). There were eight pictures of her wearing various items of skimpy underwear, some of them semi-transparent. It evoked a minor storm of protest in the press:

> *VOGUE*, the world's glossiest fashion magazine, has been accused by psychologists and other women's magazines of publishing material verging on child pornography.
>
> Kay Toon, a clinical psychologist and co-author of *Breaking Free*, a book to help survivors of child sexual abuse, said: 'It's not far from being child pornography. People who are abusers of children can use images like these to reinforce their own desires. The pictures projected women as child-like, frail and sexually vulnerable objects'.
>
> Susie Orbach, a psychotherapist and writer, said: 'She looks like a child, innocent, helpless, almost a junkie. It's just this side of porn.'
>
> Marcelle D'Argy Smith, editor of *Cosmopolitan*, said: 'The pictures are hideous and tragic. I believe they can only appeal to the paedophile market. If I had a daughter who looked like that, I would take her to see a doctor.' (Tredre, 1993)
>
> **Marion Hume** opened this month's *Vogue* to find photos she would rather not have seen

When fashion is no excuse at all

. . . voyeurisitic images of the next-door neighbour's daughter rolling around on an unmade bed, in cheap, skimpy knickers and what looked like a teen bra stretched over her flat chest.

It was intended to be a series of photographs of a range of affordable lingerie, worn by this year's top model. But we were given pictures of a pubescent child wearing the semi-see-thru sexy underwear of a knowing adult; images of a little Lolita dressed up in the private clothes of a woman. Many readers found the pictures unpleasant, calling them 'disgusting', 'dreadful', 'upsetting' and 'ugly'. *Vogue* has gone beyond the pale. (Hume, 1993)

To this the editor of *Vogue* replied

Sir: Having read Roger Tredre . . . and Marion Hume . . . on the portraits of Kate Moss in the current issue of *Vogue*, I have begun to wonder whether the *Independent* is deliberately creating a scandal as an excuse to reproduce the pictures themselves.

To date, I have received two letters and five telephone calls of complaint and three letters and numerous verbal messages of appreciation for these images. Doubtless there will be a few more of each. This, however, is slightly less response than we receive for an average lingerie shoot where a fashion magazine is traditionally criticised for depicting an unusually perfect vision of the female form and can in no way justify the 'scandal' described by Roger Tredre, nor Marion Hume's follow-up stating that 'many readers' were offended and disgusted. (Shulman, 1993)

Following that sharp clash of opinion, the *Independent on Sunday* collected a few more opinions.

TOM BLACK, sales assistant, 27: I find the pictures uncomfortable. She is very beautiful and you do fancy her, but feel you shouldn't. And the clothes are really ugly, not sexy at all – it all comes from her.

JOSE FONSECA, director, Models One: She looks like a teenager in cheap underwear and had they been in *19* magazine or *The Face* no one would have said anything.

JOEL LACY, technique editor, *Amateur Photographer*: I don't think they're any different to any other fashion photos. If she was in a bikini then they would have passed without comment. (*Independent on Sunday*, 1993)

And finally,

From Mr Alexander Walker

Sir: On learning of an anorexic-looking, eroticised child in high-fashion underwear being featured in *Vogue*'s pages, I, of course, rushed out and bought a copy of the magazine to which your writer had drawn attention and which you illustrated in your pages.

> I am bound to report that it does not live up to the prurient suggestiveness foisted upon it.' (*Independent*, 2 June 1993, p. 21)

The variety of opinion and reaction to *Vogue*'s lingerie shoot is very wide. It simply reflects the equally wide variety of different backgrounds amongst the different individuals who have been cited – their different points of view.

The American Declaration of Independence

> We hold these truths to be self-evident, that all men are created equal, that they are endowed by their Creator with certain unalienable Rights, that among these are Life, Liberty and the pursuit of Happiness. (*The Declaration of Independence*, 1776).

Although the American *Declaration of Independence* had 56 signatories, it was framed by Thomas Jefferson. So whom did Jefferson mean by 'all men'? On his plantation at Monticello in Virginia he kept slaves! Did he mean that they were to be set free as a matter of 'unalienable right'? The attitude of Jefferson and other signatories from the southern states was roughly that 'slaves not being constituent members of our society could never pretend to benefit from such a maxim' (Randolph, 1936; cited by Pacheco, 1983, p. 19).

If you were a white freeholder of Virginia, the owner of a plantation, that is the way you would have understood Jefferson's words at that time. But if you are black, even though you are also a free man, they mean exactly what they say. Benjamin Banneker was an Afro-American astronomer and mathematician. In 1791 he wrote to Jefferson, at that time Secretary of State, quoting the passage cited above from *The Declaration of Independence* and following with these words:

> Here, Sir, was a time in which your tender feelings for your selves engaged you thus to declare, you were then impressed with proper ideas of the great valuation of liberty, and the free possession of those blessings to which you were entitled by nature; but Sir how pitiable is it to reflect, that altho you were so fully convinced of the benevolence of the Father of mankind, and of his equal and impartial distribution of those rights and privileges which he had conferred upon them, that you should at the Same time counteract his mercies, in detaining by fraud and violence so numerous a part of my brethren under groaning captivity and cruel oppression, that you should at the Same time be found guilty of that most criminal act, which you professedly detested in others, with respect to yourselves. (Bedini, 1972, p. 155)

Anti-Semitism

The American *Declaration of Independence* was composed more than 200 years ago, but such a difference in point of view underpins racial prejudice in our own day and age. Lady Birdwood, aged 78, was convicted at the Old Bailey on 16

October, 1991 on ten counts of 'distributing or possessing insulting anti-Jewish leaflets, likely to incite racial hatred' (Ward, 1991b).

> The leaflets she held or distributed were an attempt by her to counter what she saw as an attempt by Zionists to mastermind the destruction of the English race by encouraging multi-racialism. They included assertions that the holocaust was a hoax, and that Jews have ritually killed Christian children.
>
> She argued in court that the Crown had not proved anyone had been incited by the leaflets. Thousands of copies were posted to MPs and members of the Church of England Synod, and put through the doors of flats in London.
>
> Birdwood said outside court: 'I am very sad and disappointed. People of my age begin to find what is happening in this country impossible. I believe in being able to speak my mind but this verdict has militated against free speech.' (Ward, 1991a)

Lady Birdwood had her supporters; there were about 30 at her trial, who interrupted the verdict from the gallery.

> The judge called for those who had interrupted from the gallery to be removed. 'I said something, I'm proud to say something, it's disgusting,' said one of them, walking out.
>
> In the corridor outside, they seemed genuinely amazed that their opinions were not more widely shared. 'I would have sworn that jury was a cross-section of the English public', said one man. 'They must have been got at by Mossad', said a woman. Outside the Old Bailey, I took down their many expressions of indignation: 'This is a religious issue, not a political one' – Mrs Cooper from Tooting. 'Not one of those people on the jury was a quality person' – Christine Yianne, formerly of the British National Party, now a Reverend in the Church of Creativity. (Barwick, 1991)

Those sharp divisions of opinion on the morality and legality of Lady Birdwood's leaflets simply reflect different points of view. Those who take one side are unable to see things from the other side – they do not even understand how there could be another side. Three years on:

> The dowager Lady Birdwood, 80, was given a three-month prison sentence suspended for two years yesterday by an Old Bailey judge for possessing and distributing a booklet likely to stir up racial hatred. She was warned that there was a very serious risk of the sentence being activated if she offended again. (Midgley, 1994)

Blasphemy

The opposition of different points of view is even more profound when they reflect cultural and religious differences. Many Muslims, for example, have very different points of view to those that I and many Britons have on the matter of Salman Rushdie's *The Satanic Verses*. This is consequent on their belonging to a different religious society. For that same reason, Muslims generally do not understand Christian attitudes, whereas Christians, again generally, do not understand Muslim atttitudes. Indeed, Salman Rushdie himself appears not to understand, even though he was born into a Muslim society. This lack of understanding provides the basis for conflict.

> The story . . . began . . . in India where Rushdie has been a celebrated writer ever since the publication of Midnight's Children, a novel about post-independence India.
>
> A copy of The Satanic Verses manuscript was sent to Delhi for Penguin's Indian subsidiary to consider publication. It decided against it and wrote to Penguin in London in July [1988] 'vaguely suggesting that Muslims in England could cause trouble'.
>
> The controversial nature of the book first emerged in public when two of India's news magazines, India Today and Sunday, published interviews with Rushdie in mid-September.
>
> Both reports caught the eye of Syed Shahabuddin, an ambitious Muslim MP. As a member of the opposition Janata party, he immediately called on the government to ban the book.
>
> . . . On October 5, soon after the book was published in Britain, the Indian government telexed Penguin in London announcing the ban. Within weeks it was followed by Pakistan, Saudi Arabia, Egypt, Somalia, Bangladesh, Sudan, Malaysia, Indonesia, Qatar and South Africa, which has a vociferous Muslim minority.
>
> The matter may have ended there, had not Aslam Ejaz, of the Islamic Foundation in Madras, already written to Faiyazuddin Ahmad, a friend in Leicester, telling him about the impending ban in India. A similar campaign, wrote Ejaz, should be mounted in Britain, which still remained largely oblivious to the blasphemous nature of the book. (Roy and Fernand, 1989)

Dr. Syed Pasha, secretary of the Union of Muslim Organisations, wrote to the British Prime Minister:

> 'Never have we encountered such a ferocious and savage attack on our Holy Prophet, using abominably foul language,' he wrote. He added that 'the Muslim community is shocked and seething with indignation'.
>
> The response from the Prime Minister on November 11 was detailed. [Margaret] Thatcher made it clear that 'there are no grounds on which the government could consider banning' the book. 'It is an essential part of our democratic system that people who act within the law should be able to express their opinions freely.' (Roy and Fernand, 1989)

A public burning of the book followed in Bradford on 14 January 1989. This sent a signal round the Muslim world, which resulted in demonstrations in many Islamic countries. On 12 February 1989 five people were killed and 60 injured when police opened fire on a riot in Islamabad; one person was killed in a similar riot in Srinagar the following day; and on 14 February the Ayatollah Khomeini issued his *fatwa*, broadcast over Teheran radio, ordering Rushdie's execution. What was the root cause of all this trouble?

The passages which give offence to Muslims occur in the dreams of the principal character, Gibreel Farishta, an Indian film-star of fading popularity. While the passages in question involve a certain amount of snook-cocking, their offensiveness does not seem, to me at least, in any way commensurate with the violence of Muslim reaction, and I conjecture that one has actually to have been brought up as a Muslim to feel the full force of the satire. As an example of the flavour of Rushdie's writing, the following will be more meaningful to British readers.

As a preliminary I need to explain that Hal Valance is a film producer, the 'creator of The Alien Show', who 'made use of his "intimate" association with the Prime Minister he referred to affectionately as "Mrs Torture".' At this point in the novel he has just entertained the hero, Saladin Chamcha, to lunch:

> When they left the secret chamber of the clavichords, the familiar Hal Valance instantly reappeared. Leaning on the balustrade of his terrace, he confided: 'The thing that's so amazing about her is the size of what she's trying to do.' Her? Baby? Chamcha was confused. 'I'm talking about you-know-who,' Valance explained helpfully. 'Torture. Maggie the Bitch.' Oh. 'She's radical all right. What she wants – what she actually thinks she can fucking *achieve* – is literally to invent a whole goddamn new middle class in this country. Get rid of the old woolly incompetent buggers from fucking Surrey and Hampshire, and bring in the new. People without background, without history. Hungry people. People who really *want*, and who know that with her, they can bloody well *get*. Nobody's ever tried to replace a whole fucking *class* before, and the amazing thing is she might just do it if they don't get her first. The old class. The dead men. You follow what I'm saying.' 'I think so,' Chamcha lied. 'And it's not just the businessmen,' Valance said slurrily. 'The intellectuals, too. Out with the whole faggoty crew. In with the hungry guys with the wrong education. New professors, new painters, the lot. It's a bloody revolution. Newness coming into this country that's stuffed full of fucking old *corpses*. It's going to be something to see. It already is.' (Rushdie, 1988, pp. 269–70)

So, is the book blasphemous, as its Muslim critics claim? It all depends on what one means by blasphemy.

> As originally defined, the crime of blasphemy meant publishing any matter which contradicted the teaching of the Church of England, and hence undermined its authority. Its twin brother was the crime of sedition – publishing matter which undermined the authority of the king within the state.
>
> In this form, the crime of blasphemy was used to suppress a large range of religious writings during the eighteenth and early nineteenth centuries.
>
> In the 1880s there were serious attempts to use blasphemy prosecutions to silence Charles Bradlaw [Charles Bradlaugh, 1833–1891, MP, 1880–1891] and

> his atheistic followers. The editor of *The Freethinker* [G. W. Foote] collected a jail sentence [12 months] for publishing a cartoon [reproduced below] featuring God's posterior, clad in a large pair of check trousers . . .
>
> These proceedings led to a powerful campaign to abolish the crime of blasphemy. The fuss died down when in 1883 the courts redefined the crime as limited to publishing a 'vilificatory' attack on Christianity, likely to 'outrage the feelings of believers'. (Spencer, 1989)

Figure 3.3 The Freethinker's cartoon, Christmas Number, 1882.

Freethinker Christmas Number

MOSES GETTING A BACK VIEW

And it shall come to pass that I will put thee in a clift of the rock, and I shall take away my hand, and thou shalt see my back parts — Exodus xxxiii.,23

Reproduced with permission from *The Freethinker*, Christmas Number, 1882. © G. W. Foote & Co.

As English law stands today, blasphemy is 'any (publication) about God or Christ or the Christian religion, the Bible or some sacred subject (which is) so scurrilous or abusive or offensive as would, if published, tend to vilify the Christian religion and could lead to a breach of the peace.' (King-Hamilton, 1988) Setting aside the technical matter that in the United Kingdom the law of blasphemy protects Christianity only – that is, transposing the protection afforded to Christianity into an equivalent protection of Islam – *The Satanic Verses* is arguably blasphemous according to the law as it stood prior to 1883, but is arguably not blasphemous according to the definition which applies today. *The Satanic Verses* is comparable, in verbal terms, to *The Freethinker's* cartoon. That cartoon was at the edge of what was considered blasphemous in 1883. G. W. Foote was tried twice as a result of a private prosecution, the Government of that day declining to take action. At the first trial the jury could not agree, and he was convicted only on the second trial. The cartoon would not be adjudged blasphemous today. In addition:

> At no point in these imaginings does Rushdie refer to the prophet Muhammad by name, nor to the city of Mecca, nor to the Sheria law, nor anything directly concerned with Islamic faith.
>
> All the fundamentalists' objections concern the *symbolic* representation of religious figures and events – as one might condemn George Orwell's fictional Ministry of Love for satirising the Ministry of Defence.
>
> What is altogether more odd is that the book's status as a novel cuts no ice with its Muslim critics. The grand sheikh of Cairo's Al-Azhar, the 1,000-year-old seat of Islamic theology, said when calling on all the nations in the Islamic Conference Organization to suppress the book that it contained 'lies and figments of the imagination' about Islam, which were 'passed off as facts', and that the Jahilia sequences were insulting distortions of Islamic history.
>
> That Rushdie has always presented his material as fictional 'figments of the imagination' is not considered an excuse. (Walsh, 1989)

What Muslims are protesting about is, according to native English criteria, a satire on Islamic authority and tradition. Muslims see it differently; they also appear not to distinguish between an assertion (that something is so) and a purely fictional creation. Instead, their concept of blasphemy appears to equate to the suppression of any publication which might undermine respect for Muslim authority. Here is another example:

> Arswendo Atmowiloto, 42, a newspaper editor in Indonesia, was sentenced to five years in prison for blasphemy against Islam yesterday because he published a readers' poll that rated pop singers, politicians and even himself as more popular than the prophet Muhammad. The paper was closed by the Information Ministry on 23 October after Muslims staged violent demonstrations across the country in the wake of the poll's publication. (*Independent*, 1991a)

The violence of Muslim reaction to *The Satanic Verses* took most people in England by surprise, not least Salman Rushdie himself. It betokens a profound difference between liberal Anglo-Saxon and Muslim points of view. Suppose someone were to write a book satirising Christian authority. Suppose, even worse, that someone were to make that book into a film in which Jesus Christ is shown making love to Mary Magdalene, again in a dream sequence!

The Last Temptation of Christ

The book is *The Last Temptation of Christ* by Nikos Kazantzakis.

> When it [the book] appeared in Greece in 1955 the Orthodox Church sought to prosecute its author. When translations came out in various western European languages, the Roman Catholic Church placed the novel on its index of

forbidden books. In the United States, fundamentalist Protestants attempted, without success, to remove the English translation from public libraries. That was in 1960. (Bien, 1988)

The film was made by Martin Scorsese and released about the same time as *The Satanic Verses*. It provoked a similar reaction.

Government ministers faced demands last night to invoke ancient blasphemy laws to stop the British release of The Last Temptation of Christ, the film denounced by American Christian protestors as the 'most evil attack on the church in the history of entertainment'.

Religious leaders, Conservative MPs and Mary Whitehouse, the campaigner for decency in the media, said the film defamed and ridiculed Christ and was deeply offensive to Christians.

The film is expected to open in Britain on September 9, six months ahead of schedule. This weekend, as the film opened in cities across America, filmgoers queued for up to five hours to see it, defying thousands of demonstrators who had called for a boycott.

The rush release in Britain is intended to take advantage of the publicity bonanza handed to Universal Studios, the producers, by the growing international furore. The film includes a dream sequence in which Jesus, played by William Dafoe, makes love to Mary Magdalene. (Sutherland and Davis, 1988)

The parallel with *The Satanic Verses* is obvious; so how do Christian and Muslim reactions to this kind of publication compare?

First, Muslim authorities exercise much greater political influence in Islamic countries than Christian authorities do in Western countries. In addition to banning the book in certain countries, and not only in Islamic countries, the Secretary-General of the Organisation of Islamic Countries sent an instruction to its 46 member states to ban all Penguin publications unless *The Satanic Verses* was withdrawn (Mills, 1988). Although the Christian protesters persuaded some cinemas not to show *The Last Temptation of Christ* (Gledhill, 1988), there was no government action in their support. 'In 1976 . . . Muslim interests successfully put pressure on a Lebanese film about Muhammad, so that it could be shown only if the prophet were not named in the title or shown on the screen; it was eventually called *The Message* and had only restricted circulation.' (Walter, 1990, p. 69) *The Last Temptation of Christ*, on the other hand, was passed uncut by the British Board of Film Classification (Morgan, 1988). This difference arises, in part, because Christian leaders were far from united in their attitudes to the film.

The Church of England said the film was not blasphemous and urged its followers to make up their own mind about whether or not to see it.

The Very Rev Michael Mayne, the Dean of Westminster, said: 'The trouble about the film is that it is in no way blasphemous. It does not make a mockery of God or the Christian faith.

'It is about the nature of temptation and the conflict of flesh and spirit. But the film is poorly served by its scriptwriter and its actors. Its portrayal of Christ mixes Scripture with pure invention and depicts him as a confused and fanatical miracle worker without much personal charisma,' he said. (Gledhill, 1988)

A second point of comparison is that both protests had counterproductive effects:

In America last night, demonstrators failed for a second day to persuade film-goers to boycott the film. It opened in major cities on Friday and long queues have formed outside cinemas in New York, Los Angeles, Chicago, San Francisco, Minneapolis, Seattle, and in Toronto, Canada.

In Los Angeles more than 3,000 movie-goers joined a mile-long queue in the 32C heat outside the city's glitzy Century City Mall. (Sutherland and Davis, 1988)

The irony is of course that *The Last Temptation of Christ* – a serious, thoughtful, intelligent, reverential and somewhat over-long religious inquest – is the kind of film which, without the furore of protest, would attract very limited audiences. It makes no concession to drama or entertainment in the conventional sense. (Robinson, 1988)

As for the Muslim protests over *The Satanic Verses*, although they got the book banned from Muslim countries where otherwise very few people would even have heard of it, sales in the West – of the hardback edition – exceeded a million, most of them in the USA (Lister, 1990). Meanwhile, in reaction to the demands of the Union of Muslim Organisations, quoted above, the Prime Minister of the day turned not a hair – not, at least, in public. If Muslim leaders had been similarly circumspect, few people, outside the literati who read Booker-prize novels, would have known of the book's existence and Salman Rushdie's satire would have been no more than a transitory verbal exercise. Instead, the Muslim authorities that organised the protests made *The Satanic Verses* into a blasphemy and broadcast it all over the world. Why did they do it?

Quite simply, Muslim authority felt threatened. The resultant furore shows, more starkly than any other single episode, how varied the attitudes of different people can be, how different the points of view from which the same book might be judged. There are systematic differences between liberal Anglo-Saxon and Muslim society. Since there have been more than a few people who have begun life in one society and subsequently migrated into the other, why is no one able to mediate between the two communities in this dispute? It needs, at this point, to be emphasised that one cannot look at Piaget's model of the three mountains (see Figure 3.2 above) from two different points of view at the same time. A child sitting at A can estimate what the doll at B is seeing, but cannot actually see it for himself without physically moving around the model to B, from where, of course, he can no longer see the model from A. While an individual might migrate from liberal Anglo-Saxon society to Muslim, or vice-versa – Salman Rushdie is one such – the process of migration is analogous to moving around Piaget's model. One can view the model from only one perspective at any one time.

While one might imagine an analogous calculation, in advance of publication, of Muslim reaction to *The Satanic Verses*, most people in England at the time entirely lacked the experience needed to envisage what that reaction might be. Salman Rushdie seemed to lack that experience too. He was brought up in a Muslim family in Bombay, but received an English education at Rugby School and King's College, Cambridge. His Muslim upbringing was essential to his being able to write satire that stung so hard; but his English education unfitted him from seeing his work as a Muslim would see it. In consequence Rushdie failed to realise how great an offence it would cause. All of us adults have been children in our time, but none of us really understands how young children see the world.

Spitting Image

Spitting Image was a satirical television show in the late 1980s and early 1990s, in which prominent people, mostly politicians, were caricatured with latex rubber puppets. The satire could be very cruel, though no more than politicians in the United Kingdom have long had to endure; and some, at least, will have viewed their impersonation on *Spitting Image* as a testimony to their public prominence.

Jesus appeared on *Spitting Image* for the first (and last) time on 11 October 1992.

> While appearances of God as a white haired old man have proved uncontroversial, the portrayal of Our Lord as a hippy has stung the Church of England, which is considering making a complaint.
>
> Last night's show included a sketch showing God looking high and low in heaven for a copy of the Bible – until Jesus suggests that he follow J R Hartley and look in the Yellow Pages. (Braid, 1992)

Here is a conventional Christian reaction from Tony Sargent, pastor of The Tabernacle, Worthing.

> This Sunday the ITV authorities are apparently allowing the producers of *Spitting Image* to depict the character of Jesus Christ. I gather there is already a regular part given over to God.
>
> And, though in no way would I wish the media to cause offence to the Muslim community, could I through your columns ask whether a puppet would be allowed to depict the person of Mohammed and permission given for a satirical treatment of the Koran? If, hopefully, the answer is no, could I be informed on what grounds this is allowed for the Bible and the person of Jesus Christ? (Sargent, 1992)

And here is a Muslim reaction.

> It was very irresponsible of the television authority to allow this degrading portrayal of the blessed Jesus. All the Muslims in Britain will, no doubt, support

> any complaint to the Broadcasting Standards Council and the Independent Television Commission. All caring Muslims and all caring Christians should stand up united and strong against this new style of 'blasphemy'. (Katme, 1992)

Summary – what it means to be a 'person'

Different people have different personal histories, different backgrounds of prior experience, and thereby come to look at a common issue from different points of view. That is why many everyday issues are contentious. Notwithstanding that we speak about 'seeing the matter from the other person's point of view', that is what none of us is able to do. We can acknowledge that other people do have different points of view – though many fail even to do that – but we cannot see things from any point of view but our own. We are all of us egocentric.

We each of us have our own individual viewpoints on many different issues, derived from our particular past experiences. It is that distinctive body of past experience and the set of attitudes derived from it that makes each of us a 'person'. It means that it is necessary to look also at the context in which each judgment is made and the relation of that context to the matter at hand, and that will occupy several chapters to come. But, first, I show that a principle analogous to relativity shapes the very world we see around us.

4 The way we see the world

This chapter introduces another basic principle; more precisely, it shows that the principle of relativity that underpins our judgments applies in similar manner to the sensory impressions on which many of those judgments are based – to the very way we see the world around us. Our sense organs – eyes, ears, fingertips, tongue and nose – and especially their connections to the brain are organised so as to be self-adjusting to the prevailing levels of illumination, background noise and odour in the atmosphere. Every mother and father who has changed their baby's dirty nappy will have found the smell, at first, intolerable. But after even a very few seconds that smell seems less, not because the concentration of malodour in the air is reduced, but because the nose has 'adapted' to the prevailing concentration. The physiologist's term for this process is *adaptation*. The manner in which adaptation is accomplished is not yet fully understood, but its most salient component is a differentiation of the signals transmitted by the sense organs along the nerves to the brain. What this means in practice may be encapsulated in this related principle.

> *Sensory experience is built up from the* ***changes*** *in the world about us. Things that stay the same cease to be noticed.*

This means that our sensory experience is itself relative to the immediate context in the same way as are judgments based upon it. We have, however, become so skilled at interpreting our sensory experiences veridically, that this differential property is not in the least obvious – until, that is, we examine our sense of balance.

The sense of balance

There is a sixth sense organ attached to the inner part of each ear, encased in the bones of the head. It is not concerned with hearing, but with balance. If you turn around quickly several times you feel dizzy; that is the balance organ making its presence felt.

The balance organ (technically, the *vestibular organ*) consists of two sac-like structures and three semi-circular canals of about 0.5 mm internal diameter, each filled with a fluid somewhat like seawater. The sacs are sensitive to linear acceleration and to the force of gravity. They enable a skin diver, out of sight of the surface, to know which direction is upwards. The three semi-circular canals are oriented approximately at right angles to each other and are sensitive to rotational acceleration. Because there are three of them, they are jointly sensitive to acceleration about any axis, irrespective of the orientation of the head.

The semi-circular canals and the sacs are not only filled with fluid, but also have sensitive cells equipped with tiny hairs. When the head rotates, the fluid in the semi-circular canals is momentarily left behind. The sensitive cells attached to the walls of the canals move with the head, not with the fluid; but the hairs attached to those cells are held back by the fluid and that results in a signal to the brain. After a short period of continuous rotation, possibly as much as 20 s, the fluid catches up with the motion of the head and the hairs straighten. This makes the cells in the semi-circular canals specifically sensitive to angular acceleration; they do not respond to steady rotation, but to acceleration. However, when a steady rotation comes to an end, the fluid carries on for a brief space of time and the sensitive cells signal deceleration, that is, acceleration in the opposite direction. Acceleration and deceleration are rates of change of motion, and the balance organ is differentially coupled to the physical stimulus (rotation). It signals changes only in the speed of rotation, not the rotation itself. This leads to some problems.

Imagine a gymnast with a highly-developed sense of balance and direction, placed blindfold in a special laboratory chair that rotates, almost without friction, about a vertical pivot. The chair is set in motion and the gymnast reports what he feels.

> I'm turning to the right. I'm turning to the right. I'm turning to the right. I'm turning to the right. Still turning to the right. Now I'm slowing down. I've begun to slow down, slowing down . . . slowing down, slower. I've stopped. (*The chair is still rotating at almost its original speed.*) I'm stopped. – Are you sure? – Yes.

The chair is now suddenly halted . . .

> Now I'm turning to the left and this time faster. I'm turning to the left. – Are you dizzy? – No, I'm not dizzy. – All right take off the blindfold. – Oh, boy! Now I am dizzy . . .

. . . and a close-up view of the gymnast's eyes shows violent nystagmus (from Moon, 1962).

The gymnast experiences no dizziness until he opens his eyes. The dizziness is therefore produced by a conflict between the signal from the balance organ in the inner ear and the signals from the eyes. The visual signals are telling the gymnast that he is stationary; but the inner ear is signalling a rotational acceleration to the left. This conflict arises because the eye signals spatial position in relation to the room in which the demonstration takes place, while the balance organ responds to the inertia of the fluid in the inner ear. The two do not always match.

'Spotting'

One profession in which this presents a problem is ballet dancing. Ballet dancers are often required to make a series of rapid turns in unbroken succession and they manage this without falling over. How? Most people can execute only one or two turns on one foot without stumbling; and I am told that, whilst learning to dance, aspiring ballerinas feel they are progressing when they can manage four or five. Ballet dancers have not always been able to do this. Auguste Bournonville was ballet master at Copenhagen from about 1830 to 1877. His ballets are still sometimes performed today, but, in respect of pirouettes and so on, they contain nothing more elaborate than single and double turns and use even those movements no more than sparingly (Lawson, 1960, p. 147). By the end of the nineteenth century, however, ballet dancers knew how to pirouette without falling over. The technique is popularly known as 'spotting'.

While the dancer's body is turning, the eyes are kept fixed for as great a part of each turn as possible on some stationary part of the auditorium or stage set. This means that the dancer's head has to be whipped around faster than her body. In practice, the head might complete its turn in about half the time taken by the body, and spend the other half of each body-turn in a stationary position, achieved by fixing the eyes on the same spot each time. As the head begins its turn with rapid acceleration there is a strong signal from the balance organ. But this is cancelled half a body-turn later by an equally strong deceleration. This recurrent pattern of acceleration and deceleration is sketched in Figure 4.1. In the upper part of the diagram the dancer's body is turning at a constant rate and the broken line shows how the sensation from the balance organ would decrease with time if her head were turning at a uniform rate, in a fixed relationship to her body. When the dancer stops, there is a sharp sensation from the balance organ signalling acceleration in the contrary direction. In the lower part of the diagram the head is whipped round quickly and then remains stationary while the body completes its turn. There is a strong sensation from the balance organ (broken line again) when the head begins its turn, but this is mostly cancelled one-third of a second later when the head comes to a halt. This cycle is repeated for each complete turn of the body. It produces an input from the balance organ that approximates the actual angular velocity with which the head is moving and thereby matches the visual signal that the dancer picks up through her eyes.

With this technique Pierina Legnani, 'prima ballerina assoluta' of the Imperial Russian Ballet in the 1890s, was able to accomplish the virtuoso feat of dancing 32 consecutive fouettés. A fouetté is a turn in which the dancer whips the free leg outwards and back in again to the knee of the supporting leg, once in each complete revolution. Accordingly, a sequence of 32 fouettés was choreographed into a number of ballets created in St. Petersburg at that time. The best known of these is *Swan Lake*. Figure 4.2 shows Altynai Asylmuratova of the Kirov Ballet,

Figure 4.1 How 'spotting' keeps the ballerina upright. The broken lines sketch the time course of vestibular sensation. The upper diagram shows what would happen if the ballerina's head was kept in a fixed position in relation to her body; the lower diagram shows the difference made by 'spotting'.

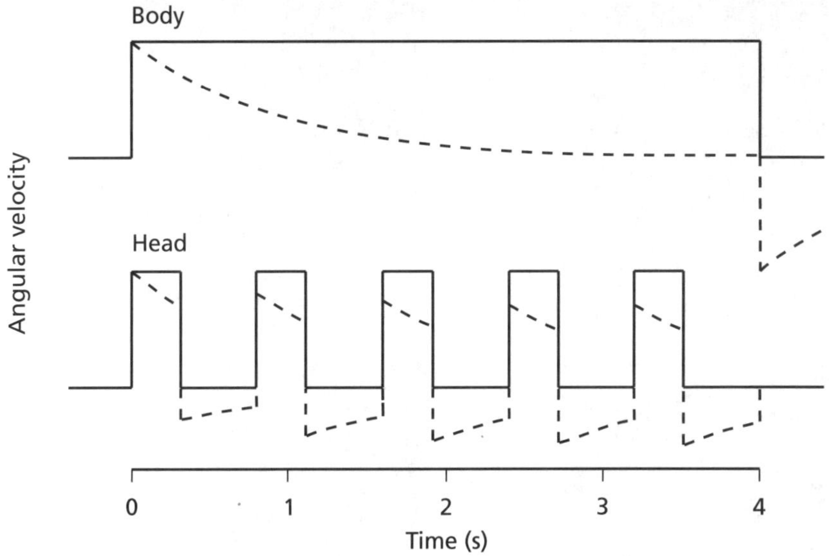

Pierina Legnani's present-day successor, dancing one of the 32 fouettés in *Le Corsaire* and shows the dancer's position at successive intervals of 1/25th second. Each revolution is completed in about 0.82 seconds. But the dancer's head does not begin to move until frame 9 in Figure 4.2 and is back to its 'spotting' position, looking out at the audience, by frame 17; therefore, the rotation of the head takes only 0.32 seconds.

Fouettés are habitually danced at about 0.8 s per revolution, and it might be thought that this rate of rotation is a compromise between the need to complete the turning of the head within a sufficiently small proportion of the revolution of the body and the need to rotate the body at a sufficient rate to preserve balance, much as a spinning top, slightly off-balance, does not fall over – instead its axis of rotation precesses. But calculations by Laws (2002, Appendix F) suggest that the angular momentum of the dancer is too small for any lack of balance to be ignored in this way. Instead, the dancer descends to demi-pointe (toes flat on the floor, frames 20 to 22 and 1 to 3) for a part of each turn to generate renewed torque for the next turn. Minor deficits in balance can be corrected at this stage in the fouetté, and the period of rotation is limited by the need for periodic corrections to balance. On the other hand, the movement of the free leg plays a very significant, possibly essential role. Laws (2002, Appendix I) calculates that when the free leg is fully extended (frames 21 to 22 and 1 to 2) the dancer's moment of inertia is increased about four-fold over its value when the leg is fully tucked in with the foot at the knee of the supporting leg (frames 12 to 14). The dancer's rate of turn varies in inverse proportion to her moment of inertia, so

1

2

3

4

5

6

7

8

9

10

11

12

13

14

15

16

17

18

19

20

21

22

Figure 4.2 A sequence of 22 video frames to illustrate a fouetté. Successive photographs show the dancer's position at intervals of 1/25th s. A complete revolution takes about 0.82 s, but the dancer's head is moving for just 0.32 s (Frames 13–20). (Performance by Altynai Asylmuratova of the Kirov Ballet Company. From *Le Corsaire* by kind permission of NVC Arts.)

that, at that point in the fouetté when the dancer's head is turning (frames 9 to 17), her body is also turning fast (it rotates about 225° in this interval), easing the task of turning the head sufficiently rapidly relative to the body.

But what sensation does the ballerina experience while she is dancing those 32 fouettés? If the rotation of the head in Figure 4.1 were instantaneous, the acceleration and deceleration of the balance mechanism would cancel exactly. But 'instantaneous' is impossible because the head has inertia. So one would expect a sensation of dizziness to build up gradually, but much more slowly than if you or I were trying to pirouette. Deborah Bull was formerly a principal dancer with the Royal Ballet. In that capacity she danced the role of Odette/Odile in *Swan Lake*, so that, when introducing a performance of *Swan Lake* by the Royal Swedish Ballet on Christmas Day, 2002 (MacGibbon and Hornblad, 2002), she was able to speak about the particular difficulties presented by this dual role, including '... let's not forget about the thirty-two *head-spinning* fouettés in the third act' (italics added. © British Broadcasting Corporation. Reproduced by permission).

Motorway driving

When the head is rotating, the signals from the balance organ and from the eye are out of kilter; but with straight forwards motion this is no longer so. The balance organ responds in the same way to linear motion as to rotation, that is, it signals acceleration, not velocity. But the response of the eye is now different. When moving in a forwards direction, the eye also responds to acceleration, not velocity, because it adapts to a steady forwards motion. This will be readily appreciated by anyone who has driven along a motorway at 70 mph.

Driving along a motorway or any other straight road at high speed produces a strong visual response to the motion of the scenery past one's gaze, followed, rather quickly, by a desensitisation. We talk about a visual *flow-field*. The response of the eye (more properly, of the entire visual system, because the effect is known to be due to the way in which the brain processes the signals it receives from the eye) is very similar to the response of the balance mechanism sketched in Figure 4.1. There is an initially strong response to the motion which 'adapts' to a point where the driver is less than fully aware of how fast he or she is travelling. That lack of awareness does not matter much until the driver leaves the motorway. At that point there is a tendency to underestimate the speed of one's car, and this is a known cause of accidents.

At some exits from motorways and on the approaches to some roundabouts a series of yellow stripes may be seen painted across the road. The stripes are 2 ft wide and extend across the full width of the carriageway. There are typically 90 stripes arranged over about a quarter mile of the carriageway, and the distance between successive stripes decreases steadily from 20 ft at the beginning of the series to 10 ft at the end. Because these stripes are placed progressively closer and closer together, they give a spurious illusion of acceleration (to a driver travelling

Figure 4.3 The speeds of vehicles entering the Newbridge roundabout on the Glasgow–Edinburgh motorway in 1971 (a) before and (b) after the installation of a COSBI (control of speed by illusion) bar pattern.

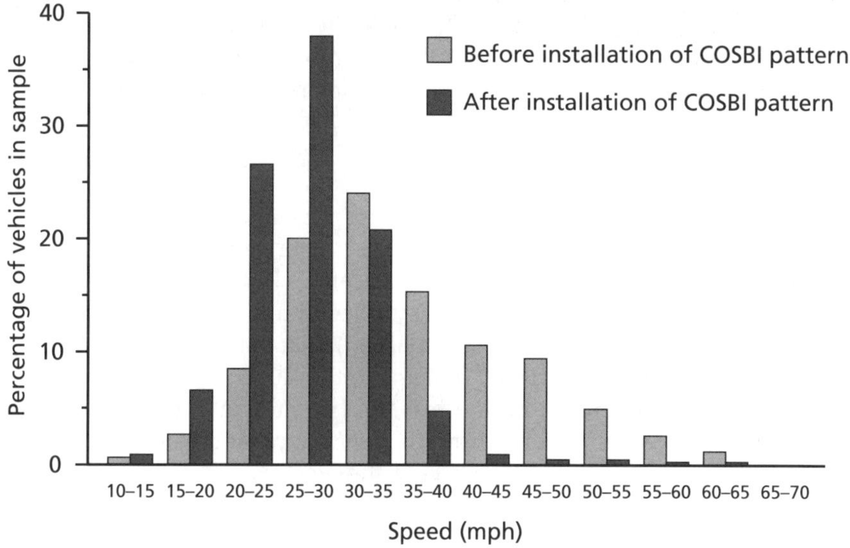

Data from Denton, 1980, p. 400.

Figure 4.4 Harmonic spiral.

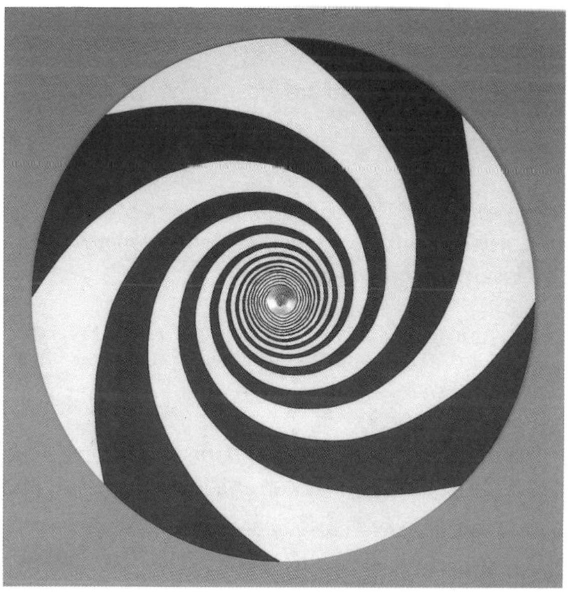

at constant speed) that counters the underestimation of speed resulting from previous adaptation. Figure 4.3 (light grey bars) shows the speeds of nearly 20 000 vehicles entering the Newbridge roundabout on the Glasgow–Edinburgh motorway in 1971. The average speed is 35.4 mph. The dark grey bars show the speeds of a further 23 000 vehicles after the pattern of yellow stripes had been installed. The average speed is now only 27.4 mph (Denton, 1980).

The sensory basis of this effect is easily demonstrated in the laboratory. When the disc shown in Figure 4.4 is rotated clockwise at about 25 rpm, the black and white stripes are not seen to go round with the disc, but instead to expand outwards. The rate of expansion increases with distance from the centre in such a manner as to simulate the visual *flow-field* experienced on a motorway. As little as 30 s viewing produces a noticeable after-effect. The sensation is somewhat like travelling through a tunnel composed of black and white stripes. When the gaze is thereafter transferred to some stationary object (I use a photograph of a set of yellow stripes on the approach to a roundabout), that object appears to be receding, notwithstanding that it visibly remains in the same spatial position. If that stationary object happens to be the exit road from a motorway, the illusory appearance of recession subtracts from the real impression of speed created by travelling along the road, and the driver estimates his speed to be less than it really is.

Sensory adaptation

The nature of sensory adaptation is most clearly experienced in the sense of smell. I put this point with a mini-playlet in two acts.

Act 1: *A young man is calling for his girl to take her out for the evening*

He: That's a lovely perfume you are wearing. What is it?

She: It's *Tendre Poison*.

Act 2: *It is three years later. The couple are now married and have a small baby. They are sitting comfortably together one evening when there is a clear eruption inside the baby's nappy.*

She: Go on! It's your turn!

He: (*Unwillingly taking the baby upstairs*) Ugh!

Happily his sense of smell rapidly 'adapts': moreover, when he returns with the baby cleaned up, he can smell his wife's Tendre Poison *once more.*

It is the sense of smell that adapts – not the perfume.

The perception of motion

The after-effect from the rotating spiral in Figure 4.4 means that the underestimation of speed as one leaves a motorway is not a simple misjudgment, but a perceptual distortion; that is to say, it occurs because of the way the brain processes the input from the eyes, rather than because of any defect in the frame of reference used by the driver in estimating his or her speed. But the site of the effect does not lie in the eyes themselves. If the rotating disc is viewed with one eye only and then some stationary object viewed with the other eye alone, that stationary object will still appear to be receding. The effect crosses from one eye to the other and must therefore be realised in the brain. This adaptation of the brain to the motion indicates a process of a physiological, even quasi-mechanical, kind. It cannot be overcome, even with appropriate training.

The after-effect also implies that the primary stimulus to the brain is the motion itself. Although, in a mechanical sense, the motion must be derived from the changing pattern of the visual field, the motion is functionally primary, a property of the motorway scene that is perceived immediately. What this means is that it should be possible, in principle at least, to experience the motion without there being any real change of position. That may sound a contradiction in terms, but it captures precisely the subjective experience of the after-effect.

This visual experience has its analogue in hearing. There is a sequence of complex tones that appears to be continuously ascending in pitch; yet, after a little while, one realises that this sequence is never going to ascend out of the audible range. In fact, it repeats exactly after every twelve tones (Shepard, 1964). There is also a continuous analogue, an endlessly descending glissando which never gets to the bottom of the scale (Risset, 1969).

The Craik–Cornsweet illusion

The disappearance of the balance organ's response to steady rotation and the diminution of the visual system's response to progression along a motorway are examples of sensory adaptation. Sensory experience in general is characterised by self-adjustment to the prevailing level of stimulation. Any ability to make absolute judgments about all kinds of sensory experiences is thereby lost, but there is, instead, a much greater sensitivity to changes about the prevailing level. On the motorway a driver tends to have only a vague idea of his or her actual speed (without looking at the speedometer), yet is immediately sensitive to a car in an adjacent lane travelling a little slower or a little faster. Likewise, photographers use exposure meters (even though, nowadays, most cameras are automatic) because they are unable to judge absolute light levels with sufficient accuracy. This happens because the eye adapts to the prevailing level of light. As a consequence, unaided judgment of light level is extraordinarily poor, but comparative judgment of changes in that level, is surprisingly good. This idea is acutely illustrated by Figure 4.5.

When the disc in the left-hand panel of Figure 4.5 is spun rapidly (1600 rpm), it is indistinguishable from the photograph in the middle panel. In that middle

Figure 4.5 The Craik–Cornsweet illusion. The middle and right-hand photographs were made from the same photographic negative, which was taken while the disc in the left-hand print was rotated at high speed. The inner disc has the same (time-average) luminance as the periphery, but it appears darker in the middle panel because at the boundary only the sharp step in luminance is perceptible.

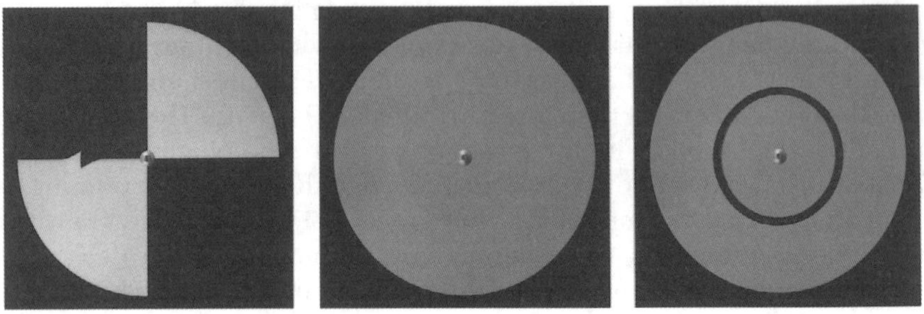

Reproduced with permission from D. Laming, *Sensory Analysis*, p. 64. © 1986 Academic Press.

panel the inner part of the disc appears darker than the annulus surrounding it; this is so, even though the centre and the periphery present the same proportionate (50:50) mixture of black and white. If, however, the boundary between these two areas is obscured by a thin opaque ring (right-hand panel of Figure 4.5), the centre and the periphery appear to be equally bright. Now remove the ring from the boundary (centre panel again) and the illusion is restored. The photograph in the right-hand panel was made by laying a thin black annulus of appropriate size on a print of the middle photograph and re-photographing the combination, so that the relative luminances of the centre and the periphery are unchanged. The difference in apparent brightness depends entirely on whether one can see the boundary between the two.

The illusion is compelling, even when one knows how it is accomplished. It demonstrates that there is no direct sensory comparison of the luminances of the central disc and of the periphery; in fact, there would need to be a difference of at least 25 per cent before that difference became noticeable. Instead, the relative brightness of these two areas is inferred from the way in which the luminance is perceived to change at the boundary. The abrupt step created by the kink in the profile of the black sector in the left-hand panel corresponds to an increase in luminance of two per cent and is easily noticeable, while the smooth ramps either side are not. On that basis the inner disc is judged to be darker. But if that entire variation of luminance in the boundary region is obscured by the ring (right-hand panel), one perceives just two equal steps in luminance of equal magnitude, one up and one down, either side of the black ring. The inner disc and the periphery now appear equally bright. Only the changes in luminance are used as a basis for judgment.

Figure 4.6 Crovitz's illusion.

(a)

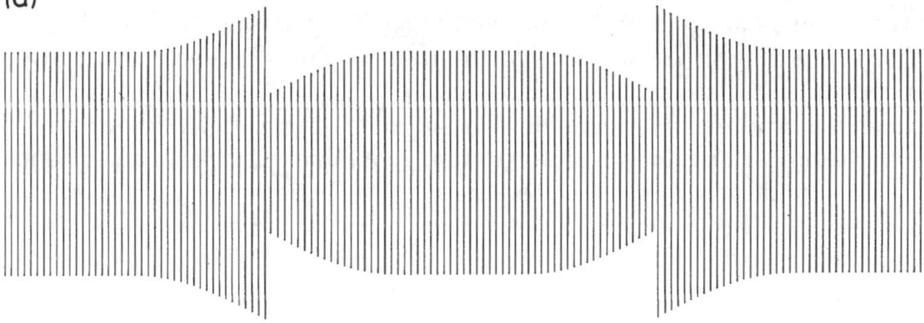

(b)

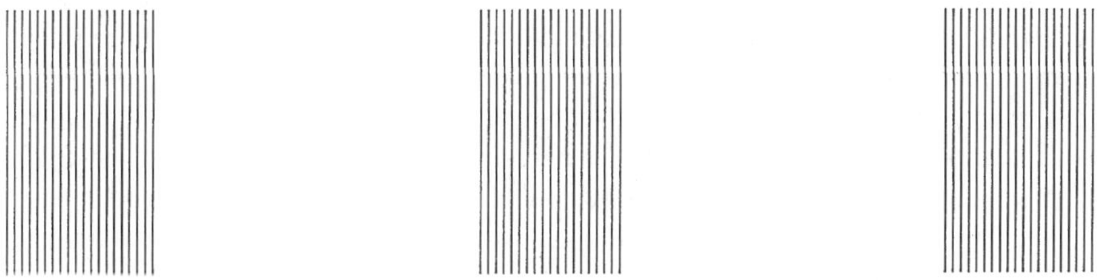

Reproduced with permission (a) from D. Laming, *Sensory Analysis*, p. 65. © 1986 Academic Press; (b) from D. Laming, 'Précis of *Sensory Analysis*', *Behavioral and Brain Sciences*, vol. 11, p. 276. © 1988 Cambridge University Press.

Crovitz's illusion

The Craik–Cornsweet illusion has analogues in other sensory attributes. Figure 4.6 shows Crovitz's illusion (Crovitz, 1976). The lines in the centre of the upper figure (a) look shorter than those at the extreme ends, notwithstanding that they are measurably of the same length. In the lower figure, where the intervening lines of variable length are omitted, this appearance is dispelled. This illusion is less compelling than the Craik–Cornsweet illusion because here there is a possibility of comparing the lines in the centre with those at the edges directly. Under such direct comparison, uncomplicated by the intervening lines of graduated length, a difference in length as small as one per cent may be noticeable, whereas the luminances of the centre and the periphery in Figure 4.5 need to differ by 25 per cent before that difference becomes similarly noticeable.

The taste of water

Today we recognise four primary tastes – bitter, salt, sour and sweet – but this is convention, not established fact. Aristotle recognised only two tastes, bitter and sweet; while in the sixteenth, seventeenth and eighteenth centuries the number of recognised primary tastes increased to as many as ten (Pfaffmann *et al.*, 1971, p. 82). If 'sweet' is a primary taste, a sweet substance ought always to taste sweet, a bitter substance ought always to taste bitter, and so on. But that is not what happens.

Bartoshuk (1968) has shown that the taste of pure, double-distilled water depends on what has previously been poured over the tongue. I demonstrate Bartoshuk's finding to my students in the following manner (though without Bartoshuk's laboratory precision). I first give them a sample of an unnamed colourless liquid to drink. What does it taste like? Acid, bitter, insipid, neutral, salt or sweet? The students are then given a slice of lemon to suck for half a minute and asked to taste the unnamed liquid again. Finally, they are each given a lump of sugar to suck; what does the liquid taste like now?

The unnamed liquid is, of course, water – double-distilled, de-ionised, the purest H_2O I can obtain. It has virtually no effect at all on the taste receptors on the tongue. This is known from the following observation. The nerve from the front part of the tongue runs through the middle ear and is exposed when the middle ear is opened up for surgery. It is then a simple matter to record the electrical response of the taste nerve to various sapid solutions placed on the tongue, and the fact that the patient is under a general anaesthetic does not invalidate those recordings. Electrical responses have been obtained to several different solutions. But when distilled water is placed upon the tongue, there is no reaction; the pattern of electrical activity that is present before the water is applied simply fades away (Zotterman and Diament, 1959). Distilled water seems indeed to be neutral, although ordinary tap water contains trace elements that give it a detectable taste.

Nevertheless, after sucking a slice of lemon, distilled water tends to taste sweet in an obvious comparison with the acidity of the lemon. After sucking a lump of sugar, water tends to taste bitter; while initially some people say it is bitter, others merely comment that it is insipid or flat. Distilled water is judged 'insipid' or 'flat' possibly because it lacks the low level of carbonic acid usually present in fresh drinking water, but the sometimes 'bitter' taste requires further explanation. Saliva is ordinarily slightly salty, with a chemical composition that varies from one person to another. Drinking distilled water dilutes the saliva in one's mouth, and the taste attributed to the water is due to the lowered concentration of salt. In a well-controlled laboratory experiment in which sapid solutions were poured directly and continuously onto the tongue, the effect is powerful (Bartoshuk, 1968). It shows that the taste attributed to the water depends on what solution has previously been poured onto the tongue. It is the change in oral environment that determines the taste. Distilled water preceded by lemon juice represents just such a change, and the resultant taste is attributed to the water.

Wine and food

In Chapter 1, and again in Chapter 2, I mentioned Robert Parker, the American wine writer. The week after his visit to London in December 1987 to promote his second wine book, Egon Ronay, gourmet and author of the restaurant guide, had this to say.

> What is the good of tasting wine without food? . . . It is a barren, abstract exercise at best, practised by a narcissistic circle admiring each other's memory and pretending it is tantamount to a good palate. . . .
>
> The wine clergy's cant annoys me. . . . bouquet . . . is a pleasant symptom, but only to be noticed in passing, not to celebrate by a highly exaggerated, Chaplinesque burying of noses in the fumes accompanied by comical mutterings parading as ecclesiastical verdicts. . . .
>
> Certain foods change the taste of wine and vice versa. The acidity of tomatoes will make a dry white graves appear to be sweetish and it is pointless to be told that the wine is magnificent. Gâteaux lend uncharacteristic dryness to liebfraumilch, while a tart apple pie sweetens it. *Coq au vin* makes a delightful sancerre watery. The tradition-bound French habit of drinking any champagne with desserts is ritualistic bunkum, the remnant of the *belle époque* when sweet champagne was widespread. Red wine is killed by curry, so is hock, but a loire is acceptable (though lager or mineral water is best). Coupling all cheeses with red wine is a worldwide fallacy: many are better with white, though to choose the right white wine with a cheese is very tricky. (Ronay, 1987)

Egon Ronay's assertion that the taste of a wine depends on the food it accompanies is supported by experiment.

Land's two-colour phenomenon

The Craik–Cornsweet illusion (Figure 4.5) works with colour as well, though with less compulsion than with black and white. Edwin Land (1974) has published a photograph showing the effect with a red and blue sectored disc. It means that our judgment of colour also is based on changes in hue across boundaries in the visual scene. That is a matter of which many women are implicitly aware – ill-chosen clothes can 'clash' horribly. It provides the basis for perhaps the most surprising illusion of all (Land, 1959).

Two black-and-white photographs are taken of the same scene, one through a red filter, one through a green. These photographs are both converted into positive black-and-white transparencies and projected simultaneously onto the same screen so that they superimpose exactly. The transparency taken through the red filter is projected through the same red filter as that which was used in the first place. But the transparency taken through the green filter is projected, not with green light, but with ordinary white light. That white light is, however, reduced in intensity in order to maintain a balance with the red-filtered transparency, and that balance is achieved by projecting the green-filtered transparency through a neutral density filter. These two transparencies, then, are exactly superimposed on the screen. Although the image is everywhere some mixture of red and white light, one sees a nearly full spectrum of hues.

To be sure, the colours are wishy-washy. The image on the screen is impoverished; that is only to be expected. What is unexpected is that the impoverishment of the percept does not correspond to the known impoverishment (shades of red/white only) of the illumination. Instead, the impoverishment is spread throughout the three dimensions (hue, saturation and luminance) of colour perception, because our judgment of colour is based on changes in the visual scene, changes between adjacent colours, and not on any one colour absolutely.

Land first demonstrated this phenomenon with a bowl of fruit, with the advantage that everyone knows bananas are yellow and grapes are either pale green or deep purple. One might suppose on that account that there might be some element of suggestion in the illusion. But this appears not to be so. Suppose the coloured filters are interchanged; that is, the transparency taken through the red filter is projected through a neutral density filter, while the transparency taken through the green filter is projected, not in green light, but in *red*. The result is a compelling colour reversal. Bananas remain yellow, but a tangerine (ordinarily bright orange) is seen to be ice-blue, even when one knows that it is a tangerine! Land's two-colour phenomenon results from the mechanical way in which our brains analyse colour. This is not a process that we can modify, not with any amount of training.

Summary – how we understand what our eyes and ears are telling us

A study of the way in which our senses work – not the sense organs themselves, but the way in which signals from those sense organs are processed by the brain – shows that our sensory experience is differentially coupled to the world around us. Although we see a solid, stable world, that picture is built up in our minds from the changes detected by our senses. The appearance of a woman's dress depends on the colours of whatever she is wearing with it. The taste of wine depends on what food we are eating with it. The apparent speed of one's car depends on how fast and how long one has been travelling along the motorway. Our entire sensory experience of the world is relative.

The principle of relativity applies both to our judgments and to our more primitive sensations. At the sensory level it is realised in a differential action of sensory analysis that is, as it were, wired in to our brains at a preconscious level. It applies to all sensory attributes and modalities. It means that any claim to a capacity for absolute judgment should be treated with scepticism.

5 The quality of human judgment

At the beginning of Chapter 2 I announced that

There is no absolute judgment. All judgments are comparisons of one thing with another.

In this chapter I add to that principle.

The comparisons are little better than ordinal;

that is, one sound may be louder, softer, or about the same as another, but that is all we can say.

A 'sliding ruler'?

As a way of explaining what 'ordinal judgment' means, let us consider a 'sliding ruler'. I have in mind a rigid ruler, but one that is not securely anchored in position and might slip sideways from one measurement to the next (see Figure 5.1 below). It cannot provide any absolute measurement of position, because it has slipped from its initial position by some unknown distance, but it does support an absolute measurement of *differences* within its span.

The measurement of longitude provides one example of a 'sliding ruler'. Position on the Earth's surface is specified by latitude and longitude. Latitude can easily be determined from the altitude of the pole star or the sun at meridian. The horizon provides a natural point of reference and measurement of the angle of altitude with a sextant is effectively absolute. Prior to radio navigation, a ship fixed its longitude by timing the transit of the sun or a star and comparing the local time of transit with Greenwich Mean Time. GMT is not available as a natural point of reference – no absolute measurement is possible – and has to be supplied from some extraneous source. This navigational problem was so pressing that in 1714 Parliament offered a reward of £20 000 (about £2m in today's money) for any means of determining longitude within 30 miles after six weeks' sailing. That meant a chronometer accurate to within three seconds per day. That prize was eventually won by John Harrison, a London clockmaker, in 1762 at his fourth attempt (Sobel, 1995).

If GMT were known exactly, longitude could be determined absolutely. The principle of relativity says that human judgment is not like that. If the error of the chronometer is not known, longitude cannot be determined absolutely;

but it is still possible to measure *changes* in longitude (i.e. each day's sailing) accurately. That would be a 'sliding ruler'. If human judgment were like that, then it would indeed be relative, because the sliding ruler has no anchorage. But a 'sliding ruler' has, as we shall see, other properties that do not accord with the results of experiment. While the idea that we are able to say no more than this sound is louder, softer or about the same as that one, might appear contrary to everyday experience, it is nevertheless forced on us by careful and precise experimental observation.

Absolute judgment of auditory frequency

Let us now see how a 'sliding ruler' might model the experiment by Pollack (1953) described in Chapter 2. In that experiment the subject was asked to identify one of nine different frequencies. Before each tone to be identified there was a reference tone: 'This is tone no. 3'. Figure 5.1 shows the equivalent number of categories corresponding to the accuracy with which each frequency was

Figure 5.1 Accuracy of identification of auditory frequency with and without a reference tone. The data points show the equivalent number of categories for each individual tone in a set of nine.

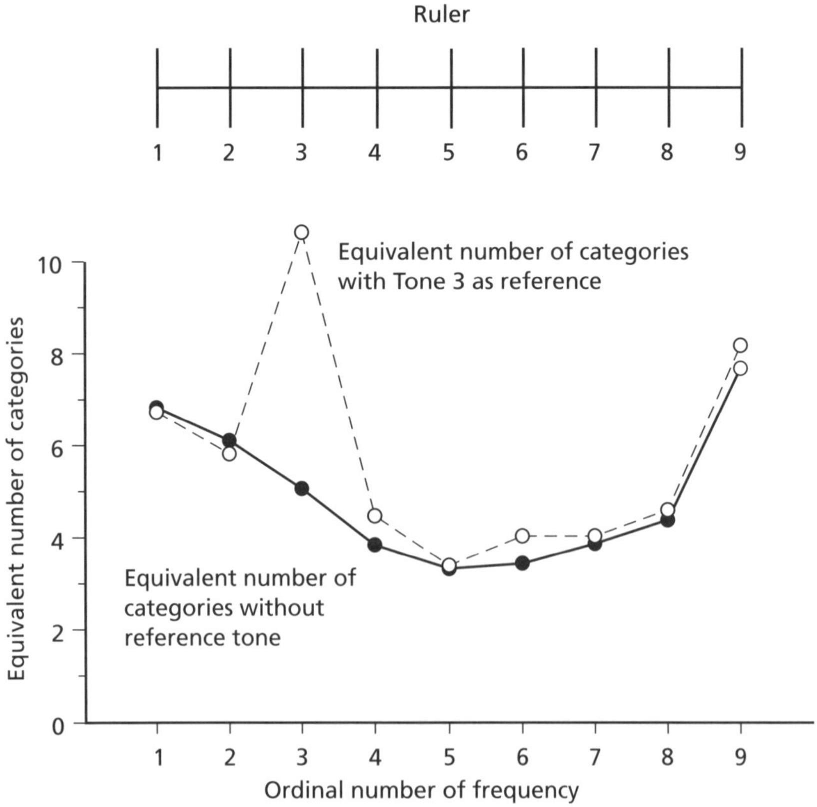

Data from Pollack, 1953..

identified. In the control condition (without the reference tone, filled points in Figure 5.1) the subjects' identifications of the extreme frequencies (Tones 1 and 9) were more accurate (equivalent to 6.8 and 7.7 categories respectively) than the middle frequency (equivalent to 3.3 categories). That could be the result of a ruler which slips and slides between successive judgments. When the ruler slips to the left, Tone 9 moves off the scale, but it can still be identified as 'Tone 9' because there is no higher frequency with which it might be confused.

With a 'sliding ruler' there is an absolute judgment of *differences*, though not of frequency itself. Errors occur because the frame of reference slides up and down the set of stimuli. But prior presentation of a reference tone ('This is tone no. 3') should anchor the ruler in its correct position and improve accuracy over the entire scale. The open circles in Figure 5.1 show the improvement in identification when Tone 3 was provided as a reference. When Tone 3 was followed by itself, the subject's accuracy was equivalent to 10.6 categories. But that improvement was specific to Tone 3 as the frequency to be identified. It did not extend to the whole set of stimuli. When Tones 5, 6 and 7 were provided as reference tones, there was some improvement in the identification of immediately neighbouring tones – to 4 and 6, 5 and 7, and 6 and 8 respectively – but still not extending over the whole set. If the principle of relativity were equivalent to a 'sliding ruler', the improvement effected by a prior reference tone would extend to the entire set of frequencies to be identified. Such an improvement is not observed; the 'ruler' is not rigid. That explains why we use tape measures and scale pans for measuring length and weight.

Chevrons on the M1

There are about 2000 nose-to-tail collisions involving injury each year on Britain's motorways. They cost the economy about £60m. The Transport Research Laboratory has conducted trials with chevrons marked on the carriageways of the M1. The chevrons were devised in France to keep vehicles apart: 'Keep apart, 2 chevrons'. A trial site in Northamptonshire was marked with chevrons at 40 meter intervals, and a distance of two chevrons equates to 2.5 seconds for a vehicle travelling at 70 mph. This is slightly longer than the Highway Code's recommended interval (two seconds) between following vehicles.

Table 5.1 Number of accidents involving injury at the Northamptonshire trial site (Helliar-Symons and Butler, 1995, p. 8).

	3 years before	1st year after	2nd year after
Test site	93	13	11
Control site	402	114	122
Percentage change at test site		–51%	–61%

Adapted from R. D. Helliar-Symons and N. R. Butler, 'M1 chevron trial – Accident study'. Project Report 118, Transport Research Laboratory, Crowthorne, Berkshire.

Table 5.1 sets out the number of accidents at the test site and at a comparable control site for three years before and two years after the installation of the chevrons. During these five years there was, of course, an increase in the volume of traffic using the motorway and hence in vehicle speeds and frequency of accidents. On the assumption that the frequency of accidents at the test site would, apart from the installation of the chevrons, have changed in the same proportion that was observed at the control site, one can calculate the percentage change shown in the bottom row of the table as attributable to the chevrons. In fact, there was a negligible effect on vehicle speed. There was a small reduction in the proportion of vehicles following another closely, but a *large* reduction in the number of accidents. Accidents appear to happen because vehicles get too close, and this includes single-vehicle accidents where one car only runs out of control. This suggests that drivers are unable to judge their distance from the next vehicle in front with sufficient accuracy. The chevrons are a crude example of a 'sliding ruler'. They are fixed on the M1, but the vehicles are moving over them. The provision of this sliding ruler reduces the rate of accidents because the judgment of the car drivers is otherwise *little better than ordinal.*

Magnitude estimation

Pollack's (1953) experiment comparing the accuracy of identification of auditory frequency, with and without a reference tone, shows that while a point of reference improves the accuracy of identification, that improvement does not extend to the whole scale of frequency. The comparisons underlying the judgments are little better than ordinal. The same inference can be justified on the basis of quite a different experimental procedure – magnitude estimation.

Magnitude estimation was originally devised by Stevens (1956) as a means, supposedly, of measuring internal sensation. In Stevens' illustrative experiment the stimulus was a 1 kHz tone. The subject had a pair of switches to push. One of them produced the 1 kHz tone at a fixed, standard, level; the other produced the same tone, but at a level that changed from one judgment to the next. The task is most readily described by means of the verbatim instructions to the subject:

> The left key presents the standard tone and the right key presents the variable. We are going to call the loudness of the standard 10 and your task is to estimate the loudness of the variable. In other words, the question is: if the standard is called 10 what would you call the variable? Use whatever numbers seem to you appropriate – fractions, decimals, or whole numbers. For example, if the variable sounds 7 times as loud as the standard, say 70. If it sounds one-fifth as loud, say 2; if a twentieth as loud, say 0.5, etc.
>
> Try not to worry about being consistent; try to give the appropriate number to each tone regardless of what you may have called some previous stimulus.

> Press the 'standard' key for 1 or 2 sec. and listen carefully. Then press the 'variable' for 1 or 2 sec. and make your judgment. (Stevens, 1956, p. 3)

The purpose of this procedure was to record the loudness of the tone as heard by the subject – the point being that the physical measure of auditory intensity (the energy of the sound) with a sound level meter is one thing, and people's judgments of loudness quite another. Averaging judgments from a cohort of subjects, Stevens obtained the relation

$$\text{Loudness} = aE^{0.3},$$

where a is a constant and E the energy of the sound. This relation is equivalent to the sone scale. Magnitude estimation has been applied to many other sensory attributes as well with the typical result

$$N = aX^{\beta},$$

where N is the (geometric) average numerical estimate and X the physical measure of the attribute. The exponent (power) β varies from attribute to attribute (see Stevens, 1975, p. 15, Table 1). This result is known as *Stevens' Power Law.*

Correlation of successive magnitude estimates

While such a result might appear to suggest some absolute internal standard of judgment, these equations relate only to the average of some very variable estimates. Much more informative for present purposes is a replication of the experiment by Baird, Green and Luce (1980), which examined the correlations between successive numerical estimates. In this experiment each stimulus was presented many different times for judgment and was assigned a variety of different numbers on those different presentations. If, on some particular presentation, the numerical estimate is high relative to what is usual for that stimulus, what happens to the estimate of the stimulus immediately following? If the stimulus is repeated, is that following estimate also high, as the principle of relativity might suggest? The correlations between successive numerical estimates tell a rather different story.

The stimuli in the experiment by Baird *et al.* (1980) were 21 different 1 kHz tones of 0.5 s duration, ranging from 40 to 90 dB sound pressure level in steps of 2.5 dB. A standard at the middle of the range (65 dB) was presented at the start of each run of 100 trials and called '100'. Now Stevens' Power Law can be written in the form

$$\log N = \log a + \beta \log X.$$

The stimulus levels (X) are evenly spaced (in 2.5 dB steps) on this logarithmic scale, and the power law prescribes that the log numerical estimates should also be evenly spaced. This makes it appropriate to look at correlations between

Figure 5.2 Correlations between successive log numerical estimates in the experiment by Baird *et al.* (1980).

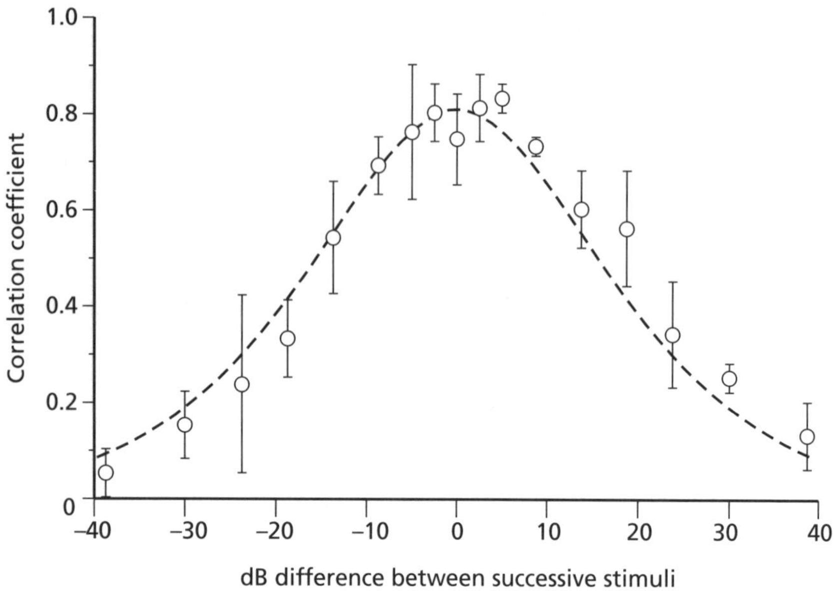

Figure adapted with permission from J. C. Baird, D. M. Green and R. D. Luce, 'Variability and sequential effects in cross-modality matching of area and loudness'. *Journal of Experimental Psychology: Human Perception and Performance*, vol. 6, p. 286, © 1980 American Psychological Association, and reproduced with the permission of Oxford University Press from D. Laming, *The Measurement of Sensation*, p. 129. © 1997 Donald Laming.

successive *log* numerical estimates. Those correlations are shown in Figure 5.2 in relation to the dB difference between the corresponding stimuli. When the stimulus level is repeated (to within ±5 dB), successive log estimates correlate about +0.8, but when there is a large difference between successive stimulus levels, the correlation disappears to almost nothing.

The 'sliding ruler' again

Consider what these results mean. There is a variety of different numbers assigned to the same stimulus on different presentations. If, on some particular presentation of the stimulus, the numerical estimate is high relative to that variety of different numbers, and if the following stimulus is of a similar level (within ±5 dB), then the next estimate is also high. Such a relationship could result from a sliding ruler that happened to have slipped downwards from its correct location, giving high measurements on two successive trials. In fact, a correlation of +0.8 means that the second assignment has inherited 64 per cent (0.8^2) of its variability from the first, which must therefore have been used as a point of reference for the second judgment. This is the most compelling evidence of all for the principle of relativity.

But note that the correlation is not perfect (+1.0). The sliding ruler (if it is a ruler) slips a little further between the first measurement and the second, and the resultant error of comparison dilutes the relationship between the two successive numerical estimates. But if the ruler were perfectly rigid, that additional slippage would be the same at all points of the stimulus scale; that is, the dilution of the relationship between the two successive numerical estimates, and hence the correlation, would be the same for all differences between successive stimuli. But this is observed not to happen.

To express the implication of this finding clearly, I set the argument out formally.

1*a*. Estimates of the same stimulus made on different trials vary; this happens because the ruler slips between trials.

2*a*. The ruler slips only a little from one trial to the next, though it can slip much further between widely separated trials. So, when a stimulus is repeated, the successive estimates are more alike than estimates from widely separated trials. This leads to the positive correlation +0.8.

3*a*. If the ruler is *rigid* (that is, if it is a *ruler*), errors arise only from slippage and, for any given position of the ruler, are the same for all differences between successive stimuli – that is, the correlation is the same for all successive pairs of stimuli .

That is manifestly not true, as a glance at Figure 5.2 quickly shows. Exit 'sliding ruler'.

Ordinal judgment

Let us examine that argument again.

1*b*. When a stimulus level is repeated to within ±5 dB, 64 per cent (0.8^2) of the variability of the second estimate is inherited from the first. So, the stimulus on the first trial and the number assigned to it provide a point of reference for the judgment on the second trial.

2*b*. The comparison of one stimulus with its predecessor is not without error. Accordingly, the correlation between successive estimates is diluted (it is less than 1.0).

3*b*. The observed correlation decreases with increasing dB difference between successive stimuli. It must therefore be that the error of comparison *increases* with the dB difference, diluting the correlation more and more. In fact, the model curve in Figure 5.2 is calculated on the basis that comparisons of successive stimuli are scarcely better than ordinal ('louder', 'softer', 'about the same'; see Laming, 1997, pp. 159–64).

Judgment of small differences

The remainder of this chapter examines some implications of this ordinal quality of human judgment, and the first point to establish is that *small differences often go unnoticed.*

In magnitude estimation experiments people tend to use round numbers to express their judgments – 5, 10, 15, 20, 50, 100, 150, etc. (Baird, Lewis and Romer, 1970). So a correlation of +0.8 between successive judgments must mean that on most trials when the stimulus level changes by not more than 5 dB, the subject simply repeats the previous response; that is to say, small differences (within ±5 dB) often pass unnoticed. This is not because the stimuli are indistinguishable; 5 dB is about 10 times the smallest difference that can be distinguished. It is just that small differences escape notice. It happens in everyday life as well.

Brian Johnston on Bud Flanagan

Brian Johnston, the veteran broadcaster, used to tell this story about his late friend Bud Flanagan, comedian, who died in 1968.

> Bud was never very clever with his money. He adored betting and lost so much that in the end he became a bookmaker in partnership with Jed Solomons. He would often go racing with Jack Hylton, who presented all the Crazy Gang Shows at Victoria Palace. Jack used to wear sporting clothes for the races and leave a smarter town suit in Bud's dressing-room, into which he would change in the evening. Bud got a tailor to come in each day and take about a quarter of an inch off the bottom of Jack's trousers. Each time he would re-stitch them to make them look as good as new. For a few days Jack didn't notice anything. Then he began to let out his braces. In spite of this the trousers climbed higher and higher up his legs. Jack became more and more puzzled and the joke lasted about a fortnight before he discovered what had happened. (Johnston, 1990)

Renata Agondi

Renata Agondi was a young Brazilian swimmer, 25 years old when she attempted to swim the English Channel on 23 August 1988. She entered the water at 8.22 am, accompanied by her coach (Judith Russo) in a small boat and a trawler carrying an official observer from the Channel Swimming Association. Ten-and-a-half hours later, six miles from the French coast, Renata Agondi was tiring and the waves were increasing. The official observer and the crew of the trawler pleaded with her coach to terminate the attempt, but neither coach nor swimmer would give up. Indeed, the trawler skipper was so worried about his own responsibility in the matter that he called the Dover coastguard to register his protest. Eventually, after three hours of fruitless persuasion, the observer from the Channel Swimming Association dived into the water to pull Renata Agondi out. But it was then too late to resuscitate her.

> The official observer of last week's fatal Channel swim attempt yesterday said that he and the crew of the support ship spent three hours trying to persuade the swimmer and her coach to end the attempt.
>
> Mr Mark Lewis, who finally dived into the water in a vain attempt to save Senhora Renata Agondi, said: 'The captain, the first mate and I were convinced she was not going to make it. She was weak.
>
> 'We were convinced of this three hours before her death. We argued with the coach to get her out of the water. The waves went from 2 ft to 6 ft and then 8 ft. Finally they were up to 12 ft, which is hard to battle. She fought waves of that size for perhaps one to three hours.' (Thomas, 1988)

Why did the coach not insist that her swimmer abandon the attempt when she was advised to? An attempt to swim the Channel involves a great deal of preparation, training and expense and neither swimmer nor coach gives up at the first sign of distress. Now the coach, Judith Russo, is very concerned about her charge, especially when the going gets difficult. She watches her swimmer *all the time* and, for that reason, does not notice the very small, but continual, increases in Renata Agondi's distress from one instant to the next. The official observer from the Channel Swimming Association and the skipper of the trawler are much less involved, emotionally, and therefore watch the swimmer only intermittently until, that is, she is in obvious trouble and needs to give up. Because they have been looking only now and again, the cumulative increases in the swimmer's distress revealed by their comparisons are much larger. They notice, where the coach does not, how exhausted Renata Agondi has become.

Skydiving over the South Pole

In December 1997 six skydivers attempted the ultimate – a dive over the South Pole. Three of them, 'accomplished and experienced skydivers', failed to open their parachutes. The odds of equipment failure of three chutes were, say the experts, 'about the same as winning the lottery twice in a row'. (McGrory, 1997)

> Human error is the likeliest cause of the skydiving deaths in Antarctica.
>
> The commonest error is failing to pull the cord to open the parachute or pulling it too late – the 'low/no pull' accident. It is the only category of accident to which experienced skydivers are more prone than beginners.
>
> A skydiver assesses altitude by working out how much of the picture he sees is occupied by sky, and how much by ground. As the ground becomes an ever-greater part of the picture, he knows from experience when to pull. But if the ground merges with the horizon, this method may fail, and the skydivers may never have realised how close to the ground they were. 'I've talked to a lot of people with low pulls', Mr Burke wrote in an Internet page on skydiving, 'and most didn't have a clue they were down to two or three seconds of life expectancy when they finally got a canopy out.' (Hawkes, 1997)

The area of the scene covered by the ground changes only slowly and, through watching it all the time, the skydiver has difficulty in judging his height above ground level.

The closure of coal mines, announced 13 October 1992

Michael Heseltine, then President of the Board of Trade, announced in Parliament on 13 October 1992 that British Coal was to close 31 pits over the next five months with the loss of 30 000 jobs. That announcement was prompted by reports that had been leaked to the press. It drew an unprecedented reaction from public and MPs alike (not least from Conservative backbench MPs). The Government was forced to retract (on 20 October), saying that 21 pits would be subject to review and the other ten were to stay open for a 90-day consultation period. Political humiliation!

> The real surprise about the reaction to the pit closures last week was not the wave of emotion which jammed the switchboards of Conservative Central Office and constituency associations in Sussex as well as Yorkshire, but the fact that the Government – and most commentators – failed to anticipate it. (Macintyre, 1992)

How did experienced ministers so misjudge the public attitude?

At the end of the coal strike in March 1985 there were 171 000 miners employed by the National Coal Board. By October 1992 that number was reduced to 41 000; an average of 17 330 jobs had been lost each year. That was not something the public had realised. On 25 September, 1992, Daw Mill colliery in Warwickshire closed with the loss of 580 jobs. But no-one protested; no-one outside the industry noticed. Over the past year (August 1991–August 1992) unemployment had risen from 2 422 500 to 2 801 500, a rate of 32 000 per month. Again, this was not something the public would have noticed. The public are not paying attention. So 30 000 jobs all at once seems monstrous. But ministers knew – it is their job to keep up with such events – and so also did the political commentators. A further 30 000 jobs over the space of five months was nothing out of the way. There was, in fact, no way in which the Government could have foreseen that this was the announcement that would blow up in their faces.

Judgment of large differences

If the comparison of each tone with its predecessor is no better than ordinal, then all that people can say is that this tone is

<'softer', 'about the same', 'louder'>

than the previous one. In fact, it is known from the experiments on category judgment reviewed in the preceding chapter (especially Garner, 1953) that people can do a little better than that. People can use up to five categories without error, which means that they can distinguish a big difference in loudness from a small one. The possible comparisons must therefore be

<'much softer', 'a bit softer','about the same','a bit louder', 'much louder'>

but still no finer than that.

The assignment of numbers to levels of sound in, for example, the experiment by Baird *et al.* (1980) must therefore go something like this:

(i) If this tone is *much softer* than the previous one, give it a *much smaller* number.

(ii) If this tone is *softer* than the previous one, give it a *smaller* number.

(iii) If this tone is *about the same* as the previous one, give it the *same* number.

(iv) If this tone is *louder* than the previous one, give it a *bigger* number.

(v) If this tone is *much louder* than the previous one, give it a *much bigger* number.

The model curve in Figure 5.2 is calculated on the basis of just that scheme of assignment (Laming, 1997, Ch. 10).

It needs to be emphasised that the absence of correlation in Figure 5.2 between successive log numerical assignments following large stimulus differences does not mean that the process of judgment is then different. Indeed, how could it be? Reworking the argument once again:

1*c*. If the difference between successive stimuli is small (±5 dB), successive log numerical assignments correlate about +0.8. So the stimulus on the preceding trial and the number assigned to it must have been used as a point of reference for the present judgment.

2*c*. Following large differences (±40 dB) between successive stimuli, the correlation between successive assignments is negligible.

3*c*. But the process of judgment cannot then be different because, until the subject has formulated a judgment, the size of the stimulus difference to be judged is unknown. So the judgment of large stimulus differences must also use the stimulus on the preceding trial and the number assigned to it as point of reference.

4*c*. The negligible correlation following a large stimulus difference must therefore mean that the additional error of judgment is then very much greater; that is to say, the judgment of large stimulus differences is exceedingly fallible. That is a natural consequence of judgment being scarcely better than ordinal.

Let us look at some practical examples.

Figure 5.3 Simultaneous contrast. The four small grey squares have all been cut from the same sheet of grey paper, but nevertheless appear to be of different greys because of the different backgrounds against which they are contrasted.

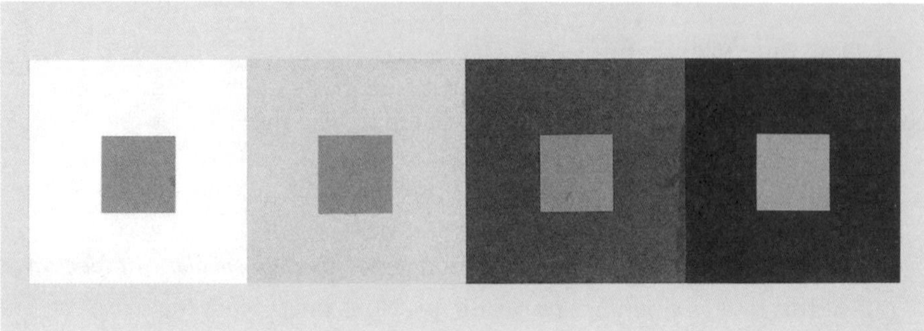

Figure reproduced with the permission of Oxford University Press from D. Laming, *The Measurement of Sensation*, p. 84. © 1997 Donald Laming. After Cornsweet, 1970, p. 279, Figure 11.7.

Simultaneous contrast

Figure 5.3 reproduces a well-known illusion from Cornsweet (1970). The four small grey squares appear to be different – the grey on the white background looks darker then the grey on the black background – notwithstanding that they were all cut from the same sheet of grey paper. Comparing the darkness of the four small grey squares means assembling a sequence of large contrasts and this cannot be accomplished accurately. Being able to say only that one grey is lighter, or darker, than another is not sufficient. Putting this succinctly, people cannot do arithmetic with contrasts. The small grey squares have to be made contiguous before they can be seen to be the same.

This illusion works with colour as well. Hurvich (1981, p. XI, Plate 13–1) exhibits a coloured counterpart in which red, purple, green and cerise discs look to be of slightly different colours against yellow and against blue backgrounds.

Clinical judgment

Such an inability to put different observations together accurately is also seen in clinical diagnosis. A doctor commonly has to take several distinct factors (symptoms) into account to identify a patient's illness. Einhorn (1972) asked four experienced pathologists to examine 193 biopsy slides taken from patients suffering from Hodgkin's disease (a cancer of the lymph system). The pathologists were asked to rate nine diagnostic signs on a five-point scale and also to judge the overall severity of the patient's condition. This judgment of overall severity was not to be an aggregate of the nine individual judgments, but a direct assessment based on all the available evidence. Since all these patients had died, it was possible to compare each pathologist's assessment of overall severity with the patient's actual survival time subsequent to the biopsy. The correlations are set out in Table 5.2.

Table 5.2 Correlation of judged severity of Hodgkin's disease with survival time (adapted from Einhorn, 1972, p. 91, Table 1).

Pathologist	Correlation	Percentage of variance predicted by diagnosis
1	–0.002	0
2	0.116	1.2
3	–0.139	1.9
4	0.143	2.0

All of these correlations should be negative because increased severity of disease leads to *earlier* death. In fact, none of them is significant; and the ability of the pathologists to predict survival time (as measured by 'Percentage of variance predicted by diagnosis') is derisory. But these pathologists' ratings of *individual* diagnostic signs *are* predictive, though the judgment is difficult. Table 5.3 shows the correlation of an optimal linear combination of assessments of individual diagnostic signs with survival time. Although these correlations (now positive) are still small – the judgment is difficult – they are all significant at 0.01. That is, a linear combination of a pathologist's rating of diagnostic signs is better than the pathologist's own judgment of overall severity!

Several studies have shown a linear combination of diagnostic signs to be more accurate than a clinician's overall judgment. Dawes and Corrigan (1974) list examples from psychiatric diagnosis, the selection of graduate students in America, and from one perceptual experiment. Indeed, the combination of diagnostic signs in these studies does not even have to be optimal. Non-optimal combinations are often obtained by regressing the *estimated* severity of disease (that is, the pathologists' overall assessments in Table 5.2) onto the assessments of individual diagnostic signs, and still the calculation surpasses the overall

Table 5.3 Correlation of optimal linear combination of diagnostic signs with survival time (data from Einhorn, 1972, p. 91, Table 2).

Pathologist	Correlation	Percentage of variance predicted by calculation
1	0.378	14.3
2	0.258	6.6
3	0.302	9.1
4	0.364	13.2

accuracy of the clinician! The reason is that the combination of diagnostic signs by the clinician is no better than qualitative; it parallels the ordinal quality of human judgment. But the linear combination uses arithmetic, and is therefore superior.

Nevertheless people resist the use of linear models to combine component judgments.

> . . . I overheard a young woman complain that it was 'horribly unfair' that she had been rejected by the Psychology Department at the University of California, Santa Barbara, on the basis of mere numbers, without even an interview. 'How can they possibly tell what I'm like?' (Dawes, 1979, p. 580).

Absolute identification

There are, however, some apparent exceptions to the idea that all judgments are relative; the best known is the sense of 'perfect pitch'. Not all musicians have 'perfect pitch', but those who do are able to judge the pitch of a note, or sing a note to order, to an accuracy of about a quarter-tone, which is equivalent to an absolute accuracy of three per cent.

Little is known about the psychological basis of perfect pitch, but an experiment by Bachem (1954) is revealing. Bachem played his subjects two tones from an oscillator for 2 s each, but separated by various intervals of time (1, 3, 15 s, 1 min, 1 hour, 1 day, 1 week). The subjects were asked, 'Is the second tone higher or lower than the first? ' Of course, the accuracy of the answer increased with the difference between the two frequencies. Interpolating between different pairs of frequencies, Bachem determined the percentage difference in frequency that would have been judged with 75 per cent accuracy.

Two subjects with acute hearing (but without 'perfect pitch') showed a continual increase in the difference of frequency needed as the lapse of time increased. Two subjects with 'perfect pitch' performed in similar manner to those without for intervals of time up to one minute, but thereafter showed no further loss in resolution. However, they showed this apparently absolute judgment of pitch only for frequencies within the conventional range of a piano keyboard (up to 4 kHz). So 'perfect pitch' is specific to the conventional musical range and does not extend outside it.

The author (who was one of the subjects with 'perfect pitch') reported using two distinct strategies. For intervals up to 1 min, he relied on a direct comparison between the two frequencies; that comparison was accurate to about 0.3 per cent, much more accurate than any 'absolute' identification. But for longer intervals he identified the 'chroma' of the note (B_3 or $F\#_4$) and remembered that instead. Identification of the 'chroma' supported a minimum accuracy of about three per cent over any and every time interval. But the sequence of musical labels repeats every octave, and the author made *occasional octave errors.*

Other cases of apparently absolute judgment include colour and inclination (nearly everybody), intensity of sound (acoustic engineers) and luminance and contrast (rare). Rowley and Studebaker (1969) described a magnitude estimation experiment with audiology students. These students had had substantial prior training in measuring sound levels and were very familiar with the decibel scale.

> The Audiology students were observed to use numbers that closely matched the decibel hearing levels of the presented tone, and thus produced a loudness curve that appeared to represent the dB . . . scale. . . . There appeared to be such a strong attachment, on the part of the audiologists, to the decibel scale that practice and repeated instructions, intended to explain the difference between the decibel and the loudness scales, did not significantly change these observers' judgments. Because of this finding, the Audiology students were excluded from the study and were replaced by other observers who were not familiar with the decibel. (Rowley and Studebaker, 1969, p. 1191)

There is one report of a visual scientist, very experienced in photometric measurements, who could make judgments proportional to physical luminance (Warren and Warren, 1958). I also know of one colleague, very practised in adjusting the contrast on an oscilloscope screen, who makes veridical judgments of contrast (Kulikowski, 1976). Other subjects do not.

Judgment of inclination

Nearly everybody has some, apparently absolute, sense of inclination. This might be consequent on the balance organ's sensitivity to gravity (which identifies the vertical) or it might be due to the preponderance of vertical and horizontal lines in our environment. An experiment by Rogers *et al.* (1947) on the judgment of inclination suggests a psychological basis for that judgment and, by analogy, for 'perfect pitch' and other cases of 'absolute' judgment.

The subject was seated in a dimly lit auditorium. Some distance in front of a plain white curtain was a circular ground-glass screen, four feet in diameter, suspended on taut wires which were not visible to the subject. The entire set up was designed to reduce extraneous horizontals and verticals to a minimum. A long thin line of light was projected onto the ground-glass screen from behind, a line extending from the centre of the screen nearly to its edge. Sitting about 30 feet away, the subject turned a hand wheel that made the line of light pivot about the centre of the screen. The subject's task was to set the line of light to whatever inclination was requested by the experimenter, inclinations ranging from –10° to 100°. The standard deviations of the different adjustments are plotted (open circles) on polar coordinates in Figure 5.4. These standard deviations are typically 3–4°, except at the horizontal and vertical where they reduce to about 1°.

The experiment was then repeated, but with a marker fixed at 30°. The marker was a similar line of light as that to be adjusted, but extending to the very edge of the screen. The filled circles in Figure 5.4 are the standard deviations from this replication. The pattern of errors around the horizontal and vertical in either version of the task is like the pattern around 30° with the marker. This suggests that judgment near the horizontal and vertical is assisted by an internal

Figure 5.4 Judgment of inclination. The open circles show the standard deviations of adjustments of a marker to an inclination requested by the experimenter. The filled circles show the corresponding standard deviations when the subject has a fixed guide set at 30°.

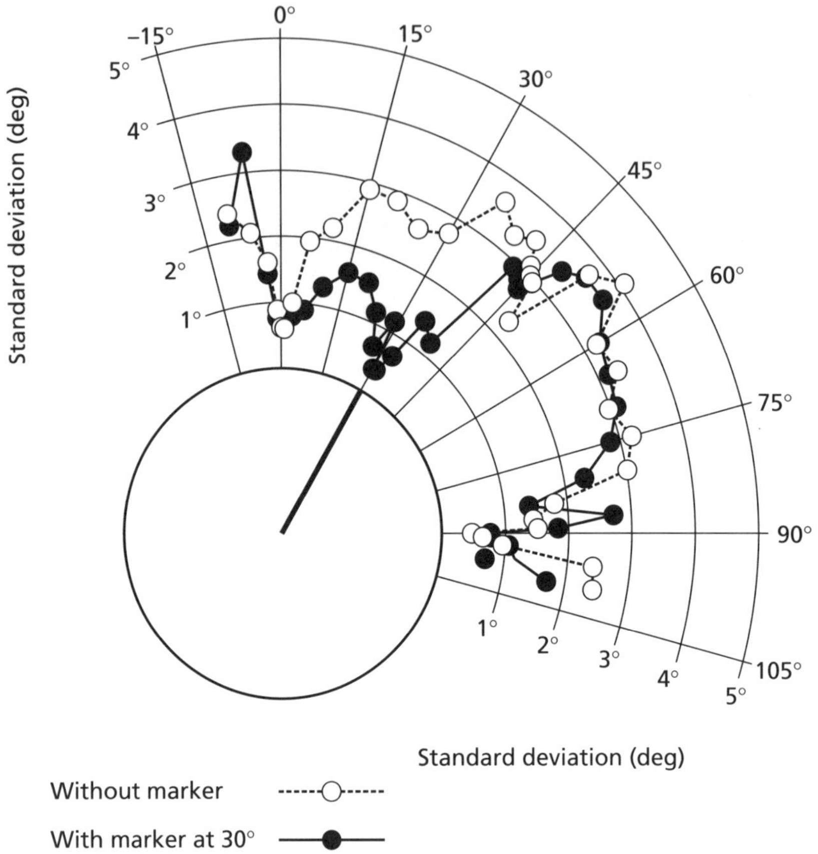

Data from Rogers *et al.*,1947, Tables XVII and XVIII.

standard. That standard could be derived from vestibular or postural sensations (though it might also derive from cues in the auditorium which had not been entirely eliminated). It provides two reliable points of reference for the judgment of inclination.

By analogy, it could be that 'perfect pitch' is mediated by 12 internal standards acquired in course of musical training (although one student explained to me that he used only two internal standards, judging the musical interval of other tones relative to one or the other of those two). This would mean that 'perfect pitch' is judged *by comparison with* an appropriate internal standard, recalled to order; the veridical judgment of sound level or luminance or contrast may be accomplished in similar manner.

Summary – the ordinal quality of human judgment

To the principle that

There is no absolute judgment. All judgments are comparisons of one thing with another

this chapter has added

The comparisons are little better than ordinal;

that is, one sound may be louder, softer or about the same as another, but that is all we can say.

This ordinal nature of human judgment was emphasised by comparison with a 'sliding ruler'. A sliding ruler does not support absolute judgment, because it may be out of position, but it does permit absolute measurement of differences. Human judgment is not like that. In consequence, chevrons placed on the carriageway of the M1 (a 'sliding ruler') can effect a large reduction in the frequency of accidents. Further consequences of the merely ordinal quality of judgment are that small differences often pass unnoticed (though not because they are too small to be noticed), and large differences cannot be assembled together accurately, leading, among other things, to the phenomenon of simultaneous contrast.

The argument of this chapter might, however, be thought to fail in the face of the sense of 'perfect pitch' possessed by some musicians. But enquiry suggests that 'perfect pitch' is mediated by a small number of internal comparators, and does not amount to an absolute judgment of auditory frequency *per se*.

One other consequence of the near-ordinal quality of human judgment is that in everyday life people often have only the slightest basis on which to make up their minds. The next chapter shows what happens then.

6 Guessing in the dark

In Chapter 2 I argued that

There is no absolute judgment. All judgments are comparisons of one thing with another.

To this we added in Chapter 5

The comparisons are little better than ordinal.

One sound may be louder, softer or about the same as another, but that is all we can say. But what happens if there is nothing with which to make comparison? Do people then make no judgment at all, or do they utter judgments at random? An experiment by Sherif (1935), in which naïve subjects were asked to estimate the distance moved by a small point of light in the dark, tells us what happens. Sherif's findings have profound implications for understanding the society in which we live.

The autokinetic experiment

Imagine yourself in complete darkness; all that you can see is a tiny pin-point of light. That light is much too weak to reveal anything else in the room; it is simply out there, somewhere in the black void. In such circumstances the light appears unstable, because there is no way of relating its location in space to your own body. This instability is known as *autokinetic movement*.

During normal vision the eyes are in continual motion. That continual motion is actually essential for seeing. If it is arranged that the image on the retina shall move with the eye so that it always falls on the same receptor cells (a *stabilised* image), seeing ceases within 2 seconds (Ditchburn, 1973; Yarbus, 1967). So the stable world which we ordinarily perceive is an interpretation of an image on a retina that is in continual motion.

It is easy to identify the visual cues that are used in that interpretation. Changes in the retinal image due to movement of the eye are necessarily coherent over the entire visual field; the world around us can be seen to be stable because it moves (over the retina) as one. That coherence also makes it easy to distinguish changes that occur because something in the world has moved – the ball at a tennis match – from changes due to movement of the eye. The tennis court on which the match is played is a part of the world around us and its motion across the retina is coherent. When the ball moves, it moves by itself, differently, and its flight can be judged relative to the background of the tennis court. But suppose the tennis court to be in darkness; suppose only a self-luminous tennis ball is visible. The visual cues needed to distinguish changes in the retinal image due to movement of the ball from those other changes due to movement of the eyes are then lacking. This is the situation in which autokinetic movement is observed. Some part of the changes in the retinal image due to movements of the eyes is then interpreted as illusory movement of the single point of light (see Gregory, 1990, pp. 101–5).

Sherif's experiment

Subjects were given these instructions:

> When the room is completely dark, I shall give the signal READY, and then show you a point of light. After a short time the light will start to move. As soon as you see it move, press the key [a telegraph key provided for the purpose]. A few seconds later the light will disappear. Then tell me the distance it moved. Try to make your estimates as accurate as possible. (Sherif, 1936, p. 95)

The light was extinguished two seconds after the subject pressed the telegraph key, indicating that it had been seen to move. Each subject made 100 spoken judgments of the distance moved, expressed in inches. But the light, of course, was stationary throughout. There was, therefore, no objective basis for the subjects' estimates – no external reason to say 'five inches' rather than 'three'. People were literally guessing in the dark. But they were in ignorance about the autokinetic phenomenon and thought they were making real judgments, albeit very difficult ones.

> 'Darkness left no guide for distance.'
>
> 'No set position from which to judge how far.'
>
> 'Didn't know direction it would move.'
>
> 'It was difficult to estimate the distance the light moved, because of the lack of visible neighboring objects.'
>
> 'There was no fixed point from which to judge distance.' (Sherif, 1935, p. 25; Sherif, 1936, p. 97)

The subjects were also asked how they had made their judgments:

> 'Compared with previous distance.'
>
> 'Judgments are all relative.'
>
> 'Compared successive judgments.'
>
> 'Approximated distance of spot from me, and used that.'
>
> 'First estimate as standard.'

'Thought of using radium dial of watch for judging distance.' (Sherif, 1935, p. 25)

When people are asked to judge the distance through which the point of light appears to move, they find that judgment very difficult. The absence of any perceptible visual world prevents the observer relating the point of light to his or her own body. In that great uncertainty people cannot help but be influenced by whatever other judgments they happen to hear, including their own past judgments. In summarising his data, Sherif reported: '. . . the *subjects subjectively establish a range and a point within that range which is peculiar to the individual* and which may differ from the range and the median point established by other individuals.' (Sherif, 1935, p. 25, emphasis original). If a subject was brought into the experimental room a second time, '. . . once a *range* and a *point* within that range are established, there is a tendency to preserve them in the subsequent sittings.' (Sherif, 1935, p. 27). If two or three subjects are first tested individually and then brought together for three group sessions in which each subject hears the others' judgments, the group converges to a common standard. Similarly, if two or three subjects are first tested together for three sessions, the common standard of the group is preserved by each subject individually when tested in a fourth session alone (Sherif, 1935, pp. 27–41).

The influence is irresistible so long as the subjects believe the illusory movement to be real. However, the influence does depend on the subjects believing that they are trying to judge real objective movement, so that there is a 'correct' estimate that is the same for all. Alexander, Zucker and Brody (1970) disabused their subjects before the experiment started. They told their subjects that the light was actually stationary and the perceived movement illusory.

> You will all be seeing the same point of light, but you should not expect to see it moving in the same direction or for the same distance.
>
> You should not be surprised if you see the light moving in a different direction and for a different distance than anyone else. In fact, you should not be surprised if the direction and distance the light appears to move changes each time you look at it. (Alexander *et al.*, 1970)

The mutual influence demonstrated by Sherif disappeared. Alexander *et al.*'s experiment showed no convergence by individual subjects, and no consensus developing between pairs of subjects. The phenomenon depends on people believing they are making real judgments.

The 'first-day syndrome'

A jury arguably constitues a real-life parallel to Sherif's experiment. Every elector from the age of 18 up to 70 is liable to be summoned for jury service except lawyers, policemen and people with a criminal record. Jurors are called, ostensibly at random, to attend court for two or three weeks during which they sit on a number of different juries trying different cases. Due to the often insubstantial basis of evidence on which juries are called to deliver a verdict, a bias towards conviction or acquittal evolves in the course of successive trials. Most people serve only once in their lifetime, if at all, so that at the beginning of each jury-session, most jurors are entirely without experience. It is well-known in the legal profession that juries trying their first case are more likely to acquit – and to acquit perversely – than more experienced juries. This is the phenomenon known as the 'first-day syndrome'. As one juror put it after the event:

> As time passed, it became apparent that acquittals were more frequent while jurors were green. If you are an accused you will do well to have your case first on the list. At that stage plenty of jurymen will believe that there is reasonable doubt if no one has actually seen you with your hand in the till. If, after long argument and with several of them still doubtful, they find you guilty and then discover that you have seventeen previous convictions for similar offences, scales tend to drop from their eyes; they become old soldiers overnight and the next accused is viewed much more circumspectly. (Barber and Gordon, 1976, pp. 97–8)

And here is a defence counsel's view of the matter:

> It was always easier to get one's way with a fresh jury at the beginning of the session. After two or three weeks' service one's jury starts to get a bit cynical: it will know, for example, that if no mention is made of a defendant's character this must mean that he has a criminal record, it will be getting doubtful about the busy long arm of coincidence around the courts and bored by constant appeals to its commonsense. (Barber and Gordon, 1976, pp. 167–8)

Manipulation of people's judgments

The fact of influence from other people is general with difficult judgments. The most dramatic and complete demonstration, though, comes in a small and very elegant experiment by Sherif (1937). Each real subject was tested in Sherif's usual autokinetic procedure in company with a confederate of the experimenter posing as a second subject. Both subjects, naïve and confederate, announced their judgments orally for the experimenter to write down. In this way the real subject was exposed to the confederate's 'judgments'. The same confederate uttered 'judgments' within a two-inch range between two and eight inches respectively, when paired with different (real) subjects. The judgments of the real subjects are set out in Table 6.1.

The effect of the confederate's pre-arranged responses on the real subjects' judgments is plain to see. Some of the real subjects were aware of their partner's influence; some were not. Some thought they were resisting the influence from their fellow subject, but not so. The real subjects were asked to come back a second day to repeat the experiment alone (second session in Table 6.1). On that repetition, in the absence of the confederate, the influence of the confederate's

Table 6.1 Median judgments and ranges (inches) in Sherif's (1937) autokinetic experiment.

'Judgments' by confederate	Norm	2	3	4	5	6	7	8
	Range	1–3	2–4	3–5	4–6	5–7	6–8	7–9
Judgments by real subjects								
1st group session	Median	3.36	4.25	4.61	5.20	5.50	5.94	7.40
	Range	1–5	1–10	2–8	3–6	3–7	3–8	4–12
2nd session alone	Median	2.62	3.77	4.57	5.21	5.42	6.18	7.83
	Range	1–4	1–5	3–6	3–6	3–7	4–8	6–9

judgments in the first session showed up even more strongly, if that were at all possible. With no basis of comparison for judging the perceived movement, there was, in fact, no way in which the real subjects could resist the suggestions implicit in the confederate's 'judgments'.

Another experiment on the same theme (Hood and Sherif, 1962) was described to the (real) subjects as being concerned with the design of tests of visual abilities under low illumination, which required 15 minutes' prior adaptation to the dark. With this excuse each subject was brought into the experimental room (in complete darkness) while a previous subject (a confederate of the experimenter) was finishing his session. The task was explained to the real subject immediately on entering the experimental room, interrupting the confederate's (fake) session. In this way each real subject heard the confederate making 18 judgments either in the range 1–5 in or 6–10 in. Figure 6.1 shows how the real subjects' judgments were divided between these two ranges. For those subjects who heard previous judgments in the range 1–5 in the median judgment was 3.98 inches, while for subjects hearing previous judgments in the range 6–10 inches it was 6.79 inches.

Provided the subjects in these experiments believe they are making real objective judgments, they are vulnerable to even the slightest suggestion. That vulnerability applies equally in the world outside the psychological laboratory. In Chapter 1 I introduced Clive Barnes, one-time theatre and ballet critic for the *New York Times* who '. . . could make or break a Broadway show' (Mercer, 1978). Clive Barnes played the role of Sherif's confederate to New York theatre-goers. He suggested what shows they should go to see and his readers followed his directions. We shall see that Sherif's autokinetic experiment provides an understanding of the effects of advertisements and of many other attempts at persuasion.

The prestige of the confederate

The influence of the confederate in Sherif's experiment is enhanced when he is introduced as someone with authoritative knowledge or prestige. This was

Figure 6.1 Percentages of estimates 'less than or equal to 5 inches' and 'greater than 5 inches' in the experiment by Hood and Sherif (1962).

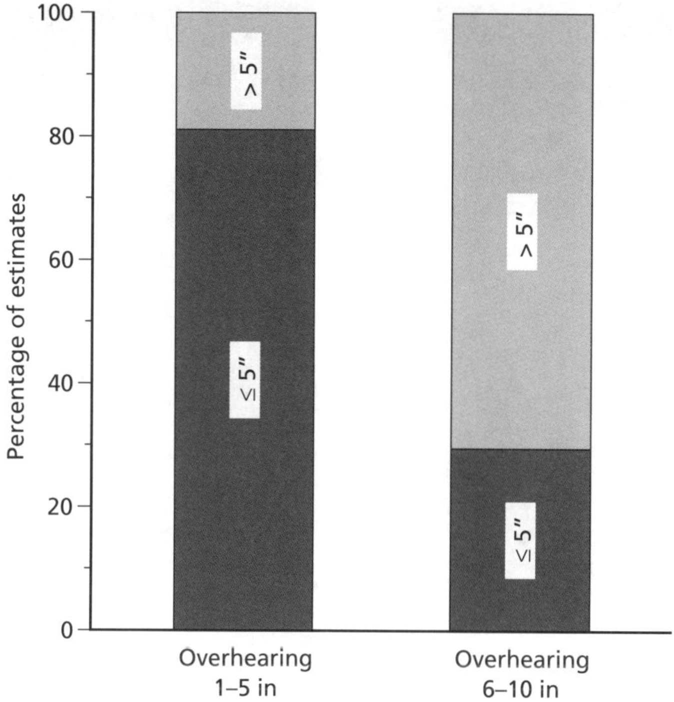

shown in a replication of the experiment by Mausner (1953) using aesthetic judgments in place of the estimation of autokinetic movement. The experiment was presented as a test of the reliability of the Meier Art Judgment Test (Meier, 1942). Each subject was asked to take this test twice so that the two scores could be compared. The test was first taken alone. At a second session a week later some of the subjects were asked to do the test in pairs in order to 'save time'. But the second member of each pair was, in fact, a confederate of the experimenter who gave systematically wrong answers.

The Meier Art Judgment Test was developed to assess people's aesthetic sensibilities. It consists of 100 pairs of black-and-white sketches adapted from selected works of art, many of them Old Master sketches. One example is shown in Figure 6.2. The respondent is asked to pick the aesthetically preferable sketch from each pair. In Figure 6.2 the right-hand sketch is to be preferred because the background pattern in the left-hand sketch detracts from one's appreciation of the line of the girl's head. The test has a reliability of 0.70 to 0.84.

Mausner compared three groups of ten subjects, previously matched for scores on the Allport–Vernon scale of (aesthetic) values. One group took the test alone both times. Subjects in the other two groups took their second test together with the confederate who was introduced to the second group as a

Figure 6.2 One pair of sketches from the Meier Art Judgment Test (Meier, 1942). Original publication of Figure, Meier, 1928, p. 192.

fellow student, but to the third group as the art director of a local advertising agency. It was arranged that the real subject should answer first on all the even numbered items, while the confederate answered first on the odd numbered items and always answered wrongly. The effect on the real subjects' judgments is shown in Table 6.2.

The first group, taking the test alone both times, turned in very similar scores. But the intervention of the confederate caused the real subjects to make more errors the second time around, doing the test in tandem, than on their first attempt alone. That increase was centred entirely on the odd numbered items on which the confederate answered first. The increase is significant for both groups. But, introduced as 'the art director of a local advertising agency', the confederate had a demonstrably greater effect than a 'fellow-student'; the subjects in the third group showed an even greater increase in errors.

Table 6.2 Mean numbers of wrong choices in the Meier Art Judgment Test (Mausner, 1953, p. 391).

Second test	Alone		With 'fellow student'		With 'art director'	
	Odd nos	Even nos	Odd nos	Even nos	Odd nos	Even nos
First test errors	14.6	13.6	13.3	13.7	10.9	16.1
Second test errors	14.8	13.9	17.0	14.5	19.6	18.2

It has long been understood by advertising agencies that the prestige of the person from whom extraneous suggestion comes matters. Agencies routinely use well-known faces in magazine advertisements and in TV commercials. But do they sell the product?

> Confronted with mug-shots of well-known product-floggers, some punters, the advertisers' dreams, confidently link Hale and Pace to Clorets mints, Jane Asher to McVitie's biscuits, and Cindy Crawford to Pepsi. Others, however, are totally blank.
>
> 'This might be Pamela Anderson,' said a baffled woman, poring over Cindy's picture. 'I don't know what she advertises. I know these are *Birds of a Feather* – they do a soap powder, but I can't remember which one. Persil? Daz?' In fact, it's Surf. 'Oh.'
>
> 'The critical question for marketing people is whether viewers will remember the personality rather than the product – it's a great source of paranoia for them,' says . . . Barry Pritchard [advertising analyst]. 'And, frankly, nobody really knows the answer.' (Lacey, 1995)

Sports personalities

The earnings of top sports stars from endorsements are rarely revealed to the public. One exception is Michael Owen, Liverpool Football Club's young international star. As of August 1998 he had a £5 million contract over six years with Umbro sportswear, an estimated £100 000 per annum from Tissot Swiss watches, an estimated £120 000 from the *News of the World* and a Jaguar XK8 convertible worth £55 000 (Kennedy, 1998). The newspaper article went on to speculate that he might eventually earn a further £6 475 000 in endorsements by comparison with what other sportsmen and women were known to be receiving. Those newspaper speculations are set out in Table 6.3.

Top tennis stars earn more off-court than they do on. Jennifer Capriati, who made her professional debut three weeks before her fourteenth birthday, is one example. The truly sensational detail of Jennifer Capriati's career up to that date was that

> A $5m five-year endorsement deal from an Italian sportswear company and another of apparently similar proportions from a racket manufacturer have made her the third-highest earner in women's tennis without hitting a ball in anger as a professional. (Rendall, 1990)

More recently, Anna Kournikova has seized the sponsorship headlines:

> With annual earnings of over £7 million Kournikova remains the second highest earner in the female game. Six years and without a title since she joined the professional tour, the Russian remains a sponsor's dream.
>
> Of Kournikova's earnings last year, £6.78 million came courtesy of Adidas, Berlei, Omega, Yonex and a dozen other licensing deals. The on-court achievements of the second highest paid woman in the game brought in just £220 000. Her career earnings have reached £25 million. (Lister and Norfolk 2002)

Table 6.3 Michael Owen's estimated earnings from sponsorship deals (as of 15 August, 1998. Kennedy, 1998).

Product	Sponsorship fee	Celebrity cited for comparison
Michael Owen's existing contracts		
Umbro Sportswear	£5m over 6 years	
Column in *News of the World*	£120 000 p.a. (est.)	
Tissot watches	£100 000 p.a. (est.)	
Jaguar XK8 convertible	£55 000	
Sponsorship deals by other people, cited to suggest what Michael Owen might receive		
Lucozade	£1.5m	Alan Shearer
Arab Milk Marketing Boards	£1m	Prince Naseem
Brylcreem	£1m	David Beckham
Impulse	£1m	Spice Girls
Pepe jeans	£600 000	Jason Priestley
Braun electric shavers	£500 000	Alan Shearer
McDonald's	£350 000	Alan Shearer
Audi cars	£100 000	Prince Naseem
Joe Bloggs clothes	£100 000	Prince Naseem
Sony video games	£100 000	Prince Naseem
Rightguard	£80 000	Desmond Lynam
Calvin Klein	£60 000	Marky Mark
L'Oreal	£60 000	David Ginola
Clearasil	£25 000	911 boy band

There is, however, no certainty that the tennis star actually likes the goods she is endorsing.

> Martina Hingis, the world's top-ranked female tennis player, is suing her former Italian sportswear sponsors for $40 million (£28.5 million) claiming tennis shoes that she endorsed injured her feet.
>
> Ms Hingis, 21, says in court papers that the company, Sergio Tacchini, gave her 'defective' shoes 'unsuitable for competition', forcing her to withdraw from several tournaments, including Wimbledon. (Peek, 2001)

'Going to Hell'

If, instead of the latest 'must have', the subject of interest is Hell, there is no-one quite so authoritative as an archbishop. In June 1991 Dr John Habgood, Archbishop of York, contributed a 'modest essay on Hell' to his diocesan newspaper under the title 'Going to Hell':

> A correspondent had asked me for an article because one of the damaging experiences of his youth had been the teaching of the sect to which he then belonged, that 'eternal conscious punishment was for all unbelievers'.

> Subsequently I had an even more powerful letter from a mother whose distressed daughter-in-law had been told by her clergyman that her stillborn child must inevitably go to Hell for eternity because it was unbaptised. How such teaching could possibly be compatible with belief in the love of God, and how the idea of eternal punishment unrelieved by any change of mind could possibly be conceived as just, are questions which demand an answer, no matter how strongly some passages of Scripture speak of an eternal divide between the saved and the lost. (Habgood, 1991b)

Dr Habgood thought of his article as no more than

> . . . present-day theological platitudes. Hence the surprise when sections of the media went beserk. Everybody wanted interviews. I was even invited to appear on *Newsnight*.
>
> The *Daily Telegraph* claimed that its readers had a particular interest in Hell, and then produced both a leading article and an item in its gossip column.

The *Yorkshire Post* also commented on the archbishop's article. But why?

As I shall later point out in Chapter 10, Dr Habgood has never been to Hell; nor has he ever had the opportunity to interview anyone else who has been there. Indeed, he has no more experience of Hell than I, and there is, empirically speaking, no reason to trust the words of an archbishop in preference to anyone else for information on such a subject. Everyone is equally ignorant of the facts. But, given that anything said on the topic of Hell is, of necessity, invention, it is reasonable to suppose that those inventions that have the endorsement of an archbishop will carry more weight. Accordingly the *Daily Telegraph* enquired in detail what the coming fashion in that department was to be.

Diana, Princess of Wales

There is no need to be a sporting champion or, indeed, an authority on anything to influence what people buy. The magic results simply from being in the public eye. In 1981, the year of both the royal engagement and marriage, many young women had a white blouse with a high frilly neck in their wardrobe. Figure 6.3 explains why.

In December of that year the Princess visited Gloucester cathedral dressed in a cossack-style coat with matching hat and muff; 'a few days after . . . Harrods was inundated with requests for muffs' (James, 1984, p. 41). On Sunday, 8 June 1986, the Princess went to Windsor Great Park to watch her husband play polo. A photograph of her arriving in polka-dot skirt and polka-dot ankle socks appeared in News Corporation newspapers the next morning. On Tuesday, the day after, the *Times* reported:

> **Polka-dot Princess starts fad**
>
> No sooner had photographs of the Princess of Wales wearing polka-dot ankle socks appeared in the morning papers yesterday than Britain started coming out in a rash of spotted socks . . .

Figure 6.3 Diana, Princess of Wales, when Lady Diana Spencer.

Photograph © Anwar Hussein.

> Sock Shop branches in London's Underground and railway stations were invaded by young women on their way to work.
> Staff said they had sold at least 500 pairs in the morning.
> Polka-dots and ankle socks are already in fashion this summer but the hosiery firm, Couture, said the Princess had done for both what she had previously done for fancy tights with bows on the seams. (Clough, 1986)

It is widely-known that a picture of a member of the royal family on the front cover of a magazine increases sales.

> Around the world, magazine editors have discovered one guaranteed route to success.
> Put the Princess of Wales on the cover.
> The highest-paid models cannot compete with Diana's international appeal. She smiles out from more front pages in more countries than any of them.
> And whether she's dressed in sumptuous designer gowns and glittering jewellery or plain jeans and sweatshirts, she sends circulations soaring. The latest portrait to capture her star quality is by Patrick Demarchelier for . . . Vogue.
> Other magazines which have given over their covers to Diana this year range from Harpers & Queen to Good Housekeeping and Woman.
> She graces the front page of Majesty more often than any other Royal. (Harrison, 1991)

On 7 June 1992, the *Sunday Times* published its first extract from *Diana: Her True Story* by Andrew Morton.

> Executives at the *Sunday Times* estimate that it sold an extra 210 000 copies last Sunday because of the claims it printed about the marriage of the Prince and Princess of Wales.
>
> At 80p a copy, this means the first part of the serialisation of Andrew Morton's book on the Princess raised additional revenues of £180 000.
>
> The increased sale amounts to approximately an 18 per cent rise on the previous week's sale of 1.14 million copies, and is being viewed throughout the newspaper industry as phenomenal. (Brown, 1992)

Sadly, all that has come to an end. In the early hours of 31 August 1997, Diana died in a car crash in the underpass at Place de L'Alma in Paris, chased by a group of paparazzi on motorcycles. When the paparazzi arrived at the scene they immediately took photographs of the crash.

> Laurent Sole, director of the SD picture agency, . . . 'I sold lots of pictures by telephone for five hours until I took them off the market on hearing the news of the Princess's death,' he said. 'I have received calls from dozens and dozens of media organisations . . . They were offering $250 000 from the States and £100 000 sterling. I am still getting calls for the pictures today.' (Bremner and Farrell, 1997)

Summary – guessing in the dark

Let me now unscramble the argument of this chapter, setting it out in reverse.

Photographs of the royals sell magazines in a way that nothing else can equal, and 'Diana is the number one commodity. She has created so many jobs. It is a publicity coup for this country' (Robin Nunn, photographer, cited in Roy, 1988). The Princess of Wales has, inadvertently, encouraged young women to buy polka-dot socks and frilly-necked blouses and everyone to buy magazines and newspapers. Top sportsmen and women collect their endorsement fees precisely because the consumer is uncertain about what product to choose. In such uncertainty, the recommendation of a friend carries weight. Tennis players, among many others, fulfil the function of such a friend. But why the uncertainty?

A tiny point of light in otherwise complete darkness appears unstable. When faced with the very difficult judgment of how far it has moved, people do not utter numbers at random. Instead they are influenced by whatever suggestions they might hear, however subtle, which might be taken as clues to the 'correct' answer. This happens when there is virtually no objective basis for judgment. So long as people think they are making a real, though very difficult, judgment, they have no defence against influence from outside. It means that there is immense scope for influencing purchasing decisions to one's own financial advantage. To that I turn next.

7 The marketplace

Brand images

In the previous chapter it was shown that, faced with a difficult judgment, people are vulnerable to extraneous suggestions from others. Celebrities are frequently used in advertisements for this purpose; even Diana, Princess of Wales, unwittingly wielded influence. But the extraneous suggestion that makes shoppers buy this or that need not come from a celebrity or a friend. The label on the goods or the packaging will also serve; and companies carefully cultivate, and also protect, their 'brand image'.

In April 1994 Sainsbury's introduced its 'own brand' Classic Cola. It was sold in a can of traditional shape and manufacture, such as *Coca-Cola* also used. The can was printed in the same red as a *Coca-Cola* can and in a very similar style of lettering.

> Coca-Cola yesterday triumphed . . . when it persuaded J Sainsbury to change the design of its own-brand 'Classic' cola to make it look less like Coke.
>
> Sainsbury is changing the typeface and removing underlining from part of the logo on the can. (Connon, 1994)

Champagne

In the run-up to Christmas 1983, Jane MacQuitty organised a tasting of non-vintage champagnes for the *Times*. The tasting panel comprised three experts engaged in the champagne trade as well as three staff members from the *Times*, and Jane MacQuitty herself. Tasting blind, they ranked the best sixteen champagnes in order. That order, together with retail prices as at December 1983, is shown in Table 7.1 below.

Top of the list came Sainsbury's Dry Champagne: 'rich, flowery and full-bodied bubbly', 'full of character', 'utterly classic', 'a glorious mouthful of champagne'. But what is of particular interest is the correlation between the rank order of expert appraisal and the retail price. The correlation is 0.034 – that is to say, for this sample of champagnes, there was no relation at all between quality, as appraised by Jane MacQuitty's team, and cost. The panel also tasted

Table 7.1 Order of 16 non-vintage champagnes as ranked by the *Times* tasting team. (MacQuitty, 1983).

Position	Brand	Price
1st	Sainsbury's Dry Champagne	£5.95
2nd	Veuve Clicquot-Ponsardin	£9.40
3rd equal	Deutz	£9.00
	Moët et Chandon's Premièr Cuvée	£8.99
5th	Mercier	£7.69
6th	Krug's Grande Cuvée	£20.00
7th equal	Tesco's Brut Epernay	£5.99
	Pol Roger	£9.60
9th	Joseph Perrier	£10.95
10th equal	Waitrose Extra Dry	£5.95
	Perrier Jouët	£10.45
	Charles Heidsieck	£7.95
13th equal	St. Michael Blanc de Blanc Brut	£7.49
	St. Michael Sec	£6.49
15th	Lanson Black Label	£8.39
16th	Laurent Perrier	£11.00

Heidsieck Dry Monopole, Bollinger, Taittinger, Pommery, Louis Roederer, Maison Royale (Victoria Wine), Mumm Cordon Rouge, Piper Heidsieck and Lambert (Peter Dominic), but these champagnes 'were not considered good buys' (MacQuitty, 1983).

Now the previous year Jane MacQuitty had edited the *Which? Wine Guide 1983*. This is what that guide had to say about the cost of champagne and Bollinger in particular:

> **The cost**
> Essentially, it is the price of grapes – always rising – and the labour-intensive skill of the champagne maker that makes champagne so costly. Special bottles, corks, capsules, and adequate maturation in bottle all add to the ultimate price. But the grapes from a vineyard rated '100 per cent' will cost more than those from one just 90 per cent (something not stated on the label), so you really do get what you pay for. To understand, try the very best BOB [buyer's own label; e.g., Sainsbury's Dry Champagne], say, against non-vintage Bollinger, for example, and note the difference. You may not prefer the more expensive wine – but you will see why it costs more. (MacQuitty (ed.), 1982, p. 242)

It appears, on some occasions at least, that what the experts say and what the experts say blind are two different things.

At the same time the selling power of the name Bollinger is beyond question:

> . . . some people who toasted Christmas and the New Year in what they thought was Bollinger champagne were, in fact, drinking Spanish sparkling wine.
>
> This failure to spot the difference may be attributable to an excess of festive spirit. It could also be proof that sometimes the label, however faulty, is all.

> An enterprising confidence trickster swapped eight bottles of what appeared to be 1983 Bollinger for spirits and cigarettes at a north London off-licence, claiming that they were an unwanted present.
>
> Dilip Patel, owner of Danbury Wines in Islington, then resold them for £21 each, about £5 less than the usual retail price for Bollinger of this vintage.
>
> One of the purchasers, Peter Bromwich, thought the bottle strange but only complained after tasting the contents.
>
> What he had actually bought was a bottle of Freixenet Cordon Negro, a sparkling wine from Spain, which sells for £5.99. Whoever perpetrated the fraud had removed the original label and replaced it with one bearing the Bollinger name. But even a fairly cursory inspection would have revealed it as a fake.
>
> The police have been told of the fraud and it remains to be seen how widespread it is. But the full extent may never be known because some people seem not to have noticed the difference.
>
> James Suckling, of the magazine *The Wine Spectator*, said yesterday: 'A lot of people who buy champagne, buy it entirely because of the label. It is the ultimate label drink.
>
> 'I would like to think that most people would have been able to tell the difference in this case but if it is really chilled then people just drink it and enjoy it.' (Bennett, 1991)

People who drink champagne on festive occasions only would, of course, have had no adequate experience with which to compare the Cordon Negro. It is likely that most of those who bought the fake bottles had no way of discovering that they had bought a qualitatively different drink, made from quite different varieties of grape.

Psychiatric diagnosis

There is something akin to 'brand image' at work when someone seeks help from a psychiatrist. There is always a presumption that such a person is suffering some kind of mental distress. But suppose an entirely sane person were to present him- or herself before a psychiatrist. Would that psychiatrist detect the sham? All the medical staff involved in the study below (Rosenhan, 1973) failed to do so. That does not matter much in a deliberately contrived experiment. But suppose someone – someone completely sane – were, by some mischance, to find him- or herself in a mental hospital . . .

In this 'experiment' it was arranged that eight sane people should be admitted to twelve different psychiatric institutions in the United States. The sham patients included three psychologists, one postgraduate student in psychology, a paediatrician, a psychiatrist, a painter and a housewife. Three of them were women, five men. They complained of hearing voices (a common mental complaint). The voices were unfamiliar, but of the same sex as the pseudopatient. They were often unclear, but appeared to be saying things like 'empty', 'hollow' and 'thud'. (These particular symptoms were chosen because they admitted interpretation as existential symptoms, reflecting a concern about the meaninglessness of life. But the notion of an 'existential psychosis' is invention, not fact.)

On admission to hospital, the pseudopatients gave correct life histories, except that all of them gave false names and some false occupations as well. Thereafter they ceased simulating any kind of mental disorder. Eleven of the twelve admissions were diagnosed as suffering from schizophrenia, the twelfth (with identical symptoms) from manic-depressive psychosis. They kept written notes of their observations and experiences in hospital. They were all discharged after periods ranging from seven to 52 days 'in remission'.

The first point to make is that none of the sham patients was ever detected as such by any member of hospital staff.

> Despite their public 'show' of sanity, the pseudopatients were never detected. Admitted, except in one case, with a diagnosis of schizophrenia, each was discharged with a diagnosis of schizophrenia 'in remission'. The label 'in remission' should in no way be dismissed as a formality, for at no time during any hospitalization had any question been raised about any pseudopatient's simulation. Nor are there any indications in the hospital records that the pseudopatient's status was suspect. Rather, the evidence is strong that, once labelled schizophrenic, the pseudopatient was stuck with that label. If the pseudopatient was to be discharged, he must naturally be 'in remission'; but he was not sane, nor, in the institution's view, had he ever been sane. (Rosenhan, 1973, p. 252)

Instead, the sham patients' life histories were reinterpreted in the light of the diagnoses:

> As far as I can determine, diagnoses were in no way affected by the relative health of the circumstances of a pseudopatient's life. Rather, the reverse occurred: the perception of his circumstances was shaped entirely by the diagnosis. A clear example of such translation is found in the case of a pseudopatient who had had a close relationship with his mother but was rather remote from his father during his early childhood. During adolescence and beyond, however, his father became a close friend, while his relationship with his mother cooled. His present relationship with his wife was characteristically close and warm. Apart from occasional angry exchanges, friction was minimal. The children had rarely been spanked. Surely there is nothing pathological about such a history. Indeed, many readers may see a similar pattern in their own experiences, with no markedly deleterious consequences. Observe, however, how such a history was translated in the psychopathological context, this from the case summary prepared after the patient was discharged.
>
> 'This white 39-year-old male . . . manifests a long history of considerable ambivalence in close relationships, which begins in early childhood. A warm relationship with his mother cools during his adolescence. A distant relationship to his father is described as becoming very intense. Affective stability is absent.

> His attempts to control emotionality with his wife and children are punctuated by angry outbursts and, in the case of the children, spankings. And while he says that he has several good friends, one senses considerable ambivalence embedded in those relationships also . . .'.
>
> The facts of the case were unintentionally distorted by the staff to achieve consistency with a popular theory of the dynamics of a schizophrenic reaction. . . . An entirely different meaning would have been ascribed if it were known that the man was 'normal'. (Rosenhan, 1973, p. 253)

Other (real) patients, however, were more perceptive:

> Finally, it cannot be said that the failure to recognize the pseudopatients' sanity was due to the fact that they were not behaving sanely. While there was clearly some tension present in all of them, their daily visitors could detect no serious behavioral consequences – nor indeed, could other patients. It was quite common for the patients to 'detect' the pseudopatients' sanity. During the first three hospitalizations, when accurate counts were kept, 35 of a total of 118 patients on the admissions ward voiced their suspicions, some vigorously. 'You're not crazy. You're a journalist, or a professor [referring to the continual note-taking]. You're checking up on the hospital.' (This and the two preceding quotations reprinted with permission from D. L. Rosenhan, 'On being sane in insane places'. *Science*, vol. 179, pp. 252–3. © 1973 American Association for the Advancement of Science.)

It would be wrong, however, to suppose that this kind of mistake could happen only in a contrived experiment.

> Maurice [Brown], now 71, lives on the first floor of a hospital for mentally handicapped people in London, but he is not mentally handicapped. Despite everything that has happened to him, he is not considered mentally ill either.
>
> Maurice was put away because he was difficult. At his father's request, magistrates sent him to an approved school when he was six (and not yet old enough to dress himself). His father . . . told the court he was beyond control. . . . he was taken to two approved schools and two military boarding schools.
>
> He went home for the first time at 20 but the return to normality lasted less than a year. He stole his father's £1 and began what has become a life sentence – 50 years in mental hospitals, including 40 years at Rampton.
>
> 'The pound was money my Dad had put by for our lass's wedding. He fetched the bobbies, they put me in front of a doctor, and he said I was a moral defective. He said I'd no sense of shame and I was barmy, but I wasn't. I've been locked up for so many years. I haven't seen anyone from my family since 1937. I'm going to die here.' (Rayment *et al.*, 1987).

Helen is another.

> At Leytonstone House, another London hospital for the mentally handicapped, Helen, a talkative if slightly cantankerous woman of 76, has been a resident for

> 48 years. She was taken there, she says, because she was carrying an illegitimate child.
>
> 'I came here just before Christmas 1939, the 23rd of December, and I've been here ever since. I'm fed up with it.'
>
> There are many examples of these social rejects. Psychiatrists say other cases include one hospital with some residents who are simply hard of hearing and a hospital in London with adults who were admitted as evacuees in the war and, for one reason or another, never left.' (Rayment *et al.*, 1987).

Once these unfortunate people had been branded as schizophrenic or 'moral defectives', all subsequent re-appraisals started from that label. Escape is very difficult. 'Give a dog a bad name and you may as well hang him.' There is, however, one apparent exception that I cannot bear to pass over.

Roy Brooks, estate agent

Roy Brooks, an estate agent, had a reputation for mocking the properties he had for sale.

> ONE OF THE FILTHIEST HOUSES I'VE SEEN FOR A LONG TIME. A crumbling corner PERIOD RES. There are many things that can be said about FASHIONABLE PIMLICO: Dingy, for instance. 9 rms (Some quite fine altho' they've kept coal in a bedroom & the Drawing rm chimney piece is sprawled across the flr.) Built in an age of elegance, contemporary I should think, with Emperor LOUIS PHILLIPE, to restore it is about the only challenge left to a rich young couple today. ONLY £8,450. Lse 80 yrs. G.R. ONLY £70. (18th December 1966. From Counsell, 1989)

It is traditional amongst estate agents to list all the advantages of a property and none of its drawbacks. Roy Brooks, in contrast, became famous for ridicule of the properties he had for sale. His reputation for disparagement put the potential purchaser in the position of one of the disabused subjects in the replication of Sherif's autokinetic experiment by Alexander *et al.* (1973). Indeed, the tactic worked to his advantage. People read his advertisements for the sake of their wit, and those who were actually looking to buy came to see what was really on offer.

The price of things

Rival manufacturers promote rival brands, and competition tends to reduce the influence of the label. How then do people make up their minds? Price is the guide to quality in absence of any other indicator. The conventional wisdom on price is summed up in this quotation that is attributed to John Ruskin, though it is not found in his works.

> There is hardly anything in the world that some man cannot make a little worse and sell a little cheaper and the people who consider price only are that man's lawful prey.

Designer paint

There are designer jeans, designer shoes, designer watches, and designer bags. Now, what about designer paint?

> Can it ever, in any circumstances, be right to spend £24 on a 2.5-litre tub of paint when you can buy the same amount of Dulux for £12.99?
>
> You can reason that designer paint is very new Labour – No 10 has reportedly been redecorated in Paint Library (£24 for 2.5 litres of matt emulsion); you can tell yourself that Kylie Minogue has Sophie Rose on her walls (Paint Library again).
>
> Rula Theocharis, a freelance colour consultant, insists that the more expensive paints are generally better. 'For example, red is one of the most difficult colours to reproduce and with, say, John Oliver, you have a purer colour.' (Bradberry, 1999)

But Dulux is a highly reputable brand of paint, very widely sold; and Dulux Colour Palette offers over 1700 different colours in a wide variety of finishes. You can have any colour you like. As of April 1999, 2.5 litres of matt emulsion, colour mixed to order, cost £13.99. So what has designer paint got going for it beyond fancy colour names – and the price?

Well,

> Dulux faces legal action after allegedly copying a range of paints produced by Farrow & Ball, manufacturers of upmarket decorating products, whose clients include the Prince of Wales.
>
> Farrow & Ball began the High Court action after Dulux issued detailed instructions in its bulletin for showroom staff on how to mix its paints to replicate the bestselling National Trust range. (Pierce, 2002)

Dulux is implicitly borrowing Farrow & Ball's colour names; it is disputable whether they are also borrowing their colours.

In the first place, the mixing process, in-store, is subject to some variability. Secondly, a customer has no way of knowing how accurately the paints actually supplied by Dulux replicate the Farrow & Ball colours. Juxtapose two panels painted with the different paints exactly side-by-side, and the customer might be able to see a difference between them. Separate the panels by even a centimetre, and no difference will be detectable. That is the message from the Craik–Cornsweet illusion (see Figure 4.5). In practice, no customer will use both paints within the one room, so what really matters is the customer's ability to distinguish one paint from the other when seen by itself. The experiment by Pollack (1952) on the identification of pure tones has been repeated with colours (Chapanis and Halsey, 1956; Eriksen and Hake, 1955b). These experiments show that people are not able to identify more than ten distinct colours when viewed in isolation. (Ten colours are distinguishable rather than five because colour vision is trichromatic. This means it has one natural reference point – arguably yellow – and five different colours can be distinguished either side of that reference.) So the differences within quite broad ranges of Dulux's 1700 colours are neither here nor there, and a few additional colours certainly add nothing to the choice. It is all in the name.

The price of champagne

Price is used as a guide to quality simply because shoppers have no other means of assessment. It has this curious consequence. Supermarket champagnes sell at about two-thirds of the typical price of a wine from one of the Grandes Marques, but do not capture the market. The best-known champagne houses have cultivated a prestige reputation for champagne.

> . . . the Grandes Marques are concerned that the price-cutting tactics of buyer's own brand (BOB) champagnes (sold under a supermarket label, for instance) are having the opposite effect [i.e. increasing sales], at their expense.
>
> Sales of cheap BOB champagnes have accelerated. But BOBs have always been resented by the Grandes Marques. To cut prices they have to cut corners, so the argument goes, damaging the prestige image of champagne. (Rose, 1989)

The Grandes Marques continue to command a premium over supermarket champagnes because they are believed to be that much better. They are believed to be that much better because they cost that much more.

The argument is circular and the champagne market correspondingly unstable. That instability is compounded by the marketing of sparkling wines from other parts of the world, especially California, New Zealand and Australia. 'There is a view that such fizz [from the New World] could never be as good as the real thing, because the pukka stuff, made in time-honoured fashion in the unique chalky hills of Reims and Epernay by master blenders, is inimitable.' (Rose, 1991) Of course, there is a mystique attaching to real champagne, and the right to use the name 'Champagne' is jealously guarded.

To show what that mystique is really worth, here are the notes made by Oz Clarke in a blind tasting of two sparkling wines produced by G.H. Mumm, one a real champagne, one a New World imitation:

> (Mumm Cordon Rosé 1985) £22.99
> Quite full salmon, no great bubble, palate rather earthy and raw. Slight sense of nutty Pinot Noir, but not much. It's too raw and rough, and made badly from poor grapes. They should (a) change their vineyard manager, (b) change their winemaker. Poor stuff.
> 11 out of 20.
>
> (Cuvée Napa Blanc de Noirs, Mumm Napa Valley) £8.49
> Fresh light pink. Palate, it's young, it's fresh, but it's very well balanced. A definite sense of Pinot Noir, touch of strawberry, good young acidity covered by

> good full cream and a little perfume. This is good commercial winemaking producing an approachable high quality product.
> 17 out of 20. (Bailey, 1991)

That kind of comment is not well received.

> Oz Clarke has started a row which reflects not only on Champagne, but on the way this kind of journalism [wine writing] is done. In October [1991] Malcolm McIntyre, director of the Champagne Bureau, which represents the governing body of the Champagne region in Britain, wrote a memo to members of the Champagne Agents' Association – who import most of the Champagne drunk in Britain – advising them to exclude Oz Clarke from hospitality and events.
>
> 'Oz's sustained criticism is, in my view, totally unreasonable because his attacks are wholesale, rather than specific,' wrote McIntyre. 'His repeated attacks have now persisted for almost a year, during which time the industry has continued to offer him hospitality, information and bottles for tasting. Our professional recommendation is that no further hospitality should be extended so long as it is so blatantly abused.' (Bailey, 1991)

Zantac

Most advertisements that mention a price seek to make that price appear a little less than it really is. There are, however, exceptions. Figure 7.1 is one of them. It looks perverse, but, presumably, it sells Stella Artois. Zantac is another.

In 1976, about the time that Glaxo's chemists were turning their attention to the prevention of stomach ulcers, one of their rivals, SmithKline, came out with Tagamet. The chemical agent in Tagamet was, of course, patented; so Glaxo had to find another compound which had to be sufficiently different from Tagamet to satisfy the patent laws, but, at the same time similar enough to have the same pharmacological effect. In 1981 they produced Zantac; but by that time Tagamet was established as the biggest-selling drug in the world.

Glaxo took three specific risks in launching Zantac. First, they accelerated its development. Second, they launched it in all the world's markets simultaneously.

> And lastly – most dangerous of all – there would be the price. Girolami [Sir Paul Girolami, later chairman of Glaxo] wanted to make Zantac more expensive than Tagamet, a decision that horrified the board.
>
> Glaxo, for all its aggression, was playing what seemed to be a weak hand. Zantac worked and it was safe, but it had few apparent advantages over the well-established Tagamet. The price, however, turned out to be a plus. As one marketing executive explained later, the doctors assumed that since it cost more it must be better; a thought bolstered by the claims of the Glaxo sales force. (Lynn, 1991b; see also Lynn, 1999a, pp. 199–200)

That tactic paid off. In 1988 'Zantac was just a whisker under £1bn in sales' – no drug had sold that much before – and contributed to a total profit for Glaxo only slightly under £1bn.

Figure 7.1 Advertisement for Stella Artois.

Sales bargains

Supermarket champagnes sell at about two-thirds of the typical price of a wine from one of the well-known champagne houses; yet the supermarket champagnes do not capture the market. But when Harrods cuts one-third off the price of its goods in its January sale, people queue outside for the opportunity to buy. What is the difference?

The difference is this: the three-seater sofa now on offer at £395 (the *Sunday Times Magazine*, 29 December 1985, inside front cover) is the very same sofa that formerly cost £600. Its former price serves as a measure of its value; at £395 it is a demonstrable bargain. Shoppers can make that comparison; even 'seconds', that is, goods with identifiable flaws, do not invalidate the comparison. The shopper can see what the difference is and weigh that difference up in relation to the reduction in price. For this reason many people think there are bargains to be had in a sale and that idea, of itself, potentiates a spending fever:

> . . . on the first day of last year's [Harrods] sale, one very happy customer clocked up the largest sale ever recorded in the china department, with the breathtaking sum of £66 400 on Limoges china . . . none of it in the sale! (Paul Taylor, deputy managing director of Harrods Ltd., 1990)

What the shopper cannot do is to compare the quality of the sofa offered in Harrods sale at £395 with that of other sofas offered regularly at about the same price in suburban furniture stores. Comparisons between the qualities of different champagnes are likewise uncertain. This is why supermarket champagnes do not capture the market, notwithstanding their 'price' advantage.

Original price measures the quality of the goods; the reduction – euphemistically called a 'saving' – the quality of the bargain. Shoppers judging the quality of goods on this basis are subject to these devious practices.

> One of the most frequent abuses involves displaying a sale price against a recommended retail price (RRP). This is allowed as long as the RRP is provided by a manufacturer or supplier 'as a price at which the product might be sold to consumers'.
>
> In some cases, however, manufacturers are in league with retailers to provide them with an inflated price so that they can make it appear they are offering a big reduction.
>
> Other techniques being used legally include:
>
> **The price elsewhere**: The code [of practice] allows a large multiple store chain to claim goods are discounted if they have sold them at a higher price in at least one of their shops for as little as a week. But a chain will put whole lines of goods on sale in one town so it can then claim to be reducing the price nationwide.
>
> **The after-event price**: A store claims to be discounting on a future higher price, saying '£99 now, £129 when offer ends'. Some shops extend this offer indefinitely.
>
> **The single unit price**: A furniture shop sells a dining room table and six chairs at a 'reduced price' because it would cost more to buy each piece individually.
>
> Retailers can use all these techniques without fear of prosecution. (Chittenden and Welsh, 1989)

There is obviously some relation between the prices at which goods are offered for sale and the costs of their manufacture. If a sufficiently wide range of goods is surveyed, this will feed through into a relation between the costs of manufacture and the quality of the product. But in any practical comparison the actual relation between quality and price is sufficiently tenuous and sufficiently open to manipulation that retail price is near useless as a guide to quality. In the champagne tasting discussed above, the correlation between expert appraisal and market price was negligible. Shoppers use price as a guide only because they have nothing else to go by. A price reduction is a powerful means of making a sale. But, just as a jury hearing a criminal trial is not allowed to know whether the defendant has had any previous convictions, in case it biases their verdict, so I am of the opinion that shoppers ought not to be allowed to know the price at which goods in a sale had previously been offered. Prohibiting dual pricing would eliminate much of the manipulation of shoppers at sale time.

Liza Bruce's swimming costumes

Exceptionally, however, shoppers will look at goods independently of their prices.

> Two years ago, Liza Bruce's turquoise and blue-dipped swimming costumes went on sale at Harrods, Harvey Nichols and exclusive little boutiques around London, Paris and New York. . . . But since Marks & Spencer put an almost identical costume on sale this spring, it would appear that sales have soared.
>
> Around the time the swimsuits went on sale at 80 M&S stores around the country, Bruce started getting letters and phone calls from customers and stockists who were angry at seeing what they thought was their £120 swimsuit on sale at M&S for a mere £21.
>
> Bruce fears that her designs have been devalued, and that in a cut-throat industry she may have future problems with orders from stores such as Harvey Nichols.
>
> 'In this country where cheap versions of designer clothes are widely available, I find that it is the designer who is perceived as the rip-off artist. People think, why does that garment have to be £100 when I can go and buy it for £20?' she says. (Blanchard, 1995)

It is now time to rephrase Ruskin's previous remark.

> There is hardly anything in the world that some man cannot package a little differently and sell for a lot more and the people who consider price only deserve to be ripped off.

The paradox of advertising

The company that plans to rely on satisfied customers coming back again and again must look to its pricing policy. All it can do to increase sales is to advertise; Figure 7.2 displays two such advertisements. I look now at what those advertisements accomplished.

In December 1985 *Which?* published the results of a blind tasting of spirits.

> Our experts – all experienced tasters, some from within the drinks' industry – were asked to try Scotch whisky, gin, and cognac in several taste tests. We

Figure 7.2 Advertisements for The Famous Grouse and for Teacher's Highland Cream.

The advertisement for The Famous Grouse © The Highland Distillers Ltd, reprinted with permission; the advertisement for Teacher's Highland Cream © Allied Domecq Spirits & Wine Ltd, reprinted with permission. TEACHER's® Scotch Whisky is a registered trade mark of Allied Domecq Spirits & Wine Ltd.

> concentrated on own-label spirits sold by the big supermarkets, and compared them with a few of the big-selling, popular brands. Our experts 'nosed' (smelled) them, and sometimes tasted them, either neat or with water. The identity of each brand was concealed from them. (*Which?* 1985, p. 552)

Within their tasting of supermarket own-label blended whiskies *Which?* included the two whiskys in Figure 7.2. As of 1986 these whiskys, together with Bell's Old Scotch Whisky, were the market leaders with 9, 13 and 19 per cent of the market respectively (*A-Z of UK Brands*, 1990, p. 307). Table 7.2 sets out the results of *Which?*'s whisky tasting, with these three branded whiskies sharing the same middle rank, described as 'Average "with some superior qualities".' So what has the advertising spend done for these three brands?

First, the advertisement reminds the reader of the product's existence. If whisky drinkers do not know about *The Famous Grouse*, they will not ask for it in the shops. Sales will fall; shops will stock other better-selling brands in its place; *The Famous Grouse* will lose market share to the point that its production becomes unprofitable. Supermarket 'own-labels', on the other hand, enjoy a certain amount of self-advertisement simply by being seen on the supermarket shelves.

Table 7.2 Blind tasting of scotch whiskies (*Which?* 1985, p. 552).

Rating	Brand of whisky
Very good	Co-op Heatherdale
Good	Co-op Arden House Co-op Majority Safeway 5-year-old
Average 'with some superior qualities'	Bell's Old Scotch Whisky: Extra Special The Famous Grouse Presto Glen Nevis Safeway Blended Teacher's Highland Cream
Average	Tesco Blended Special Reserve
Average 'with some shortcomings'	Fine Fare 5-year-old Fine Fare Strathallan
Poor	Asda Sainsbury's Blended Waitrose

Adapted with permission from 'Christmas Spirits'. *Which?* December 1985, p. 552.

Second, the advertisements attempt to commend the products in some subtle way. But it has to be said that that commendation is unrelated to quality as assessed by *Which?*'s experts tasting blind.

Third, the advertisements add about £1.50 to the price. As at December 1985 a 75 cl bottle of branded, blended whisky cost around £8, while the equivalent own-label product in a supermarket cost around £6.50.

There is a paradox. The advertisements do nothing, in return for their cost, to improve the product's quality. They simply increase the product's price. They are parasitic. Yet, at the same time, they are essential to the continued commercial viability of the product.

Economists have the concept of a 'rational man' who is always actuated by price and by profit. The cost of advertisements, especially expensive TV commercials, is a rational reason to purchase some other brand not burdened with advertising costs. Yet, contrary to this rational consideration, advertisements continue to work. This is not because consumers are perversely irrational, but because rational decisions require the consumer to be adequately informed about the different qualities of goods on offer. Advertisements continue to work precisely because that information is lacking.

Summary – persuasion in the marketplace

Shoppers rarely have opportunity to compare the qualities of the alternative goods on offer and are, most of the time, choosing 'blind'. Advertising works because it fulfils the role of the confederate in Sherif's autokinetic experiment.

(i) A well-known brand name may acquire an influence similar to that exercised by Diana, Princess of Wales. Accordingly, the French authorities go to great lengths to restrict the use of the name 'Champagne'.
(ii) In the absence of a brand name, price is what counts. This opens the way to a variety of manipulations at sale time. But when, exceptionally, objective comparison is possible between different goods at different prices, shoppers are outraged.
(iii) Shoppers' reliance on price leads to a paradox in advertising. Advertisements contribute nothing to the qualities of the goods they promote, but they do put up the price.

Similar principles apply to the appraisal of literature and art, to which I turn next.

8 The appraisal of literature and art

There are numerous anecdotes to show that appraisals, often an expert's appraisal, of some works of literature or art are based on more than just the work itself. This is always so when external evidence is cited to establish the work's provenance; but that is not what I have in mind here. I am concerned with appraisals of the work's aesthetic merit. The aesthetic merit attributed to the work depends on who is presumed to have been its author. Of course, when the author is correctly identified, there is no way of distinguishing the intrinsic merit of the work itself from the influence of its known authorship. But when, as occasionally happens, the authorship is unknown or the work is misattributed, then it becomes apparent to what extent aesthetic merit is intrinsic to the work and to what extent its assessment depends on the presumed authorship. The picture that then emerges is that people need the author's name in order to know what to say; even experts are influenced in this way as though they are also naïve subjects vulnerable to the confederate's suggestion in Sherif's (1937) autokinetic experiment.

Most examples conform to one of these five patterns:

1. A famous author publishes a novel or other work under a pseudonym and sells many fewer copies in consequence.
2. A prestigious literary work is deliberately divorced of its true author and title and is re-submitted to a publisher, usually many publishers simultaneously. In its anonymous guise that prestigious work is rejected by publishers and ignored by critics and literary agents.
3. A painting, formerly thought to be by a minor artist or anonymous, is discovered to be an Old Master and, in consequence, rises dramatically in price.
4. Conversely, a painting previously thought to be by a famous artist is discovered to be a fake. As a fake, its value is derisory, even when experts are able to tell the fake from the original only with the help of documentary evidence.
5. Works of art (invariably contemporary works) acquired by a national gallery offend the public's idea of what constitutes a Work of Art.

This chapter presents examples of each of the first four kinds of anecdote. They show that extraneous influences on aesthetic appreciation are widespread and, it must be concluded, commonplace. Examples of the fifth kind pose the more profound question: 'What is a Work of Art?' and are left to the next chapter.

The appraisal of literary work

The story of Doris Lessing's *Diary of a Good Neighbour* by 'Jane Somers' has already been set out in Chapter 1. When a book by a famous author is published under a pseudonym, its true authorship concealed, professionals engaged in the publication of literary work and critics involved in its review seem not to know what to say. It looks as though all these people are unable to recognise good writing when they see it and need the author's name to tell them what kinds of things they should be saying. To elaborate this theme I shall illustrate several different contingencies that have arisen over and over again in the literary world.

The author's name is removed from a work

Steps by Jerzy Kosinski is a short novel of 148 pages. It is described as

> The terrifying saga of a man's attempt to define himself through acts of pure violence and extreme sensuality. In a succession of brilliantly realistic scenes it explores the foundations of individual anarchy and the compulsive forces of desire and cruelty. By self-degradation and indulgence in vivid and blatant brutalities the central character seeks to liberate himself from convention and morality. (Kosinski, 1968, frontispiece)

It was first published in 1968 and won the US National Book Award for Fiction in 1969. As of 1977, when the following story begins, it was still in print and had sold about 400 000 copies.

Chuck Ross was a freelance writer in Santa Monica, California, concerned about the opportunities for authors without an established reputation, especially writers with their first novel. In May 1977 he typed out the entire manuscript of *Steps* and sent it, unsolicited, to fourteen American publishers. The retyped edition of the novel was untitled; the author identified himself as 'Erik Demos'. All fourteen publishers rejected the novel, including Random House, its original publishers in 1968, and three other publishers of Kosinski's work. Houghton Mifflin, Kosinski's current publisher at that time, replied:

> Several of us read your untitled novel here with admiration for writing and style. Jerzy Kosinski comes to mind as a point of comparison when reading the stark, chilly episodic incidents you have set down. The drawback to the manuscript, as it stands, is that it doesn't add up to a satisfactory whole. It has some very impressive moments, but gives the impression of sketchiness and incompleteness.

> We do not see our way to publishing this particular work as it is, but if you should ever have other manuscripts in progress now or in the future, we would be happy to consider them. (Ross, 1979)

One of the publishers suggested that Erik Demos should find himself an agent. So Chuck Ross repeated the exercise with thirteen literary agents; none would attempt to place the novel with a publisher. He also sent a letter of enquiry to 13 further agents. That letter included two paragraphs previously written by Kosinski himself about *Steps*. Only one of this second set of agents offered to look at the complete manuscript. They asked for a $25 reading fee in advance and then declined to attempt to place the novel with a publisher.

No-one recognised Kosinski's prize-winning book. More to the point, no-one, publisher or agent, thought it was worth publishing – a book that had already sold 400 000. That is the fate of manuscripts sent unsolicited to publishers, and of authors without reputations. American publishers receive upwards of 5000 unsolicited manuscripts each year.

> My experiment notwithstanding, the publishers all agreed that there is a dearth of decent material received over the transom (the industry's term for unsolicited manuscripts). Richard Marek . . . claims that '99.9% of over-the-transom material is junk.' Tom Wallace, editor-in-chief at Holt, Reinhart & Winston, professes that publishers are always looking for manuscripts and that readers of the manuscripts start off idealistic, but that most of the material is 'just gibberish'. Sam Vaughan, top executive at Doubleday, says that 'an unaccounted number aren't books at all – just someone's hobby bundled up.' (Ross, 1980).

The number of people who want to write and can write well enough to be published means that the volume of material submitted for publication is much greater than can be marketed. Readers, editors, publishers and critics are generally unable to discriminate. They need someone to tell them which articles and stories to accept; that is, they *actually require* someone in the role of the stooge in Sherif's autokinetic experiment. That role is commonly filled by the author's name.

Prospects for new authors amount to a 'Catch 22'. If you are already well-known, there is little difficulty in getting further work published. Publishers can estimate the likely sales by comparison with your previous work and weigh up whether your new manuscript is a commercial proposition. If you are unknown, the outcome is uncertain and publishers are loath to take the risk. For publishers as well as readers the author's name is, unfortunately, the most reliable guide.

An author's name is added to a work

Alistair MacLean (1922–1987) wrote novels of mystery and adventure. During the war, from 1941 to 1944, he served in the Royal Navy as a torpedo man below deck on Arctic convoys to Murmansk. This experience provided much material for his later writing. His particular forte was the use of the elements – the locations, machinery and ship scenes. He was best known for *H.M.S. Ulysses* and *The Guns of Navarone*.

> The critics consistently found fault; but an obedient public did not, and MacLean's books sold by the million. [He published 29 books and none of them sold less than 250 000. Renton, 1991.]
>
> In 1961 – when he was out of harmony with Collins [his publisher] – he wrote two books under the pseudonym Ian Stuart. Without the name MacLean on the dustcovers, however, *The Dark Crusader* and *The Satan Bug* enjoyed only ordinary sales. (*The Times*, 1987a)

Alistair MacLean died on 2 February 1987, leaving a number of screenplay outlines written for an American film company ten years before his death. His publishers had these outlines turned into novels by ghost writers:

ALISTAIR MACLEAN'S *Death Train* by Alistair MacNeill.
ALISTAIR MACLEAN'S *Golden Girl* by Simon Gandolfi.
ALISTAIR MACLEAN'S *Air Force One is Down* by John Denis.

> The MacLones, as they are called in the book trade, took a bit of a battering last week when Stratford Magistrates' Court ruled that it was misleading for the publisher HarperCollins to publish a book by Alistair MacNeill (very small print) from a plot once thought up by Alistair MacLean (very large print). The magistrates, concluding that reasonable people might think they were buying the real MacLean, charged the firm more than £10 000 in fines and costs. But the MacLones are undeterred.
>
> Another publisher, Chapmans, plans a new MacLone next March, by a different author. Nor will HarperCollins remove the MacNeill books from shops, although it will seek legal advice. (Cusick, 1991d)

The reason, of course, is that with Alistair MacLean's name featured prominently on the cover, the books sell far more copies than without.

> The unknown Mr MacNeill was picked to turn the outlines into books after the publishers read a manuscript of his which was considered unworthy of publication.
>
> A freelance reviewer, David Holloway, told the court Mr MacNeill was 'greatly inferior . . . he cannot keep up the suspense.' (*Independent*, 1991)

A best-selling author is no longer around to write any more books

One really cannot expect that an author who sold as well as Alistair MacLean would be meekly allowed by his publishers to 'die'. Virginia Andrews, 'who wrote seven books before she died and five afterwards', provides another dramatic example. Her first novel appeared in 1979. Here is its review from the *Washington Post:*

> FLOWERS IN THE ATTIC. By V.C. Andrews. Pocket. 416 pp. Paperback, $2.50
>
> FLOWERS IN THE ATTIC may well be the worst book I have ever read. The author, V.C. Andrews, plops four children into their grandmother's attic, where they are mistreated (neither convincingly nor imaginatively) for 400 musty pages. One of them dies up there – I suspect the only way the child could remove himself from such a silly book. This unbelievable circumstance, by the way, is what passes for plot.
>
> The principle of selection does not seem to have entered the author's head, nor her editor's. She gives us every boring thing these figures (I don't want to call them characters) say. And believe me, Andrews has no ear for dialogue – though dialogue, in long indigestible chunks, is what she uses to move the book along.
>
> The expected draw of *Flowers in the Attic*, I would guess, is the incest motif. See, dad was really mom's half-uncle, and that's why grandma's got these hang-ups. And with all that teeming adolescence up there in that attic, we know what sooner or later those kids are going to do.
>
> *Flowers in the Attic* is deranged swill, but swill with $100 000 of promotion money behind it. And if that isn't bad enough, here's more: there's a promised sequel! (*Washington Post*, 1979).

Nevertheless . . .

> When she died, in a medical sense, in 1986, Virginia Andrews . . . was one of the bestselling writers in the world. Her cumulative global sales are now [February 1991] 46 million copies. She effectively created a genre known to the book trade as Family Horror, of which the most assiduous buyers are – according to research by Collins, British publishers of her first 11 titles – adolescent females.
>
> The motherlode of the form was *Flowers In The Attic* (1979), in which, after their father's death, four children are locked away by Momma at the top of a Gothic house in Pennsylvania.
>
> By the third of the attic quintet – *If There Be Thorns* (1981) – V C Andrews was allotted first print runs in America of two-and-a-half million.
>
> When such a writer dies, it is understandable that those at their publishers feel a combination of pains: some for the end of the person, some for the end of the work. These were the feelings at Collins during the illness and death of Virginia Andrews in 1986. The corporate part of their grief was assuaged when Ann Patty wrote from Pocket Books, soon after the funeral, to say that the writer had completed 'the heart of four more books'. These . . . would, it was understood, be prepared for publication by another writer. When the last – *Web Of Dreams* – appeared in 1990, Collins was informed that this was the end of the line.
>
> Last month, however, a new Virginia Andrews novel was published in America and Britain. . . . The name Virginia Andrews was displayed in the fat

> gold lettering familiar from previous titles. The only difference was two small black letters beside the top bend of the final S. The letters were: TM. The late Virginia Andrews, novelist, had been trademarked. (Lawson, 1991)

A trademark is a name or symbol used to distinguish goods produced by one manufacturer from goods produced by competitors – a publisher's imprint, for example. It is legally registered and provides protection against counterfeit goods. An author's name is not ordinarily a trademark because an author's protection derives from the law of copyright. The name 'V C ANDREWS™' is an exception because of its proven utility in marketing the particular genre of Family Horror. A book with that name on the cover will sell millions to young women who want that particular kind of read.

The author can't write – not well enough to be published

In most cases ability to write seems not to matter; one can always hire a ghost writer. Naomi Campbell, the model, had a 'co-writer' to 'assist' her with her novel *Swan*. The author's name functions not as a guarantee of literary quality, but as a link between the book and pre-existing publicity. But in 1990 Random House contracted with Joan Collins, the actress, for two novels. They agreed an advance of $4m. In February 1996 Random House sued for the return of $1.2m already paid.

> It seems remarkably churlish of Random House, the US publishing conglomerate, to want back from Joan Collins the $1m they paid of an agreed $3m advance simply because, as some reports claim, the books she delivered are unpublishable. Most publishers who give whopping advances to celebrities know they are buying a name, not a writing talent, and get someone else actually to write the book.
>
> At her former publisher, Simon & Schuster, Miss Collins apparently 'worked closely' with her editor Suzanne Jaffey on her first novel. If, as it appears, Random House allowed Miss Collins to write the books herself, quite frankly they have only themselves to blame. (Guttridge, 1994)

Joan Collins won the case (Letts, 1996) on the grounds that the contract stipulated only the submission of two complete manuscripts, and said nothing about their quality or even that they should be publishable.

There is no author

Beginning in February 1994 a police investigation uncovered a series of horrendous murders at 25 Cromwell Street, Gloucester. Fred West and his wife, Rosemary, had, over a period of 20 years, abducted young women, subjected them to sadistic sexual rituals, then murdered them and disposed of the bodies within their own house. After his arrest Fred West confessed to eleven of the twelve murders with which he was charged. The investigation attracted great publicity, and the proceedings at the subsequent trial of Rosemary West were reported all over the world.

On 1 January 1995 Fred West succeeded in hanging himself in his prison cell. He died intestate and, because his wife was also charged with murder, the administration of his estate passed to the Official Solicitor. The Official Solicitor is under obligation to maximise the value of the estate.

> The Official Solicitor has commissioned a 'definitive' biography of Fred West and has provided the author with thousands of pages of police interviews as well as West's handwritten account of his life.
>
> The author who has been awarded what will undoubtedly prove a literary goldmine is a former *Times* journalist, Geoffrey Wansell, who recently completed a biography of the late playwright Terence Rattigan.
>
> The book – which seems certain to be one of the best-selling biographies in recent years – will be published by Hodder Headline 'some time next year' after it bid a six-figure sum for it. The account will earn West's children thousands of pounds in advance payments. (Macdonald, 1995)

Why so much interest in Fred West's biography – with seven or eight different authors clamouring to write it? Because the pre-existing publicity from the trial guarantees enormous sales.

There is no book

There was a TV commercial for Yellow Pages in which an old man is ringing around trying to find a copy of his own book.

> It all started with a good old Yellow Pages television ad eight years ago [in 1983]. There was something special about the amiable buffer hopefully searching for a copy of his long-lost book on fly fishing. And in a notoriously evanescent industry, the ad kept reappearing like spiders in the bath.
>
> It's brought huge public interest in J R Hartley. Booksellers were asked for copies, but none could supply it. One Surrey shop prints dust jackets labelled *Fly Fishing by J R Hartley* and wraps them around unsaleable books for charity. (Elliott, 1991)

The book, of course, didn't exist – but it does now. Neither does J R Hartley; the book was written under J R Hartley's name by Michael Russell. It was published in November 1991. It was reprinted three times within the first week, and it rose to the top of *The Bookseller*'s fiction list!

Publicity is everything. Books sell because of what the public is told about them, not because of any intrinsic merit. There are many similar stories of literary misjudgments. Once within the domain of publishable books, neither the reading public, nor the publishers, nor their readers and editors, nor the book critics, are able to assess literary quality with any useful reliability, and all these people are dependent on publicity, especially the identity of the author, to know what to say.

The appraisal of fine paintings

What is true of literature is equally true of fine painting. This is perhaps surprising because a book usually has to be purchased before it can be read and the reader discovers whether he or she likes it or not. Since the author contributes a personal style to the book, the author's name has functional significance. But a painting is viewed *before* purchase. Nevertheless the market price of a fine painting still depends on the prestige of the painter.

Art experts, and people generally, can distinguish different media (oils, watercolour, pastels, tempera), different subjects (portraits, landscapes, abstracts), different styles (impressionist, surrealist, cubist) and different schools of painting with little or no error. Where judgment fails is in assessing *aesthetic merit*. The history of Sebastiano del Piombo's portrait of *Pope Clement VII* was recounted in Chapter 1. A 2200-fold increase in auction price in the space of six months is exceptional, but there are other similar stories.

A painting is reattributed to an Old Master

St Lucy was martyred in Syracuse, Sicily, in 304 AD. She is known as the patroness of the eyes, so her attribute, to identify her in a painting, is a pair of eyes in a dish. This makes for a rather gory subject and maybe one should not be too surprised that, when the owner of *The Holy Family accompanied by St. Lucy* thought about selling her painting in the summer of 1987, 'Sotheby's valuation department in Bournemouth . . . valued it at £400, saying there was not much of a market for religious paintings.' (Checkland, 1987c) The owner then took it to Phillips of New Bond Street, London, who initially attributed it to a little-known painter called Sisto Badalocchio. Mr Peter Johnson of Phillips said: 'The picture is rather gruesome and is not everyone's cup of tea.' It was put up for auction on 8 December 1987 with an estimated price of £8–12 000 (that is, 20 to 30 times its original valuation).

Sisto Badalocchio (1581–1647) was an artist of the Bolognese school and a pupil of Annibale Carracci. He is said to have been a good draughtsman, but his execution was rather sketchy. After the publication of their auction catalogue, Phillips decided that this painting was actually the work of the master himself, a reattribution that was confirmed by several specialists (Checkland, 1987b). After that reattribution the picture sold for £770 000 (net of buyer's premium) to Richard Feigen, an art dealer in New York. This was nearly 2000 times its original valuation.

Two years later (but before the painting had been physically exported to America) it was sold on for £2.2m (this was 55 000 times the initial estimate) to a foreign collector.

> The probability that it will go abroad is causing an outcry. Sir Denis Mahon, the distinguished expert on 16th-century art said: 'It would be terrible if we lost a painting by one of the great innovators in the history of art. That a painting of this quality should even be at risk demonstrates the petty and provincial mentality in this country towards art.'

> Some experts think the picture's new price still makes it a bargain. Jennifer Fletcher, a lecturer in 16th and 17th-century art at the Courtauld Institute of Art, said: 'Carracci is one of the greatest draughtsmen of all time. When you think of the prices some paintings fetch, £2m seems cheap. I very much hope it will be saved for this country.' (Greig, 1989)

The original valuation of £400 was the judgment of a professional valuer. Its subsequent history demonstrates that nearly all its value resides in who is thought to have painted it. Never mind what it looks like.

A painting, formerly attributed to a prestigious painter, is discovered to be a copy

On 9 July 1987 the *Antiques Roadshow* came to the Corn Exchange in Cambridge. An elderly couple, Mr and Mrs Melville, took their picture of a hare in a snow scene to be valued. It was identified as the work of Bruno Liljefors, a Swedish painter (*b.* 1860) of animals in natural settings, especially native water birds and animals and birds of the forest. It was valued at £30–£40 000.

Mr and Mrs Melville consigned the picture to Sotheby's for auction. Initially, Sotheby's agreed the identification and valuation but after six weeks reported that the Melvilles' picture was only a copy worth £500. Mr and Mrs Melville were devastated. (Curtis, 1987)

Here is what the experts on the Antiques Roadshow said about their misattribution in an addendum at the end of the broadcast programme.

Hugh Scully	I suppose the doors had been open for an hour or an hour and a half, when a couple came in with this picture: a hare in a winter landscape which, at the time, we thought was by the Swedish painter, Bruno Liljefors. But it turned out, I'm afraid, that we were wrong. David, what happened precisely?
David Mason	Well, sadly, quite a lot Hugh; because, having satisfied myself that the picture was an example by the artist, I put a value upon it of some £30–50 000, and the charming couple then decided that they'd wished to sell the picture; and it was sought and handed over to a leading firm of international auctioneers who agreed with me – who agreed with my valuation. It was only when they'd had it some six weeks, they found the original of this picture in a collection in Sweden.
Hugh Scully	So this is copy or fake or . . .
David Mason	It's a very, very clever forgery.
Hugh Scully	Now if Liljefors himself didn't do it, have we any idea who might have done?

David Mason — I think, upon reflection, that it is what we would term to be a 'studio picture' – you see, Liljefors – I mean, to give you an idea of how prolific the artist was, when he died – at the time of his death, there were no fewer than 1000 pictures remaining in his studio. Now, I imagine that Liljefors would probably have had students and, in fact, I understand that his son was an artist who'd tinkered a bit, so it may be that this was an artist painting together with Liljefors, one of his students. It may have been, however, that – perhaps Liljefors, in fact, painted certain bits of the picture . . .

Hugh Scully — But it's certainly contemporary with him?

David Mason — Oh, yes, it was contemporary. I mean, this picture would be painted around the turn of the century. It's a very, very clever forgery. But in the main they don't get past us, but, sadly, this one did and, of course, it is a shame for the owners.
(From *Antiques Roadshow*, producer C. Lewis. BBC1 31 January 1988. © 1988 The British Broadcasting Corporation.)

Mr and Mrs Melville's painting was identified as a copy solely because the original, with an established provenance, was located in a private collection in Sweden. Two experts had been deceived by it. If experts cannot distinguish original from copy on the basis of intrinsic merit, why the 80-fold difference in market value?

A painting is discovered to be a fake

Once pictures come to be purchased as investments, rather than for their own sake, their authenticity assumes primary importance. That is what most affects their resale value. Anyone found to be passing off pictures as the work of some artist other than their creator is diligently pursued by the law.

Samuel Palmer (1805–1881) was an English painter and etcher of visionary landscapes. He was a disciple of William Blake. His best work, done at Shoreham, Kent, from 1827 to 1834, is much sought after. Figures 8.1 and 8.2 are taken from a scholarly work on Samuel Palmer (Sellars, 1974).

Geraldine Norman is a journalist and was saleroom correspondent of the *Times* in the 1970s. She noted in the early 1970s that there were an unexpectedly large number of Samuel Palmer drawings for sale. She began investigating.

> Somewhere there is a talented painter at work, and I would love to meet him. Some beautiful paintings have been created and it would be fascinating to get to the bottom of the hoax. I note in my catalogue for Sotheby's 1973 sale of 'The Horse-Chestnut Tree', I scribbled at the time three enthusiastic stars and a comment, 'the real thing'. (Norman, 1976)

Finally, Tom Keating (1917–1984) was a housepainter and self-taught picture restorer. During his lifetime he made about 2000 pastiches, including many in

Figures 8.1 and 8.2 'Pastoral with Horse Chestnut', 1831/2 (Ashmolean Museum); 'Shoreham at Twilight', (Private Collection).

From J. Sellars, *Samuel Palmer*, pp. 76, 84. 'Pastoral with Horse Chestnut', photograph © Ashmolean Museum. 'Shoreham at Twilight' © Linda Keating. Reproduced with permission.

the style of Samuel Palmer, whom he greatly admired. One of those pictures was offered by the Leger Gallery at an asking price of £15 000 in 1971; as a pastiche it was worth only £50–500. Figure 8.1 is indeed by Samuel Palmer – it has been in the Ashmolean Museum at Oxford since 1929. But Figure 8.2 is a pastiche by Tom Keating. If an art scholar compiling a definitive work on Samuel Palmer is deceived, the difference in price is not a matter of aesthetic quality.

Tom Keating stood trial at the Old Bailey in January 1979 on a charge of conspiracy to pass off his own work as that of other, more prestigious artists. The trial was discontinued the following month on account of Keating's ill health, and all charges were dropped. But why did he do it? Not for personal gain.

> At the risk of reiteration: I have made dozens of pastiches in the style of Palmer, mostly quick sketches. I signed those I felt might reach an avaricious hand with 'not S. Palmer' (the *not* being hidden under the slip of the frame); I also signed my own name in the bark of a tree, etc., or I wrote 'S. Palmer*er*', the two last letters being hidden under the slip on the right hand side.
>
> When marouflaging paper to panel I often used modern synthetic gum and signed my own name or whatever words came to me at the time, i.e., 'fake', or 'God Bless' or 'why be greedy?' – but never swear words, as Palmer was a religious man.
>
> There is, however, a matter I omitted to reckon with, namely the cleaning of these works. I have never myself seen a Palmer pastiche cleaned and revarnished, but friends who have say they are 'transformed' by the process of cleaning. It would be the matter of a moment to remove my marks accidentally. Whether this has happened with the drawings in question, I do not know – but I would be most interested to examine them if given the opportunity.
>
> As for the 'misleading inscriptions' on the backs of pictures – since I have signed my own name under paper pasted on to them and even around the edges of panels, why *not* write on the back in that archaic crabbed handwriting the poor mount-cutters used 'Mr Rembrandt will call for his Nightwatch on Thursday morning'? (Keating, 1976a)

Although Tom Keating's pastiches in the style of Samuel Palmer deceived the experts – suspicions were aroused only because there were suddenly so many of them, far more than Samuel Palmer was thought to have produced – his own assessment of his work was but modest:

> Quite frankly and with, I trust, due modesty, I cannot imagine how anyone could begin to believe that the crude daubs being marketed as Samuel Palmer's were authentic. Anyone with a true love of this kindly, generous and devout artist (who was unable to afford a pinch of snuff in his declining years) will know that he could not possibly have done this work, even on an off day. I flooded the market with the 'work' of Palmer and many others, not for gain (I hope I am no materialist), but simply as a protest against merchants who make capital out of those I am proud to call my brother artists, both living and dead. (Keating, 1976b)

In this case knowledge of a picture's provenance works in reverse. Keating, knowing which pictures were pastiches and which were not, devalues his own work in the light of that knowledge. He is too modest; experts, working without that knowledge, were unable to distinguish the pastiche from the authentic.

In 1983 Christie's paid Keating the compliment of an auction sale devoted entirely to his work, a very rare accolade for a living artist. The publicity arising from his trial and some subsequent TV programmes had turned Keating from a faker into a painter in his own right.

> Ironically, before Keating was exposed, works like his huge canvas after Turner's *Fighting Temeraire*, which Bonham's expect to fetch £12 000 [it actually made £27 500, an auction record for Keating's work; Norman, 1989], might have sold for a few hundred pounds.
>
> Few of Keating's works have appeared on the open market but, as the ultimate accolade, he would have chuckled that his name has joined the list of artists whose work is now being faked. (Alberge, 1989)

Fakes are produced en masse

Fakes are valued at the cost of labour and materials – say £500 for a good oil painting – because more can always be produced at that price. How does the artist feel about being faked? Salvador Dali is one such; his work has been faked to excess.

> Four rival gangs in Europe and America have flooded the art market with fakes of Salvador Dali's surrealist work. According to Dali's lawyer in New York, the forgeries are worth £800m.
>
> The forgers have become so brazen that one of them recently duped a Chicago collector into buying a copy of Dali's Autumnal Cannibalism. The original hangs in the Tate Gallery . . .
>
> The Chicago collector, who is thought to have paid several hundred thousand dollars for his fake, believed that Dali had been so pleased with Autumnal Cannibalism that he had painted it a second time. The collector has been too embarrassed to identify himself, though he has checked with experts in America and at the Tate to verify the swindle.
>
> Dali is so versatile – and his signature varies so much – that only the artist himself can spot some of the fakes.
>
> Dali is partly to blame for the mess. In the mid-1970s he settled a lawsuit with a publisher by paying a $400 000 debt with 17,000 blank sheets of signed paper. The publisher used these papers to run off extra prints of his work from old plates.
>
> . . . He later signed 40 000 more blank papers.
>
> Michael Stout, Dali's lawyer in New York . . . said, there are more than 400 000 fraudulent prints on the market, selling for an average $2000 each, and more than 100 drawings.

> Prices for Dali's printed work have fallen so much that even the forgers are alarmed. Stout has received 'bold' letters from one of the four gangs complaining that their fakes are being faked in turn by somebody else. (McGirk, 1985)

Proliferation of fake prints in this manner has the effect one would expect on the market for genuine works:

> Leading British auction houses are refusing to sell prints signed by the Spanish artist Salvador Dali amid mounting concern over their authenticity. There are thought to be 400 000 fakes on the world market selling for up to £2000 each.
>
> The sale of limited edition prints, authorised and signed by the artist and available at a fraction of the cost of the original, has become a lucrative multi-million pound business – hence the growing attraction for forgers. (*Sunday Times*, 12 July 1987, p. 4)

And what is Dali's reaction to all this?

> According to Descharnes [Robert Descharnes, confidant and business adviser; Dali himself was suffering from Parkinson's disease and needed round-the-clock nursing care], who has been close to Dali for three decades, the eccentric artist is extracting some surreal satisfaction from the dealers' dilemma. 'Of course he is worried about the fakes, particularly the bad ones. But when I talk to him about the problem I detect some satisfaction. He sees it as a confirmation of his fame.' (Moore and St John, 1987)

In the art market authenticity is everything. It is acceptable for an artist to print 500 copies from a lithograph. Those copies have merely to be 'authorised' and signed by the artist and they are then 'authentic'. Lithography transfers the cachet of the artist's name and reputation in a way that reproduction does not.

Summary – the Philistines are right after all!

The judgments of art experts and publishers, people who earn their living in the art market or in books, are mightily influenced by who is thought to have painted a picture or written a book. In most cases the author is correctly identified and it is not possible to disentangle the influence of authorship on expert judgment from that of the intrinsic quality of the work. But, exceptionally, the expert makes his or her judgment under a misapprehension, and it can then be seen that presumed authorship is almost everything and the quality of the writing or the aesthetic merit of the painting contribute very little indeed.

If a child's daub is compared with, say, a painting by J. M. W. Turner, the difference in execution is obvious. But once attention is restricted to marketable paintings and publishable books, the experts are as vulnerable to extraneous opinion as the subjects in Sherif's autokinetic experiment. Art and literature are two domains where even the experts are unwittingly borrowing other people's opinions, which begs the question: 'What is a "Work of Art"?'

9 What is a 'Work of Art'?

Works of Art

Quite simply, a Work of Art is a human artefact of interest to the art world – to painters, sculptors, art museums, auctioneers, dealers and collectors. That is a wickedly circular definition, but I do not think any more objective or succinct statement is possible.

Some Works of Art are irredeemably controversial. But once it is realised that different people look at the same work from different points of view – to be more precise, against different backgrounds of prior experience, especially of other Works of Art – it can at least be seen how the controversy occurs, even if the question 'What is a Work of Art?' remains unanswered.

Imagine two subgroups within society. One group, comprising the cognoscenti, accepts a new work as a Work of Art because it bears a close relationship to other works already accepted as such, and a new painter or sculptor as an artist because his or her work is perceived to follow an existing tradition. The vagaries of successive judgments will then ensure that the spectrum of works accepted by the cognoscenti is ever-increasing in variety, growing ever outwards like a spider's web. The growth of that web is constrained only by the necessity for artists to sell enough of their work to make some kind of living.

The other subgroup is the general public. They have some idea of what they think Art should be, but are not carried along with the evolution of that concept within the art world. The public are more concerned with getting value for money when they shop, and with the disposal of unwanted materials in this increasingly throw-away society. It therefore happens – indeed, it ultimately *will* happen – that the spider's web of works accepted as Art by the cognoscenti spills over into those categories which the general public sees as 'con' or even rubbish. Here are three works from the collection of modern art at the Tate Gallery, London.

IKB79 (Yves Klein)

The painting reproduced in Figure 9.1 is painted in ultramarine on fine cotton scrim over a plywood backing; it measures 55 × 47½ in. When I invite my class

Figure 9.1 Yves Klein, *IKB79*.

Tate Gallery, Exhibit T1513, acquired 1972. © 2000 ADAGP, Paris and DACS, London. Photograph © Tate Gallery. Reproduced with permission.

to guess what this painting would fetch at auction (£1–10, £10–100, £100–1000, . . . or is it a con?), they mostly select safe guesses in the range £100–100 000. One year one student knew enough about modern art to recognise what he was looking at and to give a correct answer. The rest of the class laughed politely at the suggestion that the original of Figure 9.1 would fetch somewhere between £100 000 and £1 million.

Figure 9.1 is one of a long series of blue monochrome paintings by Yves Klein. Because this particular painting is in the Tate Gallery it will never come to auction. But another of Yves Klein's blue paintings, very similar but larger (78 × 55 in), was auctioned by Sotheby's in July 1987 for £638 000 (estimate £580 000–£650 000; Norman, 1987). That price immediately raises questions: *What am I doing here spending my day at a word-processor? Why am I not on my way round to Halfords to buy a can of blue spray paint?* In fact, faking an Yves Klein painting would not be easy, because the possibility of someone else copying the idea has been anticipated. Yves Klein's blue paintings have all been carefully numbered and catalogued; their whereabouts and provenances are fully documented.

Klein experimented from June 1957 until his death in June 1962 with the production of an intense blue colour using a synthetic ultramarine pigment of high saturation bound to the surface with a weak medium – weak so as to dilute the saturation as little as possible. The ultramarine pigment was frequently sprayed onto fine cotton scrim stretched over a plywood panel, as in the Tate Gallery's example. The quality of the spraying improved over the period; the early pictures tend to have a distinctly uneven wave-like surface, whereas the later works (such as the Tate's example) are finer and more uniform in texture (Alley, 1981, p. 390). Nevertheless, Yves Klein was doing no more than mechanics in car body repair shops do every day. His work is a purely technical achievement and the Tate Gallery is a museum of modern art, not technology. So, to rephrase my question: *How does it happen that Yves Klein can sell a blue spray painting for £638 000, whereas I would not be able to sell one at all?*

Circle of Sticks (Richard Long)

This work is shown in Figure 9.2, but let us read the catalogue description first.

> 76 sticks, each approximately 11 in. long and 5/16 in. in diameter, arranged in a circle 22 ft. in diameter, to be exhibited in a space approximately 30 ft. square. Overall dimensions 5/16 × 264 × 264 (0.7 × 671 × 671).
>
> 'Circle of Sticks' was made in October 1973 for a space in the Tate Gallery selected by the artist but its display is not confined to this particular room (the present Gallery 20) – other suitable spaces may also be used.
>
> The sticks are the same kind as those Long used in his first public exhibition at the Galerie Konrad Fischer in Düsseldorf in 1968. They come from Leigh Woods, Bristol (where the artist lives). The invitation card for that exhibition shows a photograph of these woods with the Clifton Suspension Bridge in the background. In the foreground is a figure with a bicycle on the towpath beside the River Avon. A more recent photograph of the artist's source of sticks was reproduced in the catalogue of Long's one-man show at the Stedelijk Museum, Amsterdam (December 1973–January 1974), and entitled 'Along the towpath getting sticks'.
>
> 'Circle of Sticks' is accompanied by a certificate of authenticity signed and dated by the artist. (Bullock, 1975, p. 190)

With a pocket calculator you could work out that 76 sticks, 11 inches long, placed carefully end-to-end, would indeed make a circle of just 22 feet diameter.

Figure 9.2 Richard Long, 'Circle of Sticks'.

Tate Gallery, Exhibit T1783, acquired 1973. © Richard Long. Photograph © Tate Gallery. Reproduced with permission.

'Circle of Sticks' is exactly what the catalogue says. It requires no more than ordinary skill to set sticks out in a circle (which the curators at the Tate have to do every time the work is put back on show) and the arrangement reflects no particular artistic vision.

EQUIVALENT VIII (Carl Andre)

Figure 9.3 shows a neat stack of 120 firebricks, 2 high × 6 header × 10 stretcher. Each brick measures $2^1/_2 \times 4^1/_2 \times 9$ in and bears a number that indicates its precise position and orientation within the stack. These bricks were purchased by the Tate Gallery from the artist, Carl Andre, in 1972 for a sum variously reported as £4–6000. The catalogue entry for this exhibit includes:

> For his second show at the Tibor de Nagy Gallery in March 1966, Andre created an astringent environment by setting eight rectilinear mounds of 120 bricks each on the gallery's parquet floor. 120 was chosen because it was a number particularly rich in factors. The bricks had to be stacked in two layers to prevent them drifting apart and to give the pieces sufficient mass. Thus the top layer of each mound had only 60 bricks. The bricks were assembled in only four out of six possible combinations: 3 × 20, 4 × 15, 5 × 12 and 6 × 10. (In bricklaying, bricks laid end to end are called a stretcher course and bricks laid side by side are called a header course; thus the pieces may be described as 120 bricks in two courses each, i.e. 3 header × 20 stretcher and 3 stretcher × 20 header etc.) The same 6 × 10 combination, for example, could be either an elongated rectangle or a near square, depending on the orientation of the bricks. Although each of the eight shapes was different, they all occupied the same amount of space in cubic centimetres, which accounted for their visual equivalence. He therefore entitled this exhibition *Equivalents* . . .

Figure 9.3 Carl Andre, *EQUIVALENT VIII.*

Tate Gallery, Exhibit T1534, acquired 1972. © 2002 Carl Andre/VAGA, New York/DACS. Photograph © Tate Gallery. Reproduced with permission.

> Andre added on 12 May 1972 that none of these pieces was sold from the Tibor de Nagy exhibition and he afterwards returned all but 200 of the bricks to the brickyard to get his money back. The original bricks were sand-lime bricks from the Long Island City Brickworks. When he decided to reconstruct the pieces several years later he found that this brickworks had closed, so he used firebricks instead. These are approximately the same size, but yellowy-brown instead of bluish white. Only one brick piece made of sand-lime bricks survives. … He remade all the brick pieces in 1969, including a second version of this sand-lime piece. It was important that the bricks should be light in colour and solid, without holes. (Alley, 1981, pp. 11–12)

Carl Andre's *EQUIVALENT VIII* is famous in consequence of a contentious article in the *Sunday Times* in 1976 (Simpson, 1976). That article in the business section of the newspaper was questioning the Tate's stewardship of public funds. It prompted a public furore that continued in the letter columns of national newspapers and on TV for several weeks.

That furore is easy to understand. Almost anyone could stack 120 bricks neatly. There are many people (bricklayers) who earn their living stacking bricks with, probably, a greater understanding of how bricks behave in the mass than Carl Andre. Different people might well use different kinds of brick; but not even Carl Andre can now use the original 1966 bricks. It falls into the general public's conception of 'con'. So, should the Tate Gallery have bought Carl Andre's *EQUIVALENT VIII*?

> Would they have bought a similar stack of bricks from me?
> *No, that would be plagiarism.*
> Not even if I had thought of it first?
> *No.*
> Why not?
> *The Tate only collects works of art, not bricks.*
> What makes Carl Andre's stack a work of art? What is a work of art, anyway?
> *A work of art is something produced by an artist.*
> Who is an artist?
> *Someone who sells a work – a stack of bricks, let us say – to the Tate.*
> So, should the Tate Gallery have bought Carl Andre's stack of bricks?

These three works offend so obviously against an ordinary person's idea of a 'Work of Art'. They have been selected from a much larger number. Colin Simpson's article also criticised these other acquisitions by the Tate:

> 44 hazel branches, 33 strips of coloured felt, 3 ropes, and instructions for assembly.
> *Lipsticks in Piccadilly Circus, London 1966* (Claes Oldenburg): A picture of lipsticks cut out from a magazine and stuck on a postcard of Piccadilly Circus
> Five dyed hessian blankets folded by Barry Flanagan
> *Room 1970* (Victor Burgin): 18 sheets of foolscap, each with a few words typed on it.

There are many other works which might have been selected. The popular notion of a 'Work of Art' involves artistic vision and uncommon skill and technique in execution. These particular works represent ideas that are common to many people and place few demands on the executant's skill and technique. They are seen to be emperors with no clothes on. So, how did these works come to be created?

'Junk art'

If there is money to pay for art, then artists will produce it. During the 1960s and 1970s the Dutch government promoted a cultural programme that guaranteed artists a good living wage in return for some of their work. The scheme became excessively expensive and was terminated in 1988. In 1992,

> The Dutch government is about to unload 200 000 items, accumulated as part of an effort to support struggling artists.
> The programme amounted to a cultural version of the Common Agricultural Policy. . . . The scheme was described by one arts expert as 'completely barmy'. (Marshall, 1992)

The restriction on the production of new art is not artistic vision, it is money to pay the artists. This has two significant consequences. First, the young would-be artist is strapped for finance and thereby materials, especially if his or her interest is in sculpture. This has led to the creation of 'junk art' – art created from materials picked out of skips – from the rubbish that others have thrown away. For example,

> JAKE TILSON, *sculptor, was born in 1958. The V&A and the Tate Gallery have both exhibited collections of his work. He is a seasoned scavenger.*
>
> 'Finding decent street junk is getting harder. Despite what one reads, I find that the streets of New York – where I get most of my material – are getting surprisingly clean. I've been collecting junk for six years, going through skips and nipping into derelict buildings. I particularly like the letterforms from shop fronts, ventilation units, seat coverings, lots of metal. The waste is appalling. My all-time favourite find was part of a New York telephone booth.'
>
> TERRY SETCH, *the sculptor and painter, was born in 1936. He moved to Penarth in 1970, and regularly combs Welsh beaches for materials.*
>
> 'Within yards of the beach, I always find what I want – evidence of the modern world in bits and pieces that have been washed up. It's amazing what you can find on the beach: a lavatory seat, old milk bottles, old plastic, a sofa . . .' (Alberge, 1991a)

Second, the young would-be artist has, initially, to sell his work (if he can sell it at all) cheaply. Looking at the very high prices paid for some works of modern art (Willem de Kooning's *Interchange* sold for $20 680 000 in November 1989 – about £12 600 000 at the then rate of exchange; Norman and Lucie-Smith, 1990), it appears that some of the works now being produced, still available cheaply, will in course of time come to command similar prices. But which ones? The Contemporary Art Society tries to anticipate which artists and which works will prove important in the future and to acquire them at today's prices. It is a charity founded as long ago as 1911 and purchases works of contemporary art, before the artist becomes famous, with a view to giving the works to British museums.

> As well as giving a lift to their prices, being associated with the CAS brings status to an artist. Dealers give substantial discounts to get their protégés bought. The CAS is inundated with thousands of artists' CVs and slides and there are some artists who stoop to offering to donate their work. (Alberge, 1991b)

Publicity

The second question to ask about Carl Andre's *EQUIVALENT VIII* and the other works lampooned by Colin Simpson is: How did they come to be accepted as Works of Art?

Part of the answer is simply *chance*. There is a society of art cognoscenti and museums with funds to spend on works of modern art and there are contemporary artists producing such works. It is inevitable that some of those works will find their way into national museums and private collections.

But there is a second component to the answer – *publicity*. If a would-be artist can sell a work to the Contemporary Art Society or get it accepted by a museum, that is a clear step up in status and reputation. It is like having the confederate in an aesthetic version of Sherif's (1937) experiment mention one's name to the naïve subject. The Turner Prize, in the words of Nicholas Serota, director of the Tate Gallery, 'was created to draw wider public attention to the achievements of artists working in Britain and to promote discussion of contemporary art' (Gayford, 1992). The effect of the furore over *EQUIVALENT VIII* has been recorded by Richard Morphet, Keeper of the Modern Collection at the Tate Gallery:

> A really extraordinary aspect of the case, I think, is, considering all the hostility that the bricks aroused back in 1976, is that very soon after that, whenever the bricks were not on display, there were tremendous complaints from the public. And I've seen, you know, dear little old ladies going around the gallery looking at works in general, and suddenly one will see the bricks and she'll tug at the sleeve of her companion and say, 'Oh, look, dear. There are those bricks!' (James, 1991)

The very high auction prices achieved by some works of modern art themselves attract publicity, and that process is self-supporting. The best-known works are the most expensive and the most expensive works become the best known. Those works which, on the other hand, fall off the bottom of the scale of purchasability receive no publicity at all. The aesthetics of modern art are derived from the relative positions of different works on that scale of purchasability, not the other way about, and all this happens within the subgroup of art cognoscenti, in semi-isolation from the larger society within which that subgroup exists.

This isolation of public judgments from those of the art cognoscenti was exemplified in a television documentary (James, 1991). Carl Andre, interviewed in that programme, was quite unable to see his work or, indeed, any other Works of Art as the public sees them. This results from his immersion in the culture of the art world. At the same time the public, isolated from the evolution of ideas amongst art cognoscenti, do not see *EQUIVALENT VIII* as Andre sees it. That is how it happens that the art world can come to accept as Works of Art artefacts which the public see as a 'con' or even as rubbish.

> The British did not react with the generous, curious tolerance for which they are so famous. The general tenor of the ensuing frenzy was that the bricks might be *EQUIVALENT VIII* to Andre, they might be art to the Tate, but to anybody with eyes to see they were bricks *tout court*.

> Thin men with glasses from the Tate tried to explain, but it did no good. Leading articles, columns, Fyfe Robertson and the whole shooting match of outraged Anglo-empiricism fell on *EQUIVALENT VIII* like a ton of, er, bricks. (Appleyard, 1993)

Finally, in case my comment about rubbish be disputed:

The best Ad Hoc Avant-garde Chair

> An esteemed panel gathered in February 1987 to judge 387 entries in the New York Chair Fair.
>
> After some rarified discussion at the New International Design Center they awarded the prize for the best Ad Hoc Avant-garde Chair to Mr Tom Musorafita. The name was not known to any of the distinguished audience.
>
> Only when the prize was awarded did they learn that he was a construction worker on the as yet unfinished New Design Center. When he saw the entries arriving, he decided to make a seat from the leftovers in his skip as a joke.
>
> Looking at the nailed up combination of a cardboard drum, a piece of plasterboard and a green plastic lid, the award-winning craftsman said: 'I can't believe this piece of garbage won anything. I had to look up "ad hoc" to make sure they weren't yanking me around.'
>
> In praise of the judges' adventurous choice, a critic from *Design Week Magazine* said: 'It was actually quite comfortable because there was a bit of give in the cardboard drum.' (Pile, 1988, p. 148).

and . . .

Martin Creed – Work#88

Martin Creed achieved public prominence as the winner of the Turner Prize for 2001. His entry, *The lights going on and off*, was an otherwise empty room in Tate Britain in which the lights had been rigged to do exactly what the title says, neither more nor less (Alberge, 2001b).

Martin Creed has also come to public notice with his *Work#88*, a scrunched-up ball of A4 typing paper.

> A collector recently paid £2000 for the last in an edition of three scrunched-up paper balls.
>
> Creed's dealer, Martin McGeown, said that before anyone showed any interest in the artist's work, about 150 of the paper balls were sent out as unsolicited gifts to art lovers. A number of recipients, clearly failing to recognise their significance, smoothed them out or *threw them away* [italics added]. 'People who had cleaners for instance,' Mr McGeown said. (Alberge, 2001a)

Summary – why can no one say what makes a 'Work of Art'?

A Work of Art is accepted as such because of its relationship to other works, already accepted. This is simply the principle of relativity operative in the art world.

The relationship is always a matter of opinion and therefore of chance as well. Consequently, the spectrum of artefacts accepted as Works of Art increases from its existing base in random fashion. That is how 'junk' and even outright rubbish can exceptionally come to be accepted.

The increasing diversity of Works of Art exemplifies a pattern of evolution in public (strictly speaking, connoisseur) taste to which I shall return in the final chapter. The random character of that evolution means that the notion of a 'Work of Art' defies definition. Herein lies the disagreement about what makes a Work of Art.

10 Belief in God

What is 'belief'?

There is a very simple argument – so elementary that most people quite overlook it. It runs as follows:

Neither you nor I nor anyone else yet alive has any experience of 'Life After Death'. We have, none of us, ever met anyone with such experience, anyone able to tell us about it. So, when we hear a *Preacher* (by which I mean any religious authority from any religion whatsoever who professes to know) pronouncing about the World to Come or about God or Satan . . . we have no basis on which to disagree with what we are told (unless it be another Preacher we have listened to previously). We are all subjects in Sherif's (1937) autokinetic experiment and the Preacher is the confederate.

You might, of course, suggest that the influence of one person's judgment on another works only for trivial judgments, and it is indeed true that such influence has been demonstrated only in unimportant cases (for aesthetic judgments, Mausner, 1954a,b; the cutaneous perception of warmth, McCord, 1948; the duration of the spiral after-effect, Sinha, 1952; estimates of number, Bovard, 1953; and estimates of size, Bovard, 1953, and Mausner, 1954). It has never been shown to work for anything that really matters. But that is because social psychologists are responsible, ethical people. They do not use their experimental techniques to persuade volunteer subjects to part with their money, or to go to war, or to refuse medical treatment, or anything like that. But, in the real world, there are people with no such compunction, and it is Sherif's technique that they implicitly use.

You will say: 'Ah, but we are grown up; we are wise to that sort of thing!' And I will reply: 'You and I were once small children, at the mercy of the society in which we grew up – of our parents and of the Preachers our parents listened to. If you think you can now interpret the world independently of that cultural heritage . . .'. 'Give me a child for the first seven years, and you may do what you like with him afterwards' (attributed as a Jesuit maxim, *Oxford Dictionary of Quotations*, p. 647).

The thesis of this chapter is that religion works precisely because people believe they are making real, though very difficult, judgments when, in reality, they have no empirical basis for judgment at all. Sherif's (1937) experiment and other studies tell us that people are vulnerable to even the slightest, most subtle, suggestion. Indeed, they have no defence against extraneous suggestion. To tell the truth, their minds are made up for them.

Robyn Twitchell

Here is an example to illustrate that point. David and Ginger Twitchell are Christian Scientists in Boston, Massachusetts. They had a son, Robyn, who died of a bowel obstruction in April 1986 at the age of two-and-a-half after a five-day illness. The Twitchells had not called a doctor to examine their child. Now you might carelessly suppose that they were somewhat negligent, uncaring parents, but that would be quite the opposite of the truth. They both loved their child dearly and were devoted in their care. Let us listen to David Twitchell in conversation with Joan Bakewell.

David Twitchell: Friday morning after I had gone to work, Ginger called the practitioner and that practitioner helped us throughout Robyn's problem. We were in contact with her regularly and she came and visited a number of times.

Joan Bakewell: And what did she say?

David Twitchell: Like us, and even more so, her focus is prayer and healing the situation or problem or whatever it is through prayer; and so she prayed aloud with Robyn. She also just spent some personal time with him, hopefully, as a doctor or a nurse could with a child, just loving them and being a nice person with them.

Joan Bakewell: Did it ever cross anyone's mind at any point just to phone a doctor?

David Twitchell: We are not against calling a medical doctor; it's just that what I've been taught and what I've experienced is that turning to prayer, turning to God is a better, more complete and . . . more thorough healing of a problem, solution to a problem than turning to other systems. (From *Heart of the Matter: In God We Trust,* producer O. Edridge. BBC1, 14 October 1990. © 1990 The British Broadcasting Corporation.)

So, in the course of his illness, Robyn was prayed for by a Christian Scientist practitioner and looked after by a Church nurse. 'Christian Scientists turn resolutely to God, as the Master did, to effect the needed healing . . . disease hath no basis in God's kingdom.' (Eddy, 1875)

David and Ginger Twitchell were charged with 'involuntary manslaughter' by the State of Massachusetts and convicted. They were not sentenced to any term of imprisonment, but to ten years' probation, that probation to include medical supervision of their three other children. It is not certain, of course, that conventional medicine would have saved Robyn's life. That cannot be known without a medical examination. It 'depends on the cause of the intestinal obstruction. If it was caused by a malignancy, Mr Botsford's observation [that "No one . . . has suggested that conventional medicine would have saved

Robyn; no one can"] may be correct. If it was caused by a benign condition, such as intussusception of the bowel, then conventional surgery, provided soon enough, would have been curative with a high degree of certainty' (Botsford, 1990; Cherry, 1990).

Now, David and Ginger Twitchell were not experts in the diagnosis of bowel disorders. In fact, I do not suppose they knew, at that critical time, any more about it than I do. They would have had no basis for assessing different sources of advice; they were, frankly, 'guessing in the dark'. They happen to have been exposed to Christian Science teaching on the treatment of disease – teaching which prescribes prayer and prayer alone – rather than to conventional medicine. They were not in a position to follow any other course than that which they did.

Nicola Geleff

David and Ginger Twitchell were charged and convicted because they had refused conventional medical treatment on behalf of someone else. They would, of course, have been entitled to refuse it on their own behalf. Thus it was with Nicola Geleff, who was a Jehovah's Witness. Jehovah's Witnesses have a specific prohibition against taking blood into the body, either through the mouth or by transfusion.

> Mrs Geleff . . . was admitted to the maternity unit at Exeter's Royal Devon and Exeter hospital about a week ago. But she suffered a massive haemorrhage after the birth on Tuesday and slipped into a coma.
>
> [She] was brought out of a coma by doctors to make sure she did not want the life-saving treatment after the birth of her twins, it was disclosed yesterday.
>
> But Mrs Geleff, 35, insisted she did not want to be given any blood and she died in hospital just hours after the birth of a baby girl and boy.
>
> (*Independent*, 1991b)

These two stories illustrate that you, I and everyone else are subjects in Sherif's autokinetic experiment. A Preacher fills the role of the confederate partner. We have no way of resisting the Preacher's suggestion. It is simply a matter of which religious tradition each of us is exposed to. That is the gist of the argument in this chapter. But I wish to anticipate three possible misunderstandings.

(i) This chapter is about religion in the abstract, *not* about any religion in particular (even though my selection of illustrative examples might suggest otherwise).

(ii) I am not concerned with whether any particular belief is, or is not, true; I am concerned only with the *psychological nature* of belief, any kind of belief, but religious belief is much the most interesting. I shall use the word 'Preacher' to denote any religious authority from any religion whatsoever, anyone who professes to know about God and to transmit that 'knowledge' to other people. I am not concerned with whether what the Preacher says is true; I am concerned only with the psychological function of the preaching.

(iii) A person's religious belief is consequent on his or her membership of a religious community, family or culture and it is no concern of this chapter what anyone should, or should not, believe.

Life after death

The two topics that most occupy Preachers are Life after Death and (in some form or other) the existence of God. Life after Death is quickly disposed of, because there is nothing to say. Death is irreversible. You and I and everyone else yet living have no experience of Life after Death; none of us has ever met anyone with such experience. It cannot therefore be a topic in a study restricted to scientific observation of the natural world.

While I was still a student, I took a vacation job nursing in a mental hospital. I met one patient there who told me he had 'been over the other side and come back again'. He had (so he said) met the Devil, and he described to me what the Devil looked like. People who claim personal experience of Life after Death are deemed by our society to need psychiatric care.

A Preacher, of course, does not pretend to *personal* experience of Life after Death, but to *revealed knowledge*. For example, when Pope Pius IX proclaimed *ex cathedra* on 8 December 1854:

> . . . that the Most Blessed Virgin Mary, at the first instant of her conception, was preserved immaculate from all stain of original sin, by the singular grace and privilege of the Omnipotent God, in virtue of the merits of Jesus Christ . . . (Pelikan, 1989)

that is a proposition that you and I could not know about except for that revelation by the Pope. A proclamation *ex cathedra* makes it a required belief for Roman Catholics. Even so, could we have a *revealed* knowledge of Life after Death? Let us suppose that somehow (never mind how) a Preacher acquired knowledge of Life after Death. Would that Preacher be able to tell us about it?

Heaven and Hell

Beliefs about Life after Death are always expressed in images of this world, notwithstanding that they refer to an alleged world to come. The Christian conception of Hell, based on descriptions in the Revelation of St. John the Divine, pictures it as an eternal fire – a 'lake of fire burning with brimstone'. This image is, almost certainly, derived from the eruption of an acidic volcano. Brimstone originally signified the large globules of molten rock ejected by an active volcano over its brim and has come to be applied to sulphur because compounds of sulphur with unpleasant odours (hydrogen sulphide, sulphur dioxide) provide the characteristic smell of an acidic volcano. The 'lake of fire' can be physically seen when molten lava flows down the side of a volcano. But which volcano might have been the source of the image in the Book of Revelation? Vesuvius, near Naples, erupted in AD 79, which might be a little late. An alternative is Santorini on the island of Thera in the Agean Sea. Santorini erupted about 1550 BC and, more to the point, provided one of the three largest eruptions known to have occurred in historic times. Patmos, where the Book of Revelation was written, was only 100 miles away and well within the area of volcanic fallout. The magnitude of the eruption makes it plausible that it was known all over the ancient world, and since the fire was seen to have been spewed out from the depths of the earth, the image it provided of Hell (commonly thought to be below ground) would have been irresistible.

In hot Mediterranean and desert countries, fire is the greatest torment imaginable. In Norse mythology, on the other hand, Niflheim, the world of the dead, 'was a place of bitter cold and unending night' (Crossley-Holland, 1980, p. xxi). Frankly, in the frozen wastes of the far north, a large fire would have been very welcome.

Heaven, in Christian mythology, is a city (the New Jerusalem) because, if you are one of the underclass in the Eastern Mediterranean in the first century AD, the city is the desirable place to live. A city is where life is easiest. But, to Muslims, Heaven is a garden, the Garden of Delights. Life in a desert country is a continual struggle against the heat. In a garden transpiration from the trees cools the air and reduces the temperature stress on the body. Naturally, gardens are the preserve of the rulers.

If the content of beliefs about Life after Death relate so consistently to this present world, how can they relate to any world to come? Careful rational consideration reveals that the Preacher cannot possibly have that kind of knowledge. If a Preacher were to communicate some revealed knowledge to us about some other world yet to come, we would need some minimal prior acquaintance with that world in order to understand what the Preacher was saying. If you are going to learn arithmetic, you need some prior acquaintance with numbers, which young children routinely get by counting oranges and lemons. Education always builds upon existing understanding, however minimal, of the subject to be taught. We none of us have any prior acquaintance with Life after Death; for that reason any revealed knowledge about the matter would be incomprehensible. Beliefs about Life after Death are always 'made up'. That is why they differ between religions. Nevertheless, very many people, including many of undoubted intelligence, are persuaded on the basis of no empirical evidence at all. That is a problem that this chapter must address, and the key to the answer is provided by Sherif's experiments.

The existence of God

The existence of God, on the other hand, can be studied empirically through the activities of those who claim to know about Him. In every society in the world there is a religious presence. There are meeting places, usually with a characteristic architecture. There are Preachers (priests, mullahs, brahmins, etc.) who are recognisable by their distinctive dress. There are public displays of religious worship, though much more so with some religions than with others. And there is missionary work designed to increase the number of adherents. The question to be put is: What are all these people trying to do, in psychological terms? We cannot answer that question by asking them – we should only get an answer in terms of the content of their respective messages – an answer that looks from the inside outwards. I am concerned instead with the psychological function of preaching, seeking an objective answer that looks from the outside inwards. That psychological function is well illustrated by an episode from Charles Dickens' *Great Expectations*.

Controlling people's behaviour

Great Expectations opens with Pip, an orphan, visiting his parents' grave in a churchyard on the marshes beyond Gravesend. There are prison hulks moored in the River Medway and on the afternoon in question Pip is suddenly seized by 'A fearful man, all in coarse gray, with a great iron on his leg.' This escaped convict, Magwitch, can do what he likes with Pip while he physically has hold of him. But he needs food and a file and perforce has to send Pip to fetch them for him. That poses a particular problem: Supposing Pip, once out of reach, decides not to come back? Even worse, supposing Pip, once out of reach, goes to the authorities and tells them where an escaped convict may be found? That problem Magwitch solves in a very traditional manner:

> 'You bring me, to-morrow morning early, that file and them wittles. You bring the lot to me, at that old Battery over yonder. You do it, and you never dare to say a word or dare to make a sign concerning your having seen such a person as me, or any person sumever, and you shall be let to live. You fail, or you go from my words in any partickler, no matter how small it is, and your heart and your liver shall be tore out, roasted and ate. Now, I ain't alone, as you may think I am. There's a young man hid with me, in comparison with which young man I am a Angel. That young man hears the words I speak. That young man has a secret way pecooliar to himself, of getting at a boy, and at his heart, and at his liver. It is in wain for a boy to attempt to hide himself from that young man. A boy may lock his door, may be warm in bed, may tuck himself up, may draw the clothes over his head, may think himself comfortable and safe, but that young man will softly creep and creep his way to him and tear him open. I am a-keeping that young man from harming of you at the present moment, with great difficulty. I find it wery hard to hold that young man off your inside.' (Dickens, 1861, pp. 7–8)

The kind of stratagem employed by Magwitch is, possibly, now out of fashion in our society. But paedophiles are inevitably at risk of exposure by the children they abuse, and use similar threats to keep the children quiet. Following a rash of allegations of satanic abuse in the late 1980s, the Government commissioned a report from Professor Jean La Fontaine into 84 alleged cases. Professor La Fontaine found three cases of 'ritual, not satanic abuse. . . . These were cases in which self-proclaimed mystical/magical powers were use to entrap children and impress them, and also adults, with a reason for the sexual abuse, keeping them compliant' (Waterhouse, 1994).

The threat of horrendous treatment at the hands of (allegedly supernatural) beings, especially in the dark, has traditionally compelled compliance from small children. It is in no way specific to Western society. Here is an equivalent tactic witnessed among the Hopi Indians of north-east Arizona.

> Among many Indian tribes in North America we find a widespread fear of the owl; this is induced in children at an early age. They are told that the owl is a supernatural spirit who has the unpleasant habit of kidnapping children and mutilating them.
>
> I remember vividly the awestruck faces of Hopi children when, at the conclusion of a rain dance, one of the masked Katchina dancers approached and handed them a present of fruit or dolls. The children had been told that the masked and painted dancers were ancestral spirits visiting the tribe. It is customary for a Hopi parent, when a child has expressed a wish for a toy, to tell him that the spirits will bring it to him at the next dance. The parents will then secretly prepare the gift and instruct a dancer to deliver it. When these strange beings call out the child's name and bring him the present he could hardly ask for a more graphic validation of what he had been told. No less convincing is the use of supernatural sanctions in enforcing discipline. On a certain day the mesa of the Hopi is visited by a horrible clown, who arrives, carrying a huge knife and a basket, to kidnap the disorderly children and to cut off their heads. The drama is enacted with considerable realism; the clown appears at the right houses. When he knocks, the parents ostensibly array themselves on the side of the child and pretend to bar the entrance of the monster. When he breaks through, he enumerates the child's misdemeanours and moves to take him. The parents intervene in the child's behalf against the remonstrances of the clown, who is mollified only after receiving presents and the tearful promise of the terrified youngster to mend his ways. All during this scene the children in the neighboring homes have been listening to the proceedings. It is not surprising that on the day of the clown's visit, and somewhat in advance, there are few misbehaved children in the Hopi village. (Asch, 1952, p. 414–15)

The primary function of preaching is not merely to influence, but to control what people say and do. In *Great Expectations* Magwitch invokes the supernatural for the express purpose of keeping Pip obedient. Analogous techniques are used by paedophiles and by Hopi parents to command the behaviour they desire from young children.

John Wesley

Invocation of fear of the supernatural works with adults too. Eighteenth-century England witnessed a great revival of evangelical Christianity. John Wesley is the best-known of the eighteenth-century evangelists. In the course of more than fifty years of preaching he travelled all over England, Scotland and Ireland, and is estimated to have delivered about 40 000 sermons. We have no record of the words he actually uttered, but he published written sermons on standard themes. The extract below comes from his sermon (No. 54) 'On Eternity'.

> . . . in what a condition are those immortal spirits who have made choice of a miserable eternity! I say, made choice; for it is impossible this should be the lot of any creature but by his own act and deed. . . . In what condition will such a spirit be after the sentence is executed, 'Depart, ye cursed, into everlasting fire, prepared for the devil and his angels!' Suppose him to be just now plunged into 'the lake of fire burning with brimstone,' where 'they have no rest, day or night, but the smoke of their torment ascendeth up for ever and ever.' 'For ever and ever!' Why, if we were only to be chained down one day, yea, one hour, in a lake of fire, how amazingly long would one day or one hour appear! I know not if it would not seem as a thousand years. But (astonishing thought!) after thousands of thousands, he has but just tasted of his bitter cup! After millions, it will be no nearer the end than it was the moment it began! (Wesley, 1872, p. 194)

That style of sermonising was not peculiar to John Wesley; it was common in his day and age. But to give some idea of its effect (not necessarily preaching about Hell-fire) here is an extract from his journal:

> Sat. 12 [June 1742, at Epworth]. – I preached on the righteousness of the law and the righteousness of faith. While I was speaking, several dropped down as dead, and among the rest such a cry was heard of sinners groaning for the righteousness of faith as almost drowned my voice. But many of these soon lift up their heads with joy, and broke out into thanksgiving, being assured they now had the desire of their soul – the forgiveness of their sins. (Curnock, 1909, p. 23; cited by Doughty, 1955, p. 131).

And here is the testimony of one of Wesley's converts, an anonymous soldier:

> I was desperate in wickedness and did not put a restraint on any lust or appetite; till one day, as I was coming out of the country by Kennington Common, Mr John Wesley was going to preach and I thought I would hear what he had to say; for I had heard many learned and wise men say he was beside himself. But when he began to speak, his words made me tremble. I thought he spoke to no one but me, and I durst not look up; for I imagined all the people were looking at me. I was ashamed to show my face, expecting God would make me a public example, either by letting the earth open and swallow me up, or by striking me dead. But before Mr Wesley concluded his sermon he cried out, 'Let the wicked forsake his way, and the unrighteous man his thoughts; and let him return unto the Lord, and he will have mercy upon him; and to our God, for he will abundantly pardon.' I said, 'If that be true, I will turn to God today.' I immediately went home and began to read and pray, keeping

> out of bad company for about a fortnight, and hearing Mr Wesley as often as I could. (Telford, 1909, pp. 10–12; cited by Doughty, 1955, pp. 115–16).

One present-day parallel to that kind of behaviour was to be seen in Morris Cerrullo's revivalist meetings at Earl's Court in August 1993.

To sum up the argument to this point, God, and supernatural beings in general, are invoked to procure the obedience of believers to the Preacher's injunctions. What the Preacher says does not have to be true – it merely has to be believed – and the psychological basis of its effectiveness is revealed by Sherif's experiments.

Hell

Traditionally, Hell – more generally, the notion of some horrific punishment in some world to come – has been an important component of the Preacher's influence. These days, one might easily suppose the idea of Hell as an everlasting fire to be obsolete, but that would be wrong. Figure 10.1 is a propaganda poster from the 1979 Iranian revolution, showing the Shah, then still living, descending into Hell, while the Ayatollah Khomeini looks on from Paradise.

Figure 10.1 A propaganda poster from the Iranian revolution in 1979.

Even so, one might still suppose that Western society, at least, has freed itself from such an idea. That would also be wrong. Bob Kennell is a missionary working for the New Tribes Mission amongst the Bisorio people of Papua New Guinea:

> Bob Kennell believes that Satan was using fear of spirits to keep the Bisorio people in bondage. But what of the fear of Hell? Kennell does believe that the fear of Hell is an indispensable part of the message he has been commissioned to bring. Among New Tribes missionaries there is no danger that sin will be overlooked or the workings of Satan ignored. In the words of Mission Chairman Macon G. Hare: 'All Christians have a common enemy known as Satan, our

adversary, supreme evil spirit, Apollyon, destroyer, god of this world, prince of darkness, accuser of the brethren, a liar, a deceiver.' (Pettifer and Bradley, 1990, p. 60)

However, the New Tribes Mission is known to be of an extreme fundamentalist persuasion. So one might still suppose that within the mainstream of belief Hell is obsolete. That also would not be quite correct. In Chapter 6 I mentioned that Dr John Habgood, Archbishop of York, had contributed a 'modest essay on Hell' to his diocesan newspaper.

> We are well rid of those horror pictures of souls in torment, and the devils with their toasting forks, which blighted the lives of so many of our forebears.
>
> But is that all? Can we now dispose of hell? Or is there a different, and more profound, insight into its true meaning?
>
> . . . it may be profoundly immoral . . . to abandon the belief that our actions can have eternal consequences. Seen from this perspective hell is about the seriousness of moral choice, and thus ultimately about the irreducible character of human freedom.
>
> Putting it another way, hell is not an objective reality, not a place or state created by God as a means of executing his justice. Nor is it some terrible counterpart to heaven, for the reason that it has no substance, whereas heaven is the fulfilment of all God's intentions for us. Nevertheless hell is a subjective reality. We can create it for ourselves and in ourselves. (Habgood, 1991a)

Dr Habgood still felt a need to assign some substantive meaning to the idea of Hell.

Control by secular authority

Since belief in God has proved so effective a means of controlling people's behaviour, especially the behaviour of people *en masse*, it has been much used also by secular authorities.

On the first day of hostilities between Iraq and the United Nations coalition (16 January 1991) Iraqi TV broadcast a pre-recorded programme portraying Saddam Hussein, the President, engaged in a variety of activities, including his due obeisances on a prayer rug (*News at Ten*, 1991a). Saddam Hussein also called for a *jihad* (a 'Holy War') against the United Nations coalition. A *jihad* is a war fought by Muslims against infidels and unbelievers. Its particular significance is that soldiers who die in such a war are martyrs. Any evil deeds they may have done are thereby expiated; they are immediately translated to Paradise.

Iranian soldiers fighting Iraq from 1980 to 1988 were also engaged in a *jihad*. Death in that war was viewed as martyrdom and this view engendered a corresponding determination to fight (Fisk, 1982, 1987). Future martyrs, 13- and 14-year-old volunteers, were paraded at Friday prayers in Teheran (Fisk, 1986a); and '. . . the Ayatollah said war against Iraq was a religious duty, and would continue even after he was gone' (Fisk, 1986b).

The use of religious authority to encourage soldiers to fight is not, of course, a specifically Muslim practice. Western countries may do it differently, but they do it nevertheless.

> President George Bush declared yesterday that he and the coalition are on the side of God, and came as close, perhaps, as a President can to suggesting that God is on his side.
>
> Speaking to religious broadcasters the day after some of the largest anti-war protests in the United States so far, and after strong criticism from America's religious leaders, Mr Bush apparently needed to assure the world that the war is morally just, and that God is speaking through the actions of the US President and his allies.
>
> The moral and religious case for war has always been a strong element in Mr Bush's presentation of his case.
>
> He spent the first evening of the fighting with the evangelist, Billy Graham, and was at church to pray the next day. (Helm, 1991)

We do it in the United Kingdom too, every year on the Sunday closest to 11 November, very publicly at the Cenotaph in Whitehall (broadcast on TV) and at many smaller Remembrance Day ceremonies elsewhere.

Control by entrepreneurs

Belief in God is also used by some entrepreneurs to promote their business. I am not thinking here of the commercial production of religious books, icons and other artefacts, but of the much bigger business of television evangelism in the USA and of similar enterprises elsewhere. There are a number of organisations which buy TV transmission time to transmit a weekly programme of a religious nature. Their income derives from donations sent in by their audiences that may number as many as two million. Surveys have shown that viewers of these programmes tend to be elderly (over 50 years of age), living in a small town or in the country in the South or South-west of America, relatively low on the educational scale, poor, working-class and female. About six per cent of the audiences of these programmes actually send donations and the sums received average $35 (Cockburn, 1987, pp. 54, 56).

Oral Roberts

Oral Roberts was one of the pioneers of this kind of TV broadcast. He is the founder of the Oral Roberts University and of the City of Faith Medical Center in Tulsa, Oklahoma. These two institutions are reported to have cost $500 million; they were built with donations from Oral Roberts' television 'prayer partners' (Kennedy, 1987b).

Oral Roberts used to broadcast a 30-minute show called *Expect a Miracle* each Sunday morning at 9 am. As of 1986 it was viewed in 1.1m households.

Donations were about $55m in 1985, but were declining; they had been much greater in previous years. In his broadcast on 4 January 1987 Oral Roberts announced that in the previous March [1986] God had told him to raise an additional $8m 'in one year or I will call you home'. The money was required for training of medical missionaries, specifically so that they would not be burdened with residual debt on completion of their medical training, as is the way with most medical students in America. About $3.5m of that additional money had been raised as of 4 January 1987, so Oral Roberts was asking his audience for a further $4.5m.

> He told his Sunday audience, estimated at 1.6m households, that he needed 'some quick money'.
>
> 'I am asking you to help extend my life,' he said. 'We're at a point where God could call Oral Roberts home. '
>
> He also asked the viewers to send $100 immediately, saying 'you're building an account with God.' (Kennedy, 1987a).

The TV stations carrying Oral Roberts' programme were frankly uneasy at this naked appeal for 'some quick money'. Nevertheless, it worked. On 21 March, one Jerry Collins, a former state senator and owner of two dogtracks in Florida, signed a personal cheque for the $1.3m still outstanding. Meanwhile, Oral Roberts was spending a well-publicised vigil for the last ten days of March at the top of his 'prayer tower'. He continued his plea for funds beyond the $8m and eventually raised that total to $8.7m.

Jim and Tammy Bakker

Jim Bakker was another evangelist in the same line of business. With his wife Tammy he founded the PTL ('Praise the Lord') television ministry in 1974. Together they broadcast a programme called *Jim and Tammy* at 8 am on Fridays to an audience estimated at 220 000. PTL revenues in 1986 amounted to $129m, of which the Bakkers personally received $1.6m. These revenues came, in part, from a theme park called 'Heritage USA' and a 400-room luxury hotel at Fort Mill, South Carolina. The theme park received 6.1m visitors in 1986 (Cockburn, 1987, pp. 51, 54).

On 19 March 1987 Jim Bakker resigned from the PTL ministry 'for personal reasons'. Those personal reasons centred around the revelation that he had had a one-night stand with one Jessica Hahn back in 1980, and that PTL had entered into a $265 000 settlement with Jessica Hahn, one condition of which was that she, Hahn, said nothing further about the affair (Dart, 1987a). The revelation of Jim Bakker's sexual misconduct led to a catastrophic loss of donations. On 13 June 1987 PTL filed for bankruptcy, $70m in debt (Chandler, 1987).

The resulting investigation into PTL's accounts revealed that Bakker had been selling 'lifetime partnerships' in Heritage USA for $1000 a time. A 'lifetime partnership' entitled the purchaser to three nights' free lodging annually for the rest of his or her life. In fact 153 000 such partnerships had been sold, which was about three times as many as the hotel could physically accommodate. Of the money received from these sales, Jim Bakker was found to have diverted $3.7m to his own use. Bakker was tried on a charge of fraud and convicted. He was sentenced to 45 years in jail (May, 1989).

Papal indulgences

The idea of selling a timeshare to make money for religious purposes is, of course, far from new. The medieval church taught that sin in this world resulted not only in punishment here and now administered by the church (*penance*), but also divine punishment in the world to come (*purgatory*). An indulgence was 'a remission before God of the temporal punishment due for sins forgiven in the sacrament of penance.' It was possible to perform some particular good work to shorten the length of canonical public penance imposed by the church. But then:

> In the 14th century the use of *quaestores* ('commissioners' or 'promoters') to popularize indulgenced works, particularly almsgiving for the erection of cathedrals and universities, led to many abuses both in the handling of funds and in pulpit extravagances. (*Encyclopaedia Britannica*, 1989a)

> Indulgences were the commutation for money of part of the temporal penalty due for sin – i.e., the practical satisfaction that was a part of the sacrament of penance. They were granted on papal authority and made available through accredited agents. Not at any time did they imply that divine forgiveness could be bought or sold or that they availed for those who were impenitent or unconfessed. But during the Middle Ages, as papal financial difficulties grew more complicated, they were resorted to very often, and abuses grew common. Further misunderstanding developed after Pope Sixtus IV extended indulgences to souls in purgatory. The often outrageous statements of indulgence sellers were a matter of protest among theologians.
>
> The immediate cause of scandal in Germany in 1517 was the issue of an indulgence that was to pay for the rebuilding of St. Peter's in Rome. But by secret agreement of which most Germans, probably including Luther, were unaware, half the proceeds of the German sales were to be diverted to meet the huge debt owed to the financial house of Fugger by the archbishop and elector Albert of Mainz, who had incurred the debt in order to pay the Pope for appointing him to high offices. Such a prince could not afford to be squeamish about the methods and language used by his agents, and the agent in Germany, the Dominican Johann Tetzel, made extravagant claims for the indulgence he was selling. The sale of this indulgence was forbidden in Wittenberg by the elector Frederick III the Wise, who preferred that the faithful should make their offerings at his own great collection of relics, exhibited in the Church of All Saints. Nevertheless, Wittenberg church members went to Tetzel, who was preaching nearby, and they showed the pardons for their sins received from him to Luther. Outraged at what he considered grave theological error, Luther wrote

> the Ninety-five Theses [which led more or less directly to the Reformation]. (*Encyclopaedia Britannica*, 1989b)

Subsequently 'at the Council of Trent (1562) the abusive practices were ended. Five years later Pius V revoked all indulgences for which money payments or alms were prescribed' (*Encyclopaedia Britannica*, 1989a).

The Turin shroud

Except that the indulgences themselves were a confidence trick, revoking them without returning the money paid constituted a further fraud. But fraud in matters of religion is itself nothing new. The Turin shroud 'is a strip of linen 14ft long and 3ft wide, with the front and back images of a naked, crucified man, 5ft $10^{1}/_{2}$ in tall, in faint straw yellow, with a variety of red markings. Its first known appearance dates from a time when relic-making was rife – in the 1350s in France, in the possession of Geoffrey de Charnay, Lord of Lirey' (Sox, 1988). This piece of linen has long been said to be the grave cloth in which the body of Jesus had been wrapped. It was much venerated in consequence, but recent carbon-dating has shown the flax from which the linen had been made to have been harvested sometime between the years 1260 and 1390 (Sox, 1988).

Notwithstanding the precision of the carbon-dating procedure, carried out independently in three different laboratories in 1988, Catholic officials have proposed a further attempt to prove that the shroud is genuine and not a medieval fake (Owen, 2002). Such is the practical value of a relic.

Medugorje

A relic such as the Turin shroud attracts pilgrims and trade to the place where it is kept. Medugorje, a village in Bosnia, used to be another place of pilgrimage. The following report is from before the civil war.

> Since 25 June, 1981, there have been daily apparitions of the Virgin in Medugorje. At first there were six visionaries, all young, all otherwise entirely unremarkable. Only four – Ivan Dragicevic, Vicka Ivankovic, Jakov Colo and Marija Pavlovic – still have the visions, which occur with clockwork precision to the ineffable joy of the pilgrims and the steady enrichment of the townspeople.
>
> The visions have not been wholeheartedly endorsed by the Church. The local bishop, Bishop Pavao Zanic of Mostar-Duvno, has denounced them as fabrications ('It is a lie, a big lie') and dismisses the whole phenomenon as a plot . . .
>
> On the approach to Medugorje, rows of prosperous-looking villas lined the road on either side. Moira [a tour company's representative] said disapprovingly that they had been built by people who were not from the village to make money out of Medugorje, but it became clear later that almost all the villagers now live in villa-type houses, providing accommodation for tourist pilgrims. Pizzerias, hamburger joints, souvenir shops and even a pool hall cluttered the road leading to the church. (Wylie, 1991)

But the Vatican has reservations. In advance of a visit by the Pope (September 1998)

> '. . . officals said there were "doubts" about reported sightings of Mary at Medjugorje over the past 20 years, even though the shrine has become popular with pilgrims seeking miracle cures and spiritual comfort.'
>
> The latest pronouncement by the Congregation of the Faith, the Pope's doctrinal watchdog, will dismay operators of religious tours and could undermine what has become a booming business in impoverished rural Bosnia. (Owen, 1998)

These reservations by the Vatican are important because the evidential basis of the visions of the Virgin Mary are of a piece with the basis of the allegations of witchcraft in Salem, to be described in Chapter 11. It is all in the mind.

The Goddess Yellama

Such profiteering is not, of course, exclusive to Christianity. The Goddess Yellama has a temple in the Belgaum district of the state of Karnataka in India. The business of the temple devolves on *devadasis*, temple prostitutes. Although illegal, the cult continues. Irawa is a former *devadasi* who is now assisting the police in suppressing this form of worship, and the Indian government is now taking action because of the spread of AIDS.

When a girl becomes a *devadasi*, there is a religious rite. Irawa herself underwent this rite herself at the age of seven. She

> . . . does not remember much, only being bathed in a pool, clothed in leaves and taken to a plain, greenish temple devoted to the goddess Yellama. People were tossing up yellow clouds of turmeric, and dragging themselves along the cobblestones leading to the temple.
>
> Inside the Yellama temple, Irawa took an oath never to marry but to have sex with any man chosen by the priest. Usually this amounted to the priest himself and the rich men in the village, who were known to bribe the priest handsomely for this perk. Then, to complete the ceremony, a string with red and white beads was connected between Irawa and an idol of Yellama (the idols usually depicting an angelic, blue-faced woman with golden spikes radiating from her hair).
>
> This form of prostitution was banned nearly a decade ago, but the Yellama cult still has many worshippers among the lower castes in the southern states of Karnataka, Maharashtra and Andhra Pradesh.
>
> The temple priests are also protesting against the government's decision to strip them of the Yellama shrine's treasures. For almost 500 years, eight families of Brahmin priests had the temple to themselves, collecting tributes of cattle, gold and cash from the poor Untouchables. A *devadasi* rite costs 25 rupees (£0.70). (McGirk, 1991)

Religious rivalry

We now have this picture of religion. The ability to influence what people do, to solicit financial contributions efficiently, to inspire soldiers to fight, even to prohibit some forms of medical treatment, has proved a benefical exercise for those in authority. Such techniques are used by all religions, by all denominations, in varying degrees. This practice naturally brings different religions into competition for the support of potential adherents. It has always been so. There is a well-known instance from the first century AD recorded in *The Acts of the Apostles* (Ch. 19, vv. 23–41). St Paul was preaching at Ephesus, and the silversmiths of that city, who enjoyed a high standard of living from the manufacture of silver shrines of Diana, the Ephesian goddess, saw their livelihoods threatened. They rioted.

'Infidel' sheep

That first century story has its modern-day parallel.

> Algerians are being asked to choose whether to sacrifice local sheep at this month's *Id al-Adha* (the main feast day in the Muslim calendar), or to save money and endanger their immortal souls by sacrificing sheep raised by infidels Down Under.
>
> With the Australian sheep costing less than half the price of locally raised sheep this is no easy choice for many a middle-class Algerian with a large family, a small income and a traditional respect for the opinions of religious leaders.
>
> The sheep were imported by the state meat authority in an effort to keep prices down, preserve local herds and prevent speculation on the part of local sheep breeders, who traditionally raise prices during the pilgrimage season . . .
>
> But last week several fundamentalists issued fatwas (religious instructions) declaring the Australian sheep to be unfit for sacrifice or consumption at the *Id al-Adha*. Not only were the sheep raised by infidels, but they have had their tails, and in the case of males, their testicles, cut off. All this renders the Australian merinos impure. (Porteous, 1991)

No college for Panevezys

Another example, now of competition between different Christian churches, has occurred recently in Lithuania:

> Opposition from Lithuania's Catholic Church has blocked a private initiative to set up an arts and languages college in the industrial city of Panevezys: the backer, a wealthy Canadian furniture manufacturer called Art de Fehr, is a Protestant.
>
> A letter of protest from the local cardinal and bishops reads: 'We have heard that there is discussion of establishing a Protestant institute in Panevezys . . . Our opinion is that in this Catholic city it is not expedient . . . It will disturb the consciousness of believers, and harm the unity not only of the city but of the whole republic.'

According to the acting head of the Vilnius archdiocese, Bishop Juozas Tunaitis, the Church's opposition stems from fears that foreign missionaries are enjoying too much success in Lithuania. 'We have many strange sects here and we don't want another one.'

'These sects are very active and they attract young people with modern things like singing and dancing,' explained Bishop Tunaitis. (Lucas, 1991)

Evangelical infidelities

There are many other examples of competition between different Christian sects and denominations, especially in the mission field (Pettifer and Bradley, 1990). Such rivalry even occurs between ministers of the *same* denomination. The single infidelity that brought about Jim Bakker's downfall was revealed by a fellow minister, though also a rival TV evangelist. Jimmy Swaggert had 'warned the Assemblies of God denomination [the Pentecostal denomination of which they were both ministers] last [1986] summer about fellow preacher Jim Bakker's adulterous sexual encounter and urged the church to distance itself from Bakker's PTL ministries' (Dart, 1987b).

That was not the first time that Jimmy Swaggert had denounced a fellow minister; Marvin Gorman, it is alleged, had been another (Dart, 1987b).

Gorman was once a rising star, a featured guest on the former 'Jim and Tammy Show', about to hook onto the satellite and go big time. But . . . Swaggert ruined him by spreading lies about 'numerous' adulterous affairs.

Gorman . . . admitted to only one adulterous liaison, but says Swaggert pressed on to destroy him, lobbying for swift, evangelical justice. After the Assemblies of God defrocked Gorman in 1986, his TV ministry collapsed and he filed for bankruptcy with $2 million in debts. (Harris, 1988)

There is a well-known photograph of Jimmy Swaggert, with tears running down his face. The photograph was recovered from a video recording of Jimmy Swaggert confessing to 'specific incidents of moral failure' during a service at his World Faith Center, a service broadcast on TV. Swaggert had been shopped in his turn. He had been photographed leaving a motel with a known prostitute. That second photograph had been set up by Marvin Gorman to assist in a lawsuit he was preparing against Jimmy Swaggert. Permission was refused to reproduce the first, tearful, photograph of Jimmy Swaggert here; the example of Jim Bakker shows that it could have proved bad for business. As of 1987 'the weekly Jimmy Swaggert show . . . reaches more than 9m American households. From his base in Baton Rouge, Louisiana, he runs a $156m-a-year television empire which beams programmes to 140 countries, a 1000-student bible college and a 7000 seat church' (Milligan, 1988). However, that first tearful photograph of Jimmy Swaggert may be found, among other places, in Pettifer and Bradley (1990, p. 14). It shows what humiliation a man will submit himself to when sufficiently large sums of money are at stake.

Religious discipline

Continuing competition between different religions and religious denominations imposes on each a need to exercise its authority. Historically, the ultimate demonstration of authority has been putting someone to death, preferably with much publicity. In the middle ages, heretics, that is, people who openly disagreed with the established authorities in matters of faith or doctrine – the religious opposition – were routinely put to the sword or burnt at the stake.

The *auto de fé* (literally 'act of faith') was a public ceremony during which sentences passed on those who had been brought before the Spanish Inquisition were read out. The publication of offences committed and sentences passed served to impress and deter the ordinary people. The victims were most often apostate former Jews and Muslims, heretics and Protestants. Confessions to serve as evidence of guilt were extracted, under torture if need be. The extreme penalty at the disposal of the inquisitor was, in fact, only life imprisonment. But a confessed heretic could be handed over to the civil power, which would invariably oblige.

The first *auto de fé* was recorded in Seville in 1481; the last in Mexico in 1850. Initially the ceremony was simple and efficient; 750 judaizers were disposed of in a single morning at Toledo on Sunday, 12 February 1486. But in course of time the *auto de fé* became more elaborate and much longer. Here is an English summary (published in London, 1748) of a contemporary account of the *auto de fé* held on 30 June 1680 in the Plaza Mayor of Madrid.

> A Scaffold, fifty Feet in Length, was erected in the Square, which was raised to the same Height with the Balcony made for the King to sit in. At the End, and along the whole Breadth of the Scaffold, at the Right of the King's Balcony, an Amphitheatre was raised, to which they ascend by twenty-five or thirty Steps; and this was appointed for the Council of the Inquisition, and the other Councils of Spain. Above these Steps, and under a Canopy, the Grand Inquisitor's Rostrum was placed so that he was raised much higher than the King's Balcony. At the Left of the Scaffold and Balcony, a second Amphitheatre was erected of the same Extent with the former, for the Criminals to stand in.
>
> A month after Proclamation had been made of the Act of Faith, the Ceremony opened with a Procession [This procession took place on the eve, 29 June], which proceeded from St. Mary's Church in the following order. The March was preceded by an Hundred Coal Merchants, all arm'd with Pikes and Muskets; these People furnishing the Wood with which the Criminals are burnt. They were followed by Dominicans, before whom a white Cross was carried. Then came the Duke of Medina-Celi, carrying the Standard of the Inquisition. Afterwards was brought forwards a green Cross covered with black Crepe; which was followed by several Grandees and other Persons of Quality, who were Familiars of the Inquisition ['Several' is an understatement. The procession contained no less than 25 grandees, 37 nobles, and 23 illustrious persons]. The March was clos'd by Fifty Guards belonging to the Inquisition, clothed with black and white Garments and commanded by the Marquis of Povar, hereditary

Protector of the Inquisition. The procession having marched in this Order before the Palace, proceeded afterwards to the Square, where the Standard and the Green Cross were placed on the Scaffold, where none but the Dominicans stayed, the rest being retired. These Friars spent Part of the Night in singing of Psalms, and several Masses were celebrated on the Altar from Daybreak to Six in the Morning. An Hour after, the King and Queen of Spain, the Queen-Mother, and all the Ladies of Quality, appeared in the Balconies.

At Eight O'clock the Procession began, in like Manner as the Day before, with the Company of Coal Merchants, who placed themselves on the Left of the King's Balcony, his Guards standing on his Right (the rest of the Balconies and Scaffolds being fill'd by the Embassadors, the Nobility and Gentry). Afterwards came thirty Men, carrying Images made in Pasteboard, as big as Life. Some of these represented those who were dead in Prison, whose Bones were also brought in Trunks, with Flames painted round them; and the rest of the Figures represented those who having escaped the Hands of the Inquisition, were outlawed. These Figures were placed at one end of the Amphitheatre.

After these there came twelve Men and Women, with Ropes about their Necks and Torches in their Hands, with Pasteboard Caps three Feet high, on which their Crimes were written, or represented, in different Manners. These were followed by fifty others, having Torches also in their Hands and cloathed with a yellow Sanbenito or Great Coat without Sleeves, with a large St. Andrew's Cross, of a red Colour, before and behind. These were Criminals who (this being the first Time of their Imprisonment) had repented of their Crimes; these are usually condemned either to some Years Imprisonment or to wear the Sanbenito, which is looked upon to be the greatest Disgrace that can happen to a Family. Each of the Criminals were led by two Familiars of the Inquisition. Next came twenty more Criminals, of both Sexes, who had relapsed thrice into their former Errors and were condemn'd to the Flames. Those who had given some Tokens of Repentance were to be strangled before they were burnt; but for the rest, for having persisted obstinately in their Errors, were to be burnt alive. These wore Linen Sanbenitos, having Devils and Flames painted on them, and Caps after the same Manner: Five or six among them, who were more obstinate than the rest, were gagged to prevent their uttering any blasphemous Tenets. Such as were condemned to die were surrounded, besides the two Familiars, with four or five Monks, who were preparing them for Death as they went along.

These Criminals passed, in the Order above mentioned, under the King's Balcony; and after having walked round the scaffold were placed in the Amphitheatre that stood on the left, and each of them surrounded with the Familiars and Monks who attended them. Some of the Grandees, who were Familiars, seated themselves on two Benches which had been prepared for them at the lowest Part of the other Amphitheatre. The Officers of all other Councils, and several other Persons of Distinction, both Secular and Regular, all of them on Horseback, with great Solemnity arrived afterwards and placed themselves on the Amphitheatre towards the Right hand, on both Sides of the Rostrum in which the Grand Inquisitor was to seat himself. He himself came last of all, in a

> purple Habit, accompanied by the President of the Council of Castile, when, being seated in his Place, the president withdrew.
>
> They then began to celebrate Mass . . .
>
> About Twelve O'clock they began to read the Sentence of the condemned Criminals. That of the Criminals who died in Prison, or were outlawed, was first read. Their Figures in Pasteboard were carried up into a little Scaffold and put into small Cages made for that Purpose. They then went on to read the Sentences to each Criminal, who thereupon were put into the said Cages one by one in order for all Men to know them. The whole Ceremony lasted till Nine at Night; and when they had finished the Celebration of the Mass the King withdrew and the Criminals who had been condemn'd to be burnt were delivered over to the Secular Arm, and being mounted upon Asses were carried through the Gate called Foncaral, and at Midnight near this Place were all executed. (Anon, 1748, pp. 35–39; cited by Kamen, 1965, pp. 191–93. The original account is by del Olmo, 1680. The scene described above is depicted in a contemporary painting, *Auto de fe de 1680*, by Francisco Rizi, 1683).

The manner of execution is described in another contemporary account, this of a ceremony in Madrid in 1690.

> At the place of execution there are so many stakes set as there are prisoners to be burned, a large quantity of dry furze being set about them. The stakes of the Protestants, or, as the inquisitors call them, the professed, are about four yards high, and have each a small board, whereupon the prisoner is seated within half a yard of the top. The professed then go up a ladder betwixt two priests, who attend them the whole day of execution. When they come even with the aforementioned board, they turn about to the people, and the priests spend near a quarter of an hour in exhorting them to be reconciled to the see of Rome. On their refusing, the priests come down, and the executioner ascending, turns the professed from off the ladder upon the seat, chains their bodies close to the stakes, and leaves them. Then the priests go up a second time to renew their exhortations; and if they find them ineffectual, usually tell them at parting, that 'they leave them to the Devil, who is standing at their elbow ready to receive their souls, and to carry them with him into the flames of hell-fire, as soon as they are put out of their bodies'. A general shout is then raised, and when the priests get off the ladder, the universal cry is: 'Let the dogs' beards be made!' (which implies, singe their beards). This is accordingly performed by means of flaming furzes, thrust against their faces with long poles. This barbarity is repeated till their faces are burnt, and is accompanied with loud acclamations. Fire is then set to the furzes, and the criminals are consumed. (Scott, 1940, pp. 71–3; cited by Burman, 1984, pp. 154–5).

No society today can afford to execute religious opponents in so public a manner; but the practice itself continues:

> I inform the proud Muslim people of the world that the author of *The Satanic Verses* book which is against Islam, the Prophet and the Koran, and all those involved in its publication who were aware of its content, are sentenced to death. (Ayatollah Khomeini, 14 February 1989; as translated and published in Morris, Lister, and Haeri, 1989)

The Ayatollah Khomeini's *fatwa* meant exactly what it said and was in no way abrogated by Khomeini's death on 4 June 1989.

> The Japanese translator of The Satanic Verses, Hitoshi Igarashi, was found stabbed to death yesterday morning.
>
> Professor Igarashi, aged 44, an associate professor of comparative literature at Tsukuba University, outside Tokyo, had been stabbed more than 10 times in the face, neck and hands. He bled to death in a lift lobby near his university office. His body was found by a caretaker.
>
> He was the second Rushdie translator to be attacked in a fortnight. Ettore Capriolo, aged 61, who translated The Satanic Verses into Italian, was stabbed at his Milan flat on July 3.
>
> Mr Capriolo suffered cuts to the neck, arms, and chest, and was kicked and beaten on the head by a man who said he was an Iranian, police said. (Sullivan, 1991)

Summary – why does religion matter? – to all of us?

Since 1945 the world has nominally been at peace because both the Soviet Union and America realised that both countries would suffer catastrophically in any conflict between the two. At the least, there has been no global conflict, and 'victory' in a potential third world war came to mean 'not going to war in the first place'. The one exception to that restraint would be a theocratic government that believed in a better world to come. If death is followed, for 'true believers', by paradise, then the likelihood of mutual annihilation is no reason to hold back.

The reasoning underlying this caution can be summed up in four short statements.

- Belief and knowledge are, psychologically, identical states of mind.
- Knowledge is simply belief that happens to be true.
- What a person does depends on what he or she believes.
- It is irrelevant whether that belief is true or false.

Mohamed Atta piloted the plane that crashed into the north tower of the World Trade Center on 11 September 2001 and has since emerged as the leader of the entire exercise on that day. The attitude I have characterised above is illustrated by this quotation, translated from the Arabic, which comes from a hand-written document found in Mohamed Atta's baggage – baggage which, somehow, failed to be loaded onto the plane that was crashed.

> Keep a very open mind, keep a very open heart of what you are to face. You will be entering paradise. You will be entering the happiest life, everlasting life. Keep in your mind that if you are plagued with a problem and how to get out of it. A believer is always plagued with problems. You will never enter paradise if you have not had a major problem. But only those who stood fast through it are the ones who will overcome it.
>
> When you enter the plane:
>
> God, I trust in you. God, I lay myself in your hands. I ask with the light of your faith that has lit the whole world and lightened all darkness on this earth, to guide me until you approve of me. And once you do, that's my ultimate goal. (*Washington Post*, 2001)

If a government of that mindset should come to power in, possibly, Pakistan . . .

If you ask 'How can such a government be possible?' then I answer: There is, of necessity, a complete absence of personal knowledge of Life after Death. That absence of personal knowledge extends to the supernatural as well (God, Satan, . . .) because personal knowledge would convert the supernatural into the merely natural. This absence of personal knowledge provides complete freedom for Sherif's (1937) confederate; no subject in the autokinetic experiment has any basis on which to controvert the confederate. Religion is arguably the most important application of Sherif's work.

The believer is at the mercy of the Preacher, who manipulates the believer for the purposes of his or her institution and sometimes for personal purposes too. Authorities of all religions have traditionally taken it upon themselves to say what ordinary people should, and should not, do. The facility with which believers can be manipulated brings different religions into conflict. There is a long history of wars fought for religious purposes everywhere; recent conflicts in the Middle East are merely contemporary examples. Such conflict is apparent in the mission field too, albeit at a lesser intensity.

Flagrant manipulation raises its own important question: Does the Preacher – for example, Oral Roberts declaring that God 'will call him home' unless he succeeds in raising an additional $4.5m within the next three months – believe what he (or she) preaches? Since each generation of preachers is selected from among existing believers, the answer, for the most part, has to be 'Yes'. At the same time, religious authorities have been expected to conform to their own moral principles and there is a catastrophic loss of public support (e.g. Jim Bakker) when hypocrisy is revealed. The eyes of the worshippers are suddenly opened (cf. Alexander, Zucker and Brody, 1970).

If all this is so, what might one mean by 'God'? One might define 'god' (now with a small 'g') as the class of procedures by which a Preacher exercises control over his followers, maintains his authority in the community and commands the resources needed to support his lifestyle.

The next area of enquiry concerns judgments that have some material basis (unlike revelations), but an insufficient one for the accuracy desired. I look at how the material evidence on the one hand and the extraneous influences (the Preacher) on the other combine to bias the judgment.

11 Bias

Most judgments are not 'guesses in the dark'; but neither are they so clearly determined as to be obvious, so that everyone is agreed. Instead, there are many differences of opinion. The principle of relativity in Chapter 2 tells us that it happens so because people's judgments are dependent on context, and that context varies, as we saw in Chapter 3, from one person to another and from one occasion to another. In addition, many judgments are, in varying degrees, uncertain because there is no good basis for comparison. In this chapter I ask how that uncertainty combines with the kinds of extraneous influences described in Chapter 6 and exemplified in Chapters 7–10. How do other people's judgments affect our own when we have some basis on which to judge, but not a basis that is fully adequate?

The message of this chapter is this: If the material evidence is not clear enough, we cannot make a judgment without bias. I am using 'bias' in a technical sense to mean simply the involvement of extraneous information, information which is actually irrelevant to the judgment. No one is unbiased. Instead, we simply judge other people's biases relative to our own: 'All the world's barmy except for thee and me – and thou'rt a bit queer!'

The central tendency of judgment

The nature of bias is exemplified with exceptional clarity by this experiment from 90 years ago on the accuracy of movements made blindfold (Hollingworth, 1909). On each trial the subject made a guided movement with the left hand – with the left hand because the execution is then less certain, leaving greater scope for the bias to show. The subject drew a line of prescribed length; then attempted to reproduce that movement without guidance. The guidance was provided by a narrow (6 mm) slit of prescribed length cut in a sheet of cardboard, that sheet being then pasted onto another sheet to produce a 'furrow'. That guide was traced from end to end with a pencil, blindfold. Two seconds later the subject, still blindfolded, tried to draw a line of the same length on plain paper, without the guide. The left hand was supported in a sling to reduce extraneous cues arising from, for example, the pivoting of the elbow.

Seven different prescribed lengths of guided movement were presented in random order for a total of 100 times each. Three different sets of seven prescribed lengths were presented in different sessions: A: 10–70 mm; B: 30–150 mm; and C: 70–250 mm. The average lengths of the reproductions, averaged over three subjects, are shown in Figure 11.1. Within each set of prescribed lengths the reproductions of short movements are too long and of long movements too short. But 'long' and 'short' must be read with respect to the set of guided lengths presented in that session. So 70 mm is under-reproduced in the 'short' set (A), but over-reproduced in the 'long' set (C). If, however, the reproductions had been unbiased, the data points would all be lined up along the 45° diagonal.

Figure 11.1 Mean reproductions of guided movements from Hollingworth (1909). Three sets of averages are shown for three different sets of prescribed lengths. The rectangles around each set of points emphasise that the gradients of the lines are less than one. When a particular length is presented in a session by itself (filled points) reproduction is veridical.

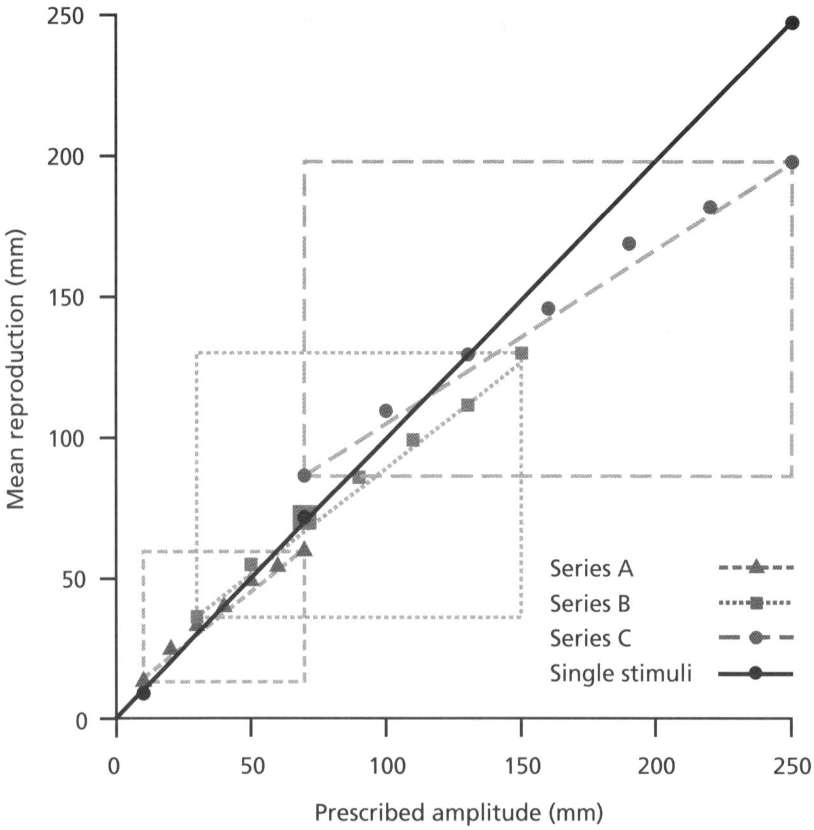

Figure adapted from D. Laming, *The Measurement of Sensation*, p. 22 with the permission of Oxford University Press. © 1997 Donald Laming.

The actual reproduction is a compromise between the particular length previously traced under guidance on that trial and the average of the lengths previously experienced within that experimental session. The lengths of furrow previously traced under guidance set up a *centre of expectation* that biases subsequent reproductions, and that bias is specific to the *set* of stimulus lengths. When 10, 70 and 250 mm were presented by themselves in a session alone (filled circles in Figure 11.1), *there was no bias*. Those data points fall on the diagonal. But when a set of prescribed amplitudes is presented in random order, the mean reproduction is a compromise between the length actually traced under guidance and the centre of the set of stimuli. This distortion of the reproductions is known as the *central tendency of judgment*.

The 'regression' effect

That kind of bias is common; it is seen in magnitude estimation as well where it is known as the 'regression' effect. Figure 11.2 presents the results of an experiment by Reynolds and Stevens (1960). The subjects in this experiment first estimated the magnitude of seven different levels of white noise; the circles in Figure 11.2 are geometric averages for 10 observers estimating the loudness of each stimulus once each, with the stimuli presented in different irregular orders. Then the same observers adjusted the volume control on the amplifier to make the loudness of the noise match six different numbers again presented in different irregular orders. The 70 dB noise was presented first and called 10. The mean matches conform reasonably well to Stevens' Power Law (see Chapter 5) and are plotted here on a log-log plot so that the power law relation appears as a straight line. But the mean estimates of loudness have a shallower slope than the mean productions. That difference is systematic. The estimates are drawn *vertically* towards a centre of expectation to give a *reduced* slope in the figure (the stimulus levels are fixed and only the estimates can distort), while the productions are drawn *horizontally* towards a centre of expectation to give an *increased* slope (now it is the numbers that are fixed and only the adjusted stimulus levels distort). The difference in gradient is usually small in data averaged over a cohort of observers, but the difference can be large for individual subjects (see Stevens and Greenbaum, 1966, p. 445, Figure 10, reproducing two individual observers' data from Stevens and Guirao, 1962).

The great storm, 15 October 1987

The central tendency of judgment does not show itself only in the laboratory; it is also apparent in weather forecasting. Here is part of the forecast for Thursday, 15 October 1987:

> Most of England and Wales will start bright although thickening cloud will soon affect the far south-west and this cloud and accompanying rain will spread quickly north-eastwards. Southern and eastern districts will see several

Figure 11.2 Magnitude estimation and magnitude production of white noise from Reynolds and Stevens (1960).

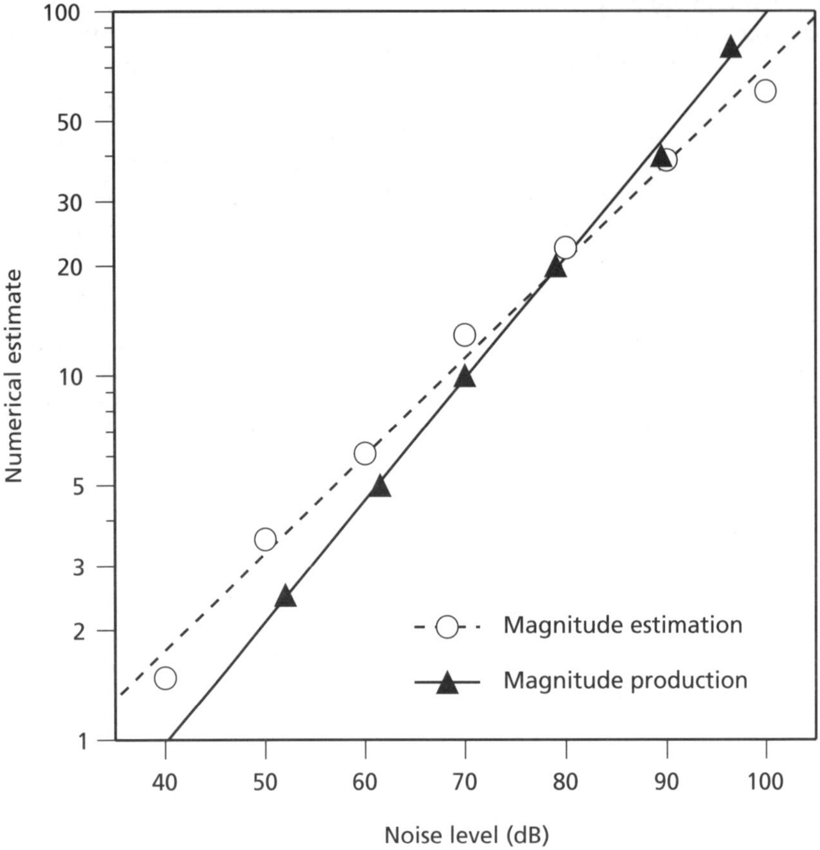

Figure redrawn with permission from S. S. Stevens and H. B. Greenbaum, 'Regression effect in psychophysical judgment'. *Perception & Psychophysics*, vol. 1, p. 441. © 1966 The Psychonomic Society Inc.

> hours of continuous rain, occasionally heavy, and it will become windy here too with gale force southerly winds affecting coasts and channel crossings. *(Times*, 1987b)

No-one reading that – indeed, no one watching the TV weather forecast at 9.30 pm that evening, just four hours before the storm broke – would have supposed that within 24 hours southern England would be experiencing its most severe storm for nearly 300 years. Some 19 people were reported killed, there was widespread disruption of services and an estimated £1000m of damage (see Ogley, 1987).

Television weatherman Michael Fish will never live it down.

> On the evening [actually, lunchtime] of October 15 . . . he beamed into the camera and said: 'A woman rang to say she'd heard there was a hurricane on the way. Well, if you are watching, don't worry, there isn't.' (Cockroft, 1988)

The storm followed a more northerly course than the meteorologists expected and, what is especially relevant here, its force was greatly underestimated. While the forecast 'gale force southerly winds' might sound alarming, it actually means a steady airflow (not gusts, which will be stronger) of only 39–46 mph according to the Beaufort scale. The actual turnout was 'violent storm', which means 64–72 mph steady airflow. At Marston, Kent, the wind averaged 69 mph over a period of ten minutes (Dawe, Wood and Matthews, 1987); and at Shoreham-by-Sea an average of 84 mph (74 knots; hurricane force) was recorded with gusts up to 111 mph (98 knots; the *Times*, 8 October 1988, section 3). What went wrong?

Meteorology is not an exact science. The meteorologists rely on observations that are always fragmentary and have to be extrapolated forwards for periods of up to 24 hours and then interpreted. That interpretation is the forecast and a human element is inevitable. The interpretation of weather data is modified by

Figure 11.3 The bias in forecasting the great storm, illustrated with reference to the Series C data from Figure 11.1.

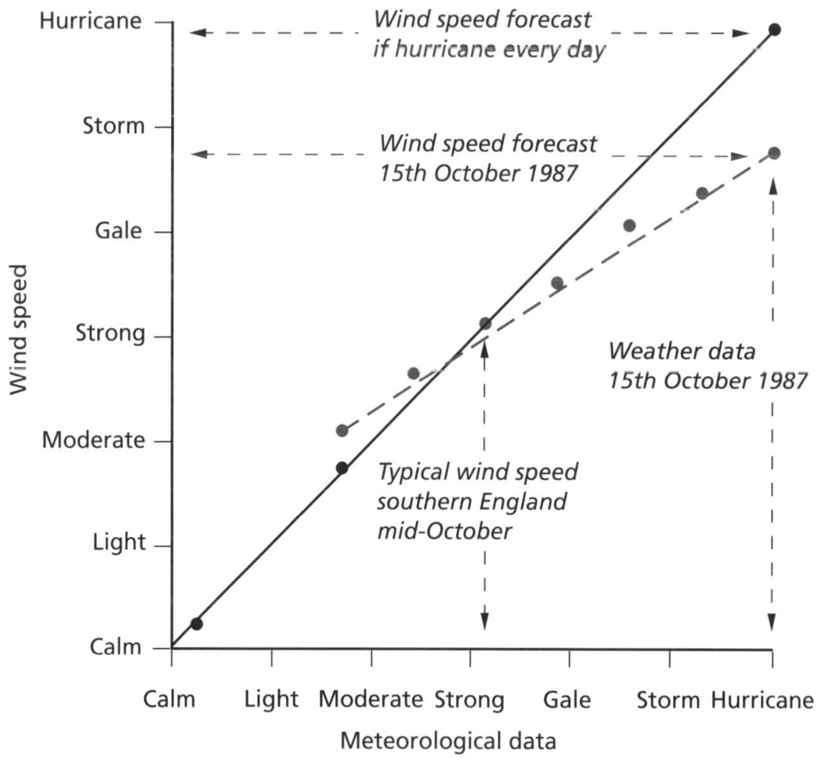

Data from Hollingworth, 1909.

past experience. Figure 11.3 shows how the meteorological data relate to the bias evident in Figure 11.1. The involvement of past experience biases the forecast towards whatever is typical for the time of year, roughly speaking, towards the centre of the ordinate scale. This generally improves the concordance of the forecast with actual turnout. But it also precludes the forecast of the worst storm for nearly 300 years. Hurricanes 'do not happen' in Britain and no meteorologist (in October 1987) was going to forecast one (his colleagues would have laughed at him). Besides, even if a hurricane had been forecast, the public would not have believed it.

Wine writers

Wine has so far been mentioned in Chapter 1 (Robert Parker's dominance amongst wine writers), Chapter 2 (why wine writers' assessments are much less precise than people suppose), Chapter 4 (why the taste of wine depends on the food which it accompanies) and Chapter 7 (the price of champagne). Now we look at bouquet.

When people describe an aroma, even professional people, they mostly use a word that specifies the source of the aroma (the smell of a rose, for example), rather than a word that describes it directly. Wine writers do the same. When describing the bouquet of a red wine, they talk about cherries, or blackcurrants or raspberries – sources that appear red or dark to the eye – and for a white wine, citrus fruit or honey or hazelnuts – sources that appear yellow or straw-coloured. Morrot, Brochet and Dubourdieu (2001) established that this was so by analysing four corpuses of tasting comments (including 7000 comments by Robert Parker). They then demonstrated that the choice of aromatic sources related to the *colour* of the wine, rather than its bouquet, in the following manner.

They asked 54 French students to describe the bouquets of two glasses of Bordeaux, one red and one white. The students selected sources to describe bouquet in the same manner as wine writers do. A week later the students were asked to repeat the exercise, ostensibly with two further (different) wines; but, in fact, on this second occasion, both wines were glasses of the same white wine that had been presented previously, except that the wine in one glass had been coloured red with an odourless red dye. The students used visually yellow sources to describe the bouquet of the white sample, but visually red or dark sources for the sample, with identical bouquet, that had been dyed.

Identifying the colour of a wine from its bouquet alone, without sight of the wine itself, is difficult (Sauvageot and Chapon, 1983). Morrot *et al.* (2001) reported only 70 per cent accuracy in this task. Consequently, when the 54 students came to describe the bouquet, they had very little empirical basis for their judgment and were accordingly biased by the colour of the wine. By implication, wine writers display a similar bias, and this finding adds support to the conclusion that the assessment of a wine is uncertain, always vulnerable to bias. But when Jane MacQuitty spelled out the natural implication – '. . . the financial arrangements which some experts have with supermarkets and wine merchants "must surely colour their judgment"' (Chittenden and Collcutt, 2000) – her fellow wine writers erupted in protest.

Let me make it clear that I, personally, am not suggesting any conscious or deliberate bias on the part of any of the wine writers. But, when it is so uncertain how some particular wine should be rated, it is inevitable that extraneous factors should enter in to bias the outcome. The existing reputation of the vineyard is one such; the source from which wines are provided for tasting is another. The influence is not a conscious one and there is no way it can be countered, except by tasting 'blind'.

However, Jane MacQuitty particularly mentioned financial interests and one of the wine writers she had in mind was Malcolm Gluck. Malcolm Gluck is wine critic for the *Guardian* and has a deal with Tesco to market 'Superplonk' wine, which has been very successful. Such an enterprise involves championing supermarket wines in general, and it may be that Malcolm Gluck has been mindful of the likely effect of his recommendations.

> He [Malcolm Gluck] infuriates wine experts by claiming, as in a Sainsbury's *Magazine* article headlined 'Are expensive legendary wines worth the extra money?' that cheap supermarket wines can be as good as a £110 bottle from a famous estate. (Kennedy, 2000)

It is easy to appreciate that cocking such a snook at reputation *per se* does not go down well with colleagues who are, in some cases at least, demonstrably biased by the label on the bottle. At the same time, the uncertainty attached to the assessment of the quality of any wine makes Malcolm Gluck's assertion very difficult to rebut.

LBW decisions in test cricket

Let us now go to Faisalabad. It is Tuesday, 8 December 1987, the second day of the second test match between England and Pakistan. At about 5.50 pm the light is almost too poor to take a decent photograph, and the batsmen are at their most vulnerable.

> Hemmings was bowling what was to be either the last or the penultimate over of the day. The timing is important because it was in his keenness to get in another over that Gatting, fielding at backward short leg, informed Salim Malik verbally and hurriedly that he was bringing Capel in from long leg. Malik was the striker and Hemmings had already started his run-up when Gatting signalled to Capel that he had come in far enough, whereupon Shakoor called for play to stop and accused Gatting of cheating. (Woodcock, 1987c)

There followed a public row on the pitch between Mike Gatting, captain of England, and the umpire Shakoor Rana. Not only did Mike Gatting not get another over, he lost the one that had started, and the match did not restart until the beginning of the fourth day, with one complete day lost (Woodcock,

1987a,b). What lay behind this fracas? There had long been allegations amongst the England team, and other touring sides as well, that the Pakistani umpires were biased. So Shakoor Rana's intervention was seen by Gatting as yet another attempt to help the Pakistani team to win an otherwise evenly-balanced match. Now it is not possible to resolve the question of bias on the part of an umpire on the basis of a single incident, but if a sufficient number of like cases can be collected, then the relative frequency of decisions favouring one team or the other is indicative. The Leg-Before-Wicket decision is the most controversial in cricket, and the relative numbers of LBW dismissals in test matches from 1967 to 1988 (partly reproduced in Tables 11.1–3) were compiled by Richard Lockwood (Lyon, 1988).

When test matches are played in Pakistan with Pakistani umpires, the visiting teams have the LBW decision go against them more frequently than do the home side (Table 11.1). When Pakistan are playing their matches overseas (the same teams, but with different umpires) there is no difference to speak of in the percentages of LBW decisions; it is much the same percentage as the Pakistani umpires allow against their own players in Pakistan. When India plays test cricket a similar pattern of LBW dismissals may be seen (Table 11.2), though no such bias can be demonstrated in the frequency of LBW dismissals in test matches between any of Australia, England, New Zealand and the West Indies. The most dramatic differences show up, as one might expect, when India plays Pakistan, which they do only infrequently. Overall, there are no differences in the frequencies of LBW dismissals between the two teams or between matches played in the two countries that cannot reasonably be ascribed to chance. But an appeal to an Indian umpire against a Pakistani batsman or, even worse, an appeal to a Pakistani umpire against an Indian batsman . . . the outcome is shown in Table 11.3.

These statistics exemplify the popular notion of 'bias' which involves an element of unfairness, with the umpire manipulating the decision to the advantage of his own country. But there are no grounds for asserting that such bias is deliberate or even conscious on the part of the umpires. This is just the way that the Pakistani cricketing community sees the game.

> There is, to say the least, a mild irony about any complaints Pakistan cricketers make about the umpiring when they are on tour after the problems England and Australia have encountered in Pakistan in the last two seasons.
>
> Intikhab Alam, their normally mild-mannered team manager, has said that he felt there were five or six bad decisions in the recent Test in Wellington [which had been drawn]. One of their party, not involved in the game, went further and told a spectator that if the game had been played in Pakistan his side would have won in four days [whereas, at the end of the fourth day the scores were: New Zealand, 447; Pakistan, 401 for 4 wickets]. (Blofeld, 1989)

I take this opportunity to emphasise that I am using 'bias' to mean the intrusion of *any* irrelevant factor, producing any systematic distortion of judgment, whether it be fair or unfair. This is to define bias in terms of the psychological

Table 11.1 Leg-Before-Wicket dismissals in test cricket, 1967–1988: Pakistan vs other countries.

	LBW decisions	Other decisions	Per cent LBW
In Pakistan (51 matches)			
Visitors	154	629	**19.67%**
Pakistan	77	542	12.44%
Overseas (67 matches)			
Hosts	111	845	11.61%
Pakistan	122	909	11.83%

Table 11.2 Leg-Before-Wicket dismissals in test cricket, 1967–1988: India vs other countries.

	LBW decisions	Other decisions	Per cent LBW
In India (77 matches)			
Visitors	183	919	**16.61%**
India	134	1011	11.70%
Overseas (69 matches)			
Hosts	92	858	9.68%
India	125	935	11.79%

Table 11.3 Leg-Before-Wicket dismissals in test cricket, 1967–1988: India vs Pakistan.

	LBW decisions	Other decisions	Per cent LBW
In India (14 matches)			
Pakistan	29	162	**15.18%**
India	23	165	12.23%
In Pakistan (14 matches)			
Pakistan	8	88	8.33%
India	33	125	**20.88%**

Tables 11.1–11.3 calculated from information in Lyon (1988).

process by which it is produced, rather than by its outcome. The operation of bias is pre-conscious; it has its effect before the individual knows there is a decision to be made. This definition includes a much wider range of applications and affords a clearer picture of how judgments are influenced.

Prior expectations

The two experiments and the failure to forecast the strength of the great storm show that a formulated judgment is a compromise between the information implicit in the immediately available evidence and what has happened in time past. One might think of past experience as setting up a *prior expectation*. That prior expectation functions as an additional (though irrelevant) source of information, and that function is illustrated in this experiment from Bruner and Postman (1949).

Identification of playing cards

People were shown playing cards, one at a time, very briefly: 'Which card are you looking at?' Some of the cards were 'normal' cards, that is, one of the fifty-two cards with which people are accustomed to play; others had been printed in reversed colours, say, a four of hearts printed in black instead of red or a six of spades printed in red. The point of the experiment was that 'trick' cards took longer to identify than 'normal' cards. The actual time measured was not, however, the time taken to make the identification, but the time for which the card needed to be exposed to view for that identification to be correct. That minimum exposure time provided an index of difficulty of recognition.

The cards were exposed in a tachistoscope, which is simply an apparatus to permit each card to be exposed for a certain, precisely limited, time – 0.01, 0.03, 0.05, 0.07, 0.1, 0.15, 0.2, 0.25, 0.3, 0.4 s, and so on up to a full second's exposure. Initially a card would be exposed for 0.01 s. If it was correctly identified, the experiment passed on to the next card; otherwise the same card was exposed for the next shortest interval, 0.03 s, and so on, the exposure continually increasing, until the card was identified correctly. So, how long an exposure is needed to identify each different card?

For a normal card an average exposure of 0.028 s was needed. That is to say, a few normal cards were recognised at the very first and briefest exposure and many more were recognised following the second exposure of 0.03 s. But if the card was a trick card, recognition took much longer. The first trick card which people encountered required an average of 0.39 s. A second trick card was recognised a little more readily (0.23 s) and a third more easily still (0.084 s). On the other hand, subjects who had already seen and recognised one or more normal cards in the tachistoscope, found the trick cards even more difficult.

Everyone is accustomed from long-established convention to hearts being printed in red and spades in black. That convention makes normal cards easier and quicker to recognise than would otherwise be the case. The price to be paid is that trick cards are correspondingly more difficult to recognise. But since trick cards never occur in honest card-play, that price is of no consequence. But the prior expectation that only normal cards will occur is very real, as this experiment made plain. At the briefest exposures people were not aware that the trick cards were abnormal. A red six of spades was seen either as a (black) six of spades or as a (red) six of hearts. At slightly longer exposures people began to be troubled; there was something wrong with the card, but they could not say what. Only at yet longer exposures did people begin to realise that their prior expectation – that all the cards would be normal – was mistaken.

The murder of Stephen Lawrence

On the night of 22 April 1993 Stephen Lawrence, aged 18 and studying for his 'A' levels, was stabbed to death by a gang of five or six white youths whilst waiting for a bus at Eltham in south-east London. A friend who was with him at the time said, at the inquiry, 'Steve did not understand that the group of white boys was dangerous or that anything would have happened.' After the attack, the friend 'tried to flag down motorists, but one car slowed down and then sped past, narrowly missing him. A couple walking down the road backed away as he pleaded for help and they later admitted they thought he would rob them' (Jenkins, 1998). Stephen Lawrence and his friend were black.

Notwithstanding the colour of his skin, Stephen Lawrence was entitled to the same care and attention in the investigation of his murder as every other citizen and that care and attention his case manifestly did not receive. Stephen's parents protested long and loud. There was an internal inquiry by Scotland Yard that identified sloppy policing (Tendler, 1997). There was a further public inquiry under Sir William MacPherson that charged the Metropolitan Police with 'institutional racism'. Briefly, if the case had been investigated with the urgency and commitment that usually attends a murder, the perpetrators would probably have been brought to book. As it was, no-one was convicted of Stephen Lawrence's murder. But, without commenting on the private attitudes of any police officer, it happens that 'More than 28 per cent of all people arrested for robbery in England and Wales last year were black. . . . The proportion was even higher in the Metropolitan Police area where 57.2 per cent of suspects arrested for robbery were black.' (Ford, 2001) Those figures relate to people arrested, not necessarily convicted. But put yourself in the position of a police officer called to an incident. The circumstances of that incident become apparent only after listening to witnesses (and witnesses frequently tell different stories) and it is inevitable that the colour of the people involved will shape the officer's prior perception of what happened and his or her decision on what action to take. Setting aside the attitudes of individual police officers, the psychological situation is analogous to forecasting the weather. Prior knowledge of the typical pattern of weather in southern England in mid-October enables most forecasts to be more accurate than would otherwise be the case. The catastrophic mismanagement of Stephen Lawrence's murder is a natural analogue of failing to forecast the hurricane on the night of 15 October 1987.

The precision of repeated judgments

Prior expectation also has the effect of increasing the *repeatability* of the judgment, as this next experiment shows. If you look at a rotating spiral fixedly, there is a curious after-effect on looking away. If the spiral has been rotating in the direction of apparent contraction, the after-effect appears as a radial expansion of whatever object one is looking at, much as the harmonic spiral in Chapter 4 generated an impression of forward motion. The sensation is one of motion in the contrary direction, but motion without change of position. It lasts for a variable, and very indeterminate, period of time. Sinha (1952) used the spiral after-effect to replicate Sherif's (1937) experiment on the judgment of autokinetic movement. Could judgment of the duration of the after-effect be manipulated in the same way?

The subjects looked at a uniform (not harmonic) rotating spiral for 30 seconds. When the spiral was suddenly stopped and they began to sense movement in the contrary direction, each subject started a stopwatch. The watch was stopped when the sensation of contrary movement ceased. Ten separate readings were taken in a session, with the subjects not allowed to see how long their respective sensations had lasted.

On a second day this procedure was repeated with two differences: First, the experimenter casually remarked, '. . . Incidentally it may be of interest to you that I have tested about fifty subjects and in the majority of cases, *the average reaction time* was found to be (here the appropriate time was given) . . .with 30 seconds exposure.' Second, the subjects were allowed to read their own watches 'as it was the final day of the test with them.' By this means each subject received some suggestion as to how long the after-effect ought to last (different durations being suggested to different subjects), and could see how long the effect actually did last, though remaining in ignorance of how long it had lasted on the first day.

The results from two subjects are shown in Table 11.4. They show that the measured duration of the spiral after-effect on the second day is systematically biased from its unconstrained duration on the first day towards the 'prescribed' duration announced by the experimenter. At the same time the variability of the ten successive readings on the second day was reduced. The indication from the experimenter, how long the effect had lasted with fifty other subjects, not only

Table 11.4 Measured duration of the spiral after-effect (Sinha, 1952).

		Mean duration (s)	Standard deviation (s)	Variance (s^2)
Subject 1	1st day	22.5	2.68	7.18
(Standard duration 15s)	2nd day	17.6	1.77	3.13
Subject 2	1st day	14.6	3.41	11.63
(Standard duration 20s)	2nd day†	20.7	0.94	0.88

†Excluding the first measurement from the series of 10.

Reprinted with permission from D. Laming, 'Prior expectations in cross-modality matching'. *Mathematical Social Sciences*, vol. 38, p. 352. © 1999 Elsevier Science BV.

biases the average duration, but also makes successive measurements more like each other. Those two changes in judgment go together.

Judgment of weight

Chapter 3 included a study by Tresselt (1948) on the grading of weights, showing systematic differences in the use of 'heavy', 'medium', and 'light' by weightlifters and by watchmakers. Figure 11.4 shows the results of another similar experiment (Tresselt and Volkmann, 1942) that displays a phenomenon similar to that in Table 11.4. In this experiment 120 students were asked to lift the same series of 12 weights (11, 60, 110, 210, . . . 560 grammes) and grade them as 'heavy', 'medium' or 'light', each weight being judged once only. Figure 11.4 now shows the *variances* of the weights judged 'medium' in successive serial positions. Different students lifted the weights in different orders, so arranged that each weight was judged equally often in each ordinal position. This means that the same set of weights were judged in each serial position, though different weights were judged by different subjects. There is a 75 per cent reduction in the variance in the course of the first eight judgments. The weights already judged to be 'medium' come to bias succeeding judgments, making them progressively less variable.

A reduction of variability equates to an increase in the repeatability of the judgment. Subjectively there is an increase in confidence; the individual feels less uncertain. That increase in confidence explains why prior expectation has the effect that it does. Where the objective basis for judgment is inadequate, the variability of the judgment is increased. That increase in variability can be contained by taking note of other (though irrelevant) information – for example, from previous judgments. We shall see in due course that these extraneous influences are irresistible.

Witch hunts

By a 'witch hunt' I mean any investigation characterised by a prior conviction so extreme that contrary evidence is disregarded. The investigator's mind is effectively made up in advance, and the psychological purpose of a witch hunt is to provide evidence sufficient to convince others to accept the conclusion to which the investigator has already come. Salem, in 1692, is the best documented historical example.

In the spring of 1692 there was a spontaneous outburst of accusations of witchcraft in Salem Village, Massachusetts (now the town of Danvers). There were sporadic eruptions of alleged witchcraft in New England at that time, and this particular eruption is remembered today because it grew to such dramatic proportions. Once accusations of witchcraft had been laid, they had to be tried, and the justices in Salem at that time scarcely knew how to proceed. After some careful discussion they decided to accept these kinds of evidence as proofs of guilt (Starkey, 1952, pp. 43-4):

Figure 11.4 Variance of weights judged 'medium'.

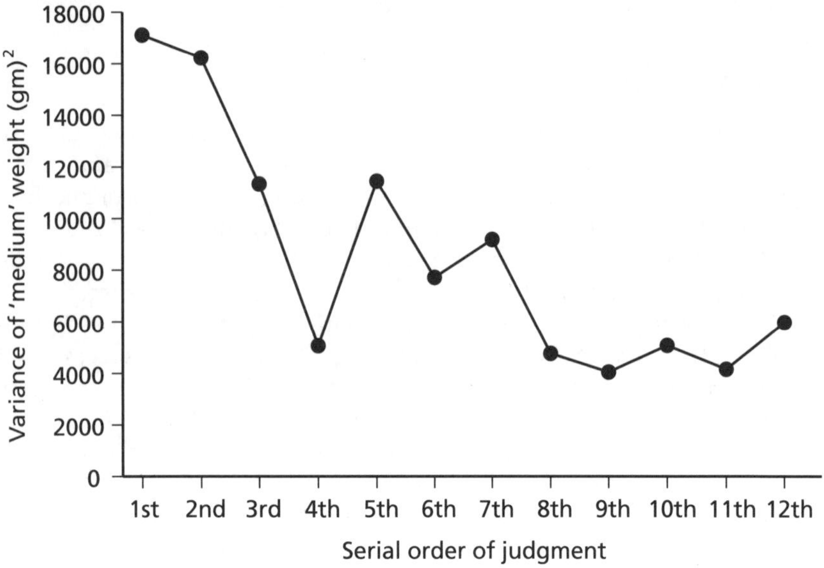

Data from Tresselt and Volkmann, 1948.

1 Any 'witch's teat' or 'devil's mark' on the body of the accused. It was believed that the Devil suckled at such an unnatural excrescence in the same way that a baby suckles at its mother's breast.

2 Spectral evidence. It was asserted that while the Devil might appear in many different guises, he could not assume the shape of an innocent person in doing mischief to mankind. This means that any hallucination, dream, or even mere fancy, on the part of some third person was taken as factual proof, not of the state of mind of the accuser, but of the guilt of the accused. Convictions for witchcraft at Salem depended almost entirely on spectral evidence; no rebuttal of such evidence was possible.

3 The touch test

> First, as to the method which the Salem Justices do take in their examinations, it is truly this: A warrant being issued out to apprehend the persons that are charged and complained of by the afflicted children, (as they are called); said persons are brought before the Justices, (the afflicted being present.) The Justices ask the apprehended why they afflict those poor children; to which the apprehended answer, they do not afflict them. The Justices order the apprehended to look upon the said children, which accordingly they do; and at the time of that look, (I dare not say by that look, as the Salem Gentlemen do) the afflicted are cast into a fitt. The apprehended are then blinded, and ordered to touch the afflicted; and at that touch, tho' not by the touch, (as above) the afflicted ordinarily do

> come out of their fitts. The afflicted persons then declare and affirm, that the apprehended have afflicted them; upon which the apprehended persons, tho' of never so good repute, are forthwith committed to prison, on suspicion for witchcraft. (Letter of Thomas Brattle, F.R.S., merchant of Boston, 1692, reprinted in Burr, 1975, p. 170)

The belief here is that the glance of a witch sends poisonous corpuscles into the afflicted and that tactile contact draws the Devil back out again.

The Salem witch trials were characterised by a belief that such evidence had a reliability almost amounting to certainty. Denials and contrary evidence, not least evidence relating to the previous godly life of the accused, were disregarded. This is simply an extreme bias. A parallel in magnitude estimation would be giving the *same* estimate on every trial, irrespective of the stimulus; such an estimate would have zero variability. Nevertheless, the bias exhibited at Salem is still of the same psychological nature as those lesser degrees of bias illustrated in earlier examples. Notwithstanding that the bias appears so extreme as to exclude all sources of relevant evidence, this is still only appearance. Two features of the Salem witch trials show this to be so.

First, witchcraft is a secret offence. It was called in as an explanation of misfortune when all other explanations failed. The only evidence of guilt that could be convincing beyond all doubt was, therefore, the accused's confession. The quality of belief in spectral evidence and in the touch test was not so certain but that strenuous efforts were made to get the convicted 'witch' to confess. Indeed, those who were accused and convicted and *then* confessed, were partially reprieved, while those who refused to confess were put to death. One man, Giles Corey, was crushed to death with stones while the authorities were trying to extract a confession from him to use against him at his trial (Starkey, 1952, pp. 179–81).

Second, people in important standing in the community, though accused, were not proceeded against; as though the evidence against them, overwhelming though it might seem to the prosecution, was recognised as being not completely watertight.

> I do admire that some particular persons, and particularly Mrs. Thatcher of Boston [Mrs. Margaret Thatcher (1625–1694), widow of the Rev. Thomas Thatcher (*d.* 1678), first minister of the Old South Church. She was the only child of the wealthy Boston merchant Henry Webb, and had been left by a first marriage the widow of Jacob Sheafe, then the richest man in Boston. Ed. note], should be much complained of by the afflicted persons, and yet that the Justices should never issue out their warrants to apprehend them, when as upon the same account they issue out their warrants for the apprehending and imprisoning many others.
>
> This occasions much discourse and many hot words, and is a very great scandal and stumbling block to many good people; certainly distributive Justice should have its course, without respect to persons; and altho' the said Mrs. Thatcher be mother in law to Mr. Corwin, who is one of the Justices and Judges, yet if Justice and conscience do oblige them to apprehend others on the

> account of the afflicted their complaints, I cannot see how, without injustice and violence to conscience, Mrs. Thatcher can escape, when it is well known how much she is, and has been, complained of. (Letter of Thomas Brattle, 1692, reprinted in Burr, 1975, pp. 177–8).

Some fifteen people were put to death in Salem before wiser counsels prevailed and the trials were stopped.

The Cooke family in Cleveland

A case of witchcraft would be laughed out of court in most developed countries today. But that does not exclude the possibility of a bias so extreme as to re-create the circumstance of a witch hunt.

On 24 June 1987 the national newspaper headlines were seized by the news that 191 children had been referred to Cleveland Social Services Department in the *past 2 months alone* on grounds of sexual abuse. The parents of 17 of those children taken into care had begun legal action for their return. The critical figure in all this was Dr Marietta Higgs who had taken up appointment as Consultant Paediatrician at Middlesbrough General Hospital on 1 January 1987. She had a particular concern for the diagnosis of sexual abuse in children; she believed that too much went undetected.

Michael and Diana Cooke (not their real names) were living in Stockton-on-Tees, Cleveland, in 1987. They had three children: Mark aged eleven, Sarah nine-and-a-half and Ben who was two. Ben had suffered from constipation ever since he had been born, and was eventually seen by Dr Marietta Higgs at Middlesbrough General Hospital in March 1987. Dr Higgs diagnosed sexual abuse on the basis of the sign of anal dilation. Dr Higgs asked to see Mark and Sarah too to examine them, and made two further diagnoses of sexual abuse on the same basis. The case was immediately referred to the police.

> A woman police constable in plain clothes arrived shortly and said she wanted to interview the children separately. Diana was told she could sit in on the interviews providing she did not upset the children or 'make things difficult'. The day clinic, at the other end of the ward from their cubicle, was made available for the interviews and Sarah was first.
>
> Diana would later describe the experience of witnessing her children being interrogated by the police as sheer torture. The questioning of Sarah began gently enough. 'I know something has happened to you, Sarah,' the woman police constable said with a smile, 'and I need you to tell me about it.' But Sarah denied anything *had* happened to her and the more she was pressed the more vehemently she denied it, all the time getting increasingly upset. 'I can't tell you anything,' she sobbed repeatedly, 'because nothing has happened.' Exasperated, the policewoman snapped, 'I know when little girls are lying, Sarah, and you're lying.'
>
> At lunchtime a detective constable arrived on Ward 9 at Middlesbrough General Hospital. Since the policewoman's tactics had got nowhere, he decided

> to try and browbeat a confession out of these two recalcitrant kids. He started on Mark, saying he was very angry with the children for wasting everyone's time. 'We've got your dad down at the police station and unless you want to keep him there you better tell us what happened.' When Mark still refused to admit that anything had happened, the detective shamelessly tried to manipulate the little boy. 'Why don't you just tell us what happened,' he said walking round and round the chair on which Mark was sitting, 'then I can go home and watch the football and you can go off and have your birthday party.' Still Mark shook his head, weeping bitterly. Sarah was no more forthcoming.
>
> At about four o'clock [on the second day] the police gave up and told the Cookes and Dr Higgs that they were withdrawing because of lack of 'secondary evidence' and that as far as they were concerned the case was closed. Michael thought 'Great, that's it, now we can all go home,' but Dr Higgs immediately stepped in and said that there was no question of them leaving the hospital since the matter was now in the hands of the Social Services. (Miller, 1988b, pp. 25–6)

Cleveland Social Services did not give up for another eight months, one week before the scheduled resumption of a hearing at Middlesbrough High Court. The children's repeated denials that they had been abused were simply not accepted.

Ignoring irrelevant information – is it possible?

The windspeed on the night of the great storm on 15 October 1987 was under-predicted because the meteorologists were influenced in their forecast by the wind strengths that were usual in southern England in mid-October. Besides the experiments cited, there are many other examples that could have been recounted. Bias results from paying attention to information that is actually irrelevant to the judgment. If the facts of the matter are insufficient, there is no way in which such extraneous influences can be excluded. The question now is: Is it really impossible to ignore such irrelevant information?

The size–weight illusion

There is a traditional trick question: 'Which is heavier, a pound of feathers or a pound of lead?' The point is that if anyone lifts a pound of feathers and then a pound of lead, they will invariably say that the pound of lead is heavier – much, much heavier. My 'pound of feathers' is a pillow, filled with polyester fibre, which is even lighter than feathers. Instead of a 'pound' of lead, I have a set of nine lead weights of graded sizes marked only with an identifying letter. A student volunteer is asked to lift the pillow on one hand and to select a matching lead weight with the other (Figure 11.5a). Different volunteers select different weights; in repeated demonstrations the pillow (720 gm) has been

Figure 11.5 (a) Selecting a lead weight to match the pillow held in the hand; (b) repeating the judgment without knowing which cord lifts the pillow and which the weight.

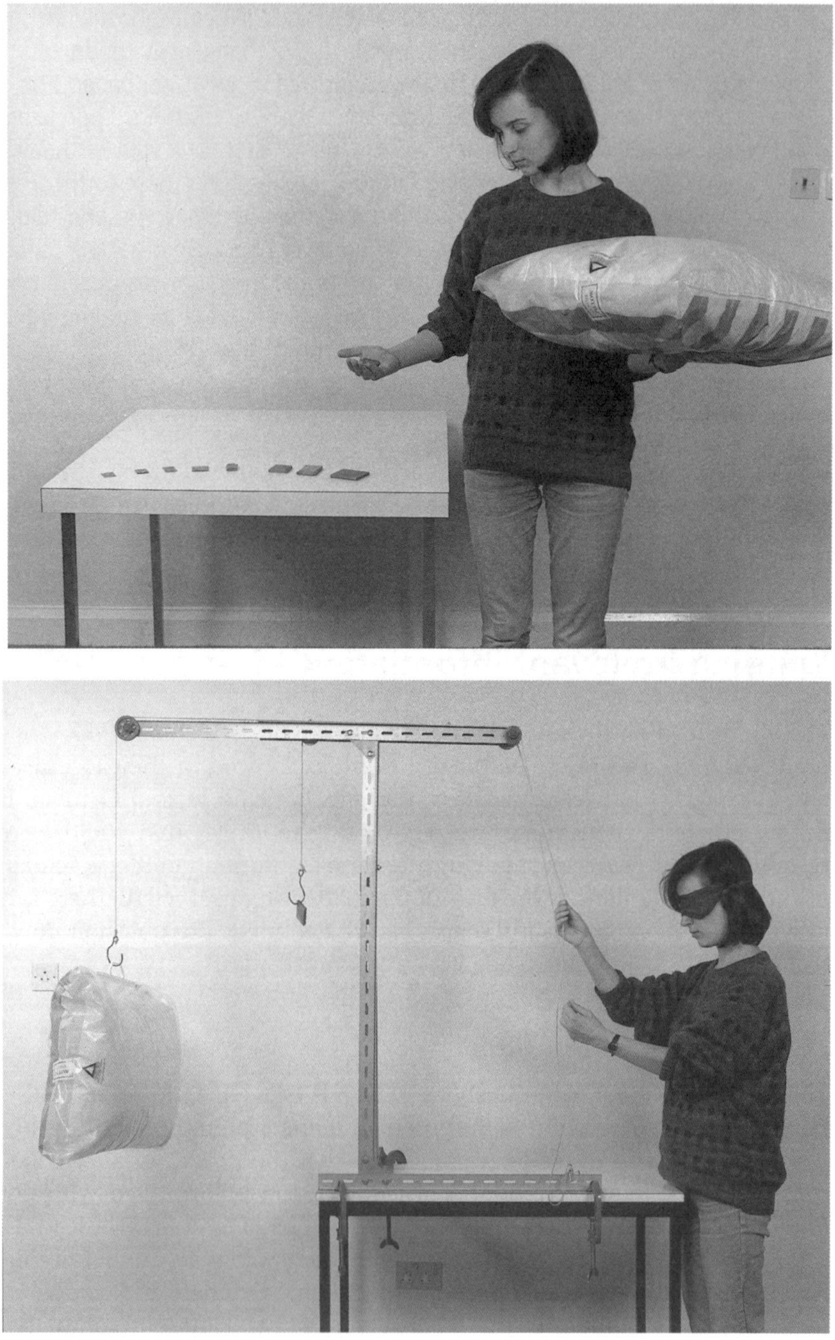

(a)

(b)

Photographs: Ian Cannell.

matched to weights ranging from 225 gm down to as little as 20 gm. The heaviest weight (320 gm) has never, so far, been selected by anyone.

I next ask the student to put on a blindfold and I hang the pillow and the weight on two cords. The cords pass over pulleys on a frame, so arranged that the student can pull on the individual cords without knowing (because of the blindfold) which is attached to the pillow and which to the weight (Figure 11.5b). Under the blindfold the pillow is always reported to be the heavier, as indeed it is. At this point I invite the student to take the blindfold off and weigh both the pillow and the matching lead weight on a set of scales. There follows an explanation that given two equal weights of different volumes, the denser weight, the one with the smaller volume, always feels heavier. This misjudgment is known as the *size–weight illusion*. I now ask the student to repeat the initial test, to balance the pillow on one hand and select a matching weight which *feels* as heavy with the other hand. The fact that the student now knows about the illusion does not make it go away. That is to say, if you can feel which is pillow and which is lead weight, you cannot help but be misled when comparing the relative weights of the two. The denser weight still feels as heavy as the pillow, even when you know (intellectually) that it is actually much lighter. The bias cannot be ignored, except when, being blindfold, you do not know which weight is which.

Figure 11.6 The thickness–length illusion – thicker logs are cut shorter.

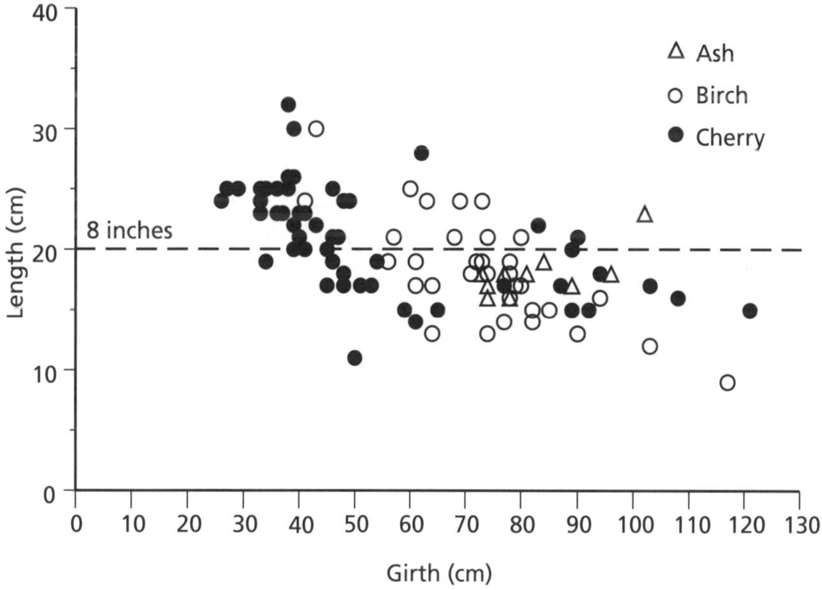

A thickness–length illusion

There is a similar, though less dramatic, bias in the judgment of length. I happened to have the remains (the trunks and limbs) of three trees in my back garden. I asked a contractor to bring a chainsaw and cut them into logs about 8 inches long so that I could burn them indoors. After he had finished, I measured the girth and length of each piece with the results shown in Figure 11.6. Thicker logs were cut shorter, showing a bias towards maintaining a constant volume.

Regina vs The Accused, Birmingham Crown Court, 5th March 1987

It is not ordinarily possible to ignore irrelevant information; that can be done only after careful training such as a legal apprenticeship. For that reason a jury hearing a criminal trial is not allowed to know whether the defendant has any previous convictions. The judge knows because such knowledge might be relevant to the conduct of the trial. But the jury do not lest it bias their verdict. Does this actually matter? Ordinarily one can never know, because in the United Kingdom it is forbidden to investigate deliberations in the jury room. Not even the trial judge is allowed to know what the jurors say to each other. So the following case is exceptional.

A young man was standing trial on a charge of rape. As the judge summed it up, the evidence stood as follows. A girl, aged 17, went to a hen party to celebrate the forthcoming marriage of a friend. The party assembled in a crowded pub and, possibly because of the crowd, gathered around a table at which the defendant was already sitting. The defendant seems to have thought himself welcomed as a member of the party; though, in truth, none of the women quite had the strength of character to tell him to 'clear off'.

The hen party moved on to a club and the defendant went with them. It thereby happened that the girl and the defendant spent some time in each other's company and eventually finished up in the front sitting-room of the home of another member of the hen party. The three of them – the girl, the defendant, and the woman whose home it was – sat talking for perhaps two hours, until the girl and the defendant got up to leave at about 3 am. After leaving together, they soon passed a block of nearly completed flats. The girl said that the defendant picked her up bodily and carried her into the flats where he forced her. The defendant said (in an affidavit – he did not himself give evidence in court) that the girl had consented.

The trial was completed within 2½ hours, but the jury clearly found it difficult to reach agreement. After 5½ hours deliberation they finally returned to court with a majority verdict – 'not guilty'. There followed some remarks from Judge Wilson Mellor.

> (*To the defendant*) You can go. Keep your hands off young girls.
>
> (*To the court*) Is the mother of the girl in court?
>
> (*A relation came forward, the girl's aunt*) I want to say something to you. You might not think it very fair that when a girl, such as this child, has to go into the witness box, that a man should be able to make allegations against her without

> going into the witness box himself, but he may. You may not understand that the jury are not allowed to know whether that man has a previous conviction for raping a young girl. That is the law.
>
> I want you to understand that as far as I am concerned, this little girl was entirely innocent of the matter and I hope that that will help you in comforting her and helping her to recover. (From Regina v. The Accused, pp. 14E–15A. Birmingham: The Crown Court, 5 March 1987. Crown Copyright. Reprinted with permission.)

Now let us look at the reaction of the jury as reported in the *Times*:

> Several members of the jury of seven women and five men at Birmingham Crown Court *held their heads in their hands* [my italics] when they realised from remarks made after the verdict that the man had been convicted before. (Seton, 1987)

If the knowledge that the defendant has a prior conviction for a similar offence so alters the minds of individual jurors, the prosecution have not proved their case 'beyond reasonable doubt', and the verdict is technically correct. At the same time, once the jurors know about the defendant's previous conviction, they are unable to put it out of their minds.

> Judge Mellor returned to the court and . . . said: 'The jury gave full and careful consideration to the evidence. I wish them to know they should not reproach themselves.' (Seton, 1987)

That particular case is exceptional, but not unique.

> Jurors cleared a family doctor of raping a girl of 15 yesterday, then gasped when they discovered that he was awaiting sentence for molesting her. At Manchester Crown Court, Dominic Jackson, 47, who ran a surgery in Adswood, near Stockport, had admitted indecent assault but opted to face a jury on the more serious charge. The jury was not told of the guilty plea until Maurice Greene, for the prosecution, stood to tell the court once they had delivered their verdict. (*Times*, 1999)

Flying 'blind'

This final example concerns an insufficiently trained pilot trying to fly in darkness or in cloud. It shows how difficult it is to ignore irrelevant information, even when it is a matter of life and death.

There are three different senses which tell us which way is up and which is down: there is vision; there is somaesthesis – the feel of the ground under our feet – and there is the balance mechanism of the inner ear. By far the most informative of these is vision. So, when a pilot takes to the air, especially in a light aircraft, that is how he or she orients the craft – until, that is, the pilot enters a cloud or darkness falls.

In cloud or in darkness flying is possible only with the aid of instruments, especially an 'artificial horizon' that displays the attitude of the aircraft to the pilot. But, even though the pilot cannot see, he can still feel the seat beneath him and still has sensations from the inner ear, which appear to be telling him which way he is oriented in space. These are the sensations that enable people to continue standing up even though their eyes are closed. However, their interpretation is fallible.

The inner ear is sensitive to gravity and to acceleration – a sensation experienced when the aircraft is banking – but not to velocity *per se*. So there is a real danger that the pilot will misinterpret his postural and inner ear sensations and, once he is no longer able to orient by sight, he is liable to sensory illusions. He will 'feel' that the aircraft is doing one thing when, in fact, it is doing something else. Judgments of aircraft attitude by experienced, but blindfold, pilots show many errors. In one study of 20 experienced US Air Force pilots:

> When attempting to judge whether the aircraft was climbing, level, or diving pilots made an average of 39 per cent errors. This is considerably more than half the number (67 per cent) that would have occurred from guessing alone.
>
> In judging whether the aircraft was banked to the right, flying level, or banked to the left pilots made an average of 37 per cent errors. The average error of their judgments (estimated bank minus true bank) was 11°.
>
> When both climb-dive and bank judgments are considered together, pilots were wrong with regard to one or both dimensions 60 per cent of the time. Estimates of right and left bank were made with equal frequency, but reports of climbing were made much more often than of diving.
>
> Pilots become adapted to the particular attitude in which an aircraft is flying and tend to report any change as if it were a change from straight and level flight. (Jones, Milton and Fitts, 1947, pp. 1–2)

When people have to walk in the dark, they rely on postural and inner ear sensations to keep their balance. Pilots naturally transfer such habits to flying an aircraft in the dark or in cloud, ignoring the instruments. But that is fatal. A series of accidents from the early days of aviation showed repeatedly that inadequately-trained pilots were unable to ignore extraneous and irrelevant sensations, even though their very lives depended on it.

> Many pilots ignore their instruments and attempt to fly contact and to rely on vestibular and kinesthetic cues under flight conditions. By so doing they are almost as seriously handicapped as if they were blindfolded. (McFarland, 1953, p. 192)

Learning to fly 'blind' means learning to disregard those postural and inner ear sensations and to rely exclusively on instruments. It might sound simple, but it turns out to be surprisingly difficult to ignore the postural sensations that one would automatically attend to on the ground. Here is a transcript of the radio communications between a pilot and ground control as that pilot lost control of his aircraft.

Narrator	. . . another pilot who was not prepared for what he encountered. This one was flying a well-equipped, twin-engined airplane. But he too is not an instrument pilot. He will lose control of the aircraft within 30 seconds after he enters the cloud.
Ground Control	Are you equipped and qualified to fly instruments?
Pilot	I have enough instruments aboard. I had maybe 18 hours, but I have not got a rating on I.F.R. [Instrument Flight Rules] as of yet
Ground Control	Roger, 64 alpha, and what are your intentions?
Pilot	I would like to come on in.
Ground Control	Roger, 64 alpha. Are you requesting an emergency authority to descend through the I.F.R. conditions to land?
Pilot	If at all possible I am requesting emergency . . . to land . . . if I could get down.
Ground Control	64 alpha, descend and maintain 4000. Over.
Pilot	Descending to four zero.
	(Alarmed; very agitated) Having difficulty! Having difficulty! (Screaming) Having . . .
Ground Control	64 alpha, make an immediate – Level off . . . 64 alpha. 64 alpha, if you are in a spin, release your controls.
Pilot	(In panic) Help! Help! Help!
Ground Control	64 alpha, are you in a spin? Over.
Pilot	(Still panicking) Yes! Yes!
Ground Control	Roger, 64 alpha, release your controls. Over.
Pilot	(Screaming) Controls released, over.
Ground Control	Roger. Straighten your rudder, please. . . . 64 alpha. Lost radar contact!
Narrator	Lost radar contact! At that moment the plane crashed and the pilot and his two passengers were killed. (From Moon, 1962).

That transcript is taken from a film, *Signposts Aloft,* made in 1962. 40 years later, on 17 July 1999, John F. Kennedy, son of the late President of the USA, left

Caldwell airfield, New Jersey, in a Piper Saratoga at 8.45 pm to fly to Martha's Vineyard, 200 miles away. He had his wife and sister-in-law as passengers. His arrival time would have been about 10 pm. The sky was hazy; it was dusk. Kennedy was not qualified to fly by Instrument Flight Rules and he did not make it. All seems to have been well until he began his descent to land at Martha's Vineyard. Then he lost control, and radar tracked the plane in a spiral dive into the sea. Kennedy and his two passengers would have experienced 30 seconds of 'pure terror' (Bone, 1999).

The dangers of flying without training on instruments are well-known, but professional helicopter pilots still fly without being qualified to fly blind. Matthew Harding, vice-chairman of Chelsea Football Club, was returning home from a football match at Bolton on 22 October 1996 by helicopter. The pilot flew into fog and crashed. All five on board were killed.

> Most helicopter pilots are unqualified to fly by instrumentation alone, leaving them vulnerable in poor weather conditions. Training to become 'instrument rated' costs £30 000, and few pilots see the need to prepare for the worst flying conditions, in which they would normally refuse to fly. (Leathley, 1998)

It is not possible to ignore irrelevant information except after special training; that is why so much attention is given to teaching a pilot to fly by instruments. It is not possible to ignore such information, even when attention to it is known, intellectually, to be fatal. A pilot cannot learn to fly 'blind' from a book. Similarly, one cannot learn to drive a car safely from a book. Driving a car is not just a matter of learning to handle the controls, the steering wheel, the accelerator and the brakes. One must also learn – most important of all – to attend to the relevant cues and ignore irrelevant sources of information when it really matters. How many of those driving on Britain's roads today could bring a car safely out of a skid?

Summary – getting it wrong

Everybody makes their judgments against a background of past experience. In a laboratory experiment that past experience includes the succession of stimuli presented for judgment and can be manipulated. In that way we can know, for sure, about the influence that previous stimuli have on present judgment.

To the extent that judgment is uncertain, past experience enters like air rushing in to fill a vacuum. That involvement of past experience makes people's judgments more repeatable and is experienced subjectively as an increase in confidence. However, except in the case that there is feedback, usually immediate feedback, the individual has no way of knowing how accurate his or her judgments actually are. It can therefore happen, and often does, that the subjective increase in confidence is accompanied by systematic error. That is *bias*.

Except after long training to specifically ignore certain sources of information, as in a legal apprenticeship or in learning to fly 'blind', people are unable to distinguish between the relevant and the irrelevant. Indeed, how could they without objective feedback? For this reason people are ordinarily unaware that they are biased. Bias is pre-conscious and cannot be resisted, even when, as with flying 'blind', it is a matter of life and death. Note, however, that I have used 'bias' here to mean the intrusion of any irrelevant information into someone's judgment. This is different from the colloquial meaning of someone consulting his or her own interests in the matter.

The next chapter looks at child protection and provides an opportunity to make the notion of bias clearer still.

12 The social workers' dilemma

Detecting child abuse

From time to time it happens, tragically, that a small child is brutally killed by her parents. Maria Colwell, Jasmine Beckford, Tyra Henry and Kimberley Carlile are children whose names featured in the national newspaper headlines for this sad reason. They were four of the 34 British children whose deaths were the subject of inquiries between 1973 and 1987. But this is only the tip of an iceberg. Registered child homicides average about 85 per annum; and the National Society for the Prevention of Cruelty to Children (NSPCC) estimates there are about '200 child deaths per annum either caused, or contributed to by abuse or neglect'. (Blom-Cooper, Harding and Milton, 1987, p. 133). Local authorities and the NSPCC maintain teams of social workers to prevent such tragedies, and for every child who dies there are many more who are saved from death or serious injury.

Social workers charged with the protection of children at risk fulfil their task best if they have the parents' cooperation. Taking a child away from its parents not only causes the child suffering and distress, sometimes quite needlessly, but is also an admission of a certain kind of failure. But if the child is left with its parents, it may be injured or even killed. At what point should a social worker intervene? Child protection is an important subject of public policy; in addition, it provides a most useful context in which to make what I mean by 'bias' even clearer.

Kimberley Carlile

As a running example to illustrate the dilemma which social workers face I have chosen the sad story of Kimberley Carlile. Kimberley had a tragically short life. She was born on 3 November 1981 in St Catherine's Hospital, Birkenhead, and died on 8 June 1986 in a council flat on the Ferrier estate in Kidbrooke, south-east London. She was killed by a blow to her left temple, quite likely a kick, which caused bleeding within her skull.

> When doctors examined the child . . . they found that 'she was literally skin and bone. She had been starved and was dehydrated. Her weight was only 24 lbs' [actually 22½ lb, not much more than half the normal weight for a child of her age, Blom-Cooper *et al.*, 1987, pp. 44–5]. Her injuries included bruising to the

> head, face, stomach, back, buttocks, arms, legs and genitals. There were scars from cigarette burns running down her spine. She also had severe internal bruising, caused by blows. (Tendler, 1987)

The inquiry found that 'physical abuse of Kimberley was inflicted almost incessantly, from about the late autumn of 1985, and continued throughout the New Year, increasing in intensity and severity' (Blom-Cooper *et al.*, 1987, p. 47).

Kimberley's mother, Pauline Carlile, had had three children including Kimberley, the youngest of the three, by her first husband who died from an accident in August 1982. She married again, to David Carlile, by whom she had one further child. She left David Carlile in December 1984 and ultimately divorced him. Thereafter she took up with Nigel Hall, a friend of her first husband, and set up home with him in the London borough of Greenwich in September 1985.

Pauline Carlile's problem was a fatal attraction to violent men. The family first came to the notice of Social Services (in the Wirral, Cheshire) when Pauline Carlile requested urgent help to escape the violence of her first husband, Kimberley's father. Her second husband, David Carlile, was known to the police as a violent man and caused Social Services to be further worried on account of the children. For example, early in their relationship he served a three-month sentence for assault; then, the day after he was released from prison, he broke his wife's jaw. In 1984 both husband and wife were sentenced to six months for fraud. Pauline Carlile gave birth to her fourth child whilst in prison but, after her release, split up from David Carlile. During this troubled period the three children of the first marriage were put into voluntary care, and Kimberley thrived.

After her release from prison, Pauline Carlile moved to London with Nigel Hall and her new baby, living first in Kensal Green and moving later to the borough of Greenwich, where a council flat was made available on the Ferrier estate. With this new three-bedroomed accommodation she was able to reclaim her other three children from voluntary care. Wirral Social Services had always seen David Carlile as the threat to the children's safety and at one point had even considered assuming parental powers by means of a Court Order. But, once Pauline Carlile had separated from her second husband, there seemed no reason why the family should not be reunited. Consequently, no particular warning was sent to Greenwich, and when the family was re-established there in October 1985 Social Services paid them only a routine visit. However, unbeknown to anyone, the problem of violence persisted in the shape of Nigel Hall and, for Kimberley, was now to begin in earnest.

There was a tip-off from a neighbour by means of an anonymous telephone call. On 7 March 1986 the clerk to the team of social workers on the Ferrier estate recorded: 'Several neighbours very concerned about the children of this family, in particular a little girl about 4. Thinks she's being beaten, cries pitifully. Sure mother drinks. DO [Duty Officer] not available at time of call, informant will ring back.' Then, under the heading of further action: 'Phoned NSPCC – not known – home visit done.' (Blom-Cooper *et al.*, 1987, p. 94).

That visit was made at about 5 pm the same day, 7 March, by two women social workers. They saw the two eldest children who appeared clean and well cared for, but were denied any sight of Kimberley. Martin Ruddock, the leader of the social work team on the Ferrier estate, paid a visit to the Carliles on the Monday, 10 March; but, finding no-one at home, left a note demanding that Kimberley be presented for medical examination within the next two days. That note provoked an hour-long telephone call from Nigel Hall the next day (Tuesday), though that call was not taken by anyone from the child abuse team. It resulted, however, in an appointment for Martin Ruddock to visit the Carlile home at 4 pm the following day (Wednesday). But that appointment was pre-empted by the Carlile family turning up, unannounced, at the Social Services offices on the Wednesday morning. The consequence was that Martin Ruddock had to interview the family of six in a room just 7′ 4″ square within the Social Services offices. He recorded that Kimberley appeared 'withdrawn, sallow, pasty and still', but otherwise had no opportunity to examine her. Nevertheless Mr Ruddock's suspicions were partially allayed by the family turning up at Social Services of their own volition.

When there is concern about a child possibly suffering abuse, the standard procedure is to call a Case Conference. This is a meeting of all those who have professional knowledge of the child – doctors, paediatricians, health visitors, police and social workers – who pool their knowledge and decide jointly what action should be taken. A Case Conference can put a child on the register of children 'At Risk'; this ensures monitoring of the child by a specified social worker. Thereafter, only another Case Conference can take the child off the register. In more urgent cases a Place of Safety Order provides immediate, but temporary, protection. It is a short-term detention order granted by a magistrate for up to 28 days. In the longer term the Local Authority can apply for a Care Order, which confers powers of supervision, but does not necessarily remove the child from the family.

Martin Ruddock failed to call a Case Conference, and he believed that there was insufficient evidence to justify a Place of Safety Order. As a result, the case drifted. This is not to say that the case was put on the shelf or otherwise dismissed, but it was not allocated to any particular social worker and, in default, fell to Martin Ruddock, the team leader, as his personal responsibility. There was sporadic further contact with various members of the Carlile family. On one visit Martin Ruddock was allowed a brief glimpse of Kimberley and the baby [Pauline Carlile's child by her second husband] through a glass light above a bedroom door, but that was all. The Carlile parents contrived to evade close examination by Greenwich Social Services, whom they repeatedly put off with excuses. They made it clear that attention from Social Services was unwelcome. Eventually a Case Conference was convened for 9 June, but that turned out to be the day after Kimberley was killed.

At their trial Nigel Hall was sentenced to life imprisonment for murder and Pauline Carlile to twelve years for assault and causing grievous bodily harm. Greenwich Borough Council set up an inquiry into the circumstance of Kimberley's death, chaired by Louis Blom-Cooper, QC. That inquiry blamed almost all of the social workers involved in the case, but especially Martin Ruddock, the leader of the team responsible for Kimberley Carlile. Their report recommended that Mr Ruddock 'should not in the future perform any of the statutory functions in relation to child protection' (Blom-Cooper *et al.*, 1987, p. 22). Mr Ruddock resigned his appointment.

But how did Martin Ruddock himself see it? Was he (to use his own words) 'an excuse-giving bumbling idiot' or did 'job pressure and its resulting stress undermine [his] ability . . . to intervene and save Kimberley Carlile? (Ruddock, 1998, p. 93) It is not denied that at that time Martin Ruddock's team was overworked. Two of its experienced members had just left the team, leaving 50 per cent more work for each of the other four. Consider the consequence: the increase in case-load made each individual member more and more tired, with less and less ability to give due consideration to any one case.

> The level of pressure during those months became so intense that instead of being faced with a manageable number of tasks which required a major effort of me but which I was able to deal with to my satisfaction, I was faced with an overwhelming body of work which meant I could deal with none of it to anything approaching the degree of competence which I would normally demand of myself and was forced to adopt a method of working where by some tasks were not dealt with at all. (Ruddock, 1987; cited by Ruddock, 1998, p. 94)

But that is not the real point.

Interviewed at an earlier point in time, Martin Ruddock said:

> I blocked. I mean, I should have seen! . . . I didn't think it would happen to me. . . . My immediate reaction when I heard of Kimberley's death was, 'This is my mistake.' I think I was prepared to be honest partly because my immediate feeling was so gutted and I needed actually just to – maybe, in part, just weep about it. It hurt. I had to go home, tell my wife that a kid had died, and I had to live with that for the rest of my life. (From *Everyman: There but for the Grace of God,* producer A. Kaye. BBC2, 22 April, 1990. © 1990 The British Broadcasting Corporation.)

That is the sort of thing people say when they realise they have somehow made a mistake, but do not understand how or why. The inquiry did not understand either. That is the central issue in this chapter; its nature is brought out very clearly by some laboratory experiments on 'signal detection'.

Signal detection

A submarine underwater cannot be seen; it is invisible to radar, but it can be detected by reflected sound. Figure 12.1 shows how this is accomplished. There is a transducer mounted underneath the hull of the frigate. It emits a pulse of high-frequency, usually ultrasonic, sound which is reflected off any solid object (here a submarine) in its path. The shape of the sound beam results from the

Figure 12.1 Active sonar beam detecting a submarine.

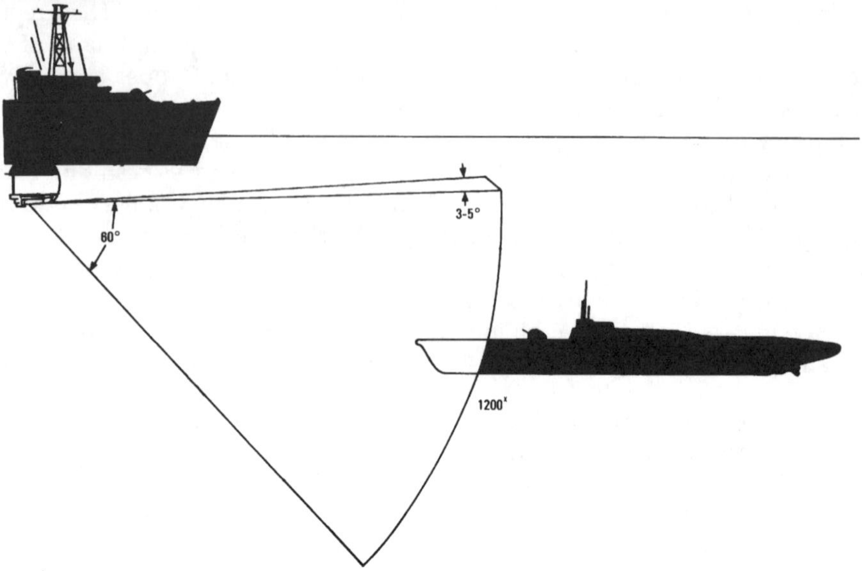

Adapted with permission from W. Hackmann, *Seek and Strike*, p. xxxii. London: HMSO. © 1984 Board of Trustees of the Science Museum.

design of the transducer and the wavelength used, and the ocean can be searched by stepping the beam round through 360 degrees. Any echo is picked up by a hydrophone and today the acoustic waveform output from the hydrophone is analysed by computer. However, before the advent of small computers, a naval rating had to listen for the echo through headphones. Herein lies a problem because the sea is noisy and, even though there is no ship or other object in the path of the sound beam, there is still an input to the hydrophone. That input sounds like a mistuned radio – ssshhh – and a weak echo has to be picked out from that background of noise. Sometimes that echo is less than clear: is there a submarine there or not?

Radar detection presents a similar problem. The radar transmitter emits a pulse of high-frequency radiation and the receiver then looks for a reflected wave. Again, the input to the receiver is noisy and a weak reflection may be missed. Noise (in the technical electronic sense) can be analysed mathematically; the 'Theory of signal detectability' (Peterson, Birdsall and Fox, 1954) is a mathematical theory of the detection of weak signals in noise and applies equally to radar and to sonar detection. It identifies optimum strategies for deciding whether a received waveform contains a reflection from a target or not, and specifies how the weakness of the echo limits the accuracy that can be achieved. Herein lies the relevance to child protection; social workers also lack clear indications of which children are truly at risk.

'Signal detection' is a transposition of the task of detecting a submarine underwater, or an aircraft or ship by radar reflection, into a simple laboratory experiment. Because that experiment reproduces the uncertainty intrinsic to the detection task, it also simulates the social workers' dilemma. As a comparison it is oversimple, but it does expose the nature of the decisions with which social workers are faced.

There is a continuous background of noise, such as one gets from a mistuned radio. Periodically a small light flashes to indicate a 'trial'. Coincident with the light a brief weak tone (the 'signal' – often a 1 kHz tone of 0.1 s duration) may, or may not, be added to the noise. After each stimulus the subject is asked to say, 'Yes' or 'No', whether the tone was present or not. Thereafter the subject is told the correct answer and waits for the next trial. Figure 12.2 presents the data from one such experiment.

There are two kinds of error that the subject in such an experiment might make. He or she might fail to report a signal when it is present (a *missed detection*), or he might report a signal when it is not there (a *false positive*). It is conventional to plot the proportions of correct detections ('Yes' when a signal is presented) against the proportion of false positives ('Yes' when there is noise alone). The coordinates of the data points are determined as follows:

Figure 12.2 Signal detection performance by one subject in the experiment by Tanner, Swets and Green (1956). Successive data points represent different blocks of trials with different costs and payoffs.

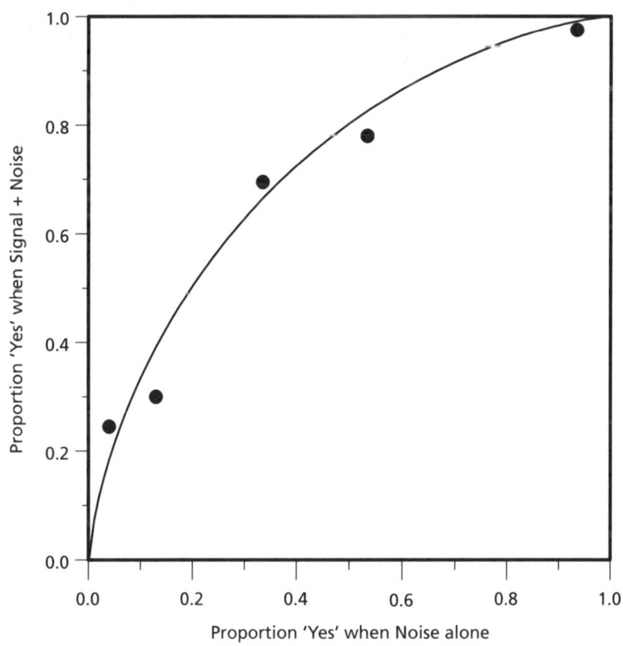

Redrawn with permission from D. M. Green and J. A. Swets, *Signal Detection Theory and Psychophysics*, p. 89. © 1966 J. A. Swets.

	'No'	'Yes'
Noise alone		*Abscissa*
Signal + noise		*Ordinate*

The curve in Figure 12.2 represents a limit to what the observer can do. For example, 35 per cent of the signals can be detected if one is prepared to accept 10 per cent false positives. But, if one is prepared to accept as many as 38 per cent false positives, then 75 per cent of the signals can be detected. There is a trade-off between missed detections and false positives. The incidence of the one can be reduced only at the expense of increasing the other. That trade-off results from an uncertainty intrinsic to the combination of signal and noise. (Mathematically, any example of a signal in the noise background could be a sample of noise alone, but with a reduced probability, and any sample of noise alone could equally be an example of a signal, but again with reduced probability.) So, *in the absence of sufficient information, it is impossible to be correct every time.* Social workers also frequently lack adequate information because child abuse is a private offence, not at all obvious to outside observation.

The different data points in Figure 12.2 correspond to different trade-offs between missing a signal and uttering a false positive. They represent different biases, either towards reporting a signal or towards noise alone. *Every observer is biased in some way*. In this experiment the subject was paid different amounts for correctly detecting a signal and identifying noise alone, and suffered different deductions for a false positive or for missing a signal. These different payoffs were used to manipulate the observer's bias. The five different data points in Figure 12.2 result from five different payoff schedules (see Green and Swets, 1966, p. 90). A social worker also has to make decisions in the face of uncertainty and finds it impossible to be correct every time. Martin Ruddock's failure to seek a Place of Safety order for Kimberley Carlile reflected a bias against removing a child from its family. If he had been generally more ready to remove children thought to be at risk, Kimberley might have been saved; but, other children under his surveillance might have been taken from their parents unnecessarily, with all the distress that such a separation involves. The possible outcomes for the social worker are therefore

	Leave alone	Place of Safety Order
No danger		*Court action*
Child at risk	*Child dies*	*Child saved*

A Place of Safety Order authorises the removal of the child from its family for a period of up to 28 days. It is a last resort. In practice, the social worker's task is both easier and more effective if he can win the cooperation of the parents. In that sense a Place of Safety Order is a defeat. It is something to put off, as Martin Ruddock put it off, while there is still some hope of getting the parents to co-operate without it. But if parents will not cooperate . . .? The comparison with signal detection shows that it is impossible to distinguish those children truly at risk from those who are not, without sometimes getting it wrong. If a social worker fails to remove a child truly at risk, that child may be seriously injured, even killed, by its parents. But if a social worker removes a child not actually at risk – a child who has not suffered any abuse at all – the parents will take action to secure the child's return and the social worker will be castigated in the press and the media. The social worker does, however, have a third option and that is to wait for further evidence.

Putting the evidence together

Martin Ruddock was unable to tell from his one interview with the Carliles that Kimberley was really at risk. But surely the succession of events that were traced in retrospect should have been decisive? The ability to put different incidents together, each one less than decisive by itself, has also been studied in a further signal-detection experiment.

The subject listened, as before, to a continuous background of noise, punctuated with observation intervals marked by flashes of light. After each observation interval the subject said whether he thought there had been a signal or not. There was just one difference from the procedure described above. The observation intervals came in sixes. Either all six had the signal added to the noise, or all six were samples of noise alone. This was well known to the subject. In fact, it was heavily emphasised with specific instructions to take advantage of this relationship. The point of this experiment (Swets and Green, 1961) was to discover how well an observer could put together the less-than-decisive indications from a series of six linked observation intervals. Can the subject use the earlier observations to improve the accuracy of answers later in the series?

Mathematical theory provides a single number, d', to summarise a subject's performance in detecting a brief weak tone in a background of noise, irrespective of the subject's bias. That number, d', measures how close the curve in Figure 12.2 approaches to the top left-hand corner, a corner that corresponds to error-free performance. As the signal is made stronger so d' increases. It also increases if the subject is allowed two or more 'looks' at the signal. In fact, mathematical theory specifies that, ideally, d' should increase in proportion to the square root of the number of 'looks'. Figure 12.3 shows the improvement in performance during a series of six linked observation intervals (all six either signal plus noise, or noise alone) by three different subjects. The numbers of looks are spaced on the abscissa in proportion to their square roots, so that the theoretical relation to d' becomes a straight line through the origin. The three subjects were able to assemble the less-than-decisive information from successive observation

Figure 12.3 Increase of detectability (*d*') with the number of looks in the experiment by Swets and Green (1961).

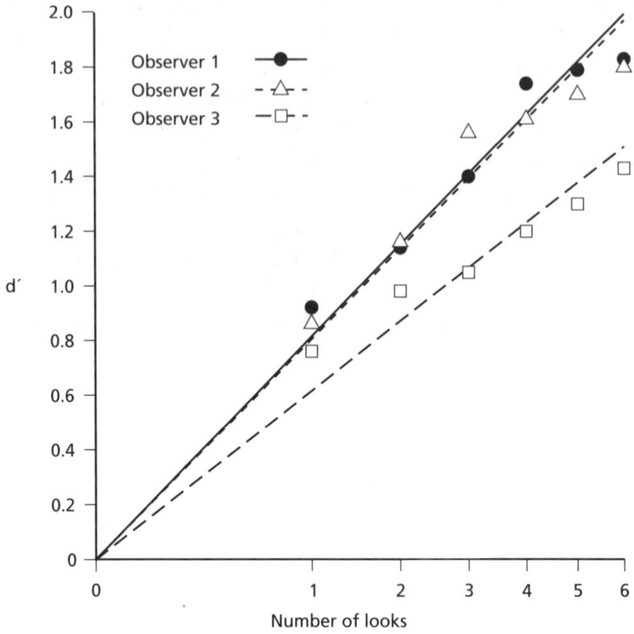

intervals much as the mathematical theory said they should; but these results obscure a much more important point.

The experiment I have described was, in fact, the *third* such experiment employing the same subjects. The first two experiments presented a slightly different task and lacked emphasis in the instructions on putting information from different observation intervals together. So far as one can tell from the data, in those first two experiments the subjects simply waited until an observation interval was sufficiently decisive by itself, either clearly a signal or equally clearly noise alone, before coming to a decision. That is to say, although after some training the subjects were able to put the information from different observation intervals together, without special instructions they did not naturally do so. That experimental finding has this implication: although after suitable training social workers should be able to recognise particular patterns of indicators, each indicator less than sufficient by itself, as evidence that a child is at risk (for example, the little girl who displays sexual knowledge beyond her years), ordinarily, without such training, one must expect them simply to wait for an episode that is clear enough by itself to justify a Place of Safety Order. Unfortunately, in Kimberley's case, that one episode was the call for the ambulance.

This difficulty that one person by him- or herself has in putting things together underscores the value of the Case Conference. As I have explained, a Case Conference brings together all those people with some professional knowledge of the family. They each report what they know, exchanging their collective knowledge and impressions. In addition, those contributors with an historical knowledge of the case, especially the social worker in charge, are required to review their knowledge for the benefit of the other members of the conference. That review causes the social worker, or whoever else it might be, to see the events in a new light – in short, to put them together more effectively than he or she did before. The inquiry repeatedly said that Martin Ruddock should have called a Case Conference. It might have made the difference.

The inquiry

When a child dies in such piteous circumstances, public concern is satisfied only by a formal inquiry to determine what went wrong and who was to blame. A second task for this chapter is to look at some of that inquiry's conclusions. There are two general problems that beset all such inquiries endeavouring to reach fair and effective recommendations after the event. The report of this inquiry illustrates them both.

In the first place, the inquiry has the benefit of hindsight. It would not have been convened if Kimberley Carlile had not been murdered, so the hindsight is inescapable. Knowing that Kimberley Carlile was, at the time in question, undergoing systematic maltreatment of a brutal nature makes sense of many episodes leading up to her death – for example, the anonymous telephone call on 7 March 1985; Nigel Hall's anxious over-response on 11 March to Martin Ruddock's note demanding that Kimberley be presented for medical examination; and the Carlile family's pre-emptive visit to Social Services on the morning of 12 March. Those different incidents, each insufficient to justify action by itself, are seen in retrospect to fall into a coherent pattern of parents hiding an escalating level of physical abuse. But that is to argue from the subsequent knowledge of Kimberley's death to the interpretation of those prior episodes. When Martin Ruddock had to make up his mind, he did not have that hindsight. And to say, 'Yes, but surely he should have been suspicious!' simply misses the point.

The analogy with signal detection tells us that the question which especially needed to be asked was whether the indications that Kimberley was being abused constituted a sufficiently strong 'signal' in relation to the many other signs for concern (possibly 'noise') from other families living in a rough area of suburban London. The inquiry did not make that comparison; it looked at the management of Kimberley's case in isolation from those other cases that came to Martin Ruddock's attention at the same time. Now, the Carlile home was reported to be clean and tidy. The two eldest children, aged nine and seven, and also the baby (18 months) when she was seen, appeared clean and well-cared for. These are not the kinds of indicators that would ordinarily alert a social worker to a serious risk of injury or death. While a child's death, when she should have been protected, is reason for an inquiry, it is not necessarily of itself reason for some particular person to be blamed. A social worker may reasonably be criticised for systematically misreading signs of abuse, but not for one chance error, however serious that error might be. In a state of uncertainty some errors are inevitable. That is what the analogy with signal detection tells us.

To be fair to the inquiry, they were aware that they, but not the social workers, had the benefit of hindsight. In a number of places they cite that distinction in absolving certain participants, though none of the principals, of blame. Yet their hindsight continued to colour their reading of all the events leading up to Kimberley's death simply because, like the rape trial jury in Chapter 11, once it is known that Kimberley has been tortured and killed by her parents, there is no way that that fact can become unknown or excluded from consideration. Hindsight also biased Martin Ruddock's judgment so that, after the event, he was unable to understand how he came to get it wrong. The inquiry could have attempted to calculate how the social workers would have seen things at the time, but such calculations are neither accurate nor reliable. It would have been, at best, like the child faced with Piaget's 'three mountains' task trying to calculate what the doll would see. That lack of precision creates the second problem an inquiry has to face.

The public are concerned, are angry, about the failure to protect a child at risk. That was reflected in newspaper and TV reports. The headlines in the tabloid newspapers said things like:

> 'Social workers gave up . . . and Kim died' (*The Evening Standard*)
> 'The man who let Kimberley die' (*The Star*)
> 'You must never work with kids again
> Kimberley worker barred' (*The Sun*)
> 'Ban Kimberley case bungler for ever' (*Daily Mirror*)

> There was so much anger and almost hate. I felt easily the most hated person in the country. There were people threatening to do to me what Kimberley had done to her. There were vicious phone calls and letters, and people outside, and pressmen phoning and ringing the doorbell at 2 o'clock in the morning and later – and it was very, very frightening. (From *Everyman: There but for the Grace of God*, producer A. Kaye. BBC2, 22 April 1990. © 1990 The British Broadcasting Corporation.)

Such a public attitude is a source of bias for the inquiry. In the absence of clear and reliable calculations of the view that social workers could have had of the case at the time, that bias cannot be resisted. This is apparent from the inquiry's verdict on Martin Ruddock, which was curiously ambivalent.

> Mr Ruddock's behaviour before us and his general professionalism lead us to say that, in spite of the criticism that attaches to his handling of the Carlile case, we regard him as an intelligent social worker, conscientious and hardworking, although **we recommend that he should not in the future perform any of the statutory functions in relation to child protection**. We suspect that part of the problem was that he over-worked, to the detriment of his professionalism. Our view was more than amply confirmed by the receipt of his

> written statement. It is not only an outstanding document of insight into the nature of a social worker's tasks. But it was also well written, movingly reflective and self-critically analytical. It avoids casting blame on others, in circumstances where it might have been expected. Our appreciation of its work can be reflected in **our recommendation that Greenwich Borough Council, Mr Ruddock's employing authority, should make the document available as an educational tool for the training of social workers generally, and for those involved in child abuse particularly**. (Blom-Cooper *et al.*, 1987, p. 22; bold face type original)

In his television interview, Martin Ruddock displayed the love of children, the passion, and the commitment that one always hopes for in a child-protection worker:

> For anybody who's had kids, or knows kids: Do you picture kids playing and laughing and giggling and bouncing and everything in that joy which is childhood? I think children in part represent hope for us. It was over, I mean, for that child, and just having to look at it felt . . . it's hard to find a word to describe. I'm not getting to the word to describe it, but it is very, very, very painful – wasteful. And if those childhood dreams, you know, when you watched the Lone Ranger and Tonto as a kid – kind of saving people, were gone and you just totally failed to do that, which was one of the hopes of being in a profession like social work. And you had to live with that from now on. (From *Everyman. There but for the Grace of God,* producer A. Kaye. BBC2, 22 April 1990. © 1990 The British Broadcasting Corporation.)

Reading between the lines of the inquiry's report, one can readily conclude that it prematurely terminated the career of a dedicated, and by then specially experienced, social worker.

The message to other social workers

The inquiry may have had one other consideration in mind. It may have felt concerned about standards of child protection work in general and may have wished to send a message to social workers nationally. This the inquiry did, with consequences which I explore in the remainder of this chapter. The manner in which those consequences follow from warnings, such as those implicit in the inquiry's report, is exemplified in a third signal-detection experiment.

The primary analysis of signal-detection data consists in calculating the proportions of missed signals and of false-positives in each block of trials. This third experiment (Tanner, Rauk and Atkinson, 1970) differed in two important respects from the pattern of Figure 12.2. First, the authors picked out those trials in which the subject had missed a real signal, or reported a signal that was not there, and looked at what happened on the *following* trial. Second, they included a block of trials in which their subjects were not told whether they were right or wrong (immediate knowledge of results is usual). These two circumstances enable us to see what effect immediate knowledge of an error has. (In addition, the subjects were asked to distinguish between two levels of a 1 kHz tone, presented without any noise background, but this further difference is no more than incidental. The relative levels were adjusted to permit about 70 per cent correct responses.)

The left-hand diagram in Figure 12.4 presents the results from an initial 4200 trials in which the subjects received no feedback, not knowing when they had been correct and when wrong. After a missed signal (filled circle) the subjects missed 39 per cent of the signals on the following trial, but said 'Yes' only 26 per cent of the time when no signal was presented. But after reporting an imaginary signal (filled square), the subjects missed only 14 per cent (cp. 39%) of the signals on the following trial, but reported a false-positive 55 per cent of the time (cp. 26%). The frame of reference, the bias, is different in these two cases – that is, after a missed detection and after a false positive. The picture suggested by this experiment is that the bias fluctuates, though only slowly with respect to successive trials. Errors occur chiefly at extreme swings of the bias.

The centre diagram in Figure 12.4 presents the next 4200 trials in which the subjects received the usual knowledge of results. After a missed signal, the subjects missed only 28 per cent (previously 39%) of the signals on the following trial, but said 'Yes' only 20 per cent (previously 26%) of the time when no signal was presented. After reporting a false positive, the subjects now missed 21 per cent (previously 14%) of the signals on the following trial, but reported a false-positive 32 per cent of the time (previously 55%). There is an overall improvement in discrimination (the curve has moved towards the top left-hand corner) and, especially important, performance following an error (of either kind) has shifted towards the centre of that curve. These shifts in performance are emphasised by reproducing, in the centre diagram, the operating points from the left-hand diagram for those trials that followed an error and connecting them by arrows to the new operating points. The knowledge that one has just made a mistake shifts the frame of reference for the next trial in such a way as to make a repetition of that particular mistake less likely; but that change in bias simultaneously increases the likelihood of the alternative kind of error.

This effect of the knowledge of having just made an error appears even more clearly in the right-hand diagram in Figure 12.4. That right-hand diagram summarises performance from a further 10 500 trials without feedback. The improvement in discrimination (due to practice) is maintained, but the absence of feedback means that performance following an error, of either kind, is again at an extreme swing of the bias. This difference is again emphasised by reproducing the operating points for trials following an error from the centre diagram. The clear conclusion is that being told one has just made a mistake shifts one's bias for the next judgment. The inquiry into Kimberley Carlile's death castigated the principal social worker involved. That message was received and understood by social workers at large. Rene Rafferty was one child who felt its effects.

Figure 12.4 Performance following each kind of error and correct response in the experiment by Tanner, Rauk and Atkinson (1970). The left-hand diagram presents the results of an initial 4200 trials without feedback; the centre diagram shows the results of the following 4200 trials *with* feedback; and the right-hand diagram a final 10 500 trials, again without feedback.

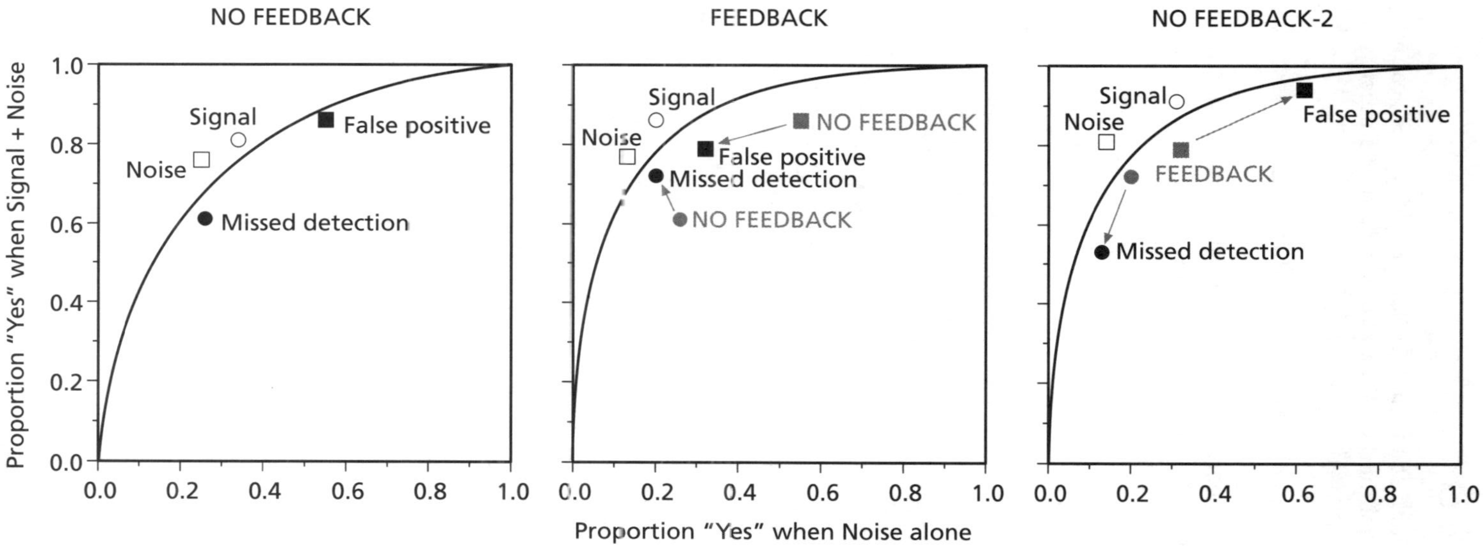

Rene Rafferty

Rene, aged four, spent August Bank Holiday, 1991, camping in Sussex with her mother, her mother's father, and her mother's much younger brother, Philip, aged 7. They played a game:

> . . . blowing dried peas at one another through peashooters made from cow-parsley stems.
>
> Rene soon developed horseshoe-shaped marks and blistering on her body [see Figure 12.5] and was sent by her GP to the hospital last Monday [2 September 1991]. After a spell in isolation, she moved to a children's ward, apparently perfectly healthy. But when Mrs Rafferty decided to take her daughter home, she was warned that the child could be taken into care if they left the hospital.
>
> Catherine Rafferty, 25, claims she and her daughter, Rene, were kept virtual prisoners last week at the Royal London Trust hospital on the orders of social services staff. The ordeal ended when a conference of police, health and social workers [a Case Conference], hastily convened to consider Rene's future, was interrupted by a consultant dermatologist who confirmed what Rene's mother had suggested was the cause – cow-parsley. (Jones, 1991)

Mrs Rafferty knew that her daughter had not been abused; she was in the position of an experimenter who knows that this particular trial contains only noise. But the social workers were in the position of subjects who were not sure; they were not sure because they had not seen how the marks and blisters on Rene's body had been caused. They could not take her mother's word for it, because the mother might be covering up abuse, as the Carlile parents had done. They had to wait for the dermatologist to provide the additional information that resolved their uncertainty. Meanwhile, the social workers held Rene, just in case:

> Catherine's mother, Muriel Neesam, arrived with Philip at the hospital on Thursday morning to show them his marks. 'My daughter was treated abominably and made to feel like a criminal,' said Mrs Neesam. 'The whole situation was handled most unprofessionally. The bottom line seemed to be that unless they could find a medical explanation, Rene would be taken into care.' (Jones, 1991)

Actually, the case was handled most professionally – according to the new professionalism engendered by the recommendations of the Kimberley inquiry. It showed a strong bias towards assuming the worst, generated in part by the castigation of Martin Ruddock for failing to read a pattern of events the like of which he had never seen before. The Tower Hamlets social workers were determined not to repeat that mistake; so likewise were social workers in Islington.

William McGowan

> Marian McGowan is a consultant community paediatrician who routinely diagnoses child abuse. Michael McGowan is an insurance agent and a graduate

Figure 12.5 Rene Rafferty.

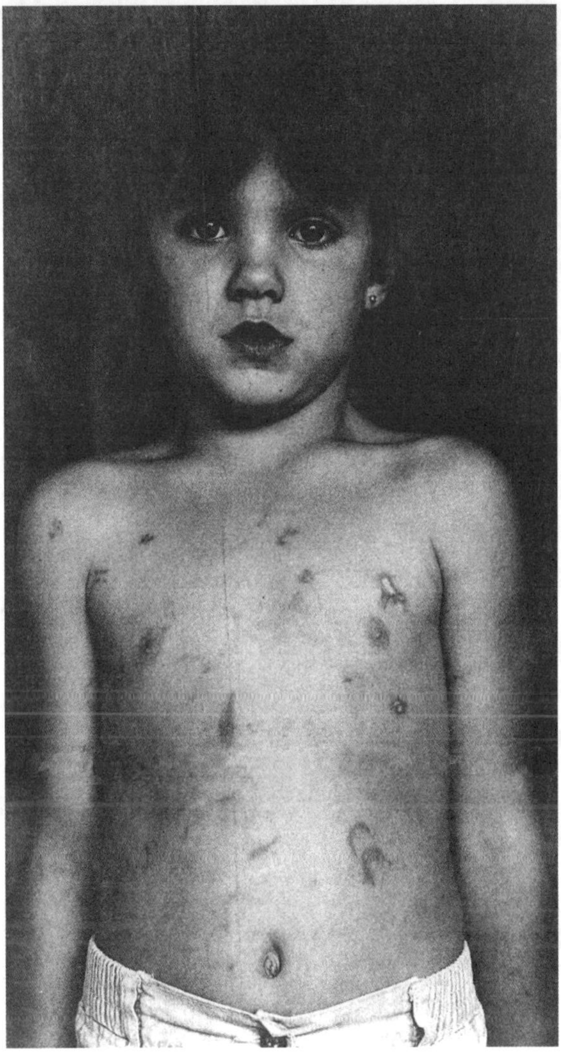

Reproduced with permission from J. Jones, 'A little girl caught between cow parsley and the climate of our times'. *Independent on Sunday*, 8 September 1991, p. 1. Photograph Geraint Lewis. © 1991 Independent Newspapers (UK) Ltd.

> in social administration. They have an apparently healthy 20-month-old son.
>
> Last week, however, they were told that the local authority was considering taking the boy, William, into care. They have not been told why, nor have they been allowed to defend themselves. (Kelsey, 1990)

Because both parents work full-time, they employ a nanny to help look after their five children. They think their troubles actually began before William was born with an anonymous telephone call, possibly from a disgruntled former nanny, accusing them of neglect. That telephone call remained on the NSPCC's records and covert monitoring continued after William was born in 1989. William was a small child – all their children are small – and developed at less than the normal rate. Nevertheless, his mother, whose profession this is, saw no cause for alarm. But in December 1990:

> . . . they received a letter informing them that a child protection case conference had been convened. The letter arrived on 7 December; the conference was held last Monday [10 December].
>
> This was a serious development: the conference has the power to take children into care, or put them on the 'at-risk' register. Dr McGowan would have been forced to resign her job had the social services decided William was the victim of abuse.
>
> The case has been adjourned until January pending an investigation into the child's health. The family was told by one doctor who attended the meeting that 'if we had been a single parent, in a high-rise block, we would have lost the child. It was that close.' (Kelsey, 1990)

Happily, a further Case Conference on 22 April 1991 exonerated the McGowans of neglecting their children, although records of the investigation remain on file. But in this post-Kimberley-Carlile-report era, it seems that no child is safe.

Ritual sexual abuse

The inquiry into Kimberley Carlile's death complained of a reluctance to use legal procedures to force access to children believed to be at risk and to remove them from their homes if necessary. That message was received and understood by social workers at large, especially in Orkney.

South Ronaldsway is one of the Orkney Islands. It has a population of about 1000 people, most of them living in St Margaret's Hope, the remainder in scattered farms and houses. South Ronaldsway appeared in the national headlines at the beginning of April 1991 because at 7 pm on 27 February nine children from four families had been seized in a dawn raid and taken into care. They had been immediately flown to the Scottish mainland in a chartered aeroplane.

> The children were in 'moral danger'. They had been exposed to 'lewd and libidinous practices'. There had been sexual and simulated sexual intercourse in ceremonies involving 'ritualistic' music and dance.
>
> The 64-year-old local minister in St Margaret's Hope had his manse searched by police. They removed his coloured graduation hoods and black funeral cloak. Although no charges against the Rev Morris Mackenzie have been brought, it was implied that in the 'hours of darkness' ceremonies he played a central role, choosing children from a ring by hooking them with his shepherd's crook. (Cusick, 1991b)

In the background to these events there is a fifth family, the children of which are known to have been sexually abused by their father. The children from the four families first mentioned were seized and taken into care solely on the basis of statements from three children of this fifth family, statements made under interrogation by officers of the Royal Scottish Society for the Prevention of Cruelty to Children (RSSPCC). The seizure of the children from the four families was vigorously contested by their parents until, on 4 April, Sheriff David Kelbie in Kirkwall, Orkney, ruled that the applications for care warrants in respect of the nine children were 'fatally flawed' and 'incompetent' and dismissed the social workers' case on technicalities. The children were returned to their parents.

> Back in their village house, sitting on a stone in the back garden, the boy, almost a teenager, is not reluctant to discuss what has happened over the last five weeks.
>
> While his sister kicks a ball on the grass, he says of those who interviewed him: 'They were bullying me. They said they knew what had happened, because people had told them. They were trying to put words into my mouth.'
>
> His voice is low, but he is not shy or confused. 'They sniggered at me. I don't know why they sniggered at me.'
>
> There are complaints about postcards he sent to his sister which she did not get, letters that his parents sent that were not delivered.
>
> Casting their minds back to the day they were taken away is easy. They [brother and sister] remember the first interviews taken by a person they refer to as 'fag-ash Linda'. The boy says: 'She smoked all the time she talked to us. She kept asking about a place, a quarry where people dressed up.' And barely able to pronounce the next few words, he says, 'lewd and libidinous', as if they belong to a foreign vocabulary. At the end, he says: 'I told them I didn't know what they were talking about.' (Cusick, 1991c)

Two further families were interviewed on the television news.

Mrs. B.	And they actually came and took my children and there was not a thing I could do to protect them from what was happening. That had to be the worst moment in my life possible.
Ken Rees	The couple's teenage daughter described the allegations as nonsense.
Wendy B.	What I've got to read in the paper, it sounds most stupid. (*Laughing*) Some kids made up a story about us.
Ken Rees	This family had two of their four children taken. They had no contact with them; didn't know where they were; their teenage son among them. (*To the teenage son*) What did they say to you, I mean, in general terms?

Sam M.	We have reason to believe that you were sexually abused and just that sort of stuff – just . . .
Ken Rees	And what was your reply to that?
Sam M.	Well, it's nonsense. Nothing happened.
Ken Rees	The eleven-year-old said he'd only heard about the alleged satanic rituals a few days ago.
Jonathan M.	. . . about, it was meant to be ritual dancing or, it was meant to be in the quarry, or anything.
Ken Rees	And what about all that? What's your response to those allegations?
Jonathan M.	Stupid! No truth in them at all. (Reproduced with permission from *News at Ten*, 1991b. © 1991 Independent Television News Ltd.)

The testimony, on the basis of which the nine children from the four families were seized, alleged ritual sexual abuse, an idea much in fashion at that time.

> The four families [seized on 27 February] were subjected to the same process that the [fifth] family had been through – with no parental access or communication of any kind, the children were subjected to repeated, and leading, questioning. In police interrogation, the parents learnt of their alleged part in the ritual sex dances in a shallow quarry, overlooked by several neighbouring farms.
>
> One mother was said to have dressed in white, another to have had sex with a boy of eight. The Rev MacKenzie, with his bad heart and colostomy bag, was alleged to have hooked children into the centre of the ring for sex. (Hilton, 1991)

If you are interrogated about something of which you know nothing at all, you nevertheless have to make up answers to satisfy your interrogators, and those answers have to be made up about somebody. It helps to choose someone of not too high a standing in the local community, otherwise one's made-up answers might not be accepted. All the four families implicated by the testimony of the children from the fifth family were 'incomers' from England (Cusick, 1991b). Made-up answers also have to be constructed out of actual experiences. There was an inquiry (Clyde, 1992) and during the second week of hearings details emerged of the disclosures on which the social workers had acted:

> New details also emerged of the disclosures, made by three children from the [fifth] family while in care, which first made the Orkney authorities believe they had uncovered a child sex ring. Mr Lee [Orkney's director of social work] read out transcripts of an interview with a [fifth family] girl. Describing a sex ritual,

> the child went into detail about children dressed in Girl Guide, Brownie, and Boys' Brigade outfits. Some dressed as cowboys and danced round in a circle while the local parish minister had sex with a child in the centre, she said.
>
> The inquiry was told that parents and children from the four families at the centre of the case took part, and the minister was identified by the inquiry as the Rev Morris MacKenzie. The child from the [fifth] family said the minister's wife, Jan, had taken part in the rituals.
>
> Interpretations of what such descriptions mean differ in Orkney. For example, at Kirkwall golf club last week, the chat suggested that statements from the inquiry had influenced opinion in favour of 'surely something must have been happening.'
>
> But in South Ronaldsway reaction was more dismissive. A former Brownie leader offered a different opinion. During the Hallowe'en holiday last November, the week before the three [fifth family] children were taken into care, the school hall in St Margaret's Hope held a children's fancy dress party organised by the local Brownies, Guides and Boys' Brigade. Over 50 children attended, mainly from South Ronaldsway and Burray. Jan McKenzie drove children from the [fifth] family to the party in her car. Some children dressed as cowboys. Some of the adult leaders were in Brownie uniform. A few of the children dressed as witches – in tall black hats, black cloaks, carrying turnip lanterns. There were games, with skittles arranged in a circle. Those competing stood round the circle. (Cusick, 1991a)

Not only do one's made-up answers have to be made up about somebody, they also have to be constructed out of actual experiences. Novelists do not write in a vacuum and children's stories are never complete fantasy. The testimony of the three children from the fifth family reads like a dream. A dream draws on material from diverse sources, all of them part of the dreamer's experience, and blends them into one. Part of the children's testimony appears to relate to the Hallowe'en party; the resemblance is so close that it is difficult to suppose it could be from any other source. But many other people were present at that party, and the elements of ritual sexual abuse must have come from elsewhere. That other source may well have been questions asked by the interrogators. They were frankly looking for evidence of sexual abuse and thereby contrived to manufacture it.

No other evidence was adduced that the nine children seized on 27 February had been subjected to any kind of sexual abuse. Such evidence might have come from medical examinations of the children or from other people on South Ronaldsay, not otherwise involved in the allegations. Nevertheless, the social workers decided to remove those children in a dawn raid.

The relation of that decision to the warnings implicit in the findings of inquiries such as that into Kimberley Carlile's death needs some further explanation. Looking back at Figure 12.2 it can be seen that optimum signal-detection performance is achieved with an operating point in the middle of the characteristic where about 70 per cent of decisions about both 'signal + noise' and 'noise alone' will be correct. This choice of operating point minimises the total number of errors. If one kind of error is deemed to be more expensive than the other, there is a formula (see Green and Swets, 1966, p. 91) that identifies a different operating point at which total *cost* is minimised. Over the long term this is the criterion that social workers should be using. But the criterion that a particular social worker does use results from that individual worker's experience. It is not at his or her disposal. Rather, the social worker's bias is manipulated in one direction or the other by extraneous events. Moreover, an inquiry into a child's death is not concerned with social workers' discharge of their duties in general – it is concerned only with the handling of the one particular case. So it is inevitable that the report of such an inquiry will push social workers' judgments towards one extreme or the other, rather than guide it towards the desirable optimum. It is therefore no wonder that the social workers in Orkney acted as they did for fear of castigation if they were subsequently found to have overlooked an actual paedophile ring.

Summary – protecting the children

Social workers engaged in protecting children against abuse believe they are on a hiding to nothing.

> **Social workers can never win**
> From Mr Norman Warner [Director of Social Services, Kent County Council]
> Sir: Recent coverage of social work activities in the Orkneys illustrates why social services' morale sometimes takes a dip. The media has a penchant for reporting the down side.
>
> A good example of this was the way that only one national newspaper reported the handling of a child sexual abuse network in Kent last year involving about 70 children and the prosecution of more than a dozen adults.
>
> This case was larger than any of the episodes in Nottingham, the Orkneys or Rochdale, all of which have been reported in depth. The trouble with the Kent case was that it showed the police and social services working closely together, observing sound procedures, and achieving convictions. Pretty boring stuff really – just some routine incest and buggery.
>
> Through much of the Seventies and Eighties, the media has hammered social workers for not protecting children. There is engraved on the hearts of most social workers a roll call of dead children who were not removed from the tending loving care of one or both of their parents. It is not surprising that social workers are anxious to protect children. (Warner, 1991)

But that letter misses the most important reason for the public's attitude.

The social workers charged with the responsibility of a case of suspected abuse do not know the truth of the matter. They can only make a tentative judgment on such evidence as is available to them. Nevertheless, if their judgment is later found to be wrong, they are liable to be castigated. People, including the inquiry sitting in judgment, do not appreciate the limit that is imposed on appropriate choice of action by less than adequate information.

But the children's parents *do* know whether their children have been abused or whether it is all in the minds of the social workers. Parents know because child abuse is usually within the family. In cases where the abuse is real, the parents usually accept whatever care orders and sentences the social workers and the courts hand out. Protest would only expose yet more of the parents' wrong doing to the public gaze. Such parents do not usually talk to the press.

But if the abuse is imaginary, the parents know they have been wrongfully accused and seldom give up their attempts to clear their names and to secure the return of their children. They seek whatever publicity they can get; they have nothing to hide. This elevates the case into the national interest as additional details emerge.

Imaginary cases arise because child abuse is a private offence and social workers rarely have conclusive evidence. They have to decide in a state of uncertainty and some mistakes of one kind or the other are inevitable. In such uncertainty, social workers are inevitably subject to bias. Public inquiries, such as that into the death of Kimberley Carlile, make social workers more ready to intervene. The inquiry into their intervention in Orkney had the contrary effect. Rene Rafferty, William McGowan and the recent events in South Ronaldsway are part of the price the public has had to pay.

The next chapter looks at bias in the marking of public examinations, where some simple arithmetic measures its magnitude.

13 Examinations

In August each year the education correspondents of the national newspapers turn their attention to A-level results.

> **Where A-levels can be unfair**
> The season of indignation over A-levels is at hand. As the brown envelopes were torn open last week, thousands of sixth-formers discovered they had not made the grade for a university place.
> The search for a scapegoat has already begun. Surely, say angry parents, the marking was unfair, the standards were higher, more clever people sat the exam. (Judd, 1984)

A-level results are seen to frustrate the ambitions of many sixth-formers, and for that reason this kind of invective against the public examination boards is popular with the readers of national newspapers. But most parents and, it would appear, most politicians and education correspondents, have little understanding of the technicalities of marking examinations. In this chapter I explain some of the elementary technicalities as a contribution to an increased understanding. That means looking at the way examiners make judgments about examination scripts. I shall also look at public judgments about the way examiners carry out their work. So this chapter looks at examinations on two distinct levels: first, how judgments about examination scripts are made and, second, at judgments about the fairness of judgments about examination scripts. This enquiry will clarify yet further the notion of 'bias'; indeed, it will even be possible to do some simple arithmetic to evaluate the contributions from different sources of bias.

Marking examinations

The numbers of candidates sitting most public examinations are so large that a team of examiners is required. Different scripts are marked by different examiners and this presents a problem in aligning the standards of marking applied by different individuals.

> . . . public examining bodies who have to employ large teams of examiners to mark their examinations use various procedures to standardise the marking of these examiners. Chief Examiners and Senior Assistant Examiners are appointed and their job is to supervise the marking of teams of Assistant Examiners. This is done through marking schemes, the sampling of scripts, standardisation meetings and finally through adjustments made to the marks of individual examiners.
>
> Assistant Examiners are provided with detailed marking schemes, by their Chief Examiner, outlining the way in which they are expected to mark individual questions. They also attend standardisation meetings where the interpretation of this marking scheme is explained to them by their Chief Examiner with reference to the actual scripts which they are going to mark. As a check on whether the Assistant Examiners are complying with the standards set down by the Chief Examiner in the marking scheme, they are required also to send in sample batches of scripts during the marking period. These are scripts, which they have already marked, but their marking is then checked by the Chief Examiner or one of the Senior Assistant Examiners, and they are then returned to the Assistant Examiner with comments.
>
> If, at the end of the marking period, it is still considered that particular examiners have consistently marked either too strictly or too leniently, then the Chief Examiner may decide to adjust all of the marks of these examiners accordingly. This is the final method by which the Chief Examiner attempts to bring into line the marking of his team of examiners, and if these procedures are successful then the final set of marks awarded will reflect the marks which the Chief Examiner would have awarded to the scripts if he had marked them all himself. (Murphy, 1978, p. 196)

Marking schemes

To illustrate what is meant by a marking scheme I reproduce three examples. First, from O-level English Literature.

Question:

HARDY. *Far From The Madding Crowd*

Hardy tells us that Oak's 'defects were patent to the blindest', while his 'virtues were as metals in a mine'.

By close reference to incidents in the novel, illustrate the truth of this statement.

Marking scheme:

Mark as a whole, out of 20.

The quotation comes at the beginning of Chap. 29.

The question demands close reference to incidents. For an unpointed character sketch or an obviously prepared answer, award a maximum of 8.

Give up to 12 for good reference to three or four incidents chosen to illustrate different characteristics. Reserve the top marks for candidates who discuss the quotation.

They may well disagree, particularly as far as his defects are concerned, though he is obviously homely, blunt, and tactless. Some of his virtues are equally obvious. But it remains true that, the better we know Gabriel, the more we admire him.

The candidate must make his own selection.

Next, from A-level Pure Mathematics:

Question:

A high vertical wall is on level ground and is in an east-west direction. A vertical pole, 5 m from the wall and on its south side, is 10 m high. The sun is at an elevation of 50° in a south-westerly direction from the pole. Calculate the length of the shadow of the pole on the wall, giving three significant figures in your answer.[6]

Marking scheme:

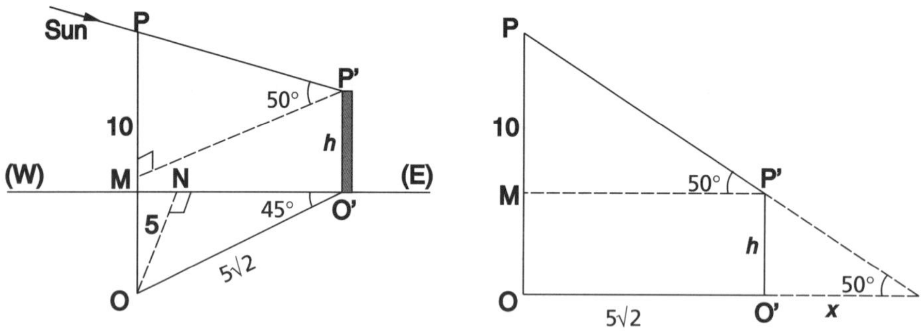

OO′ = $5\sqrt{2}$ [B1]

A right angled triangle showing 50° correctly [B1]

Complete Method for h from a <u>correct</u> figure [M2]

$h = 10 - 5\sqrt{2} \tan 50°$ [A1] (any correct form)

= 1.57 [A1] (correct answers only)

(condone failure to round off to three significant figures)

(Marked out of 6. There are three kinds of marks: 'M' marks are awarded for any method which would give the correct answer if correctly worked; 'A' marks are for accuracy of working and are not awarded without the relevant 'M' marks; 'B' marks are independent of 'M' marks; 'Correct answers only' marks are awarded if the answer is correct and all the relevant work is correct.)

Finally, from A-level History (English History 1450–1964):

Question:

> Why did Britain go to war for Poland in 1939, but not for Czechoslovakia in 1938?

Marking scheme:

> While the form of the question relates to the eleven months between Munich and September 1939, it is basically a question about appeasement and the change of British policy in March–April 1939. Candidates could legitimately devote two-thirds of their answer to explaining appeasement as practised by Baldwin and Chamberlain and to a debate on 'Munich', but it is to be hoped that they will also go on to the period from March to September 1939.
>
> (This question was marked out of 25. There were, in addition, some general directions, applicable to all essay questions in this examination, of which I reproduce the following:
>
> Every point worth a mark must be ticked in the margin. Every point worth half a mark must be indicated by a dash in the margin.
>
> For most answers the final mark will be the accumulated total of ticks and dashes. . . . But examiners are allowed to adjust marks upwards and in exceptional cases downwards.)
>
> (From GCE examinations set in 1985 by the University of Cambridge Local Examinations Syndicate. I thank OCR for their permission to cite these examples.)

To put the matter succinctly, the examination is devised and set by the Chief Examiner, but marked by a team because the volume of marking is much too great for any one person to undertake alone. The marking schemes and standardisation meetings are the procedures by which the Chief Examiner teaches his or her assistants how he/she wants the examination to be marked. The reliability of assessment by such a group of markers ought not to be taken for granted and the Associated Examining Board published some studies conducted to check this matter.

The reliability of public examinations

Samples of 200 scripts were selected at random from GCE examinations after the completion of the normal summer marking period. All existing marks and comments were removed. The scripts were then distributed amongst certain Chief Examiners and Senior Assistant Examiners who had all been involved in the normal marking of the respective examinations, with instructions to mark the scripts as though they were seeing them for the first time, keeping to the marking scheme and standards previously agreed for the examinations. This procedure yielded two marks for each script, the mark originally awarded in the examination and the further mark from the Chief Examiner on re-examining the script for the purpose of this study.

These marks provide, for all practical purposes, two independent assessments of the script. The second mark was assigned in ignorance of what the first mark had been. If the two marks always agreed, they would suggest that, if the entire examination had been re-marked, the outcome, especially the grades awarded to individual candidates, would have been exactly the same. If, on the other hand, the two marks varied, then a re-marking of the original examination would have given proportionately different results, with some candidates moved up a grade and others moved down. How big a difference might such a re-marking make?

Mental test theory (Gulliksen, 1950) tells us that the correlation r between two independent examiners measures the proportion of the variance in either set of marks that is attributable to the scripts themselves; the remainder $(1–r)$ is the proportion attributable to differences between the examiners. The argument runs as follows.

> Let the 'true score' for a script be t.
> Let Examiner X's mark be $x = t + a$.
> Let Examiner Y's mark be $y = t + b$,

where the components a, b, and t are all independent of each other.

$$\begin{aligned}\text{Covariance}(x, y) &= \text{Cov}([t + a], [t + b])\\ &= \text{Var}(t),\end{aligned}$$

because a, b and t are all independent of each other

$$\begin{aligned}\text{Correlation}(x, y) &= \text{Var}(t)/\sqrt{\{[\text{Var}(t)+\text{Var}(a)][\text{Var}(t)+\text{Var}(b)]\}}\\ &= r\\ &= \text{proportion which Var}(t)\text{ is of total variance,}\end{aligned}$$

i.e. of the squared differences between marks

Reliability and validity

The correlation r is the proportion of the variance of the marks that can be attributed to differences between the scripts. It is the *reliability* of the examination, estimated from the extent to which independent examiners agree. *Validity* is the extent to which the examination is assessing whatever it is supposed to be assessing. It may be less than the reliability; it cannot be greater.

On behalf of the Associated Examining Board, Murphy (1978, 1982) conducted 24 re-marking assessments, using scripts from both O-level and A-level examinations. For O-level mathematics and physics, the two sets of marks agreed almost perfectly (correlation 1.0), while, at the other extreme, A-level English, A-level Government & Politics, A-level History and O-level English Language correlated only 91 per cent. Of the 24 re-markings, only three showed a reliability less than 90 per cent. To achieve such reliability in the marking of questions that called for essays by way of answer seems to me very satisfactory. But let us see what Judith Judd in the *Observer* made of it.

> Surely, say angry parents, the marking was unfair, the standards were higher, more clever people sat the exam. In general, if not in particular, they are right. The A-level grading system is unfair. Despite some checks and balances, nobody pretends that the process of allocating grades is scientific. It is done by discussing a selection of papers at a chief examiners' meeting after all scripts have been marked by teachers who themselves have pupils sitting the exams.
>
> In subjects such as English and History, opinions vary widely and there are obvious problems. Last year's answer on Charles Dickens has to be compared with this year's on D.H. Lawrence. This year's question on Disraeli may be trickier than last year's on Henry VIII. The examiners adjust the marks to allow for easier papers but this again is a matter of human judgment. (Judd, 1984)

The adjustments that examiners make at their final meeting result in some borderline candidates being moved up a grade, with a consequence that I look at next.

Standards in public examinations

Since 1965 there have been a succession of comparisons between the grades awarded by different boards in particular subjects (Bardell, Forrest and Shoesmith, 1978; Forrest and Shoesmith, 1985). For the most part these studies have failed to reveal any systematic difference between the standards required by the different boards. But making a valid comparison is more difficult than it at first appears.

It is not sufficient to simply compare pass rates. The former Oxford and Cambridge Board drew 90 per cent of its entrants from independent schools; its pass rates (Grade C or better at O-level) were the highest of all. The Associated Examining Board, on the other hand, drew 36 per cent of its entrants from the further education sector; its pass rates were typically 20 per cent lower (Bardell *et al.*, 1978, p. 11). But this difference in pass rates might be no more than a reflection of the different qualities of the respective entries.

If a valid comparison is to be made between the standards set by different boards, there has to be some common ground between them. In 1966 some 6343 candidates were found to have sat the examination of two boards in the same subject within the same examination period. At A-level 75 per cent (of 762 candidates) received the same result (pass or fail) from both boards; at O-level the proportion was 72 per cent (Bardell *et al.*, 1978, p. 16). If the examinations from the different boards had related as closely to each other as did the independent markings of the same scripts in the AEB's re-marking study, one would have expected 86–90% of the results to have matched (except for the fact that some candidates would have been better prepared for one examination than the other). The reliability of the individual examination sets an upper limit to the concordance one can expect; but the correlation between different examinations (in the same subject) might easily be less than that.

Cross-moderation

Double entry is now very much less common; moreover those candidates who did enter twice were an atypical sample. Consequently, the public examination boards have turned to cross-moderation exercises as a means of comparing standards. Examiners from different boards scrutinise each other's examinations, often re-marking a selection of scripts and 'awarding' their own grades. The only common element is the examiners; the candidates and the examinations are different. Such an exercise presupposes that each Chief Examiner has a precise and stable idea what standard of work merits each different grade – A, B, C, etc. – independently of the particular examination. In view of the experiments and examples cited in the first five chapters of this book, that supposition is most unlikely.

The popular view of a candidate who fails to get the grades that he or she was expected to get is that such failure is probably due to human error (other than by the candidate) in the examination process. Accordingly, examination boards review borderline candidates at their final meeting. That review has this consequence that showed up in a cross-moderation exercise looking at the C/D borderline in O-level history:

> The broadest finding to emerge from this report is that, to varying degrees, all Boards thought all other Boards to be generous in their fixing of the C/D borderline. . . . It has been suggested to us that while each team of examiners honestly believed that the standard it imposed on other Boards' work was its own standard, in practice, because of negotiated compromises made at awarding meetings which invariably end up favouring candidates, the standard which emerges and is applied is *below* what the team believes it to be. (Garrett and Wood, 1980, p. 7, cited by Forrest and Shoesmith, 1985, p. 35)

Maintaining standards

The press and the public are inclined to make all kinds of allegations about examinations on no evidence at all. For example,

> **Teachers praised for record increase in GCSE pass rate** (Judd, 1992).
>
> **GCSE examiners blamed for 'erosion of standards'** (MacLeod, 1992).

If there were known to be some way of fixing a standard objectively, the examination boards would already be doing it.

> In practice, public examinations (and in particular GCE) are not norm-referenced; that is to say, it is not true that grades are awarded to conform to predetermined proportions, any more than it is true that the pass mark is

pre-determined. Each board's practice involves, for example, the re-reading of scripts at critical regions of the distribution in order to make judgements of quality about where the grade cut-off points should come. In doing this, the boards' principal concern is to maintain the same standard from year to year, although that standard is nowhere explicitly laid down: it lies instead in the experience and minds of those teachers and administrators whose task it is to carry the standard across time.' (Forrest and Shoesmith, 1985, p. 23)

Except when a cohort of candidates takes the same examination in successive years, there is no basis for quantitative comparison. But, even so, such a cohort would not be comparable with itself as it was 12 months previous. In Chapter 5 I showed that small differences, small changes from year to year, pass unnoticed. But a succession of small changes can amount to a large change.

There was a report prepared for the London Mathematical Society (Howson *et al.*, 1995) in response to growing concerns that the standards of mathematics set by public examinations were slipping.

> Standards are falling – this time in school maths. Academic mathematicians declared last week that students arriving at university to read maths and science were hopelessly ill-equipped.
>
> They did not understand the meaning of proof and they failed to grasp that maths was a subject requiring precision. They were unable to do numerical algebraic calculations accurately and incapable of solving problems involving more than one step. Most had little notion of what maths was all about. (Judd, 1995)

As a consequence, most universities now have four-year mathematics courses.

But there is another point of view.

> Steve Robinson, a maths teacher for 24 years, says: 'Standards haven't slipped. But there is a difference. Students now are being taught a much wider range of maths and, for the student, that has to be right.
>
> 'We may not go into the same depth always. A- and O-levels were set up for the universities – they used to write them. It is the universities that have not adjusted.' (Berliner, 1995)

So what is meant by a 'standard'?

National assessment of seven-year-olds

The general level of competence in public comment about examinations is illustrated by the national assessment of seven-year-old children, which was first carried out in the summer of 1991. The results from 105 education authorities were published on 19 December of that year. The best and the poorest of those results are shown in Table 13.1.

> Richmond-upon-Thames comes top, with 88 per cent of pupils scoring average or above, and Bradford is at the bottom with 59 per cent.

Table 13.1 National assessment of seven-year-olds, 1991.

	Level 1	Level 2	Level 3
Richmond	12%	64%	24%
103 others	. . .	. . .	. . .
Bradford	41%	54%	5%
Average	21%	64%	15%

> Richmond said yesterday it was 'thrilled' by the results, which reflected great credit on the high quality of its teachers, who used a variety of teaching methods.
>
> But Bradford attacked the validity of the tests. 'There is no national checking or monitoring of the way papers are marked [by teachers],' said John Ryan, chair of the education committee. 'It is like asking pupils to award themselves exam marks or asking learner drivers to decide whether or not they should pass their driving test.'
>
> Jack Straw, Labour's education spokesman, said: 'The results have turned out to be a test of the Government's record in education. They've failed badly. These children have been educated during record teacher shortages, rising class size, crumbling buildings, cuts in the share of national wealth devoted to education and, above all, one ill-thought-out change after another.'
>
> The National Union of Teachers said there was nothing new in a quarter of pupils having difficulty at school.
>
> Mr Clarke [Secretary of State for Education and Science] said yesterday that in publishing the results he was making 'a small piece of history. This is the first time in this country that we have clear evidence on a national scale about what children can do when they are seven.'
>
> He went on: 'The results that worry me the most are the considerable differences in maths and science . . . Too many primary schools do not apparently believe in teaching children the times table. That I fail to understand. They are short-changing their pupils. It is almost a prejudice against imparting knowledge.' (Crequer, 1991)

Different children of the same age differ in their ability; they differ widely. Many quantities which vary in nature – a child's score on a test of ability is one of them – approximate a particular pattern of variability which statisticians know as the normal distribution. That pattern suggests two principles to guide the construction of a test. First, the test should be centred on the average performance of (in this case) seven-year-olds. Second, it is especially meaningful to divide the range of scores into three broad categories so that 16% fall into Level 1, the lowest level, 68% into Level 2, which is 'average' in the sense of being typical of what a seven-year-old can do, and the final 16% into Level 3, the top level. This pattern is illustrated in Figure 13.1. The large proportion assigned to the middle category corresponds to a range of ±1 standard deviation either side of

Figure 13.1 The 'levels' in the national testing of seven-year olds (the abscissa is scored in units of standard deviation).

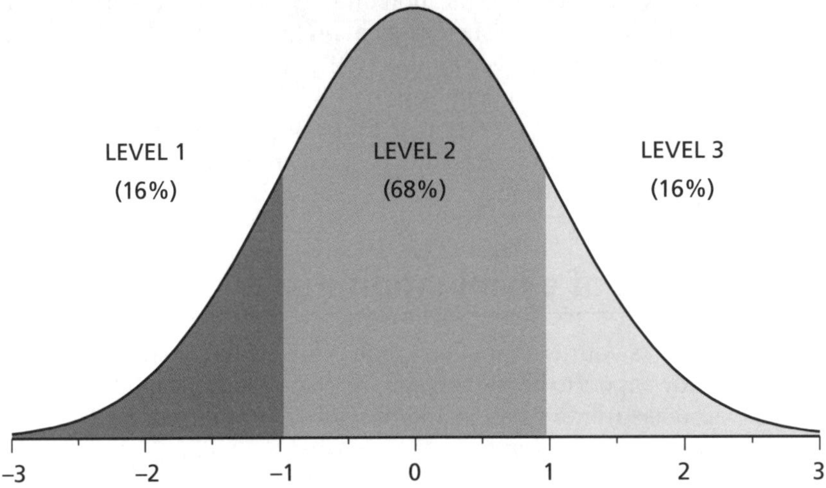

the mean. It can now be seen why Bradford, the authority with the poorest results, nevertheless had 59% scoring 'average or above'. 'Average or above' covers two broad categories which taken together are intended to embrace the top 84%.

These national tests were designed to be administered and marked by the children's own teachers. That opens the way for some variation in implicit standards between one teacher and another. Some variation in the results from different educational authorities is to be expected, if only for this reason. The average proportions in the table above are therefore commendably close to the desired 16, 68 and 16 per cent. So what do the results really tell us? They tell us chiefly that the experts who devised these tests knew exactly what they were doing. That was accurately characterised in a preview of the results the previous day.

> Shameful! say the tabloids. Unacceptable! says Kenneth Clarke. Shocking! says the Labour Party. Yet the results of this summer's tests for seven-year-olds, due to be published today, are noteworthy mainly because they are so utterly unsurprising.
>
> On BBC radio at the weekend, the Secretary of State for Education and Science tried to use the results to support his case for bringing back traditional methods in primary schools. Jack Straw, Labour's education spokesman, said they were an indictment of 12 years of Tory rule.
>
> They are both wrong. The results for reading tell us very little. They show that 28 per cent of pupils failed to reach the average [i.e. typical] standard for a seven-year-old, 51 per cent were average and 21 per cent reached level 3, the most advanced for their age. This is a normal distribution curve. As Clare Burstall, director of the National Foundation for Educational Research, points out, you would get a similar curve if you compared children's height. (Judd, 1991b)

National tests for seven-year-olds are a political clothes' peg. Publication of the results of the national assessment of seven-year-olds provides an occasion when the Secretary of State for Education and Science and his Labour shadow (and any other politician who wishes to get in on the act) can say whatever they want about state education (never mind whether it has any genuine relevance to the test results) and have it fully reported in the press, just like a child at school hanging his or her clothes on a peg. Education correspondents and politicians appear to have little understanding of the technicalities of marking examinations; most parents have none.

Re-assessment of examination marks

If your school thinks your examination grade is lower than it should have been, it can ask for your papers to be re-marked. The cost varies; the grade is increased (it is never decreased) in a small proportion of such applications. Here is one angry parent writing to the *Times:*

> I have recently discovered (for reasons that will not be hard to guess) that the scope for pupils to question the grades they obtain is rather unsatisfactorily limited.
>
> The examination boards are autonomous bodies (providing, it may be pointed out, work and money for the examiners). They are under no obligation to allow a re-mark by *an independent authority* (and they do not do so).
>
> For payment of a handsome fee (£25) and after presentation of a case by the pupil's school, they will have it re-marked by a different examiner, often the chief examiner in the subject.
>
> One could well imagine that the examination boards have a vested interest in keeping the number of re-marks that result in a changed grade to a minimum – in order to preserve their credibility. The numbers requested are relatively few, perhaps not surprising in view of the cost, tardy response, and very low percentage of changes – about 3 per cent I am told.
>
> Given the vagaries of marking and the qualitative nature of much of it, this figure is suspiciously low . . . (Barbour, 1985).

This parent has a point. If the reliability of marking were 90 per cent, one would expect 7 per cent of re-markings to result in the award of a higher grade. When the reliability rises to 95 per cent, the proportion of higher grades ought still to be 5 per cent. There is, however, a reason why, in practice, the proportion of grades changed is lower.

Marking a public examination offers many opportunities for slips of the pen. One precaution taken is to write the marks awarded on each candidate's script in red ink. Red is easy for the eye to pick up and helps in the clerical checking before the results are issued (and the marks are checked very carefully indeed. It would be only too easy to omit the marks for one question from the total). If, now, there is a request for a re-mark, the relevant script is simply handed to the Chief Examiner with the Assistant Examiner's marks and comments *still clearly visible in red.* The re-marking is supposed to be independent; but do those original marks bias the re-assessment?

Murphy (1979) selected a GCE O-level examination in which the candidates had answered four out of a selection of essay questions. Two samples of 100 scripts were selected, each sample evenly distributed across the original examiners, to protect against any systematic differences in the original marking. All previous marks were removed from one of the samples, but not the other. Both samples were then given to two Senior Examiners with instructions to re-mark 'as though they were being marked for the first time'. The differences between the original and the new marks were twice as great when the old marks had been removed from the scripts. The examiners were clearly biased by the original marks, when they were left on.

Measuring the bias

Figure 13.2 shows two scatter diagrams plotting Examiner 1's re-mark against that of Examiner 2. Each data point represents one script; its ordinate is Examiner 1's re-mark and its abscissa Examiner 2's mark. If there had been perfect agreement between these examiners (correlation +1.0), all the data points would lie on a straight line. Differences between the examiners throw points off that line, to one side or the other. The spread of the data points away from the line increases with the extent of disagreement between the examiners, and that disagreement may be measured by the correlation between their respective sets of marks. The shaded ellipses in Figure 13.2 indicate the shapes of the joint distributions of marks, with correlation 0.94 when the marks are left on the scripts for the examiners to see and 0.87 when they are removed. The difference in relationship between the marks in the two sets is clear and it provides a means of measuring the bias.

1. Correlation between the two re-markings with the original marks removed = 0.87

So Proportion of variance due to examiner = 0.13

& The ratio (Variance due to scripts : variance due to examiner) = 0.87:0.13

2. Correlation between the two re-markings with the original marks left on = 0.94

So Proportion of variance now due to examiner = 0.06

& The ratio (Variance due to scripts + variance due to original marks : variance due to examiner) = 0.94:0.06

3. If the original mark be given equal weight with the new (re-)mark, the triple ratio
<Variance due to scripts : variance due to original marks : variance due to examiner> should be 0.87:1.00:0.13
Whence the ratio <Variance due to scripts + variance due to original marks : variance due to examiner> should be 1.87:0.13
0.935:0.065

Figure 13.2 Scatter diagrams, Examiner 1 vs Examiner 2, from the re-marking of O-level scripts.

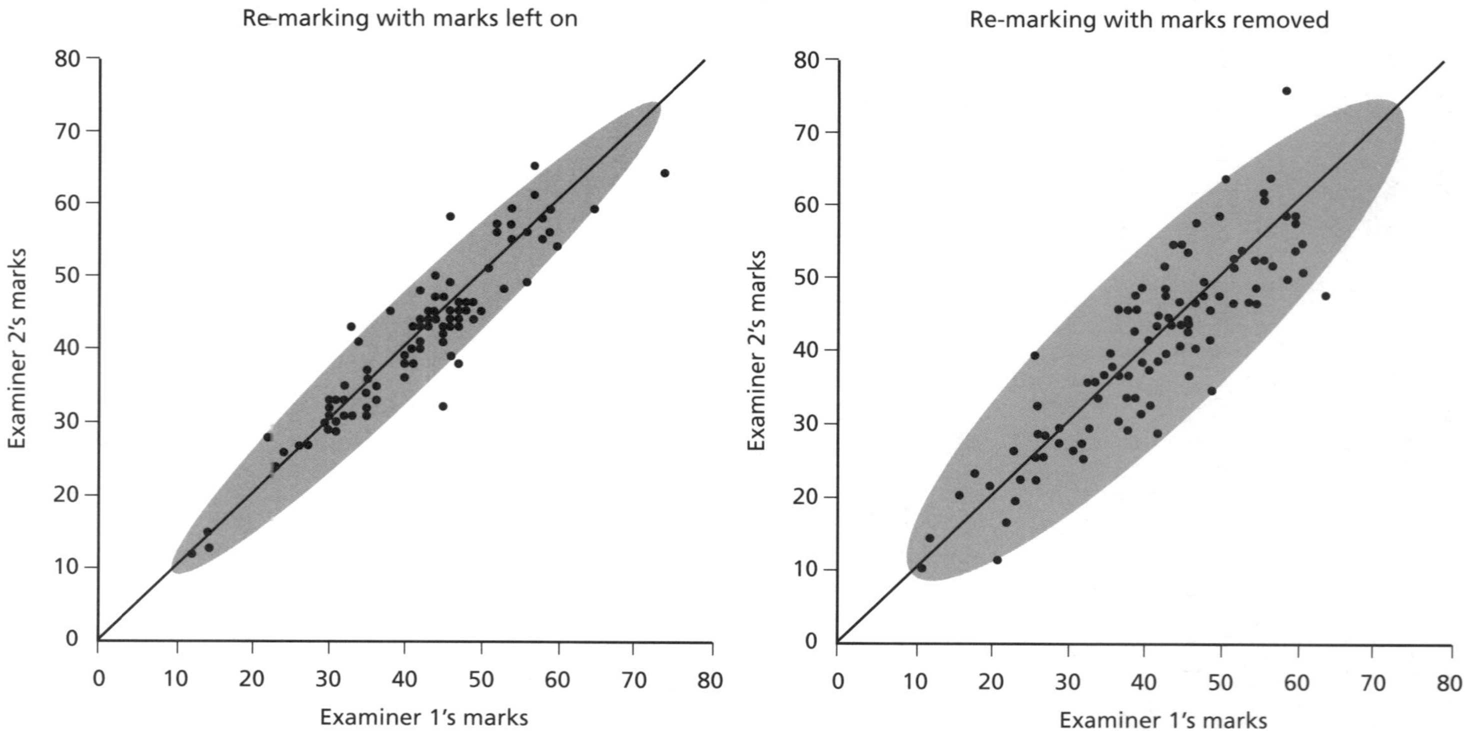

Redrawn with permission from R. J. L. Murphy, 'Removing the marks from examination scripts before re-marking them: does it make any difference?' *The British Journal of Educational Psychology*, vol. 49, p. 75. © 1979 The British Psychological Society.

In this examination the reliability is 0.87 and the contribution from the examiner's vagaries of judgment 0.13. That is to say, most of the marks are determined by what the candidate has written; but there are places, especially in an examination involving essay questions, where the marking scheme leaves the examiner uncertain. Different examiners make different choices, and those differences account for 13 per cent of (the squared differences between) the marks. When the original marks are left on, the examiner undertaking the re-marking can see what choice the original examiner made and takes that choice into account. Comparing the 0.065 with the 0.06 above, it can be seen that when the original marks are left on, the original examiner's mark is given a weight equal to the new mark in the re-assessment. Since the same original marks are available to both senior examiners, both are biased in the same way and the level of agreement rises to 94 per cent. This means that a re-marking with the original marks left on is only half a re-marking and it produces only half the number of revisions of grades previously awarded that one would otherwise expect. It happens that way because, when an examiner is uncertain, he or she is unable to disregard the manner in which his or her predecessor resolved that uncertainty.

The actual proportion of requests for a re-mark that successfully led to upgrading has varied over the years. In 1989 the Joint Matriculation Board had 80 000 A-level entrants. There were 3400 requests for a re-mark, of which 250 (7 per cent) resulted in an increased grade (Judd, 1991a). But recently, consequent on public pressure from parents, as in the letter reproduced above, the handling of requests for a re-mark has changed. The examination boards (now called 'awarding bodies') are required to deal with all such requests within 40 days (30 days where the re-mark might impact on admission to university); there is also an opportunity to appeal against the outcome. Looking specifically at requests for re-marking of an individual candidate's examination scripts (there are other categories of request), in the summer of 2000 there were 24 219 enquiries about A-level gradings of which 4343 (18 per cent) resulted in an upgrade. At AS-level there were 809 enquiries of which 148 (18 per cent) were successful, and for GCSE there were 20 819 enquries of which 4002 (19 per cent) resulted in an upgrade (Qualifications and Curriculum Authority, 2001). The success rate of requests for a remarking has now risen to about 18 per cent, whereas calculations (above) based on the reliability of public examinations suggest that no more than 7 per cent should be successful. That means that it is possible, for a fee of £25, to buy a small statistical advantage in GCSE and in A-level.

University examinations

Newspaper education correspondents write as they do about A-level examinations because A-level results are of great concern to the parents who buy the newspaper. They do not write about university examinations in the same way because the concern is not there. That does not mean that university examinations are above the kind of criticisms that beset A-levels; indeed, quite the contrary!

A-level scripts are marked once only by one of a panel of examiners according to a carefully standardised marking scheme. University examinations, on the other hand, are commonly marked twice, by the same examiners throughout, but (except for subjects like mathematics, engineering and physics) without any prior marking scheme. Does it make any difference?

There is a long history of disquiet over the reliability of university examinations, beginning with a study by Hartog, Rhodes and Burt (1936). They asked 17 examiners to mark a history examination comprising four three-hour papers, different examiners marking different papers. The correlations, calculated for individual papers, between the marks awarded by pairs of examiners ranged from +0.85 (satisfactory for a single three-hour paper, comparable to the reliability of public examinations) to –0.14 (that is to say, the two examiners were in actual disagreement). The median coefficient was +0.38, which has subsequently been found to be typical for an examination in which the candidates write essays (cf. Cox, 1967). Examinations in which the questions consist of problems to be solved (e.g., mathematics) pose less of a problem; reliability is then typically +0.95 or better.

Let us look at one university examination in detail (Laming, 1990). This examination consists of four three-hour papers. There are a large number of questions on each paper, each requiring an essay-type answer. The questions are divided into five sections, which cover different areas of the subject. The candidates are required to answer three questions from each paper taken from at least two different sections. There are five examiners, and each section is given to a different pair of examiners to mark. Initially the examiners mark each answer independently, without consultation and without entering any mark or comment on the scripts, and then meet in pairs to agree joint marks. The only published results from this examination are the class lists, which provide no grist at all for an education correspondent's mill. But a comparison of the examiners' original marks, that is, of the provisional marks as they stood before any consultation, affords some estimates of reliability.

The correlation between the marks independently awarded by pairs of examiners ranged from +0.13 to +0.72. But that understates the reliability because those independent marks are subsequently combined. Assuming, for simplicity, that the mark actually awarded by agreement between each pair of examiners is the average of their individual marks, that range of correlations converts into +0.23 to +0.84 according to the Spearman–Brown formula.

The Spearman–Brown formula

As before,

Let the 'true score' for a script be t.
Let Examiner X's mark be $x = t + a$.
Let Examiner Y's mark be $y = t + b$,

where the components *a*, *b* and *t* are all independent of each other. The average of Examiner X's mark and Examiner Y's mark is $t + \frac{1}{2}(a + b)$, and $\frac{1}{2}(a + b)$ has only half the variance of either *a* or *b*. So,

> if the ratio of Var(t) to Var(a) is r : 1–r,
> then the ratio of Var(t) to Var{$\frac{1}{2}$(a + b)} is r : $\frac{1}{2}$(1–r);
> and the ratio of Var(t) to the total variance is r : $\frac{1}{2}$(1+r).
> The improved reliability is therefore $2r/(1 + r)$.

This is the Spearman–Brown formula (Gulliksen, 1950, p. 63).

Even so, the reliability of the examination as a whole is still understated because the reliabilities so far calculated relate to single answers, a single hour's work in the examination room, and the fact that each candidate writes twelve answers altogether. Combining twelve marks, each of a reliability between +0.23 and +0.84, ought to be satisfactory. The Spearman–Brown formula for combining 12 independent marks is $12r/(1+11r)$ and it gives, in this case, a range of reliabilities from +0.78 to +0.98. But these reliabilities are not attained in practice.

The reason is that each candidate typically answers some questions much better than others. This variation in the quality of the answers from an individual candidate increases the apparent reliability of the marking of individual answers without improving the ultimate assessment of individual candidates. A more sophisticated calculation, taking this variation into account, gives a reliability for the assessment of individual candidates in this examination somewhere between +0.50 and +0.90; except that there were three cases (out of ten pairs of examiners – marks from two separate years were analysed) in which the examiners were in operational disagreement about the relative merits of the different candidates. It compares poorly with the reliability of public examinations.

This is not generally appreciated, not even amongst teachers. Here is the headmistress of South Hampstead High School complaining about A-level examinations.

> The truth is that A-levels, although the principal means of selection for university entrance, are not good predictors of degree success; again and again institutions have found poor correlation between A-level grade and degree class. (Burgess, 1991)

True – but it is the university degree examinations that are wobbly.

Degree standards

Each university examination is set and marked by examiners internal to the university, but in consultation with one examiner from outside. Given a continual and unsystematic interchange of external examiners between different universities, there ought, so the reasoning goes, to be a convergence of degree standards. In practice, this cross-moderation does not work. One external faced with five internal examiners cannot exert much pressure for change if he or she disagrees. So it is not surprising that the proportion of first-class honours and upper seconds (second class, first division) awarded in the same subject at different universities varies greatly. In one survey of university degrees in psychology the percentage of 'good' degrees was found to vary from 22 to 73 (Connolly and Smith, 1986), and another survey of degrees in geography revealed proportions ranging from 21 to 69 per cent, averaged over the 18 years from 1973 to 1990 (Chapman, 1994). From 1981 to 1990 there was a systematic increase in the proportion of 'good' degrees across all of the higher education sector, in geography, from 40 per cent (1973) to 52 per cent (1990). Nevertheless, 'the most striking result of the analysis is the stability of the position of individual departments relative to the overall mean' (Chapman, 1994, p. 96).

This might, of course, reflect differences in the quality of the student intake. But the relation between the proportion of 'good' degrees and A-level results is very tenuous, as also is the relation with every other factor that has been examined. Bee and Dolton (1985), analysing the degrees awarded throughout England in 1981, found that the proportion of 'good' degrees correlated +0.94 with the proportion in the same examination averaged over the past five years, but bore no demonstrable relation with anything else, not even with the A-level performance of the candidates three years previously. Each university examination is a law unto itself.

That lack of consistency between different university examinations applies also to comparisons from year to year. University examinations evolve. Tarsh (1990) compared the degree classes awarded by UK universities from 1981 to 1988. That survey provided education journalists with something to write about.

> Students have dramatically improved their performance over the past 10 years, with a substantially higher proportion gaining first and upper second class degrees, according to a study of academic results published today.
>
> The upper second has now become the 'typical' degree of university graduates.
>
> The Department of Education and Science analysed exam results of about 70 000 university graduates a year. Between 1981 and 1988, the percentage gaining firsts and upper seconds rose from 32 to 44 per cent for men and from 33 to 47 per cent for women.
>
> No one has been able to identify the reasons for the apparent improvement in standards (Whitfield, 1990).

There is no doubt about the increase in the level of published degree classes. But Tarsh identified 'a controversial but unavoidable possibility . . . that there has been a reduction in the standard required either just for firsts or throughout the degree class distribution' (p. 500). There is no way in which that possibility can be shown to be unfounded; indeed, in the absence of any enduring standard, the argument of Chapter 5 makes it only too plausible.

Summary – examining the examiners

The assessment of public examinations, especially those asking for essay-type answers, is necessarily subject to some uncertainty, leading to less than perfect reliability. This is not appreciated either by education journalists, or by politicians, or by parents, who attribute the vagaries of examination results to less than sufficient care and attention on the part of examination boards and their examiners. While insufficient care and attention might contribute some part of the variability of examination outcomes, there is also a variability intrinsic to the process of assessment. To the extent that the assessment of examination scripts is uncertain, that assessment will be biased. Bias is shown up in the re-marking exercises, and this is so notwithstanding that the public examination boards achieve a commendable standard of reliability. The special point of this chapter is that it is possible to measure the bias with simple calculations.

However, what is really lacking is any control over examination standards, both between boards and, more seriously, from one year to the next. In fact, it is difficult to see how standards could be effectively controlled, or even monitored.

The next chapter looks at another area of public life that has long been known to be subject to bias – the identification of a suspect by an eyewitness.

14 Eyewitness identification

A crime is committed.
Some people see a man running away from the scene.
'What did he look like?'

Later, a man is arrested.
The witnesses are called.
'Is this the man you saw?'

There is an insuperable difficulty in describing a face in words so that someone else can identify it at sight. We do not have sufficient words in our language for distinguishing the variety of different faces; nor do we use those words that we do have with sufficient consistency. Although, having once seen someone's face, we can often recognise that person again on next meeting, we are unable to communicate that memory to anyone else with useable accuracy (except in the case of some unusual deformity such as a large scar). That inability applies even to faces that we know very well, such as a wife or husband. We can all recognise some faces with great accuracy, but we cannot pass that accuracy on to anyone else.

The murder of P. Sgt Speed

P. Sgt Speed was shot in Kirkgate in the centre of Leeds while on duty on 31 October 1984. The murder of a serving police officer calls forth the utmost of investigative effort and persistence on the part of his colleagues. Nevertheless, Leeds police were unable to find the perpetrators. Their only leads depended on eyewitnesses recognising one or other of the two gunmen, who had escaped. There were many eyewitnesses, including one police constable who saw one of the gunmen very clearly, face to face. Yet the perpetrators could not be traced.

Some two and a half years later David Griseworth, the man who had actually shot P. Sgt. Speed, was arrested in connection with another crime, and his arrest led to the apprehension of his accomplice, Paul Guest. In this case it is known with certainty who the killers of P. Sgt. Speed were. With that knowledge it was possible to evaluate the many attempts at eyewitness identification in the course of the investigation, and the retrospective evaluation was sufficiently interesting and instructive for the entire investigation to be recreated for Crimewatch File

(Cleeve, 1988). I shall use the murder of P. Sgt Speed as a running example to illustrate the difficulties of identification by eyewitnesses.

P. Sgt. Speed and P. C. Thorpe were asked to investigate two men who had been reported to be acting suspiciously near a yellow Ford Cortina saloon. P. C. Thorpe grappled with one of the men who drew a revolver and shot Thorpe. Notwithstanding his very serious injury, P. C. Thorpe was able to radio a description of the gunman to the police station. Meanwhile the gunman walked away, but was intercepted by P. Sgt. Speed in a churchyard nearby. P. Sgt. Speed was shot dead. Further shots were fired as both men made their escape. (Cleeve, 1988).

P. C. Thorpe was in hospital, too ill to be interviewed, for six weeks. Nevertheless, there were about a hundred other people who had caught some glimpse of one or other of the gunmen as they escaped.

Police Officer	You see the man – that drew the gun . . . ?
Witness	I saw the man, yes.
Police Officer	What did he look like?
Witness	Just medium build, I would say.
Another witness	The man with the hat would have been about six foot, I would think.
Police Officer	Would you know him again if you saw him?
Second witness	No.

(From *Crimewatch File: The Murder of P. Sgt. Speed*, producer L. Cleeve. BBC1, 12 October 1988. © 1988 The British Broadcasting Corporation.)

The police have a variety of different descriptions; which one do they put out to the public at large, asking for information? There are many witnesses who saw one or other of the men, but none who is confident of recognising them again.

Six weeks after the murder P. C. Thorpe was sufficiently recovered to give an account of what had happened that day to the investigating officers. He was asked, in particular, if there was anybody in the room that was of a similar build to the gunman.

> Would you come out then, Peter, please? This is the type of man that we're looking for, the heavily built man, round about thirty-eight/forty, big shoulders, very strong. When you knock on the next door and you see a man of this description, you want to be giving him a really good look. (Cleeve, 1988)

Photofit

A face cannot be described in words so that someone else can recognise it. Accordingly, police forces have developed systems which enable witnesses to express what they remember in terms of a standard alphabet of facial components. Photofit is the British system. It consists of segments of photographs of faces, which can be fitted together in any required combination. There are

195 different hairlines and ears to choose from, 99 eyes and eyebrows, 89 noses, 105 mouths, 74 chins and cheeks, and a range of accessories. Additional details such as a scar can be drawn on a transparent cover placed over the photographic components selected.

The alternative is an artist's sketch drawn to the eyewitness's direction, and that is still sometimes used. After Stephanie Slater, an estate agent's negotiator from Birmingham who was abducted on 22 January 1992, had been released a week later, she spent about ten days being debriefed by the police. During that debriefing an artist drew a sketch of her abductor to her specification, but it took several days before the police had a sketch they deemed worth publishing (Kirby, 1992). The advantage of photofit is that it dispenses with the need for an artist's skills. But it is still sufficiently complicated that an experienced operator is needed to help in constructing a photofit according to the witness's direction.

However, we still need to ask how reliable identification from a photofit is. In one experiment (Ellis, Shepherd and Davies, 1975), photographs were taken of 36 men, all of them white. Six of these photographs were selected at random and given to six different people with a request to construct a photofit of each one. So there are six sets of six photofits, each set made by a different person to match the same six originals. Each set of photofits was now given to a group of twelve subjects with a request to pick out the six photographs (from the original 36) which they thought the photofits had been constructed to match. There were 72 subjects, each picking six from the original 36 photographs, making a total of 436 choices. Fifty-four of those choices were correct; that is, one in eight. Bearing in mind that someone who had never seen the photofits at all would nevertheless get about one in 36 correct by chance, this can hardly be considered 'good'.

One of the difficulties with a photofit is that the very visible boundaries between the components disrupts the perception of it as a face. In a further experiment (Ellis, Davies and Shepherd, 1978) people were tested on their recognition of photographs from the original collection of 36 faces and also on photographs of photofits made to match those faces. The original photographs (87% correct) were recognised more easily than the photographs of the photofits (75% correct, making the recognition in this latter case, not with respect to the original photographs, but to photographs of the photofits). The difference was due to the lines dividing the segments of the photofits, since recognition of original photographs with random lines superimposed (73% correct) was about the same as photographs of photofits.

Photofit has now been superseded by 'E-Fit' (Electronic Facial Identification Technique), which enables combination of the same graphic elements, but on a computer screen and without the dividing lines. Figure 14.1 below shows an example.

Alexandra Griffiths

On 11 January 1990 at about 7 pm Alexandra Griffiths, then about 36 hours old, was taken from her cot in St Thomas' Hospital, Lambeth, by a bogus 'health visitor'. The baby's mother, Dawn Griffiths, gave a description to the police who asked an artist to draw a sketch of the abductor according to the mother's instructions. That impression is reproduced in Figure 14.2. An artist's sketch was used in this instance because it was impracticable to ask a mother, still recovering in hospital after childbirth, to cope with the multitude of elements that make up the photofit system. The artist's sketch (Figure 14.2) was issued on 14 January, three days after the abduction, and published in the national press. The baby's mother subsequently recorded her recollection a second time in the E-fit shown in Figure 14.1.

Comparison of these two pictures gives some idea of the repeatability of a pictorial impression constructed by one person according to another's recollection. There are two sources of variability. First, in constructing the E-fit the mother was required to select from the alphabet of facial components stored in the computer, while, in directing the artist who produced Figure 14.2, she was effectively choosing from an analogous and implicit set of components that comprised, as it were, that particular artist's repertoire in the depiction of faces. As we have already seen, a verbal description alone is quite inadequate. So Dawn Griffiths' directions to the artist had to take the form of asking for changes in an already existing preliminary sketch (the principle of relativity again) and were thereby relative to what the artist had already drawn. Moreover, any direction to the artist to change this or that detail had to be given in words and interpreted by the artist according to his or her experience of human faces. The witness is as much restricted by the artist's experience and style of drawing as she is by the alphabet of facial elements available in the computer.

Figure 14.1 The E-fit of the abductor of Alexandra Griffiths compiled under her mother's direction.

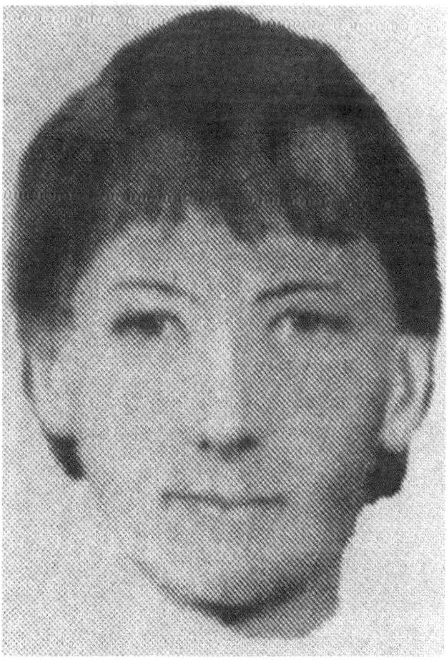

A second source of variability subsists in the accuracy of the mother's recollection. In endeavouring to express her memory in pictorial form, Dawn Griffiths would have viewed many different trial faces as possible representations of her baby's abductor. Successive comparisons of that sort open the way to confusion. After a while the witness might begin to recall one of the trial faces in place of the original or, at least, an amalgam of the two. The recollection can evolve. The chin in Figure 14.2 is much more pointed than it is in Figure 14.1. Which is correct? Indeed, is either correct?

The E-Fit in Figure 14.1 was published in the national press and broadcast on television in the hope that someone would recognise the abductor and lead the police to her. And that is how the case was resolved. After fifteen days a tip-off led police to where the baby and her abductor were living; and Alexandra Griffiths was restored to her mother. The abductor, Janet Griffiths (no relation to the baby's mother) appeared briefly in court on 29 January and afterwards the sketch in Figure 14.3 was drawn by Julia Quenzler from memory. It provides a check on the fidelity of both the E-fit (Figure 14.1) and the original artist's sketch (Figure 14.2). Figure 14.3 is not a photograph; it is constrained by Julia Quenzler's style in drawing faces, much as an E-fit is restricted to the alphabet of facial components stored in the police computer. But in Figure 14.3 the error, introduced into Figure 14.2 when an eyewitness communicates her recollection

Figure 14.2 An artist's impression of the abductor drawn according to the mother's instructions.

Figure 14.3 Janet Griffiths – the abductor, not the mother.

Artist's sketch by Julia Quentzler from her memory of Janet Griffiths' appearance in court.

to an artist in words, is eliminated; the eyewitness and the artist are one. Moreover, this is an eyewitness who has been trained to observe and reproduce faces and who had attended court especially for that purpose.

Honor Loudon

But the real point of this story concerns Honor Loudon who at that time was the mother of a four-month-old baby.

> When I was shopping at a big south London supermarket the next day, I thought nothing of it when the cashier asked me how old the baby strapped to my front was. I was only slightly surprised when I was packing the shopping into the back of my car to be asked again, by a passer-by, how old my baby was.
>
> When, the following day, I was asked five times during a brief walk down Putney High Street how old my baby was it dawned on me that I was in south London, with short brown hair and a pointy face and was carrying a young baby on my front half-hidden by my coat.
>
> My reaction was to feel pleased that the public was being so vigilant and that everyone was keeping their eyes open. I felt less pleased and more disturbed as

Figure 14.4 Honor Loudon.

Reproduced with permission from H. Loudon, 'When the wrong face fits'. *Independent*, 31 January 1990, p. 13. Photograph Richard Smith. © 1990 Independent Newspapers (UK) Ltd.

> the days went by and I continued to be questioned by passers-by wherever I went. When two policemen came to the door one afternoon, I was relieved to discover they were following up a query from a member of the public about my baby and were not there because some disaster had befallen my other two children, who were at school, or my husband, who was driving across England at the time.
>
> No one could resent his or her identity being mistaken in this way, though of course it is slightly unnerving to discover that people are following you home in order to give your name to the police. (Loudon, 1990)

The comparison between Figures 14.1, 14.2, 14.3 and 14.4 provides one practical impression of the fidelity of photo-identification methods.

It has to be said that sometimes a E-fit or an artist's sketch does lead to the apprehension of the offender.

> The skills of an elderly portrait artist have helped to catch a burglar who forced his way into her home armed with a knife.
>
> While the image of the intruder was fresh in her mind, Patricia Mynott sketched the outline of his face on the back of an envelope. Her drawing of the

> gaunt, fair-haired burglar, knife in hand, was so accurate that it was recognised by detectives as the face of a convicted criminal, Stephen Lawson. (Horsnell, 2002)

At the same time, an E-fit may resemble some entirely unconnected person. The misidentification of Honor Loudon alerts us to the possibility, well known to the law, that someone might be apprehended and even convicted as the result of a mistaken identification. It is clear that constructed faces are better than mere verbal descriptions, but they are not good enough by themselves and do not compare for reliability with recognition by the original eyewitness. So, if at all possible, that original witness must view the suspect directly to effect an identification. But the problems are not over yet, not even when an eyewitness views a suspect directly.

Show-ups

There are two procedures traditionally used by police forces for obtaining an eyewitness's verdict on the identity of a suspect; there is the 'show-up' and the 'line-up' or (in the United Kingdom) 'identity parade'.

Alfred Hitchcock's film *The Wrong Man* reconstructs for the cinema a true story that took place in New York in January 1953. In his book *Hitchcock* François Truffaut describes this film as 'a fairly faithful account of a real-life news story', and Alfred Hitchcock, whom he is interviewing in that book, does not disagree. Hitchcock explains:

> . . . for the sake of authenticity everything was minutely reconstructed with the people who were actually involved in that drama. We even used some of them in some of the episodes and, wherever possible, relatively unknown actors. We shot on the locations where the events really took place. Inside the prison we observed how the inmates handle their bedding and their clothes; then we found an empty cell for Fonda and we made him handle these routines exactly as the real inmates had done. We also used the actual psychiatric rest home to which the wife was sent and had the actual doctors playing themselves. (Truffaut, 1968, p. 199)

Early in the film Manny Balestrero is helping the New York Police with their enquiries. There have been a number of hold-ups in the neighbourhood, all pulled off by the same man, and Balestrero is taken by car to two of the stores where the hold-ups took place. Balestrero is instructed to 'Walk in, walk to the back of the store, turn around and come out again.' The storekeeper, of course, is expecting him. 'Is this the man who robbed you?' (Hitchcock, 1956).

The storekeeper, of course, cannot help but know that this is the police suspect. Is such a procedure fair? How many men other than the perpetrator would have been identified as such under those circumstances? If no-one ever recognised anyone else wrongly, a show-up would be satisfactory. But mistaken identifications do happen (and Manny Balestrero was one such, which is the point of Hitchcock's film). Each of us can identify a small number of people without error; and while there is a much larger number of people whom we are sure we have never seen before, there are yet others about whom we are unsure. The nature of eyewitness identification is such that the perpetrator usually falls into the witness's 'unsure' group. If there is uncertainty about recognising the perpetrator face-to-face, there is necessarily room for bias. 'This is the man the police suspect.'

At the very least, an identification resulting from a show-up has to be treated with great caution. If an eyewitness confidently says 'No', the police have most likely got the wrong person, but if the witness says 'Yes' or 'Probably', that evidence should be treated as no more than circumstantial. Nevertheless, show-ups still sometimes take place.

Sammy Davis

Sammy Davis was jailed for six years in 1987 for the rape of a Swedish student in a mini-cab office in North London. There was no dispute that the rape took place, or that it occurred in a mini-cab office, or that the attacker was black. But Justice, the law reform organisation, questioned the identification of the mini-cab office by the victim when she was driven around the area by the police. If the identification of the mini-cab office was correct, then so also was the identification of the rapist; but there were sufficient inconsistencies and inaccuracies in the victim's story to cast doubt on that identification.

Once he had been accused, Sammy Davis unwisely volunteered to meet – indeed, insisted on meeting – the victim face-to-face in a show-up. The victim thereupon identified Davis as her attacker. If Davis had had nothing to do with the attack (a matter that only he can know for certain), he would have reasoned that if the victim were actually to see him face-to-face, she would immediately realise that she had never seen him before. But not so. Sammy Davis is black. Sweden has a very small black population, and the victim failed to distinguish between one black mini-cab driver and another. The victim admitted to little experience of black people and partly for this reason could not attempt to put an age to her assailant (Justice, 1990, §32). It has, indeed, been shown that people recognise faces of their own race best. It is thought that this happens because prior experience of similar faces provides a basis for distinguishing between one face and another (Chance, Goldstein and McBride, 1975). That basis becomes crucial in a show-up. Suppose the Swedish victim had been faced with two or more black taxi-drivers; she would, at the least, have realised how uncertain her identification was.

Identity parades

A line-up, or identity parade, addresses the principal criticism of the show-up. The police suspect is placed in a line with several other people of similar appearance. If the eyewitness is unable to make a reliable identification, he or she may well pick someone whom the police know to be uninvolved, or may decide that he or she cannot be sure whether the perpetrator is present at all. But that does not, of itself, mean that the line-up is free from criticism.

Prior to his arrest by the police Manny Balestrero had visited his life assurance office to find out how much he could borrow on his wife's insurance policy. While he was at the office counter, two women clerks identified him, to each other, as the man who had tried to rob the office two weeks previously. They informed the police, and that was how Manny Balestrero's troubles started.

Back in the police station after the show-ups, Manny Balestrero is ushered into fourth place in a line-up of six men, all similarly dressed in hats and overcoats. The two women clerks from the insurance office observe the men through a doorway, from another room. 'Please look at the men from right to left; count them off, and when you come to the one you can identify, stop.' (Hitchcock, 1956) Now, is such an identification procedure fair?

(i) The police do not know who carried out the robberies they are investigating. They believe Manny Balestrero to be responsible, but that belief is not knowledge. So it could be that the line-up is wholly comprised of innocent men. But in the absence of any warning to the contrary, an eyewitness is likely to assume that the perpetrator of the crime is one of those present – otherwise why should the police hold such a parade at all? – and so select the member of the parade most resembling the perpetrator. This will usually be the suspect.

The Devlin committee (Devlin, 1976, §5.63) looked in detail at two then recent cases of certain misidentification against a background of increasing concern about the reliability of identification procedures. They recommended that the police explain to each witness that the person who actually committed the crime might not be in the parade at all, and an identification should be made only if the witness was certain. No such warning was given in the episode recreated in *The Wrong Man*.

(ii) The two identifications by the women clerks were not independent; the second woman had already heard the identification made by her colleague. If identification is difficult, overhearing someone else's identification will bias the witness's judgment. The autokinetic experiment by Hood and Sherif (1962; see Chapter 6) speaks directly to this point.

(iii) But in *The Wrong Man* these first unfairnesses are no more than academic in relation to the third. Both women clerks had seen Manny Balestrero the previous day; there is no question about that – Manny Balestrero had been traced by means of the insurance policy he submitted for inspection. Moreover, both women had taken a very careful look at Manny Balestrero while he was at the office counter because of the suggestion by one to the other that this was the man

> who had previously tried to rob the office. The likelihood of a mistake in their identifications was tiny. The women's identifications were then taken as positive evidence that Manny Balestrero was, in truth, the criminal; but, in fact, the women were simply identifying Manny Balestrero as the man they had seen in the assurance office the previous day. Their identifications did not tell the police anything they did not already know.

In *The Wrong Man* Manny Balestrero is ultimately proved innocent when the real criminal is caught in the course of a further robbery.

Carole Richardson

The women clerks in *The Wrong Man* identified Manny Balestrero in the line-up because they had seen him only the previous day. In other contexts, if the witness has seen a photograph of the suspect in a newspaper, perhaps, the witness's judgment is likely to be compromised.

On Saturday, 5 October 1974, at about 8.50 pm a bomb exploded in the Horse and Groom, Guildford. Five people were killed and more than 50 injured. Later the same evening, at about 9.35 pm, a similar bomb exploded in the Seven Stars, about two hundred yards away. In the first phase of their investigation the police traced and interviewed almost everyone who had been present in either pub on that evening. They were told about a 'courting couple' who had been sitting in the Horse and Groom just where the bomb later exploded, but who had not come forward to be identified. They had twelve witnesses ready to attend an identification parade if that couple could be found.

The second phase of the police investigation began with a tip-off and led in the course of five days to the arrest of more than forty people, one of whom was Carole Richardson. The police believed that she had been the female partner in the courting couple and put her on an identity parade. None of the twelve witnesses picked her out. Nevertheless, at the trial of the Guildford Four in October 1975 Carole Richardson was sentenced to imprisonment for life.

Continued public concern over the safety of all the Guildford Four's convictions led to a second and ultimately successful appeal in November 1989. In preparation for that appeal the police re-interviewed the eyewitnesses who had attended the identity parade in 1974.

> Among those who attended the parade were Eileen Burns, her husband Robert, and their daughter Carol. They were called in because they said they had been in the Horse and Groom pub in Guildford shortly before the bomb exploded on 5 October 1974. They had arrived at 7 pm and had seen a courting couple, sitting where the bomb was planted. Mr Burns said the couple left at 7.40 pm.
>
> Police alleged at the time that the courting couple were Carole Richardson and Paddy Armstrong. But the Burns family, like all the other witnesses, failed to identify Miss Richardson in the line-up. [Only Carole Richardson had been put on parade.]

> In the new statements from the Burns family . . . Mrs Burns, recalling the parade, says: 'I did, in fact, recognise one of the girls as being one I had seen in the pub at Guildford on the night of the explosion. Because I was not 100 per cent certain, and because I was very nervous of the situation, I did not, in fact, make an identification.'
>
> She added that after the parade all the other witnesses agreed with her, although none had picked Miss Richardson out.
>
> Mrs Burns also said: 'When the trial of the accused people was under way at the Old Bailey I saw news photographs of a woman who was accused of planting the bomb in the pub.
>
> 'I am certain that the woman in the photographs was the same woman I had seen on the identification parade and in the pub at Guildford on the night of the explosion.' (Helm, 1989)

Much of the ground truth of this crime is known, and it is certain that Carole Richardson was not one of the courting couple in the Horse and Groom that night. But, subsequent to the identity parade, Mrs Burns saw newspaper photographs of Carole Richardson and recognised her (quite correctly) as the person she had seen on the parade. She also (incorrectly) referred that identification backwards in time to the woman (the real perpetrator) she saw in the pub. Because she had not seen the newspaper photographs before she attended the identity parade, she was unable to make any identification at that time.

How accurate is eyewitness identification?

The stories recounted above raise these questions: How accurate is eyewitness identification? Is it safe to convict solely on a single eyewitness identification? There have been a sufficient number of miscarriages of justice for the answer to the second question to be clearly 'No'. Supposing the eyewitness was confident that his or her identification was correct? There have been a sufficient number of mistaken identifications when the eyewitness was confident, that the answer is still 'No'. Indeed, it is a matter of experimental research whether confidence has anything to do with accuracy at all.

There has been continuing experimental research on the accuracy of eyewitness identification and on the factors that might bias it. It may be taken for granted that show-ups are too unreliable to be worth experimental study, and all the studies which follow look at the accuracy of identification from an identity parade. Even so, there are problems of comparability.

In the outside world, the perpetrators of a crime are initially seen live and, often, only very briefly. Experiments in a laboratory with volunteer subjects who know what it is about, who are primed to report what they see as accurately as they can, are not really comparable. Likewise, the crime or other incident in a laboratory experiment is often presented as a sequence of slides or as a video recording, with the volunteer subjects having a clear view of what is going on; that also fails to achieve comparability with the world outside. These problems persist because it is difficult to circumvent them. But here is one of the more realistic studies.

Buckhout (1980)

> A scenario was developed for a stimulus crime film to create a fast-moving crime, with a limited view of the face of the perpetrator of the crime, some distractions, and a high level of mundane realism. Based on statistics on street muggings in New York City, the whole incident, involving a victim being knocked to the ground and a purse being stolen, took only 13 sec, including 3.5 sec in which the face of the 'perpetrator' was clearly visible. The film was shot by a professional camera crew from WNBC News, using 16-mm color/sound film and studio lighting.
>
> The scenario has a young woman (the victim) walking down a hallway, with the perpetrator lurking in a doorway. Suddenly, the man runs up behind the woman, knocks her down, grabs her purse, and runs forward toward the camera, while the woman screams. The perpetrator wore a hat, a leather jacket, jeans, sneakers, and a small mustache. To test recognition, a separate filmed lineup was shot by the same film crew. Five stand-ins were recruited who matched the general physical features and appearance of the perpetrator and stood with him in the lineup. The perpetrator had removed his mustache and changed to ordinary sports clothes similar to that worn by the stand-ins. The lineup film pictured an overall view of the six men standing against a wall. Each showed a number from 1 to 6 on his chest; the perpetrator was in the number 2 position.
>
> The crime film was shown on the air during a special 5-min segment of the local news program devoted to the problems of eyewitness testimony and recognition testing. Following a discussion of the problems, the crime film was shown, and members of the viewing audience were informed that they were all witnesses to a crime. Approximately 2 min later, the announcer presented the lineup film, asking the viewers to look carefully at each man and decide if they recognized anyone. They were shown an overview of the lineup and a close-up of each man. A special phone number was flashed on the screen, and the viewers were urged to call and report their lineup choice number to one of our student volunteers. If they were convinced that the perpetrator was not in the lineup, viewers were to state the number '0'. . . . The response was overwhelming, with jammed phone lines, over 2000 recorded responses, plus numerous comments. (Reprinted with permission from R. Buckhout, 'Nearly 2000 witnesses can be wrong'. *Bulletin of the Psychonomic Society*, vol. 16, p. 308. © 1980 The Psychonomic Society Inc.)

Of the 2145 viewers who phoned in, 302 picked the correct man in the line-up. As a proportion of the total, 302 is very close indeed to the 1 in 7 that one would expect by chance (six men in the line-up plus the option of saying that the perpetrator was not there). Further showings of the film at legal conferences

Table 14.1 Eyewitness identifications from Buckhout (1980).

Group	Position in line-up						Not in line-up	Total
	1st	Mugger	3rd	4th	5th	6th		
TV Audience	322	302	221	285	314	145	556	2145
Conferences	64	58	25	27	49	11	59	293

provided additional identifications falling into much the same pattern. So, when the problems of comparability with real street incidents are attended to in earnest, the level of recognition is not distinct from chance.

Buckhout's study tells us that in many actual cases eyewitness identification will be very difficult indeed. It will be comparable to judging the extent of autokinetic movement, with witnesses much influenced by extraneous suggestion from, for example, someone else who has just viewed the same identity parade. The kinds of extraneous suggestions or unwitting assumptions that might bias someone's identification include:

> 'The police believe they have the criminal in this line-up' – (of course they do); and (in a show-up)
>
> 'This is the police suspect.'

Egan, Pittner and Goldstein (1977)

To put Buckhout's study into perspective, here is another, more conventional, experiment.

> Subjects were brought into a small conference room in groups of from five to ten, and were seated directly in front of a large one-way mirror. They were informed about the general nature of the study, and were instructed to role-play an eyewitness to a crime. The role-play instructions portrayed the subjects as accidental witnesses to a crime in which two men robbed and shot a store proprietor while the witnesses remained hidden from view. Subjects were told to imagine that each was the sole witness and that their identification of the criminal would be crucial.
>
> Subjects viewed two confederates, who were the 'criminals' (hereinafter called 'targets') in the hypothetical robbery. The two targets entered the room on the other side of the glass partition, stopped in front of the mirror, then left the room. Both targets were dressed alike in blue jeans and white T-shirts, and were visible to the subjects for approximately 15 seconds. (Egan *et al.*, 1977).

Identification was tested with either a live five-man line-up or a photospread of the same size. All the men in the line-up or in the photospread were dressed alike in jeans and T-shirt, but only one had been a target. The other four were stand-ins whom the witnesses had not seen before, so it was possible for one of the stand-ins to be identified as the second target. The target was detected 98% of the time in the live line-up (only one subject failed to pick him out) and 85% with the photospread. That is hardly suprising when subjects have been primed and have a clear view of the participants, but, at the same time, they tend to mistake one of the stand-ins for the absent second participant. This happened on 67% of the identification tests.

Whether or not the 'witnesses' have a clear view of the 'criminals' and whether or not they have been primed in advance make a great difference to the accuracy of the subsequent identification. In a laboratory study the 'witnesses' are of necessity volunteers, from whom it is difficult to hide the nature of the experiment. In real life the crime happens without any public warning and witnesses are, of necessity, unprepared. That lack of preparedness means that witnesses in real life tend not to get a good view of the criminals because they do not realise, until after it has happened, what was going on and, therefore, what it would have been useful to have noted carefully.

P. C. Thorpe

The one exception is when the witness is a policeman, especially a policeman who knows or suspects he may be apprehending a criminal. Not only is he primed (like the witnesses in the second laboratory study), but he is also trained to observe those details that might assist subsequent identification. How did P. C. Thorpe perform in the task of identifying the man who shot P. Sgt. Speed?

P. C. Thorpe was shown 9872 faces and, though his assailant was in that file, he failed to pick him out. Ultimately, David Griseworth was arrested in connection with a series of armed robberies at supermarkets. In the course of his arrest Griseworth accidently shot and killed himself. P. C.Thorpe was asked to go and look at the body, but still could not positively identify him as the guman.

> I felt very bad when it came out that Griseworth had been the gunman, because I hadn't identified him. All this time, this two-and-a-half years, I been telling everybody that I would know this man, that I would recognise him. And I didn't recognise him. (Cleeve, 1988)

Instructions to the witness

Inaccuracies in eyewitness identification, especially false identifications, have long been a matter of concern because they can lead to a defendant being convicted of a crime of which he or she is innocent. In 1976 the Devlin Committee recommended that police should explicitly warn witnesses viewing identity parades that the perpetrator they had seen might not be present. But does it matter? Here is another experiment.

> Approximately 350 students from introductory courses in behavioral science and psychology were assembled in a large lecture hall for a biofeedback demonstration. During a pause in the demonstration an act of vandalism was staged. The vandal, a male confederate of the investigators, entered the room, spoke with the instructor, and was asked to wait next to a rack of apparatus. The vandal changed a switch setting on the apparatus, and the instructor asked him not to. The vandal, however, changed settings twice more, to which the instructor responded with increasing anger. The vandal responded to the last of these by shouting an obscenity, pushing the electronic rack to the floor, and escaping through a rear door. The vandal was visible to the audience for 85 sec. The audience's response was a distinctly audible gasp. Twenty minutes after the vandalism a state police officer arrived and interviewed faculty members and a few persons who were seated close to the vandalism. The audience was then told that the vandalism had been staged and that the vandal was a confederate of the investigators. A questionnaire was distributed, and members of the audience were asked to volunteer to attend one of the lineups to be held on the following three evenings. One hundred witnesses (74 women, 26 men) appeared for these lineups. (Malpass and Devine, 1981, p. 484)

There were two different kinds of instruction given to the witnesses who attended the line-ups. The biased instruction read:

> 'We believe that the person who pushed over the electronics equipment during the EEG demonstration is present in the lineup. Look carefully at each of the five individuals in the lineup. Which of these is the person you saw push over the equipment? Circle the number of his position in the lineup below.' The eyewitnesses receiving this instruction were provided with five numbers (1–5) from which they could choose. Witnesses who wished to reject all five of the persons in the lineup had to ask how to indicate their judgment because no place was provided for such a response. Those witnesses who did ask were told that 'if you believe that the vandal is not one of the people in the lineup, write that on the identification form'.

The unbiased instruction, however, explicitly provided the witnesses with a 'no choice' option. It read:

> 'The person who pushed over the electronics equipment during the EEG demonstration may be one of the five individuals in the lineup. It is also possible that he is not in the lineup. Look carefully at each of the five individuals in the lineup. If the person you saw push over the equipment is not in the lineup, circle 0. If the person is present in the lineup, circle the number of his position.' The witnesses receiving this instruction were provided with six numbers from which to choose (0–5). (Malpass and Devine, 1981, p. 484)

Some of the hundred witnesses were tested with the vandal present in the line-up and some without; their respective identifications are set out in Table 14.2. There was no difference between the two sets of instructions, biased and

Table 14.2 Identifications in a 5-man line-up from Malpass and Devine (1981).

Group	Vandal	Foil (4 out of 5)	Not in line-up	Total
Biased instructions:				
Vandal present	21	7	0	28
Vandal absent	—	17	5	22
Unbiased instructions:				
Vandal present	19	0	4	23
Vandal absent	—	9	18	27

unbiased, in the frequency with which the vandal was identified when he was present. But when witnesses failed to identify the vandal or when he was not present, those who had received the biased instructions were much more ready to identify one of the stand-ins, whom they had not seen before, as the person who pushed over the rack of electronic equipment. There were very few witnesses with the biased instructions who said the vandal was not present; but with the unbiased instructions witnesses were ready to say the vandal was not present, sometimes even when he was there, and identifications of stand-ins (in real life these would always be innocent people) were much fewer.

One might argue that because the additional participants brought in to make up a real-life identity parade are known to have nothing to do with the crime, (mis)identification of one of these stand-ins does not matter. But that misses the point, which is that the police cannot know whether or not they have the real perpetrator in their parade. This means that the police suspect might be, effectively, another stand-in, with the real criminal absent. If witnesses tend to identify an innocent stand-in as the person they saw at the scene of the crime, they will equally tend to identify the police suspect in the case that he also has nothing to do with the crime; and, because the police suspect is not known to be innocent, his or her identification could ultimately lead to a miscarriage of justice.

Realism of the line-up

Notwithstanding that the act of vandalism in the course of a university lecture was realistically staged, the audience were told that it had been staged and so knew that there were no legal consequences depending on their identifications. In real life, on the other hand, such identifications are always made with a view to accumulating evidence against a suspected criminal. Does it matter that the audience know that the incident has been staged? Does such knowledge invalidate a comparison with real-life identity parades?

This question was addressed in another study. Subjects were engaged, one at a time, to take part in an experiment. They were told they would be playing a TV game and taking a test of perceptual ability as part of an investigation of game strategies. But, in reality, they were there to witness a staged crime.

> The subject was told the room number for the experiment and told that he/she would be allowed to practice in private for a few minutes. As the subject entered the room, the perpetrator was in the final process of disconnecting the TV game from the TV. The perpetrator appeared startled and hurriedly put the TV game under his jacket. The perpetrator then dropped his screwdriver, picked it up while looking at the subject, and brushed past the subject as he ran out of the room. As the perpetrator ran down the hall, he looked over his shoulder three times to see if he was being followed. After a few minutes, the experimenter arrived and discovered that the TV game was missing. The experimenter told the subject that a theft had occurred and that Campus Security would be called.
>
> After supposedly calling Campus Security, the experimenter told the subject–witness that 'Campus Security says other things have been stolen from this building recently, and Campus Security thinks there may be a connection between the thefts and all the maintenance work that is being done in the building lately. They say that they have pictures of the maintenance men who have been working in the building and have been waiting for an opportunity to show the pictures to someone. Campus Security says that they'll be right along and that they want you to wait for them' (Murray and Wells, 1982, p. 46).

The subject–witnesses were asked to make identifications from a six-man photospread. Half the subjects were told that the theft had been staged; the other half were left uninformed. Half of each half saw a photospread with the perpetrator included; the others saw a photospread with the perpetrator replaced with an additional stand-in of similar physical appearance. The most obvious difference in the identifications in Table 14.3 (it has nothing to do with knowing that the

Table 14.3 Identifications in a 6-man photospread from Murray and Wells (1982).

Group	Vandal	Foil (5 out of 6)	Not in photospread	Total
Informed witnesses:				
Vandal present	20	6	20	46
Vandal absent	5*	16	25	46
Uninformed witnesses:				
Vandal present	12	17	17	46
Vandal absent	5*	12	29	46

* Choice of stand-in, similar in appearance to thief

theft had been staged) was that the additional stand-in (the real perpetrator being absent) was selected much less frequently than the perpetrator was when he was present. Instead, subjects selected one of the other five members of the photospread (the same five stand-ins in every case) or declared that the perpetrator was not present. But there were some other, lesser, differences that did depend on whether the witness had been informed that the theft had been staged. Briefly, those witnesses who were told that the whole incident was part of an experiment picked the perpetrator out more often when he was present, and picked one of the other five stand-ins less often, than did those witnesses who had not been so informed. Knowing that the whole affair had been staged has, possibly, the contrary effect to what one might expect.

Witness confidence and accuracy

Eyewitness identification is known to be unreliable. For that reason the police will ask, 'Are you sure?' In court a witness will often be asked whether he is confident that his identification is correct, and juries tend to suppose, in cases of conflicting evidence, that those eyewitnesses who declare themselves confident are more likely to be correct. But is that supposition borne out by experiment?

In each of the last two experiments (Malpass and Devine, 1981; Murray and Wells, 1982) the subjects were asked, in addition to the question about identification, how confident they were that their identification was correct or, as the case might be, their assertion that the perpetrator was absent from the line-up. 'How sure are you that this is the man?' or 'How sure are you that none of these is the man?' In the second of these experiments (Murray and Wells, 1982) involving the staged theft of a TV game, some witnesses were informed that the theft had been staged as part of the study, while others were left thinking that they had witnessed a real crime. Among the first group of witnesses, who knew that the incident had been staged, there was some small relationship between confidence and accuracy (correlation +0.280, small, but significant at 0.01); but amongst the second group, who thought it had been a real crime, there was no relationship at all (correlation –0.004).

If that lack of correlation between witness confidence and accuracy sounds counter-intuitive, the levels of confidence expressed by the subjects in the experiment by Malpass and Devine (1981) show how it comes about. In that experiment a vandal had knocked over a rack of electronic apparatus in a staged incident during the course of a lecture. Some witnesses viewed a line-up containing the vandal, while others viewed a line-up from which the vandal was missing. Those witnesses who generally lacked confidence did not make an identification. This was so whether the vandal was present in the line-up or not. Confident witnesses, on the other hand, did make an identification and, when the vandal was present in the line-up, were usually correct. Taking all the witnesses together – the confident with the less confident – when faced with a line-up in which the vandal was present, there was a strong positive relationship between confidence and accuracy. But when the vandal was absent from the

Table 14.4 Correlations between witness confidence and accuracy from Malpass and Devine (1981).

Instructions to witness	Vandal present	Vandal absent
Biased	0.43	–0.84
Unbiased	0.95	–0.85

Overall correlation –0.06

line-up, the confident witnesses still made an identification that was, of necessity, wrong; and in this second case (with the vandal absent) there was an equally strong inverse relationship between confidence and accuracy. Now, in any real identity parade the police cannot know whether they have the criminal present or not, so these two cases, vandal present vs vandal absent, cannot be separated. The relationship that needs to be noted, then, is the correlation between confidence and accuracy irrespective of whether the vandal is present in the line-up – and that overall correlation turned out to be negligible. The correlations from Malpass and Devine (1981) are set out in Table 14.4.

An case of mistaken identity

As an example of how eyewitnesses can be both confident and mistaken I cite this actual case (Davies, 1991). The original writer is a barrister.

There were two cousins – let us call them Mr Owner and Mr Driver, because Mr Owner owned a Skoda that he regularly allowed Mr Driver to drive, notwithstanding that Mr Driver had no driving licence and was not insured. One day Mr Driver was involved in an accident. He gave the other driver, Mr Third-Party, his cousin's, Mr Owner's, name, address and insurance company, writing these details down for him. But he quickly drove off when he heard that the police were on their way, because he was not insured and had no licence.

That evening, an officer called at Mr Owner's address and met, not Mr Owner, but his cousin, Mr Driver, who pretended to be Mr Owner. Mr Driver could not produce a driving licence (of course), so the policeman left a form requiring the licence to be produced for inspection at a police station. That form Mr Driver passed to Mr Owner, who duly went to the police, believing that the request for a driving licence related to some other matter.

Three months later the case came to court. Mr Owner was charged, but denied the offence; he did not bother with representation by a lawyer. But Mr Third-Party identified him in court and he was convicted. Mr Owner then engaged a lawyer, who brought an appeal on the ground that the identification was fallible – it was a 'show-up'. Nevertheless, the judge allowed the identification to stand as evidence, and also admitted an identification from the police officer who had visited Mr Owner's address nine months before. Both Mr Third-Party and the police officer laughed at suggestions that they could have been mistaken. Mr Third-Party claimed that he was 'well known for his ability to remember faces' and the police officer said he 'took special note' of the man he met at Mr Owner's address. Mr Owner then insisted on bringing Mr Driver into court to be identified by the two witnesses. Mr Driver was already in detention and came unwillingly. Both witnesses looked at him and said, no, he was not the man. Moreover, Mr Driver denied being the driver of the car; he had no licence, nor insurance.

Mr Owner was in a spot. Both the witnesses were clearly convinced of the truth of their testimony. But a former Home Office handwriting expert of 26 years' experience put quite another gloss on the case. Given a sample of handwriting produced in the witness box by Mr Driver, and unwillingly too, he pointed to certain letter formations in the original note containing details of Mr Owner's address and insurance company that were identical to formations in Mr Driver's sample. Making a similar comparison with a sample of Mr Owner's handwriting, the expert was certain the original note was not his work. This evidence astonished everybody in court. But the Crown accepted the expert's testimony and Mr Owner was cleared of his conviction. If, however, Mr Driver had dictated the details for Mr Third-Party to write down, Mr Owner would have had no chance of reprieve.

To set eyewitness confidence in its proper place: a witness cannot know what was the original source of the memory he or she is at present recalling – it is merely that for some reason the person seems familiar – and cannot so guard against error, except in so far as additional details are recalled which exclude certain erroneous interpretations. And even those additional details are not foolproof because they might have been recalled from quite extraneous sources – the witness has no way of knowing whether they are themselves relevant or not. So a witness is not confident because his or her identification is correct; rather, the witness makes an identification because he or she is confident, there being little or no relation between confidence and accuracy. I intend no suggestion that confident witnesses are careless or biased or otherwise untrustworthy. It is just that 'As Lord Devlin, the former Law Lord, has written: "The highly reputable, absolutely sincere, perfectly coherent and apparently convincing witness may, as experience has quite often shown, be mistaken."' (Cited by Jenkins, 1990a)

Severity of the crime

Of necessity, staged incidents in a laboratory experiment involve relatively minor misdemeanours, while the crimes for which the police appeal for eyewitnesses include murder and armed robbery. In real life the eyewitness may have some thoughts about the penalty that could depend (at least in part) on his or her identification. Does it make any difference whether the crime being investigated carries a heavy penalty upon conviction?

There was another staged incident similar to the disruption of the biofeedback demonstration described above, but at a different university. To assist the investigation 42 witnesses attended line-ups organised by the police. At this point none of the witnesses had been told that the incident had been staged; they all believed the vandalism to be real. Each witness attended alone to view the line-up, and prior to each viewing the police officer in charge had a conversation with the experimenter about the likely consequences for the perpetrator if he was identified.

> While the officer was walking between the lineup viewing point and the witness, RSM [the experimenter] approached and asked what would happen to the vandal if he were identified. The officer responded with a variation on one of the two following scripts.
>
> *Trivial consequence*: 'Well, the College is really mad about it. They've had a lot of vandalism here this year, but I think they'll end up dropping charges and taking care of it inside the College. He'll probably just catch hell from the Dean.'
>
> *Severe consequence*: 'Well, the College is really mad about it. They've had a lot of vandalism here this year and I think they'll want to make an example of him if we get him. The College is going to press charges and he probably will have to pay for the equipment. And prosecution could mean a felony conviction and some time in jail.' (Malpass, Devine and Bergen, unpublished manuscript, p. 6).

This conversation was private, but arranged so that the witness attending to view the line-up would overhear it. Its effect is set out in Table 14.5. Those witnesses who were led to believe that the college would take stern action were much more ready to make an identification, at the expense of saying that the perpetrator was not in the line-up. They were not necessarily more accurate at identifying the perpetrator – simply more willing to identify someone, more 'confident'.

To sum up, eyewitness identification in the laboratory differs from that in real life in several important respects. First, in real life witnesses seldom get a good view of the criminal and do not usually realise that a crime is being committed until after the event. Policemen, of course, are trained to be observant and, especially, in what to look out for; even so, P. C. Thorpe was unable to identify his assailant positively, notwithstanding that he had seen him face-to-face. It is difficult to capture that elusiveness in a laboratory study; the subjects know that

Table 14.5 Identifications in a 5-man line-up from Malpass, Devine and Bergen (unpublished manuscript)

Group	Vandal	Foil (4 out of 5)	Not in line-up	Total
Mild penalty	1	4	14	19
Severe penalty	9	10	4	23

they have been engaged for a purpose and are primed to attend to everything around them. Second, in real-life identity parades the police cannot know whether or not they have the real criminal – the one the witnesses actually saw – so there is a possibility that witnesses will mistakenly identify an innocent person. Laboratory studies show that possibility to be increased if the witness is not warned that the real perpetrator may not be in the line-up. Third, in laboratory studies the witnesses often know that the act of vandalism they saw had been staged, so their identifications have no legal consequences. Those witnesses who are informed that nothing hinges on their identifications seem, paradoxically, to be more accurate. Finally, one might expect witnesses to be concerned in proportion to the seriousness of the penalty that might result from their identifications. Curiously, for a serious offence witnesses seem to be more willing to make an identification, although they are not necessarily more accurate.

Identification by voice

It occasionally happens, when a witness has not actually seen the criminal, but merely heard him speak, that identification is attempted by voice. This presupposes that voices can be identified with some useful accuracy; these are not voices that one knows well, such as the voice of one's spouse, but voices that one has heard once only. That question arose in an especially famous trial.

Colonel Charles Lindbergh engaged the world's attention on two separate occasions. In 1927 he flew an aircraft, *The Spirit of St Louis*, from New York to Paris, becoming thereby the first man to fly across the Atlantic Ocean. He became a national hero, he was awarded a Congressional medal of Honour and he entered into a socially prestigious marriage. Then on 1 March 1932 his two-year-old son was kidnapped. A $50 000 ransom was paid, but the child was later found murdered.

In 1935 Bruno Hauptmann, a German immigrant carpenter, was brought to trial for the murder of Charles Lindbergh's son. One element of the evidence against Hauptmann was Lindbergh's assertion that he had recognised Hauptmann's voice as the voice of the man who had collected the ransom money. Instructions for the payment of that ransom required the $50 000 to be thrown over a particular cemetery wall at night by an intermediary acting for Charles Lindbergh. In the course of making sure that the location was correct, the man collecting the ransom had been heard to say 'Hey, Doctor'. Lindbergh had heard this, though only from a car parked some 80 to 100 yards away.

To test Lindbergh's recollection of the voice, his lawyer had arranged an interview with Hauptmann at which Lindbergh was surreptitiously present, within earshot but out of sight. Hauptmann was asked to cry out 'Hey, Doctor' several times so that Lindbergh could hear. On that basis, Lindbergh asserted on the witness stand that Hauptmann had been the man who cried out over the cemetery wall at the time the ransom money was paid over. But the interview arranged by Lindbergh's lawyer did not take place until two-and-a-half years after the event; moreover, it amounted to a show-up with no stand-ins. Is recollection of a voice, heard only once, good enough that such an identification can be relied upon?

The conviction of Bruno Hauptmann prompted an experiment on the accuracy of voice recognition (McGehee, 1937). The subjects heard someone reading a paragraph of 56 words behind a screen. They knew there was some kind of memory test to come, but did not know what was to be tested, and there is a presumption that they would have been expecting to be tested on the content of the paragraph rather than the voice in which it was read. Later, after various different lapses of time from one day to five months, the subjects were asked to listen to five speakers reading the same paragraph behind the same screen and to say which of the five they had heard originally. The percentages of correct recognitions are shown by the open circles in Figure 14.5. The filled circles are percentages from a replication of the experiment using voices recorded on 75 rpm gramophone records (McGehee, 1944). After one, two or three days, or even a week, recognition of the original voice from amongst the five was more than 80

Figure 14.5 Percentages of correct recognition of voices after various lapses of time.

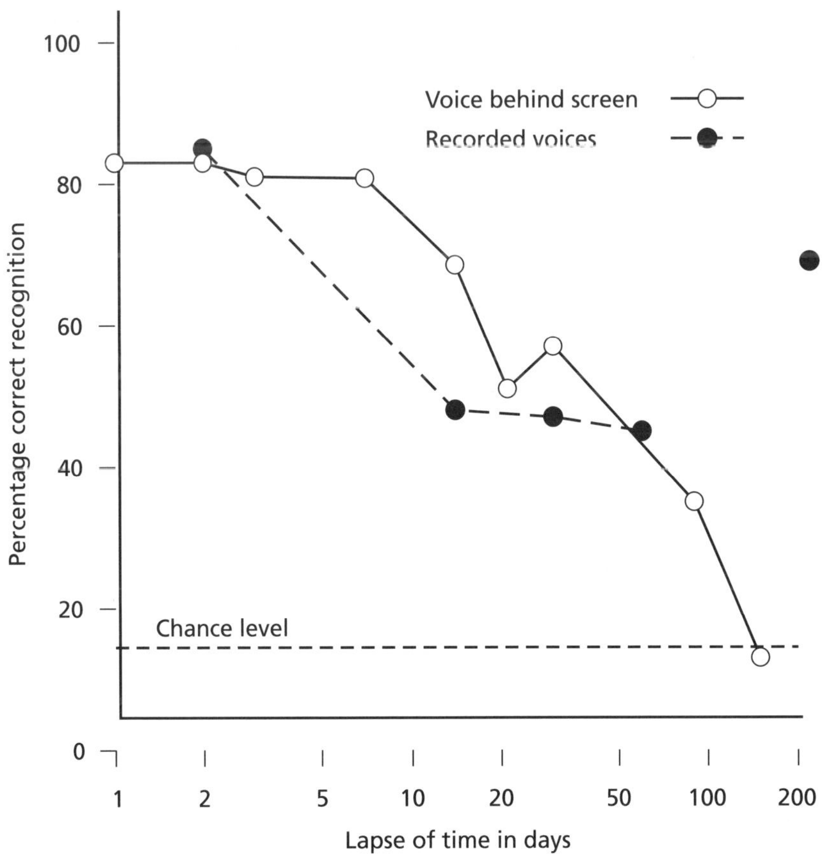

Data from McGehee, 1937,1944.

per cent accurate. If guesses had been distributed evenly amongst the five speakers, one would have expected 20 per cent of them to be correct by chance. In fact, guesses were not distributed evenly and by omitting the middle position (3) for the speaker, McGehee reduced the chance level to about 14.5 per cent. After five months (150 days) recognition was at that chance level. Charles Lindbergh's identification was made after two-and-a-half years.

In this early experimental study the subjects knew full well that their memory for the passage read behind the screen was to be tested in some way or other, although they did not know how and probably expected to be tested on its content. The accuracies of voice recognition in this experiment were perhaps the best that one might expect; in the real world, and with attention to the matter of the witness not being prepared, accuracy of recognition might be somewhat lower. This has been confirmed in a more recent and much more realistic experiment (Clifford and Fleming, unpublished manuscript, cited by Clifford, 1983, p. 207 and Bull and Clifford, 1984, p. 120).

A confederate of the experimenter entered a bank or a shop, introduced himself, and explained that he had lost his cheque book and card and asked what he should do. Then, either immediately, or after a delay of one hour, four hours, or one day, an experimenter approached the bank clerk or shopkeeper and asked if they remembered the incident. Given that the incident is recalled, the experimenter then asked if the clerk or shopkeeper would attempt to identify the voice of the confederate from a recorded voice parade that included a sample of the confederate's speech along with nine other stand-ins. The proportions of correct recognitions were:

Immediate test	50%
After 1 hour delay	33%
After 4 hours' delay	17%
After 24 hours' delay	*c* 10%

That is to say, after a whole day's delay the clerk or shopkeeper might just as well have been guessing. If the subject is not primed to remember the incident at the time, subsequent identification can be very poor.

Summary – identification of the suspect

In those cases that especially matter, witnesses have usually had only a fleeting glimpse of the perpetrator. Laboratory experiments mostly fail to reproduce the fleeting and unprimed quality of witness observations. In such circumstances identification is very open to bias. A show-up is not to be trusted and an identity parade needs particular care.

The courts commonly ask a witness if he or she is confident about his or her identification. Confidence equates to readiness to make an identification, but is largely irrelevant to accuracy. This is because the police can never know whether they have the perpetrator in their line-up or not, and cases where the confident witness makes a correct identification are inextricably mixed with those in which an innocent suspect is picked out. The identification of unfamiliar voices heard only once is much like that of faces, only more fallible.

The next chapter looks at yet another source of bias – a logical argument.

15 The power of argument

In Lewis Carroll's *Through the Looking-glass and What Alice Found There* Humpty-Dumpty talks about 'a nice knock-down argument'. This turns out to be an argument that fails to address the question at issue. People are often convinced by a 'good' argument. We like to think that we, that people, are rational. Point people in the right direction and they can see for themselves how things are. But do we really think rationally? There are two difficulties. First, some remain unconvinced even by the simplest, most obvious argument – all right, those are people who just cannot see things straight. But, more seriously, there are others who advance fallacious arguments, particularly arguments which fail to address the point at issue, clearly believing their arguments to be sound. How come that such people are unable to perceive their own fallacies?

This chapter looks at several examples – at arguments advocating the advantages of special loudspeaker cables, 'pound/cost' averaging, the European Monetary System and an independent central bank. The allegation of cheating in an examination levelled at Francis Foecke at Bristol University in 1986 constitutes a particularly acute example.

A nice knock-down argument

The prototype for an argument that fails to address the point at issue is to be found in the conversation between Alice and Humpty-Dumpty in *Through the Looking-glass and What Alice Found There* (Carroll, 1872). Alice has been looking quizzically at a certain garment tied around Humpty-Dumpty's middle (Humpty-Dumpty is an egg), wondering whether it was a belt (around his waist) or a cravat (about his neck).

> 'It's a cravat, child, and a beautiful one, as you say. It's a present from the White King and Queen. There now!' . . . 'they gave it me – for an unbirthday present.'
>
> 'I beg your pardon?' Alice said with a puzzled air.
>
> 'I'm not offended,' said Humpty-Dumpty.
>
> 'I mean, what *is* an unbirthday present?'
>
> 'A present given when it isn't your birthday, of course.'
>
> Alice considered a little. 'I like birthday presents best,' she said at last.

'You don't know what you're talking about!' cried Humpty-Dumpty. 'How many days are there in a year?'

'Three hundred and sixty-five,' said Alice.

'And how many birthdays have you?'

'One.'

'And if you take one from three hundred and sixty-five what remains?'

'Three hundred and sixty-four, of course.'

Humpty-Dumpty looked doubtful. 'I'd rather see that done on paper,' he said.

Alice does the sum on paper.

'. . . that *seems* to be done right – though I haven't time to look it over thoroughly just now – and that shows that there are three hundred and sixty-four days when you might get unbirthday presents –'.

'Certainly,' said Alice.

'And only *one* for birthday presents, you know. There's glory for you!'

'I don't know what you mean by "glory",' Alice said.

Humpty Dumpty smiled contemptuously. 'Of course you don't – till I tell you. I meant "there's a nice knock-down argument for you!" '

As I have already explained, this chapter is about 'nice knock-down arguments', arguments that convince, especially the originator of the argument, although they fail to address the question at issue.

Loudspeaker cables for hi-fi systems

High-fidelity sound reproduction is all about reproducing the recorded sound without distortion of any kind. The best amplifiers today have less than 0.001 per cent total harmonic distortion, so attention has passed to the cables that connect the amplifier to the loudspeakers. While one might think that a cable is an entirely passive device that does nothing except connect two components in the system, theoretical analysis of the physics of electrical conduction tells us otherwise.

AudioQuest (1992) list these effects that act to 'colour' the sound reproduction.

1 *Skin effect*. There is a frequency-sensitive increase in impedance below the surface of a copper conductor. For a frequency of 20 kHz, for example, there is a 63 per cent current reduction at a depth of 0.467 mm, that is, at the centre of a 0.934 mm strand. This limits the diameter of copper strand that can be used for high fidelity reproduction and means that the cable has to be composed of several strands.

2 *Magnetic interaction*. The current passing through a cable strand generates a magnetic field that induces current in neighbouring strands.

3 *Conductor quality*. Loudspeakers are low impedance devices, and a cable of high impedance would introduce power losses. Copper and silver

offer the lowest resistance, but even so they contain impurities which increase the resistance. AudioQuest offer cables made from oxygen-free, high-conductivity copper, from 'long grain' copper in which the crystaline structure is much simplified by careful manufacture, and from 'long grain' silver.

4 *Directionality*. All cables are directional – it matters which way the music travels along the cable from amplifier to speakers. (Cable directionality is not well understood, but is thought to be related to the asymmetric structure of the drawn conductor material.) 'The difference will be clear, in the correct direction the music is more relaxed, pleasant and believable.' (AudioQuest, 1992)

Of course, these high-fidelity cables are expensive, but if you want perfect reproduction of your recorded sound . . .

To put these claims in perspective, there is a well-known and widely-available 79-strand, twin core, PVC-insulated cable, with cores 1.78 mm diameter spaced 4 mm centre to centre, with an resistance about 0.0137 Ω/m and inductance about 0.7 μH/m – tiny in relation to the impedance of any loudspeaker. So, can anyone hear the difference? If the difference is not detectable, it is hardly worth paying 'several thousand pounds in some cases that have been advertised' (Blake-Coleman and Yorke, 1993) for high-fidelity cable.

The 'Golden ears' hypothesis

The effects in question are mostly of a theoretical kind, not ordinarily detectable by physical measurement. So we are dependent on the subjective judgments of reviewers of audio equipment and these people, who might be supposed to have 'Golden ears', know what they are listening to. Does that colour their judgments?

Blake-Coleman and Yorke (1993, p. 391) reported informally on some listening tests, comparing different loudspeaker cables. 'Each of us compared the virtually instantaneous switch over from one unknown cable to the other. The first results were crushingly disappointing. No immediate difference could be detected, nor any when a carefully conducted set of double-blind tests followed.' This is hardly surprising. A physical difference of about 0.5 dB is needed before any change can be detected; this is so whether the test is carried out with white noise (Miller, 1947) or with a pure tone (Jeffress, 1975).

Now, a 'virtually instantaneous switch over' provides the most sensitive paradigm for comparison between the two cables. An ordinary listener and, presumably, a professional reviewer will not listen in that sharply comparative way, but simply compare performances heard on different occasions. This would make the comparison analogous to distinguishing the difference between two separate luminances (see Figure 4.5, right-hand panel), rather than detecting an edge (middle panel). But a discrimination between two separate luminances is much less precise (about 25 per cent difference required) than the detection of an edge (about 2 per cent). Moreover, even if there were a noticeable difference between cable systems, listening to one system for even a short period of time would induce adaptation to the sound colouration it produced, after the manner illustrated in Chapter 4. Given that sensory experience is differentially coupled to the sensory input, in this case the output of the loudspeakers, any colouration contributed by the cables would simply drop out of the comparison. So, what are the 'Golden eared' really saying?

It is likely that they are expressing a preference for a particular colouration of the sound. It used to be claimed that the sound reproduced by valves is inherently superior to that from any semiconductor, but it has been known for a long time that listeners often prefer to hear a small amount of second-harmonic distortion (King, 1978) and that is what many valve amplifiers supply, consequent on technical problems of linearity.

But the worst is yet to come. A loudspeaker is an electrical–mechanical–acoustical interface with a necessarily complicated frequency response. In comparison to the colouration of the output due to the characteristics of the loudspeaker, any contribution from the interconnecting cables is negligible.

'Pound/cost averaging'

AudioQuest are by no means the only company to use 'a nice knock-down argument' to sell their products. The investment industry does it too. Investment houses of all kinds encourage savers to put by a fixed sum regularly every month rather than a lump sum as and when the idea occurs. The reason is obvious – without a regular savings commitment the money would be spent on other things, a holiday or the latest fashion in consumer goods. But that is not the argument that is used.

> Investing a regular amount each month in unit trusts rather than investing one single lump sum could work to your advantage in terms of the number of units purchased due to a factor known as 'pound/cost averaging'. Unlike a lump sum investment, the buying power of a regular monthly investment is exposed to stockmarket fluctuations over the course of time. So when stockmarket prices are low, a regular monthly amount will buy more units than when stockmarket prices are high. This means that over the longer term, the total investment may purchase more units than if an equivalent amount had been invested as a lump sum . . . which, of course, means more units within your Plan. (Perpetual, 1994)

I have quoted from one particular investment house, but the use of this argument is widespread.

Let us do some sums to see what it means. Suppose I agree to invest $300 per month. I begin by buying 300 units at $1 per unit on 1 January; but when 1 February arrives, the price of units has risen to $3 each, so my second $300 buys me only 100 units to give a total of 400. But, suppose that instead of investing my $600 in two monthly instalments, I had invested it all in one lump sum, buying my units at the average of the January and February prices. That average price is $2 and my $600 investment would have bought 300 units – less than the 400 I have purchased from two separate monthly instalments. Some more sophisticated mathematics will show that the total number of units bought with any number of equal monthly instalments will always be greater than the number bought in one go at the *average* monthly price. The only exception is when the price is unchanging throughout. That is what 'pound/cost averaging' is about and it looks good to be paying those regular monthly instalments.

But the argument is fallacious, because no investment house is going to trade at an average price. Typically, the price of units varies from day to day. An average price will invariably be either above, or below, the current price, and only one party will want to trade at that average price. Units are always offered at their current daily price. The actual choice facing the investor is either to invest $600 on 1 January, when it will buy 600 units, or on 1 February, when it will buy 200. The better choice is obvious – except that as of 1 January I do not know what the price will be on 1 February. It might, for example, be 50¢, in which case, by holding off until February, I could purchase 1200 units instead of 600. All that one can say is that by choosing 1 January or 1 February at random, I may *expect* to purchase (as a statistical mean) the same number of units as I would get by dividing my investment equally between those two dates (and again some more sophisticated mathematics will show that the total number of units bought with any number of equal monthly instalments will always be equal to the expected number obtained by investing a lump sum on an arbitrary chosen one of the monthly instalment dates). A regular monthly investment conveys no advantage in the mean – merely a slightly reduced risk. But that is not what the 'pound/cost averaging' argument says.

An independent central bank

On 8 October 1991 Britain entered the European Monetary System at a parity of DM2.95 to the pound. The pound rose sharply following that announcement; that allowed lower interest rates and cheaper borrowing for the Government, ultimately on the assumption that the pound would retain its value vis-à-vis other European currencies. For example, central banks of member states within the European Monetary System undertook to intervene to prevent any currency falling below a 'floor' (which was set at 6 per cent below the highest valued currency in the European Monetary System).

On 17 September 1992 British membership of the European Monetary System was suddenly suspended as the pound sunk below that 'floor' (then at DM2.7780, 6 per cent below DM2.95). An increase of interest rates from 10 to 12 per cent failed to revive the pound, and one might well ask: Why? The reason was that British inflation at that time was more powerful than both the setting of interest rates by the Government and the support of other European central banks.

At that time the deutschmark was the benchmark currency and interest rates in Germany were set, not by the German Government, but by the Bundesbank. That led to this argument, espoused most notably by Norman Lamont, then recently resigned as Chancellor of the Exchequer, on the *Channel Four News* (26 November 1993):

- Germany has an independent central bank.
- Germany has a low rate of inflation.

ergo Britain needs an independent central bank,

specifically with interest rates set by the Bank of England.

The point Norman Lamont made was that politicians' manipulation of interest rates are actuated too much by political considerations, rather than economic. Possibly!

However, inflation results from many component decisions about prices made by different companies and individuals within the economy. If the money is there to pay for goods, companies will put up prices to whatever level the market will bear. If interest rates rise, house owners have less to spend after servicing their mortgages. It makes no difference whether interest rates are set by the Government or by an independent Bank of England. High interest rates will send the country into recession just the same.

Not everyone was taken in by this argument. Sir Bryan Hipkin was Head of the Government Economic Service and Chief Economic Advisor to the Treasury from 1974–77.

> Under our present arrangements, the control of inflation rests ultimately on maintaining unemployment at a high level. Conferring independence on the central bank would not remove this central dilemma of policy. It would only transfer from politicians to bankers a share in the vital decision about the level of unemployment the country should accept in order to keep inflation under control. This is not the sort of decision that ought to be entrusted to bankers.
>
> The proposal to set up an independent central bank is a gimmick and a distraction. (Hipkin, 1992)

Britain now has both an independent central bank *and* low inflation, but the low inflation is not consequent on the independent central bank because the low inflation arrived first. What will happen to the independence of the bank if inflation rises again?

'Cheating' in a university examination

The examples cited so far concern companies in the business of marketing a product or politicians pressing a point, and one might readily suppose that such people are not too concerned about the relevance of their arguments provided only that they have the desired effect. In a university, on the other hand, one would expect more accurate and rational considerations to prevail. Not so! This

Table 15.1 Foecke's results in April 1986 (from Miller, 1988a, p. 22).

Subject	Mark (%)	Comment
Algebraic Number Theory	159 (sic)	By answering all six questions when only four were required.
Computer Architecture	90	Examiner: 'The best paper I have marked in the last ten years.'
Computer Construction	90	
Double project in computer speech synthesis	70	
Foundations of Mathematics	91	
Logic	84	

next example shows that university dons are as much taken in by a 'nice knock-down argument' as anybody else.

Francis Foecke was accused of cheating in his final mathematics examinations at the University of Bristol. In 1983, at the age of 25, Foecke began a three-year degree course in mathematics and computer science. Students who return to an undergraduate course after a break earning their own living often have difficulty getting back into the habit of studying. Francis Foecke was no exception. He failed his examinations at the end of his first year. He was made to resit the worst of his papers and failed again, so he was taken off the honours course. He was deeply resentful of the examination system that had failed him.

In his second year Foecke was frequently at odds with his tutor, who reprimanded him for not attending lectures. 'There was a basic disagreement between us about my style of working. I have a very individual study style. I felt able to study on my own very effectively and thought a huge amount of time was wasted by lectures.' But Foecke's individual study style was not too successful; he just scraped through with 43 per cent. But that was enough, just, to reinstate him on the honours course (Miller, 1988a, pp. 20–2).

In his third year, notwithstanding strong discouragement from the teaching staff, Foecke announced that he would sit 13 papers in his final examinations and also offer a double project in computer speech synthesis. If he were to gain a first class degree (his ambition), this much work was necessary in order to compensate for his very poor marks in his first two years. Foecke's results in the first round of examinations in April were astounding. They are set out in Table 15.1.

Despite discouragement, lest he should dilute his hitherto excellent performance, Foecke insisted on continuing with eight further papers in the summer, with the sensational results set out in Table 15.2.

But four days before the results were due to be announced, Foecke received a letter to say that he was suspected of 'dishonest conduct'. That suspicion had been raised by Dr E. J. Collins, the tutor with whom Foecke had been so frequently at odds during his second year. While marking his 'Linear Models' script, Collins noticed a striking similarity between Foecke's solution to one of the problems and the examiner's model solution. He thereupon checked the

Table 15.2 Foecke's results in June 1986 (from Miller, 1988a, p. 22).

Subject	Mark (%)	Comment
Advanced Computer Architecture	75	
Graph Theory	100	
Linear Models	91	Marked by Foecke's second-year tutor
Linear Programming	98	
Operating Systems	95	
Programming Methodology	100	
Statistics 2	78	
Stochastic Processes B	96	

remainder of the script for further such similarities and reported his suspicions to Dr E. V. Evans, the head of the mathematics department. What these two said to each other is not known, but following their conversation disciplinary enquiries were rapidly put in hand. Dr Evans asked the examiners to check all 13 of Foecke's examination scripts to see whether there was 'any possibility that he might have had prior access to the questions or solutions'. On the very same day the university wrote to Foecke telling him he was under suspicion of 'dishonest conduct', without waiting for any results from this inquiry. None of the examiners reported any 'positive evidence of fraud', except Dr Collins, whose suspicion about the Linear Models paper had started the whole inquiry off, and Dr G. R. Grimmett, who discovered similarities to the model solutions in Foecke's Statistics script.

There followed a succession of committee meetings and tribunals that do not need to be recounted here until on 15 October a special meeting of the Board of Examiners in mathematics decreed that none of the written examinations Foecke had sat in his third year were acceptable towards the award of an honours degree; and the project and results in Foecke's first and second years qualified him for an ordinary degree only. Even worse, a sub-committee set up to determine what disciplinary action should be taken decided on 8 December that simply refusing to award an honours degree was not sufficient penalty by itself 'as it was impossible to be certain that he would have reached honours standard if he had not cheated'. It was resolved, in addition, that Foecke's name should be withheld from the pass list for an ordinary BSc degree for a period of five years from 30 June, 1986 (Miller, 1988a, p. 25).

To anticipate possible confusion, let me emphasise that Francis Foecke was *not* found in the examination room in possession of unauthorised notes (that is how most cheats are discovered), nor was he caught in the act of smuggling prewritten examination answers, written on the special papers that universities keep only for examination scripts, into any examination. In fact, there is no evidence that he had breached any of the examination regulations at all. All the evidence was circumstantial, internal to the examination. Briefly, his written performance was simply judged 'too good to be true'. The tribunal decided 'that out of 10 answers [investigated] in four scripts, four were highly suspicious and three could not have been written unless Foecke had seen the model solution. "We conclude that a breach of examination regulations has taken place, in that Mr Foecke has, beyond possible doubt, employed knowledge of the examiners solution *which could not have been honestly obtained* [my italics]." ' (Cited by Miller, 1988a, p. 25).

However, what a candidate writes in his scripts tells the examiners what he was capable of in the examination room on that day. It says nothing about whether that capability was obtained exclusively by honest study or whether some part of it was acquired contrary to the examination regulations. A concordance between what the candidate wrote and the examiners' model solution needs to be explained, but such a concordance is not of itself evidence of dishonesty. It may be, for example, that the model solution, on the one hand, and the candidate's answer, on the other, derive from some common source, access to which was entirely legitimate. That was agreed to be so for one disputed answer (Furmston and Higgins, 1989, p. 64). The examination papers were set, and the model solutions devised, by members of staff at the University of Bristol who also taught the students. Part of that teaching comprised worked examples that illustrated model solutions. If an examiner includes a question in an examination paper which is similar to, or even identical with, a worked example previously used in teaching . . . of course, the very industrious candidate who has prepared for that examination thoroughly will turn in an answer very similar to the model. That is what teaching students is about. There is, however, one answer that requires more careful consideration.

The model answer to Question 5 on the second paper of the Statistics 2 examination contained a number of errors that reappear in Foecke's script (see Miller, 1988a, pp. 22–3). While producing a correct answer according to the model pattern is what the examination is indeed about, reproducing the examiner's errors looks too much of a coincidence. Indeed it is. Foecke

> produced lecture notes he had borrowed from a previous third year student which contained, in a sampling theory problem sheet, an exact replica of the model solution to one of the 'suspicious' questions in his Statistics paper. The lecture notes also repeated the error – a simple transposition of two numbers – in the model solution. Foecke explained that he had been revising from the lecture notes right up to the last minute before entering the examination room and he had simply remembered the solution, along with the error.
> (Miller, 1988a, p. 23)

If a student has a copy of the model solution in his possession, a copy *honestly acquired,* the argument that he has had unauthorised access to the copy in the examiner's filing cabinet simply evaporates.

Examinations are written under pressure of time. That pressure is especially acute in a mathematics examination because one may have to spend an indeterminate time merely thinking how to solve a problem. If, therefore, a candidate finds a question on the paper to which he already knows the answer, he will write that answer out as quickly as possible (I speak from personal experience of university mathematics examinations) and move on to another question. That is what Foecke did. If the examiners are sufficiently lazy that they put worked examples, used in teaching students in previous years, straight into the examination paper without amendment or checking, and if they are sufficiently incompetent that the model solutions to their worked examples contain errors, that is what happens.

'We conclude that a breach of examination regulations has taken place, in that Mr Foecke has, beyond possible doubt, employed knowledge of the examiner's solution which *could not have been honestly obtained* [my italics].' The examiners at Bristol University did not say what breach of the examination regulations has taken place. 'We have not considered it to have been within our remit to have considered how this might have taken place.' (Dr A. Paterson, chairman of the internal tribunal of inquiry, cited by Horsnell, 1988). Certainly there was an unexpected concordance between Foecke's examination scripts and the examiners' model solutions, but that is not of itself evidence of dishonesty. Even Bristol University recognised that. So there is a profound question that needs to be asked: Why was Francis Foecke accused of cheating in the first place? The reason why he was first accused and the evidence ultimately put before the tribunal may be quite different. But, without that initial accusation, there would have been no convening of a tribunal; and, since a tribunal is not convened without grave cause, that initial accusation feeds through covertly to colour the evidence.

I repeat that an excellent examination performance by itself is not sufficient; there has to be some other input as well to single Foecke out from all the other outstanding students at Bristol University. The nature of that other input may be inferred from the fact that the initial accusation was raised by Dr E. J. Collins – Foecke's erstwhile second-year tutor, the tutor with whom Foecke had so frequently been at odds – while marking Foecke's Linear Models paper. Dr Collins then had a meeting with Dr D. V. Evans, the head of the mathematics department, in the course of which he must have convinced Dr Evans that there was a *prima facie* case of cheating. What could Dr Collins have said? Mere excellence of examination performance is not, by itself, sufficient. Dr Collins has to have said that Foecke was a poor student (on the basis of his tutoring of Foecke during the second year) who was a doubtful candidate for any kind of honours, let alone a first class degree. That input reappears in the penalty imposed by the subcommittee above: 'it was impossible to be certain that he would have reached honours standard if he had not cheated'. That additional input is *essential* to any case for Foecke having cheated, but it also poses this problem, to which the examiners at Bristol University failed to offer any adequate answer: What kind of cheating would enable a mediocre candidate of doubtful honours standard to turn in a consistently super-first-class performance throughout thirteen written papers?

In a dossier entitled *The Case of F. Foecke*, Dr Grimmett, head of the department of statistics, explained that the examination papers and the model solutions were kept in a filing cabinet in the office of a Dr Walker on the third floor of the University's Mathematics and Computer Centre. The doors at the bottom of the stairs were locked at nights and at weekends, preventing access out of hours to the upper floors. But it would have been possible to hide somewhere on the upper floors during the day, in a service duct perhaps, until the doors were locked and then have unrestricted access to all the offices. But this could not be done without a master key . . . there was a key, kept under a bucket in the ladies lavatory on the ground floor, that disappeared. This key opened the cleaners' cupboard, adjacent to the lavatory, where a master key could be found in the pocket of one of the cleaners' overalls. With that master key and by hiding in a service duct during the day, Foecke could have had access to the upper floors. But even if he knew where the examination material was kept, he still had to get into Dr Walker's filing cabinet. First he would have to open Dr Walker's office with the master key, then take another key from a tray in Dr Walker's desk, go outside into the secretary's office and use the second key to open a cupboard, where a key to the filing cabinet with the examination papers was kept. Easy!

There were four keys involved; and Foecke would have needed to know the whereabouts of each key and what to do with it before even venturing, without authority, into the upper floors of the building. Who told him about those keys? Until Dr Grimmett's enquiries no one person knew about all of them. Moreover, Foecke would have needed to know of the existence of the model solutions and where to find them. Inside Dr Walker's office he would have had some 400 pages of questions and model answers to copy out by hand, and that without using the room lights for fear of detection. The story is ludicrous, especially ludicrous because there is a much, much easier and safer way of obtaining advance sight of examination papers and model answers. *The candidate buys them from a member of staff with access to the examiner's filing cabinet!*

At this point I emphasise that I make no suggestion that any member of the staff of the mathematics department at Bristol University acted in any way contrary to the examination regulations in revealing any examination material to Francis Foecke. I, personally, do not believe that Foecke ever had any unauthorised sight of the examination material, but if Dr Evans, the head of that department, did believe that the integrity of the examination had been compromised, there were certain inquiries that it would have been his duty to make. While Dr Grimmett appears to have interrogated the cleaning staff, it has not been reported that Dr Evans asked corresponding questions of the academic staff – questions that would have been embarrassing, to say the least, and would most certainly have been resented. Dr Grimmett's far-fetched scenario is an attempt to answer the question how Francis Foecke might have obtained advance access to the examination papers without making the obvious suggestion, for which Dr Grimmett had no evidence and which might have proved libellous. There is some doubt, therefore, whether the members of staff who prosecuted the case against Foecke actually believed that the integrity of the examination had been breached.

There is also another problem that has gone unanswered. The case against Foecke rests, not only on the concordance between some of his examination scripts and the examiners' model answers, but also on the assumption that his ability was mediocre, possibly not even of honours standard. Even if Francis Foecke did have illicit access to the examination material, he has still got to carry the model answers in his head into the examination room and write them out there. He would need an exceptional memory. Even so, his allegedly mediocre mathematical ability would lead to errors. One would particularly expect to find complete lines of argument omitted, as when a copy typist skips a line of text because some word or phrase recurs on the following line; there might also be transposition of adjacent lines of argument – a mistake that a competent mathematician would never make. It has not been alleged that he made any errors of these kinds. Indeed, such errors are incompatible with a score of 100 per cent for Graph Theory and for Programming Methodology. Putting this objection more simply, there is an undoubted advantage to a dishonest candidate in having prior sight of the examination papers and the model answers, but not so great an advantage as to make the difference between just deserving honours, on the one hand, and a super-first-class performance, on the other. It is very doubtful whether, given only the examination scripts, examiners would be able to distinguish between candidates who had had prior sight of the examination papers and candidates who had not.

So, the allegation that Francis Foecke cheated runs into all sorts of problems to which the University of Bristol failed to provide answers. It is the kind of allegation that can be sustained only on the basis that there is no possible alternative. But there is an alternative – a much, much simpler explanation – moreover, an explanation that is in accord with all the published facts. This explanation did not occur to Dr Collins as he was marking Foecke's script; well, it wouldn't, would it? Nor apparently did it occur to Dr Evans, though it ought to have done so, when Dr Collins confided his suspicions to him as head of department.

A student who returns to academic life after a break earning his living experiences difficulty in getting back into the way of study. I have experienced that myself. That is sufficient to explain Foecke's poor performance in his first year, though one would expect him to be showing his true ability by the end of his second year. Foecke's second-year tutor appears, so far as Foecke is concerned, to have put in a less than professional performance. (I make no comment on Dr Collins' treatment of any of his other pupils.) There are two consequences. First, Foecke is effectively left to look after himself at a time when he is, in fact, especially in need of help. He therefore continues to perform poorly in his second year. Second, Dr Collins fails to discover how brilliant a student he has under his charge. In fact, he makes a gross professional misjudgment about Foecke's ability. So, when at the end of Foecke's third year, Dr Collins finds himself marking Foecke's Linear Models script, he cannot believe what he is reading. He cannot give it less than 91 per cent because he has a marking guide to direct him. He therefore accuses Foecke of cheating, without stopping to consider whether that is a tenable assertion or whether there might be any other explanation, more in accord with the facts.

I do not suggest that Dr Collins was actuated by any kind of malice; there is no need for malice – simply an erroneous belief about Foecke's ability that was incompatible with what he read in Foecke's script. At this point it is well to remember that the examination is marked by examiners who know the candidates personally. But the examination is about what the candidates write in the examination room, not about how well they did the previous year, nor about any other personal matters. It is therefore important that the marker does not know the identity of the candidate whose script he is marking, to preclude extraneous matters entering into the examiner's marking, just as the jury trying a criminal case is not allowed to know of any previous convictions which the defendant might have. Once such details are known, it is not possible for the jury, or the examiner, to put them out of their minds. So, Bristol University's examination should have been marked blind.

From the moment of Dr Collins' initial accusation onwards, or perhaps from the moment when he successfully persuaded Dr Evans to investigate his allegation, the University's conduct of that investigation has been characterised by a curious lack of objectivity. There are two distinct questions to consider: first, whether the correlation between Foecke's scripts and the model answers was significant in the statistical sense of that term and, second, whether, in addition, there was any evidence of dishonesty, because, as statisticians know well, correlation does not imply causation. The Board of Examiners and the Appeal Tribunal looked only at the first question and the evidence established that correlation beyond all reasonable doubt. But the charge against Foecke related only to the second. Truly a 'nice knock-down argument'.

One would have expected such intelligent men to perceive the distinction; instead, they contented themselves merely with compiling a case against Francis Foecke sufficient to convince the Board of Examiners. For example, 'On June 12, Dr Evans returned all 13 of Foecke's exam scripts to the respective examiners with a covering letter asking them to check whether there was "any possibility that he [Foecke] might have had prior access to the questions or solutions" ' (Miller, 1988a, p. 22). That exercise produced some additional opinions to be counted. But a script by itself tells one nothing about whether the candidate's expertise was gained entirely legitimately or whether the candidate had been guilty of some breach of examination regulations. As a guide to the truth of the matter, those opinions are worthless.

Allegations of cheating are determined by committee. In a committee it is chiefly numbers of heads that count. The evidence, such as it is, will influence the way individual members of the committee vote, but when a committee upholds a charge of cheating on no direct evidence at all, only on circumstantial evidence, one might well enquire as to how clearly the committee members understood what they were doing. In particular, the entire case was predicated, even if only implicitly, on Dr Collins' estimation of Foecke's ability. That estimation seems to have gone entirely uncontested.

Summary – do people think rationally?

There are arguments that convince because they look like sound logical arguments – convince, notwithstanding that they fail to address the point at issue. Such arguments are believed, especially by their originators. How can this be?

Logical argument, indeed any argument, rests on a series of judgments that each successive step follows from its predecessor. 'Rationality' subsists in learning which steps follow from which previous steps, that is, learning what leads to what in the real world; it is acquired, not innate. Once a false argument has been accepted, it is liable to be reproduced as 'correct' on some subsequent occasion. It becomes an acquired pattern of erroneous judgment and successive reproductions make it increasingly difficult to see the fallacy.

I turn now to one domain – gambling – where fallacious arguments prove especially compelling.

16 Luck

Gambling is an ancient and continually popular pastime. The roulette wheel was introduced into Paris in 1765 as a gambling device that would be proof against the tricks of card sharps. Playing cards are older. They evolved into their present form, four suits of thirteen cards each, about the year 1500, but were commonplace in an earlier form in twelfth-century China. Dice are older still. They were popular with the Greeks and Romans, and also appear in Greek and Egyptian myths. In addition, large numbers of approximately dice-shaped bones (*astragalia*) have been recovered from prehistoric archaeological sites (Epstein, 1967). Gambling appears to predate history.

Table 16.1 shows the prevalence of gambling in this country in 1995/96. If you went to a casino or 'did the horses', you could expect to have about 80 per cent of your stake money returned to you as winnings. Much more popular, though, was the National Lottery which returned only 50 per cent as prize money. But nine million people staked a total of £556m on football pools of which only £128m was returned as winnings – only 23p for every pound staked. So, why do so many people repeatedly make so disadvantageous an investment?

Common intuitions about how and why people learn suggest that, if you lose your money often enough, you will eventually give up. In this respect, commonsense coincides with psychological insight, and what makes gambling so profound a puzzle is that in this particular case psychological insight is wrong. Gamblers do not give up!

Utility theory

In this chapter I look first at the traditional academic answer to the question: Why do gamblers persist in gambling? That answer invokes the notion of utility, a notion introduced by von Neumann and Morgenstern in 1944 in their seminal book *Theory of Games and Economic Behaviour* as a way of measuring the value, to the individual recipient, of an economic reward. The essential idea is that the subjective reward-value of different sums of money may not be exactly proportional to those sums expressed in pounds or dollars. If you were to win £2m on the football pools, the second million will not be quite so easy to spend as the first because, by then, you will already have done the most obvious things you

Table 16.1 Prevalence of gambling in Britain, 1995/96.

Gamble	Number of participants	Amount staked	Exchequer	Profits and expenses	Returned to punters	Per cent return
Casinos	—	£2548m	£80m	£370m	£2098m	82%
Gaming machines	4 201 000	£9000m	£130m	£1670m	£7200m	80%
On-course betting	708 000	£761m	£448m	£881m	£5315m	80%
Off-course betting	3 174 000	£5883m				
Bingo	2 787 000	£1161m	£94m	£255m	£812m	70%
National Lottery	31 684 000	£5260m	£583m	£732m (& £1473m to good causes)	£2472m	47%
Instants	12 505 000					
Football pools	8 990 000	£556m	£131m	£297m	£128m	23%

Reproduced with permission from D. Laming, *Understanding Human Motivation*, p. 263. © 2004, Donald Laming; published by Blackwell Publishing.

might do with your win. It would have a somewhat lesser utility. Likewise, if you should be so unfortunate to have your home burned down, the £250 000 or so required to reinstate your house will then seem a much bigger sum (assuming you to be uninsured) than £250 000 arriving unexpectedly as first prize in a Reader's Digest sales promotion. Utility theory attempts to massage the subjective values of different sums of money in such a way as to make gambling appear (subjectively) rational, and I must begin by explaining what 'rational' means in this context.

The expected value of a bet

Suppose I am offered a gamble that wins me \$$x$ with probability p and \$$y$ with probability $(1-p)$. My expected winnings would be:

$$\text{Expected winnings} = \$\{px + (1-p)y\}, \qquad (1)$$

and this is the most that a rational man should be willing to pay to participate in this particular gamble. If I pay more than this, then, in the long run, I shall be out of pocket. But gamblers repeatedly flout this principle – they buy bets for more than their expected values – and it is necessary that they should do so to provide a margin for the casino or the lottery promoter. Gamblers keep on gambling despite losing. Here is one at the Casino Club, Lytham St Anne's.

Maggie Harding	I've lost for about the last three months, I would say. And I've just won tonight, so that's good.
Interviewer	You've lost pretty solidly, as well?
Maggie Harding	Yes, yes.
Interviewer	So totting that up, what's it come to?
Maggie Harding	What's sixty times twelve? About six hundred, seven hundred pounds.

(Reproduced with permission from *Cutting Edge: Casino*, producer M. Nelson. Channel 4, 15 February 1998. © 1998 Channel 4 Television.)

It will turn out that utility theory is not able to accommodate the spectrum of gambles – those which gamblers will accept, and those they will not – without the introduction of a *subjective* probability; and if (subjective) probability is available for massage in the same way, the notion of utility is no longer needed. What matters is the accuracy with which ordinary people can assess the likelihoods of different events (in the light of Chapter 2, this will be very poor) and the biases to which they are subject (in the light of Chapter 11, this will be profound).

Expected utility

Suppose that \$$x$ has, for me, a utility (subjective value) u and \$$y$ utility v. The expected utility of the bet is then:

$$\text{Expected utility} = pu + (1-p)v. \qquad (2)$$

If that expected utility is equivalent to the utility of $z, then that is what I might be expected to pay to participate in this gamble. Utility theory endeavours to find a relation between (objective) sums of money and their (subjective) utilities such that the expected utility of a bet which a gambler accepts is never less than the utility of the stake.

It is not known what a workable relation between money and utility would need to look like; Figure 16.1 sets out one conjecture. The important point is that utility theory allows us to invoke whatever relation we please between different sums of money and their utilities in an attempt to make gambling appear rational.

Now, suppose your home is burned down. If you did not have the money to reinstate it, that would be a very grievous loss; you would be destitute. So people pay a much smaller sum, the insurance premium, and, in the case that they suffer a specified loss (their house is burned down), receive a much larger

Figure 16.1 Conjectural relation between money and utility.

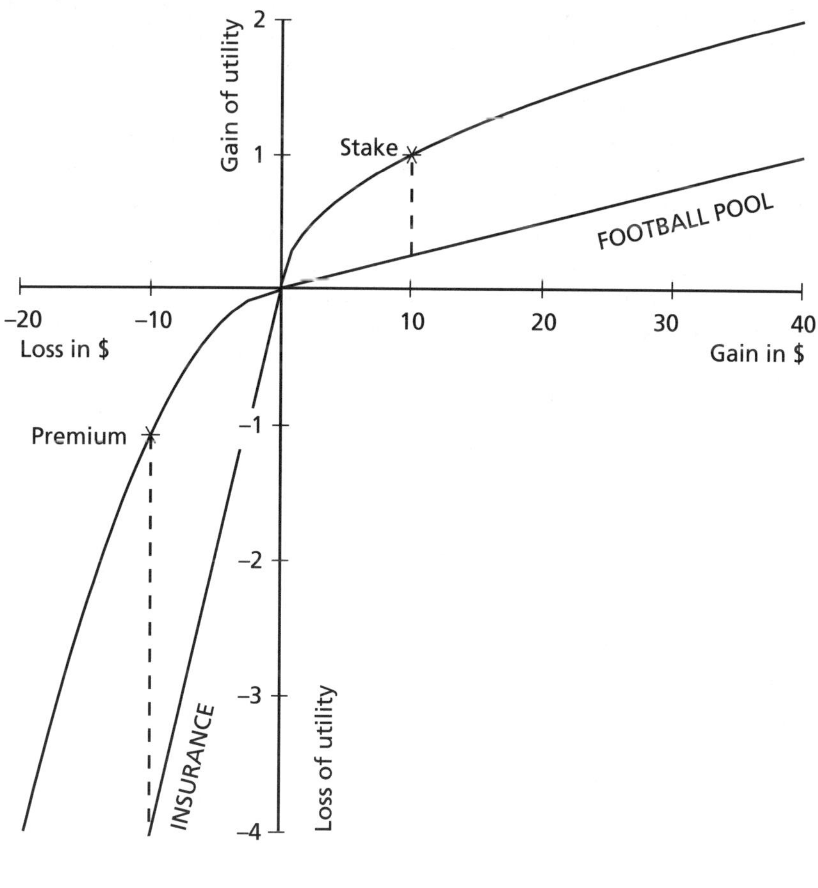

agreed sum to reinstate it. Of course, if your house is not burned down (most people's houses are not) the premium is lost with no return. Nevertheless, most people deem insurance to be worth buying, especially against really huge potential losses. Insurance is bought because the subjective value of the loss is deemed to be disproportionately greater than its monetary value. But a football pool is the exact contrary of insurance (see Figure 16.1). People pay a small sum (the stake) to buy a bet which pays a very large sum at very long odds. Buying insurance and simultaneously investing in football pools, as many people do, is paradoxical. It is difficult to see what kind of utility function would simultaneously make both these gambles appear rational. There is another reason as well why utility theory will not do; this centres on a paradox proposed by the French economist Maurice Allais in 1953.

Allais' paradox

Suppose you are asked to choose between the gambles A and B in Table 16.2. Most people choose B; in one experiment (Kahneman and Tversky, 1979) 59 out of 72 participants (82%) preferred B. But offered a similar choice between gambles C and D, most people prefer C. In the same experiment 60 of the same 72 subjects (83%) preferred C. Moreover, 44 of those 72 subjects (61%) chose both B from A and B, and C from C and D. But this combination of choices is indisputably irrational.

With gambles A and B, you receive $2400, 66 times out of 100, whichever way you choose. In those 66 cases your choice is irrelevant; only the other 34 cases actually matter. In those 34 cases you are actually choosing between gambles E and F in Table 16.3. That is the real choice. With the second pair of gambles (C and D) you receive nothing 66 times out of 100, whichever way you choose. In those 66 cases your choice is again irrelevant. But in the other 34 cases you have exactly the same choice as before, between gambles E and F. So both choices in Table 16.1 (A versus B and C versus D) present the same *real* choice.

Table 16.2 Allais' paradox. Data from Kahneman and Tversky (1979, p. 265).

Gambles	A	B
Choose between . . .	$2500 with p. 0.33 $2400 with p. 0.66 Nothing with p. 0.01	$2400 with certainty
No. choices (out of 72)	13	59
Gambles	**C**	**D**
Choose between . . .	$2500 with p. 0.33 Nothing with p. 0.67	$2400 with p. 0.34 Nothing with p. 0.66
No. choices (out of 72)	60	12

Table 16.3 Allais' paradox – the real choice.

Gambles	E	F
Choose between . . .	£2500 with p. 0.33 Nothing with p. 0.01	£2400 with p. 0.34

When that choice is dressed up as A versus B most people (82 per cent) choose F, but when it is dressed up as C versus D a similar proportion choose E. Since it is the same real choice that is taken in opposite directions in the two cases, no postulated relation between money and subjective utility will distinguish between them. Exit utility theory.

Allais' paradox is not restricted to monetary rewards. Table 16.4 presents the results of another experiment by Kahneman and Tversky (1979). The *relative* proportions of the probabilities of the different outcomes are the same in each case, so that if one prefers B to A, one ought also to prefer C to D. But preferences seem to depend on the *absolute* probabilities, even when the relative probabilities are the same. That suggests that people do not perceive probabilities in strict proportion to their objective values and that we need to think about the subjective perception of probabilities.

Table 16.4 Allais' paradox with non-monetary rewards. Data from Kahneman and Tversky (1979, p. 267).

Gambles	A	B
Choose between . . .	50% chance to win a 3-week tour of England, France and Italy.	A 1-week tour of England with certainty.
No. choices (out of 72)	16	56
Gambles	**C**	**D**
Choose between . . .	5% chance to win a 3-week tour of England, France and Italy.	10% chance to win a 1-week tour of England.
No. choices (out of 72)	48	24

Subjective probability

The expected utility of a gamble (Equation 2) is independent of whatever other gamble it might be combined with. This is so whatever relation one proposes between money and utility. So the respective contributions of gambles E and F in Table 16.3 to the expected utilities of gambles A and B in Table 16.2 are the same as their respective contributions to gambles C and D. The difference in utility between gambles A and B is the same as that between C and D, and utility theory provides no basis for the different frequencies of choice in the two experiments by Kahneman and Tversky (1979).

Allais' paradox can only be resolved by introducing subjective probabilities. Suppose that an objective probability p is perceived subjectively to have value s. The subjective expected utility of the bet in Equation 2 is now:

$$\text{Subjective expected utility} = su + (1-s)u, \tag{3}$$

and we have two arbitrary relations, that between money and utility ($\$x$ and u) and that between objective and subjective probabilities (p and s), with which to make gambling appear rational.

It has often been suggested that very small probabilities are consistently overestimated. How do people estimate the probability of having their house burnt down? Why, from stories they hear on television and read in the papers. That kind of probability seems greater than it objectively is, and insurance appears a good bargain. Likewise, the probability of winning the jackpot on the National Lottery ('Maybe I'll be lucky this week') is also seen to be much greater than it is in reality, and Camelot, the lottery company, fosters that overestimation by giving as much publicity as it can to previous jackpot winners. Systematic overestimation of very small probabilities can explain why people both buy insurance and also stake money on football pools or buy lottery tickets. The notion of utility is not needed.

But we do need to ask: How accurately can people estimate probabilities? In the experiments by Kahneman and Tversky (1979) the probabilities were given explicitly; but that only happens in laboratory experiments. In practice, people have to estimate likelihoods from experience. How accurately can that be done? And how subject to bias are people's estimates? When people are asked to identify different notes on the piano or different levels of sound, they are unable to distinguish more than five without error. When estimating probabilities it must be even worse, because a probability is not something one can experience like a note on the piano or a sound. It is a mathematical abstraction; it can be estimated only from analysis of a large number of like cases.

Contraceptive pills

The manner in which ordinary people (that is, excluding statisticians) appreciate probabilities is shown by the reaction of many women to the announcement on 18 October 1995 by the Committee on Safety of Medicines that third generation contraceptive pills, compared to second generation pills, had been found to carry an increased risk of thromboembolism. Women using third generation pills (about 1.5m women) were advised to consult their doctor to review their prescription and switch to another brand on completion of their present monthly course. This warning was issued in the form of a letter to doctors (Laurence, 1995).

Figure 16.2 Risks of thromboembolism from contraceptive pills.

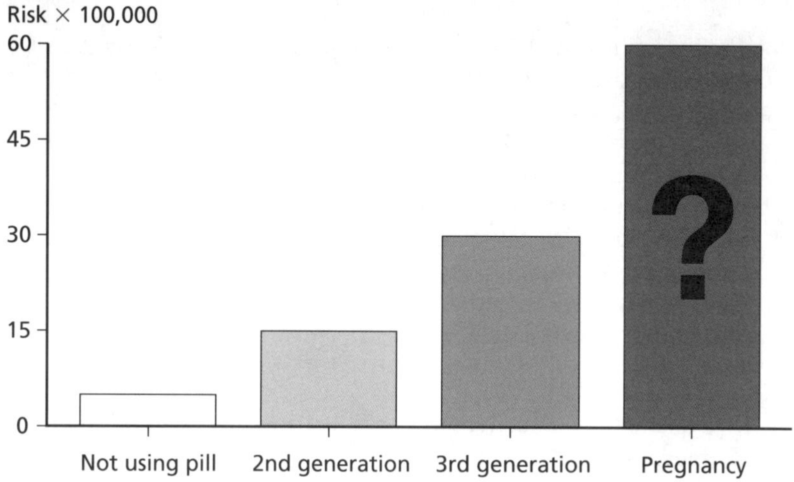

Redrawn with permission from *Understanding Human Motivation* by D. Laming, p. 267. © 2004, Donald Laming; published by Blackwell Publishing.

> The telephone lines were jammed and the queue never shortened yesterday at the Margaret Pyke centre in central London, as worried women tried to find out if they were at risk from their Pill.
>
> Telephonists and advisers at the family planning clinic had been doubled to cope with demand; the centre stayed open late yesterday and even considered opening over the weekend to help frightened callers. (Cooper, 1995)

> The panic that followed is estimated to have led to about 3000 abortions in Britain, while a baby boom is predicted for June and July [1996]. This week, it emerged that more than 800 extra abortions were carried out by the British Pregnancy Advisory Service alone, which also said that 41 per cent of women stopped taking the Pill immediately and 61 per cent did not finish their course as a result of the scare. (Dobson, 1996)

Figure 16.2 sets out the facts of the matter. First, the risks are tiny – typically three in 10 000. Second, they are greatest during pregnancy. But gradations of probability are not appreciated by ordinary people (that is, people who are not statisticians). Either the pill is 'safe' or it is 'risky'. There is no 'in between'.

Extended warranties

The sale of extended warranties on electrical appliances (actually insurance policies against breakdown) provides another example of inability to estimate likelihood.

> Nearly all the profits made by Dixons Group last year [1992], and nearly all it is expected to make this year [1993], came from the sale of extended warranties

on its electrical products – an extra that has been described by the Consumers' Association as 'a waste of money'. (Nisse, 1993)

A Sunday Times survey of warranties being sold by stores including Comet, Tempo and Dixons reveals that the policies can commonly add 90% or more to the price of products such as televisions, computers, washing machines, dishwashers and vacuum cleaners.

In its latest report on the issue, Which? magazine found that shoppers were being subjected to a 'range of misleading facts and pressure-selling tactics'.

Methods employed by staff at stores such as Comet, Currys, Dixons and Tempo included exaggerating a product's unreliability and offering discounts on the policies if consumers agreed to sign up to them on the spot, the magazine said. (Nuki and Corbishley, 1998)

So, to summarise the argument:

(i) If we talk about subjective probabilities, the previous notion of utility is no longer needed.

(ii) Experiment shows that people are not able to make absolute judgments of simple stimuli, nor even comparative judgments beyond a crude ordinal level. Probabilities are no different, so 'subjective probability' can have at most five different values, as in Figure 16.3.

Figure 16.3 Five different levels of subjective probability.

Contraceptive Pill	Horses
Certain	
Dangerous	'Sure Thing'
Risky	'Maybe'
Safe	'No Way'
Impossible	

Reproduced with permission from *Understanding Human Motivation* by D. Laming, p. 266. © 2004, Donald Laming; published by Blackwell Publishing.

In what follows I look at real gamblers staking their own real money in real casinos, and that enquiry is possible by virtue of research published by Willem Wagenaar (1988). Experimental studies with simulated gambles in a laboratory (e.g. Coombs, Dawes and Tversky, 1970, Ch. 5), or even in a casino (Lichtenstein and Slovic, 1973) are of doubtful validity, because in those studies the probabilities are given to the subjects numerically. An important element of real gambling turns on the individual's inability to estimate likelihoods accurately from informal observation, and that element is not present in such experimental studies.

Blackjack

The two most popular games in a casino are blackjack and roulette. Blackjack is the casino version of Pontoon or 21. The rules vary slightly from one casino to

Table 16.5 The rules of Blackjack.

- Four decks of cards are shuffled and placed in a holder ('shoe').
- A plastic card is inserted about three-quarters of the way down the shoe, at which point play stops and the cards are reshuffled.
- All cards are dealt face up, two to each player, only one to the dealer.
- Cards count at point value, and all court cards are worth 10, except for an Ace which may be either 1 or 11.
- The objective is to obtain a total greater than that of the dealer, but never exceeding 21.
- Ace and 10 (or court card) makes a blackjack which beats any other hand.
- Each player may either stand or hit (that is, draw additional cards, one at a time).
- If the two cards dealt to a player have identical values, the player may split and play two hands separately.
- If a player's total is 9, 10 or 11, the player is allowed to double his/her stake and draw just one more card.
- If the dealer's card is an Ace, each player may place an additional side bet (insurance) that the dealer will complete a blackjack.
- If a player busts (exceeds 21), the stake is lost.
- When all players have finished, the dealer takes a second card. The dealer must hit at 16 or less, and must stand at 17 or more; that is, the dealer plays mechanically.

another; the rules that applied in the Dutch casinos in which Wagenaar studied are set out in Table 16.5.

The fact that the dealer plays entirely mechanically means that there is an optimal strategy, known as 'Basic'. For each total held by the player and each card turned up by the dealer, Basic identifies the most profitable action: 'stand', 'hit', or 'double' (where doubling is allowed). To use Basic a player simply needs to memorise all the optimum combinations, which are set out in Table 16.6.

Basic gives an expected loss equal to 0.4 per cent of the stake. It is a better strategy than 'never bust' (i.e. always stand with a total of 12 or greater, which loses 8 per cent) or 'mimic the dealer' (i.e. stand at 17 or greater, but hit at any lesser total; this loses 6 per cent), but is not so good as 'counting'. 'Counting' means keeping a count of which cards have been played (all are played face up), chiefly the proportion of 10s and court cards. In this way the card-counter can distinguish situations that are favourable to the players from those that are unfavourable. This is possible because all cards are dealt from a 'shoe' containing four packs shuffled together. Knowing which cards have already been dealt means knowing which cards remain to be dealt and their respective probabilities can be modified accordingly. Court cards and 10s are especially favourable because two of them together make a hand worth 20, which is a very desirable score. 'Counting' enables the player to win in the long run at a rate equal to somewhere between 0.5 and 2 per cent of the stake. This is achieved by laying the minimum stake in unfavourable situations, and the maximum stake in favourable ones (the maximum and minimum being set by the house), but card

Table 16.6 Basic strategy for Blackjack.
(*'H' denotes 'hit', that is, draw another card; 'D' denotes 'double', that is, double one's stake and draw just one more card; 'S' denotes 'stand'*).

Players' total	Dealers' card 2	3	4	5	6	7	8	9	10	Ace
8	H	H	H	H	H	H	H	H	H	H
9	H	D	D	D	D	H	H	H	H	H
10	D	D	D	D	D	D	D	D	H	H
11	D	D	D	D	D	D	D	D	D	H
12	H	H	S	S	S	H	H	H	H	H
13	S	S	S	S	S	H	H	H	H	H
14	S	S	S	S	S	H	H	H	H	H
15	S	S	S	S	S	H	H	H	H	H
16	S	S	S	S	S	H	H	H	H	H
17	S	S	S	S	S	S	S	S	S	S

Reprinted with permission from W. A. Wagenaar, *Paradoxes of Gambling Behaviour*, p. 19. © 1988 Psychology Press.

counting is hard work, especially if one is doing it for eight hours a day, five days a week.

How gamblers play blackjack

Keren and Wagenaar (1985) studied 112 players in a small casino in Amsterdam and recorded a high percentage of plays which violated Basic strategy.

> Blackjack players repeatedly explained to me that the decisions prescribed by the Basic strategy are only made by inexperienced players. (Wagenaar, 1988, p. 82)

> One player told me: 'Listen, I have seen one of those card counters play. He lost his very first bet!' (Wagenaar, 1988, p. 110)

Wagenaar met a professional blackjack dealer who played blackjack during his leisure hours.

> Asked how he could hope to win both as a dealer and as a player, he explained that the whole secret is in knowing the order of the cards in the deck. He had discovered that two successive cards add up to 10, 11, or 12: after a six comes a five, after a two comes an eight. When I expressed some disbelief, he took me to the blackjack table, and indeed, his rule was confirmed frequently. A quick computation shows that about one-quarter of the possible pairs confirm the rule, whereas three-quarters do not. (Wagenaar, 1988, p. 108)

What these remarks show is that the view which habitual players of blackjack have of their game is out of kilter with reality. Indeed, many players see blackjack as a team sport. 'A bad player can spoil the game for everyone' (Wagenaar, 1988. p. 107).

> The illusion of a match between players and dealer is encouraged by expert dealers, who attempt to create the atmosphere of a 'good fight'. Many players object less to losing after they had a good fight, because it offers the excuse that the dealer was too strong. The illusion is also shared by some pit bosses. They have a tendency to change dealers rapidly when the house is losing, as if bringing in 'fresh' dealers would wear out the players. (Wagenaar, 1988, p. 108. This and the preceding quotations reprinted with permission from W. A. Wagenaar, *Paradoxes of Gambling Behaviour*. © 1988 Psychology Press.)

But there are a few players who know what's what.

> Ken is a professional card counter – a member of an élite band of mathematical geniuses who make a living from memorising sequences of cards.
>
> Casinos hate Ken and will try to ban him as soon as he crosses their portals, which is why he is so secretive. In order to reach him you first have to call his mum in Birmingham, who then relays a message by fax to whichever casino he happens to be holed up in.
>
> Ken switched to blackjack. He knew little about the game but worked out what is known in the US as 'basic strategy': the mathematically correct way of playing. He immediately won 14 nights in a row, clocking up a £400 profit.
>
> Then on the fifteenth night, disaster. 'I lost £225, which in those days seemed like a fortune,' recalls Ken. 'I stayed at home and licked my wounds for a few days. But then I realised that not even the casino can win the whole time and decided to battle on.'
>
> It was not until 1978, however, that Ken began making serious money.

> 'I was playing Cromwell's in Birmingham and now other players were copying me. If I bet, everyone else piled on money, too. At first the casino loved it, but 16 months later when they saw how much they'd lost, they weren't so pleased and I was barred.'
>
> By now Ken was playing professionally, but he was having to travel farther and farther to get a game. Today, he cannot get a game anywhere in Britain.
>
> . . . mastering the maths is only half the battle. Card counters also need nerves of steel. Most casinos keep watch for sudden swings in betting that indicate you are counting. You also have to be psychologically prepared for bad runs of luck even when your count tells you that you should be winning.
>
> Card counting takes its toll in other ways, too. Ken rarely gets to bed before 6 am and lives in constant fear of being roughed up in a casino backroom. His only companions are fellow card counters but he cannot acknowledge their presence, at least not while working, for fear of being caught. (Honigsbaum, 1992)

There are much easier ways to earn a living.

Roulette

The other popular casino game is roulette. Again, there are variations from one casino to another how the game is played. Table 16.7 sets out the rules in the Dutch casinos in which Wagenaar studied gamblers' ways of playing.

Table 16.7 The game of Roulette.

- A disc with 37 pockets numbered from 0 to 36 revolves within a bowl.
- The croupier projects a ball around the rim of the bowl in the opposite direction to the rotation of the disc. After several rotations, the ball leaves the rim of the bowl, hits one of the spoilers and finally falls into one of the 37 pockets on the disc.
- Players may bet on single numbers, on various combinations of 2, 3, 4, 6, 12 or 18 different numbers, or on the 'simple chances' (RED or BLACK, or EVEN or ODD, or HIGH or LOW).
- The expected loss is always 1/37 (2.7 per cent) of the stake, no matter how it is split between different numbers (except for a special provision when betting on the 'simple chances').

Betting patterns

A 'betting pattern' is a combination of numbers on the roulette grid – a combination of bets on a single spin of the wheel. E.H.M. Terheggen's book *One Hundred Winning Moves at Roulette* is a book of betting patterns – instructions which the croupier will immediately understand. In the long run one must always expect to lose 2.7 per cent (1/37) of one's stake; but the degree of risk,

Figure 16.4 The number of cells covered and the consequent spread of risk for 29 roulette players studied by Wagenaar (1988). The horizontal and vertical arrows indicate the standard deviations of each subject's choices.

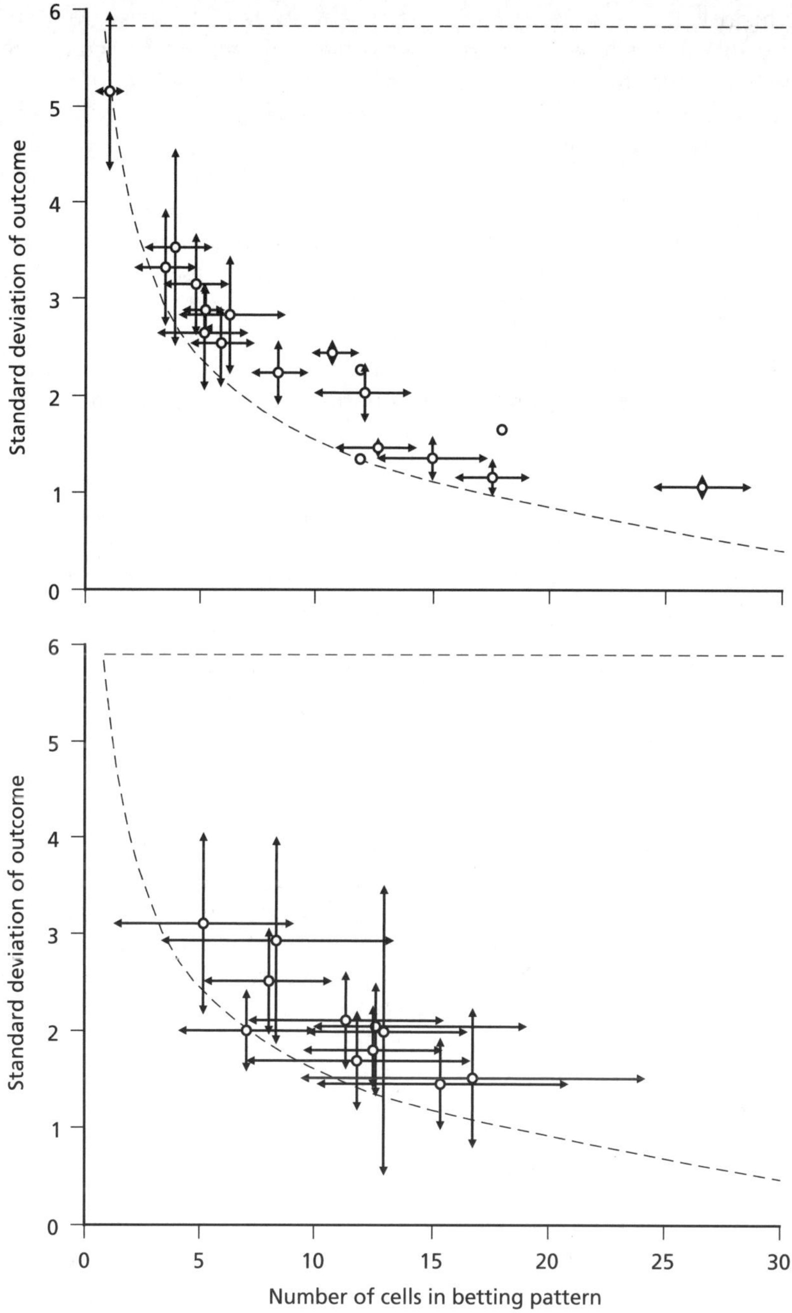

Reproduced with permission from W. A. Wagenaar, *Paradoxes of Gambling Behaviour*, p. 54. © 1988 Psychology Press.

which depends on the number of cells covered, can be varied. If the stake is spread evenly over N cells, the probability of winning something is N/37, but the amount won is smaller – 36/N times the amount staked. In this way a player can reduce his risk.

Figure 16.4 shows how different players show different idiosyncratic preferences between the different degrees of risk. Each player tends to prefer a consistent pattern of bet, spreading the stake over a similar number of numbers, on successive plays of the game. But the riskiness of the bet, remarkably stable for each individual, varies widely from one player to another. This is a pattern of behaviour shown by Sherif's subjects (see Chapter 6) when they were asked to estimate the distance apparently moved by a point of light, seen for a few seconds in otherwise complete darkness. Those estimates were idiosyncratic because there was no sensory basis at all for the numbers uttered by the subjects. In roulette all bets carry an expected loss of 2.7 per cent. The expected loss is not affected by the way in which the bet is spread across different combinations of numbers, and the degree of risk sought is entirely a personal preference.

Betting systems

Whereas a betting pattern describes the distribution of the stake money over the different numbers on a single play of roulette, a 'betting system' specifies how one should vary the bet, especially the amount staked, from one play to another. The most common principle is to increase the size of the bet after a loss in order to recoup and, in some cases, to make a small profit. But every play is a statistically independent event. Every play carries an expected loss of 2.7 per cent. All systems are equally good (or bad). Why then do players bother to use them?

Luck

The answer to that question is 'Luck'.

In popular parlance we have notions of both 'luck' and of 'chance'. While statisticians can elaborate the notion of chance quite precisely, it will appear from what follows that 'luck' has no foundation at all in nature. It is a purely artificial concept and I am concerned here to explain how it arises. To illustrate its source, Table 16.8 shows sample sequences of 25 black and 25 white dots, with the proportion of repetitions (white-white and black-black) equal to 0.2, 0.3, 0.4, 0.5, 0.6, 0.7 and 0.8 in successive rows (after Wagenaar, 1988, p. 92). Now, which of those sequences looks the most random? Imagine that I have tossed a fair coin 50 times; which of those sequences looks most typical of the succession of heads (white) and tails (black) that I should generate?

A fair coin not only produces about as many heads as it does tails (average 25 in 50 tosses), but also produces as many heads as it does tails following a head (or a tail) on the preceding toss. For this reason, sequence D is the correct answer; it has been constructed to have as many repetitions as it has alternations; but people tend to select sequence C (62.5 per cent alternations) or even B (75 per cent alternations) as typifying their notion of randomness.

Table 16.8 Sample sequences of white (heads) and black (tails) dots.

A	○○●○●●●○○●○●○○●○○●○●○●○●○●●●○●○●●○●○●○●○●○●○●○●○
B	○●○●●○○●●○●○●○●●●○○●○●●●○○●○○●○●○●○○●●○○●○●○○●○○●●
C	●○●●●○○●●○○●○○○○●○○●●●●○○●●○○●○●○○●○●○●●○●○●○●○○●●
D	●○●●○●○○●●●○●●○○○○●●○●●○○○○○●●○○●●●○●○○○●●●○○●●○○●
E	○○○○●●●●○○○○●●○○●●●●○○○○●●●○○●●●●○○○●●●○●○○●○●○●●○
F	○●●○○●●●○○○○○○●●○○○○○●●○○●●●●○○○●●●●●●●○○●●●●●○○○○
G	○○○●●●●●○○○○○○●●●●●○○○●●●●○○○●●●●●○○○○○○○●●●●●●○○○

Reprinted with permission from *Understanding Human Motivation* by D. Laming, p. 273. © 2004, Donald Laming; published by Blackwell Publishing.

Wagenaar (1970) prepared 16 different sets of strings (as in Table 16.8, but with 100 dots in each string) and asked 203 subjects to select the one most likely to have been produced by tossing a coin. The median judgment of a large majority (86 per cent) favoured a sequence with less than 50 per cent repetitions (i.e. A, B, or C in Figure 16.4). Most people expect a small number of tosses of a coin, or a small number of plays at roulette, to conform more closely to the average than actually happens in nature. Consequently, a truly random sequence contains more long runs of losses or successes than people expect. Some other factor must therefore be operative to produce those long runs of repetitions. That other factor is LUCK.

Jean Dearden believes in luck.

> 'Well I think it's 'im up there, and if 'e says it's your night, it's your night. And whatever you do, you can't lose. This is over twenty years and we've – don't we say that? – over twenty years, if it's our night, we've won a fortune on stupid things. But when it's not our night, can't do a thing.' (Reproduced with permission from *Cutting Edge: Casino,* producer M. Nelson. Channel 4, 15 February, 1998. © 1998, Channel 4 Television).

The essence of this popular misconception of randomness is easily characterised: people expect a small number of tosses of a coin, or a small number of plays at roulette, to conform more closely to the average than actually happens in nature. This misplaced expectation is commonly known as the 'gamblers' fallacy' or, satirically, as the 'Law of Small Numbers'.

> Since players do not expect long runs of wins or losses, they perceive good and bad luck as the cause of these runs. The conviction that good and bad luck last for a certain period of time changes the perceived nature of the game considerably. Instead of seeing the game as determined by fixed odds, they now feel that their task is the detection of good and bad luck. In this manner losses will be attributed to lack of skill, rather than to adverse odds. Consequently players can always assure themselves that next time they will be more alert. (Wagenaar, 1988, pp. 112–13)

There are, therefore, laws of probability that specify the relative frequencies of chance events, in this case runs of wins and losses, and there is also a popular conception of how those relative frequencies should be. That popular conception does not match the frequencies actually observed in nature, and the notion of 'luck' is invoked to 'explain' the difference. That difference is entirely a matter of popular misconception, as also is the source of the notion.

Keren and Wagenaar (1985) interviewed many players about various aspects of gambling:

> . . . we learned that one cannot force luck to happen. You should wait till luck appears, and in that sense it is much like chance. On the other hand you can lose your luck easily by using it unwisely. You can also fail to utilise it when it happens, for instance by not even noticing that this is your lucky day, or your lucky deck, or your lucky dealer. Finally, one can also ruin the effect of good luck by not noticing that it ended, thus losing everything that was won. In this sense the utilisation of luck is more like a skill. The special nature of luck explains why it is difficult to attribute the outcome of gambles to chance or skill only. When subjects were asked to divide 100% over three causal factors, chance, skill, and luck, the following results were obtained (Keren and Wagenaar, 1985): chance 18%; skill 37%; and luck 45%. (Wagenaar, 1988, p. 93)

How then can luck influence the motion of the roulette wheel? It doesn't.

> . . . it should be realised that the outcome of a gamble is the result of a coincidence between a choice made by the gambler and a random event beyond the gambler's control. . . . From my discussions with gamblers I learned that most do not, in fact, believe that they can influence the roulette wheel. Neither that luck will influence the roulette wheel or any other randomising device. But luck may influence the player's choice. The chance outcome of the roulette wheel is the same for all players, but betting is not. Good luck may help one player to bet on the right number, whilst as a result of bad luck other players bet on the wrong number. In this manner the concept of luck does not run counter to a purely physical explanation of how randomisers like roulette wheels, dice, and cards work. But belief in luck makes all reasoning based on the physical definition of a game irrelevant. (Wagenaar, 1988, p. 101. This and the preceding quotations reprinted with permission from W. A. Wagenaar, *Paradoxes of Gambling Behaviour*. © 1988 Psychology Press.)

'Luck' is by no means the only imaginary concept to arise in this way.

> Mr Warham knew his cerebral system must one day scoop a jackpot on the football pools and, as wretched [Albion] Rovers conceded an equaliser with only four minutes of the match remaining, the Post Office sorter from the Potteries could justify his modest little flutter – which has amounted since 1974 to putting more than half his wage packet where his system is.
>
> 'I have spent years perfecting the system, including many hours on a computer,' Mr Warham, 56, said. 'I always knew it would come right in the end.'

> Six other regulars [at the Black's Head, Stoke-on-Trent] shared in a Littlewood's payout of £2m. They have nicknamed Mr Warham 'Magnus Pike' for his scientific approach to the pools. 'I used the same numbers every week. There is something called the cluster effect when draws come together in twos and threes,' he said. (Foster, 1992)

Many people comment on many different kinds of events that they seem to happen in twos and threes – but that is only appearance. Randomness is the absence of any systematic variation. It subsists in there being nothing to see and for that reason it is not itself noticed.

Luck, then, does not correspond to any property existing in nature, and its estimation is necessarily based on entirely irrelevant considerations. But people are unable to ignore the irrelevant. In games of chance 'A large number of players do indeed believe that their results depend on personal skills' (Csikszentmihalyi and Bennett, 1971). Why then do people gamble? Because they estimate that the combination of chance, luck and skill is favourable. But there are other people – Willem Wagenaar is one – who can see that that combination is always unfavourable. Such people are correct; but how do they reach their conclusion?

The conservation of expected loss

Jean Piaget devised a now very well-known problem as a means of testing the intellectual development of young children. The contents of a glass (A) are poured into a narrower glass (B) or a wider glass (C). Four- to six-year-old children think that the amount of liquid increases or decreases as the level is higher in the second glass (B) or lower (C). However, by the age of seven or eight the child says:

> 'It is the same water.'
> 'It has only been poured.'
> 'Nothing has been taken away or added.'
> 'The water is higher, but the glass is narrower, so it's the same amount.'

Or, particularly,

> 'You can put the water in B back into A where it was before' (Piaget and Inhelder, 1969, p. 98).

By about seven or eight years of age the child has acquired the principle of the conservation of (liquid) volume, applicable when water is poured from one vessel into another. Piaget saw that acquisition as indicative of a significant stage in intellectual development.

To bring out the psychological nature of Piaget's problem, I put it to my class (university students who are all very well acquainted with Piaget's ideas on conservation) in inverse order. They are first shown the two beakers in Figure 16.5, part filled with milk: which beaker contains the most milk? Because the beakers

Figure 16.5 Piaget's 'Conservation of Liquid' problem. Which beaker has the more milk in it?

Photographs: Ian Cannell.

are of different diameters, that is an exceedingly difficult judgment. Answers from different students are more or less random. The contents of the wider beaker are now poured into the second narrow beaker, of the same shape and size as the first. At that point, but not before, it becomes clear that the wider beaker had contained the greater amount of milk. The psychological structure of the problem can be set out as follows.

Accurate comparison of the two quantities of milk is very difficult. No-one can compensate for the differing widths of the two vessels without precise and detailed measurements of the two. But the action of pouring the liquid into the second narrow glass, together with the principle of conservation of liquid volume, constitutes a 'trick' which enables the question to be answered correctly. It is like a mathematical theorem. The young child, four to six years old, has not yet discovered this means of solving the problem. Such a child is in the same position as my students before they see the milk poured from the wide beaker into the second narrow one. But the older child of seven or eight has learned that particular trick and can answer correctly, as also could all of my students after they had seen the pouring completed.

The principle of conservation is functionally extraneous to the visual comparison of the two liquid volumes. It is actually a bias. But calling it a 'bias' is liable to mislead because it happens to deliver the correct answer, where otherwise people would be more or less guessing in the dark. Piaget has explored other principles of conservation relating to number, length, mass (or substance), weight and other quantities besides. These different principles are not all acquired at the same time, but gradually, one after another, as the child grows up and gains increasing experience. Indeed, the conservation of energy is a profound scientific principle which students learn about at university; it enables solutions to many difficult physical problems.

In the present context, simple calculations based on probability theory show that the expected value of a gamble in a casino (card counting at blackjack excepted), or on a football pool, is always negative; on average the punter should always expect to lose. By the 'conservation of expected loss' I mean the use of formal (but usually very simple) probability theory to calculate one's expected return. This is an abstract idea, and many adults have failed to master it. It displaces the sensory basis for judging one's likely winnings; it is, in fact, the extraneous factor, like the principle of the conservation of liquid above, which biases an otherwise very difficult judgment, to enable the correct answer to be discovered.

One might suppose that anyone who goes near a casino needs a prior grounding in probability theory. That is not necessary, because the calculations are often no more than common sense. Neither is a grounding in probability theory sufficient as the following example shows:

> Peter lost everything through gambling 15 years ago – his house, his wife and family. He believes his problem is that he is addicted to his own adrenalin.
>
> Peter, who has rebuilt his life with the help of Gamblers' Anonymous, said: 'It's nothing to do with the money. It is to do with the need to be in action. I would sit at the roulette wheel for hours with my heart pounding. I sat next to the same people for years and have no idea who they were. If I won at 4 am when they closed I went home totally depressed because I did not want to stop when I was winning. If the croupier tried to stop the wheel a minute before time I would be very angry.
>
> Peter, *who has a degree in statistics* [my italics], knew all about probability but he could not believe that it was any help in winning casino games. 'I could never believe that each number had an equal chance of coming up. I would notice that the ball was not falling on one part of the wheel and would believe that those numbers would come up next. So I piled my money on. I liked blackjack too because the casino would stop you if you played too skilfully. It was more important to me to play and take the risk than to play well.' (Gillie, 1990)

Another story concerns an accountancy student who, although not actually studying probability, might be expected to be competent at the simple calculations involved.

> An accountancy student who gambled away his loans hanged himself after losing £500 on the tables of a Leeds casino, an inquest was told.
>
> Barry Partridge . . . was a regular customer of the city's casinos. He hanged himself after losing the loan money within three days of cashing the cheque.
>
> Nicholas Girling, a friend and neighbour, said Mr Partridge had a gambling habit he could ill-afford. 'I've been . . . with Barry on numerous occasions and he gambled quite recklessly. He was never much good with money,' he said. (*Independent*, 1991a)

Under most circumstances people learn naturally from their experiences, and thereby acquire a practical knowledge of how the world works. They learn what leads to what; a mistake once made tends not to be made again. But when someone is observing the numbers generated by a roulette wheel or the succession of wins and losses at the blackjack table, they discover, it seems to them, curious properties of the succession of events they are witnessing. 'There is something called the cluster effect when draws come together in twos and threes' (John Warham, cited by Foster, 1992). The natural ability which all people have to pick out what leads to what in the world in which we live, causes the same people to 'detect' trends in the outcomes of games of chance which are, in fact, no more than chance, but which are interpreted by the gambler as the effects of some other agency. That other agency is 'luck'. Paradoxically, the one thing about the outcomes of games of chance which people's natural talent for informal learning will never teach them is that there is nothing to be learned. For that reason gamblers' judgments of likely winnings are biased by irrelevant factors from which they cannot escape. An estimated nine million people stake money on the football pools for an average return of 23p in the pound. One of the irrelevant factors in this case is shown in Figure 16.6.

Figure 16.6 Advertisement for Littlewood's football pool.

Summary – why do people gamble and keep on gambling despite repeated losses?

The outcome of the next bet presents a very difficult judgment. Ordinary people's appreciation of probability accommodates at most five distinct levels of risk. Consequently, judgment of the next bet is much subject to bias. There is bias from hearing about other people who have won the jackpot in the National Lottery ('It could be you!') or the football pools, and the promoters encourage the maximum of publicity for their winners. Likewise with the purchase of insurance; hearing the news of someone's house being burned down or seeing a road accident increases people's estimate of the risk. Intuitive appreciation of likelihoods from relevant events that one has heard of leads to systematic overestimation of small probabilities, especially very tiny ones. Multiply those overestimates by the sum of money that might be won and, to more than a few people, gambling becomes irresistable. Only a careful application of probability theory can achieve an accurate assessment of risk.

17 Predicting the future

To summarise the argument of this book:

I began with a principle of relativity, which says:

- There is no absolute judgment – all judgments are relative, comparisons of one thing with another. This was illustrated with an escape from East Berlin and with the removal of children's tonsils. It also explains how different people with different points of view can express different judgments about the same thing – about Salman Rushdie's *The Satanic Verses*, for example.
- Sensory experience is differentially coupled to the physical world so that only changes in sensation are available as a basis for discrimination. This was illustrated with the Craik–Cornsweet illusion and with the taste of water.
- The comparisons (of one thing with another) are little better than ordinal; that is, one sound may be louder, softer, or about the same as another, but that is all we can say. This was illustrated with the effects of chevrons painted on the carriageway of the M1 and with the phenomenon of simultaneous contrast.

Next, I looked at what people say when, unbeknown to them, there is no objective basis for comparison. What people do in such a situation is elegantly exposed in Sherif's experiments with the autokinetic phenomenon. People are then vulnerable to even the slightest and subtlest suggestions from others; indeed, they have no defence against extraneous suggestion. Such influence between one person and another pervades our everyday life; it underlies advertising, the appraisal of literature and art, and, perhaps most important of all, religion.

In most practical situations, however, there is some material evidence on which to base a judgment, but not so firm a basis for comparison but that some doubt remains. In such cases, judgments are biased by whatever extraneous influences there happen to be. This was illustrated with the underforecasting of wind speed on the night of the great storm, 15 October 1987, and with the identification of playing cards printed in the wrong colour. Bias of this kind can be seen in many areas of public life – in the investigation of child abuse in

Cleveland and elsewhere; in marking examinations; and in identification by eyewitnesses. Indeed, bias can be excluded only to the extent that the material evidence is decisive. This was illustrated with two trials on charges of rape and with the accidents that invariably occur when an insufficiently trained pilot suddenly and unexpectedly has to fly 'blind'. It also explains why people gamble.

Now, in this final chapter, the limited reliability of peoples' judgments and the possibility of errors accumulating from one judgment to another pose the question of how far we can predict the future of human society. The motion of the planets in our solar system can be calculated and predicted with great accuracy; but to the extent that a human society evolves through the judgments and choices made by its members, its evolution is unpredictable, random. Different individuals have different points of view and are subject to different influences, most notably from the different people they know and meet. While the choices of some one individual might be amenable to study and become predictable, the aggregate of the choices of an entire society, especially when members of that society influence each other, is beyond calculation. The vagaries of peoples' judgments mean that the society of tomorrow is forever beyond our purview.

Prediction

There is an important distinction to be made between predicting the future behaviour of physical systems such as the motion of the sun and moon and predicting the evolution of human societies.

Those aspects of the future which depend on the extrapolation of purely physical principles, such as the motion of the Earth and planets around the sun, are, of course, accurately predictable. Keeping the calendar has long been an important activity in human society; and the accuracy which can now be achieved is elegantly illustrated by a calculation in reverse by Dr Leslie Morrison of the Royal Greenwich Observatory and Dr Richard Stephenson of Durham University. These two astronomers have studied records of lunar and solar eclipses on 2500 year-old clay tablets excavated in Babylonia and in Chinese records from between 500 and 1200 AD. Their calculations show that days are getting longer by about 1.7 thousandths of a second per century, because the eclipses were recorded as occurring at slightly different times to those which backward calculation gave on the basis of a constant speed of rotation of the Earth at its present-day rate. The lengthening of the Earth's day is due to friction with the tides. This slows the Earth's rate of rotation, and it is calculated that about six hours has been 'lost' since the time of Homer, 3000 years ago (Berry, 1993; *Independent*, 1993).

Where the future depends on human choice, however, the quality of prognostication is very different. During a general election campaign there is intense interest in its likely outcome, not least because political parties reassess their strategies in the light of their projections. Several organisations publish opinion polls almost every day, and that sampling of public opinion is possible because political preferences do not change much over the course of three weeks. This is so, notwithstanding the blandishments of the politicians. But over a longer period of time more radical changes occur. Indeed, the political structure of society itself evolves.

So, when a question is asked about some aspect of the future which depends on the evolution of human choice, prediction over a sufficiently long period of time becomes impossible. The future appears random, unpredictable. And in some instances 'sufficiently long' turns out to be surprisingly short. The 100-hours war in Kuwait was one of them.

The 100-hours war

To set the scene in 1990, Iraq has been at war with Iran for eight years and was very short of foreign exchange. Its chief source was from exports of oil. But Kuwait's overproduction of oil, in excess of a quota agreed amongst the OPEC countries, was allegedly holding the price down (to $16 per barrel) and thereby reducing the amount of foreign currency that Iraq might otherwise earn. So Iraq revived an ancient border dispute with Kuwait (Fisk, 1990); specifically, Iraq claimed two islands (Warbah and Bubiyan), which would give it marine access to the Persian Gulf, uncomplicated by any agreement with Iran, and a swathe of Kuwaiti territory which would give it all of that part of the large Rumeila oilfield not already in Iraqi possession.

In late July 1990 Iraq assembled 100 000 troops on the border with Kuwait (Berger and Cockburn, 1990). This was seen in the West as a tactic to bring pressure on Kuwait during talks about to be held between the two countries. But, on 2 August 1990, Iraq invaded Kuwait, occupying not merely the two-mile swathe covering the southern tip of the Rumeila oilfield, but the whole country. This took everybody in the West by surprise, including April Glaspie, the American ambassador to Iraq, who, after a talk with Saddam Hussein, the president of Iraq, the week before the invasion, 'felt sufficiently confident to leave Baghdad . . . for a summer holiday'. (Hughes and Morris, 1990; see also Darwish, 1990). The invasion was described as a 'political masterstroke' in the *Independent* (Cockburn, 1990a), 'catching all of Iraq's enemies in the Gulf and the world at large, by surprise'. Now, if Iraq had contented itself with occupying the disputed territory only, there would probably have been insufficient will in the West to take military action in response; that *would* have been a 'political masterstroke'. But, being so greedy as to occupy the whole country and to plunder it withal ought to have been a political disaster.

At about this time intelligence reports were repeatedly uncertain about Saddam Hussein's intentions, trying to make strategic sense of what he had done (Bellamy, 1990). One letter writer, referring particularly to Saddam Hussein's attempt to link his invasion of Kuwait with the Palestinian question, described his strategy as 'shrewd' (Labib, 1990). 'A shambles' would have been a more apt description. The difficulty faced by the intelligence people arose precisely because there were no well-considered strategic intentions for them to discover. This is illustrated by the Iraqis' vacillation over the several hundred Westerners they took prisoner when occupying Kuwait.

Iraqi TV broadcast personal interviews between Saddam Hussein and some of these prisoners, including children (Helm, 1990). The Iraqis may have thought this would be good propaganda, but, frankly, it caused nothing but revulsion in the West. Presumably, the purpose of keeping Westerners hostage was to deter military action against Iraq, in which case the piecemeal release of the prisoners threw away whatever advantage had been gained, without reversing the feeling of revulsion (Dowden, 1990). A visit by Sir Edward Heath in October secured the release of 33 prisoners (Beeston and Anon, 1990), and other elder statesmen and celebrities followed, almost forming a procession. Again, one supposes the Iraqis thought it good publicity. All the remaining hostages were released in time for Christmas (Cockburn, 1990b), and that final release appears to have been made in the hope of averting the coming war. But, if that was its purpose, it was much too little; Saddam Hussein was not yet willing to relinquish Kuwait.

Meanwhile, Iraq had been building immense fortifications to defend Kuwait. When, on 17 January 1991, the UN ultimatum expired, air attacks began against Iraq and against its forces in Kuwait. At this time Western analysts were still unable to make sense of what the Iraqis were doing.

> Sometimes it seems as if two different wars are being fought at once. The allies are fighting a textbook war and have braced themselves for textbook responses that have failed to materialise.
>
> They are perplexed by an enemy taking military measures that appear to be either self-defeating or derisory [most notably, flying most of the Iraqi warplanes to Iran]. As a result, these measures are coming to be judged largely according to their political impact, raising the nagging question as to whether the Iraqi President is very clever or very stupid.
>
> Much air-time and newsprint have been devoted to making sense of Saddam Hussein's strategy. Because it has such a high political content, every time he does something irrational in military terms he is given credit for great political imagination. (Freedman, 1991)

The answer to that quandary is very simple. Saddam Hussein was quite out of his depth, not knowing what to do and what not. He also had no conception of the effectiveness of US firepower. All that is evident from what followed. On 15 February Iraq made a conditional offer to withdraw, which was rejected; again too little was offered. The US and its allies knew by then that they could eject Iraqi forces from Kuwait unconditionally with very little trouble. The 'Mother of Battles' began on 24 February. The Iraqi forces were quickly routed and President Bush called a halt after exactly 100 hours, perhaps motivated by the thought of possible public revulsion at the slaughter of retreating Iraqi forces, especially at the Mutla ridge (Bulloch, 1991, p. 13).

Up to this point it would appear that all the miscalculations were on the Iraqi side. Not so. Allied intelligence estimated that there were more than 600 000 Iraqi troops in Kuwait at the beginning of the air offensive. After the war that estimate was scaled down to below 400 000; but mass desertions make 200 000 to 300 000 a more plausible figure. Iraqi battlefield casualties were originally estimated at 25 000 to 100 000, with the most conservative estimate at 15 000. But that estimate was ultimately revised downwards to 1500. 'US forces, in their rapid advance, found and buried only 577 Iraqi corpses' (Bellamy, 1991).

Miscalculation also entered into estimates of the battlefield effectiveness of the US Air Force.

> . . . on 30 January 1991, the US central command held a press conference at which it showed a video taken by a F-15E fighter-bomber. It was claimed they had hit between three and seven launchers [mobile launchers for Scud missiles], but these were probably fuel trucks.
>
> Widely shown on television, the film gave the impression that the US Air Force, equipped with laser-guided bombs, could hit any target with total accuracy.
>
> In fact, according to a new survey reluctantly released by the USAF, its planes flew 1500 missions against mobile Scud launchers, but failed to hit any. (Cockburn, 1993)

An obviously desirable outcome to this war would have been the removal of Saddam Hussein. However, it is not diplomatic etiquette to seek the removal of a foreign head of state (killing him would have been murder, whereas killing Iraqi soldiers in battle is not), so that when President Bush called on the 'Iraqi people and the Iraqi military to take matters into their own hands, to force Saddam Hussein the dictator, to step aside' (Doyle, 1991), there was some allied protest. Nevertheless, the sentiment was widely shared, in Iraq as well as in the West. But, equally nevertheless, Saddam Hussein survived in power, ruthlessly suppressing revolutions in the north (from the Kurds) and the south (from the marsh Arabs) and resisting compliance with those UN resolutions calling for the destruction of Iraq's nuclear and chemical war capability – resolutions to which Iraq had specifically agreed as a part of the armistice. After the rout of the Iraqi army it would have been only too easy for the US forces to carry on to Baghdad and take over the whole country. Why did they hold off? Robert Gates, then the director of the CIA, explained:

> . . . official explanations have focused largely on three factors: that US troops would take more casualties in an extended drive on Baghdad; the administration's mistaken belief that he would soon be overthrown in a post-war coup; and that the United Nations coalition supporting action against Iraq had been put together strictly to reverse the Iraqi invasion of Kuwait, not to install a new Iraqi government.

However,

> The idea was rejected largely because officials feared that he would go into hiding, as Panama's Manuel Noriega had done during the 1989 US military intervention, and that troops occupying Iraq would be unable to find him. (Mann, 1993)

Saddam Hussein has continued to govern Iraq, very much in control, for 12 further years. While much of his development of biological, chemical and nuclear weaponry was dismantled by UN inspection teams, those teams were subsequently expelled from the country and the web of restrictive sanctions began to crumble. It is clear that Saddam Hussein made a disastrous miscalculation of Western reaction to his invasion of Kuwait and of Western capability to reverse it; and western political commentators made equally gross (though not disastrous) miscalculations of the consequences of Iraqi actions. But the Americans miscalculated as well. Who, after the rout of the Iraqi forces in Kuwait, foresaw the personal survival of Saddam Hussein as president for 12 further years? No-one. And who, apart from Osama bin Laden and senior members of al Qaeda foresaw the suicide attacks on America on 9/11? Or that those attacks would provide an opportunity for America to renew its war on Iraq? And what (as of 27 March 2003) will the outcome of that war be? People cannot foresee the future.

The Amy Fisher story

It is quite easy to see the unfolding of events in Iraq as the result of miscalculation, rather than an essentially unpredictable 'chance'. If the Western allies had *known* . . . they would have acted differently. But, in some cases, the critical trigger from which, in retrospect, all else seems to have followed can be seen, again in retrospect, to be the sort of occurrence whose consequences no-one could possibly foresee. Here is how a chance remark created a box-office success.

Amy Fisher, 17 years old at the time, was having an affair with a married man, Joey Buttafuoco. On 19 May 1992 Amy went to the Buttafuoco home and shot Mrs. Buttafuoco in the head. Mrs. Buttafuoco somehow survived, though with damaged hearing and sight. Amy Fisher was quickly arrested and pleaded guilty to attempted murder. She was sentenced on 1 December 1992 to between five and 15 years in prison – an unappealing and mundane story.

During the investigation of her crime Amy Fisher explained that she had been having an affair with Joey Buttafuoco and said that he had encouraged her to kill his wife. On that point, Daniel Severin, a Nassua county detective-sergeant, remarked in the course of a press conference 'that the case looked like a "near-*Fatal Attraction*", referring to the box-office mega-hit starring Michael Douglas, with Glenn Close as the *femme fatale*' (Usborne, 1993).

What followed was dramatic in more senses than one. Three national networks in America very rapidly made film versions of Amy Fisher's story. There was *Amy Fisher: My Story* (NBC, 28 December 1992), *Beyond Control* (ABC) and *Casualties of Love: The 'Long Island Lolita' Story* (CBS, both 3 January 1993).

> With viewing figures running to 80 million, these were the most-watched 'faction' movies of this winter season. (Usborne, 1993)

Compelling drama?

For the unplugged-in, this chart [a blow-by-blow comparison of the three TV films] shows what you missed: six hours of vidiocy. (Corliss, 1993)

The Guildford Four

The story of the Guildford Four is another example of the role of minor chance; but this time chance leads not to an insignificant outcome like 'six hours of vidiocy', but to a Royal Commission on Criminal Justice. The message of this final example is that minor and seemingly insignificant factors can lead to profound consequences. The future of our society truly is unpredictable.

The crimes

On Saturday, 5 October 1974, at about 8.50 pm a bomb exploded in the Horse and Groom, Guildford. There was no warning. Five people were killed and more than 50 injured. Later the same evening, at about 9.35 pm, a similar bomb exploded in the Seven Stars, about two hundred yards away. No-one was killed this time because the publican, hearing of the first explosion, had had the fore-

Figure 17.1 The Horse and Groom, Guildford, after the explosion on 5 October 1974.

Figure 17.2 The Seven Stars, Guildford, 5 October 1974.

© The Chief Constable of Surrey. Reproduced with permission.

sight to empty his pub; but eleven people were injured. Figures 17.1 and 17.2 are photographs of the two pubs after the explosions. These two pubs had been selected by an IRA 'active service unit' because they were popular with servicemen and women from nearby training camps at Pirbright.

Five weeks later on 7 November 1974 at about 10 pm a bomb was thrown through the window of the King's Arms, Woolwich. That pub was also popular with servicemen, being close to the Royal Artillery depot. Two people were killed and 27 injured. All three bombs were the work of the IRA. In fact, the Guildford bombs marked the beginning of a fresh and especially ferocious bombing campaign in London and south-east England.

The police investigation

The police investigation fell into two quite distinct phases. In the first phase the police traced and interviewed almost everyone present in either pub on the night of the bombs. There were about 380 people to be interviewed. The police reconstructed the detailed sequence of events prior to each explosion – who was sitting where in each pub and for what period of time. The witnesses reported a 'courting couple' as having been in the Horse and Groom, sitting where the bomb later exploded; this 'courting couple' had not come forward to be identified. There was, of course, no way of finding them. In such circumstances police routinely 'start from the other end', bringing in possible suspects for interrogation. I emphasise that the selection of a suspect in such circumstances is entirely a matter of *chance*.

The second phase began with the arrest of Paul Hill in Southampton on 28 November, some 54 days after the explosions in Guildford. The reasons why Paul Hill was arrested are unclear. He had come to England with his sister and girlfriend on 23 August. He had some prior association with the IRA and was thought to have come to England on a bombing mission. The movements of known IRA members and their associates are, of course, monitored by military intelligence in Northern Ireland. The address in Southampton at which Hill was arrested was obtained from military intelligence and it was said that 'a sum of money was later paid to the source who had first produced Hill's name'. (McKee and Franey, 1988, p. 88).

The truth of the matter was that Paul Hill was wanted for questioning by the Provisional IRA in Belfast in connection with a Armalite rifle which they believed he had misappropriated. He was also wanted for questioning by the RUC in connection with the murder of one Brian Shaw, a charge on which he was later convicted. His journey to England was therefore an escape, undertaken at the insistence of his family (McKee and Franey, 1988, pp. 71–4). He was anxious to remain in England. Once arrested by Surrey police, however, there was the possibility of repatriation to Belfast. He therefore talked. What would such a suspect say?

An author writing a novel draws on his or her personal experiences, constructing characters from an amalgam of acquaintances. A dream is constructed in similar manner; that also is an amalgam of previous experiences. Carole Richardson (one of the Four) was interrogated in total for over 20 hours. 'I was trying to think of people I didn't know. I thought of people I had seen in the past week and tried not to describe them. I didn't want any of my friends to be arrested.' (Kee, 1986, p. 139) But Paul Hill was not so circumspect; under interrogation he implicated several other Irish acquaintances, including Gerard Conlon. Conlon, under interrogation in his turn, implicated the MacGuire family, to whom he is related, Paddy Armstrong and Carole Richardson, among others. Carole Richardson, who is English, not Irish, was simply Paddy Armstrong's girlfriend. Paul Hill also mentioned Armstrong and Richardson. So, five days after the tip which led to Paul Hill, more than forty people were under arrest on suspicion of complicity in the Guildford bombings. Twenty of those suspects had been living in squats in the Kilburn area of North London, the others were relatives or acquaintances of the Guildford Four (McKee and Franey, 1988, p. 131).

Why these four?

Of those more than forty suspects only Paul Hill, Gerard Conlon, Paddy Armstrong and Carole Richardson were ultimately brought to trial (though the

MacGuire family were subsequently tried for possession of explosives). Why only these four?

These four were brought to trial because they confessed under police interrogation. They were very nearly the *Guildford Five*.

> Brian Anderson . . . was originally charged with murder on the strength of Hill and Conlon's statements. He thus recounts how he very nearly made a confession himself.
>
> As a preliminary he describes some of the attendant circumstances. He says he was questioned for about two hours on each of four days, being kept in a cell at nights in which he was only once given a mattress, once a pillow and never any blankets. He refers to being 'slapped about'. These details, however, seem of minor significance compared with the psychological pressure to which he testifies. He thus described it:
>
> 'They kept going on at me telling me that I had to admit that I was one of those who went down to Guildford and planted the bombs and I wouldn't do so. Eventually it got to the state where I was ready to say that I had planted the bombs at Guildford. I just couldn't take any more. What happened was the police officer brought me out from the cell and said that he was going to give me a last chance to tell the truth or else, and if I didn't tell the truth it would be the worse for me. He told me that I had to tell the truth about what part I had played in the Guildford bombings. I was so tired and confused by this time that I thought that the only way that I would get any peace was to say what he wanted me to say. Just as I was about to tell him, someone came into the room and told him he had a telephone call and he told me that he was going to put me back down in the cell to think about it for an hour and then he would ask me again. I went back down to the cell and during that time I managed to recover control of myself and when I was brought out of the cell about an hour later to see the same officer I told him exactly the same as I had told him before, namely that I had nothing to do with it and didn't know anything about it.'
>
> (Reprinted with permission from R. Kee, *Trial and Error: The MacGuires, the Guildford Pub Bombings and British Justice*, pp. 124–5. © 1986 Fairrealm Ltd. Reproduced by permission of the author c/o Rogers, Coleridge & White Ltd, 20 Powis Mews, London W11 1JN.)

Brian Anderson was charged with murder and taken to Winchester prison. But he was cleared in the magistrates' court on 3 February 1975 because of insufficient evidence (Kee, 1986, p. 159). But for that telephone call to his interrogator at that critical moment, the Guildford Four would have been the Guildford Five.

Selecting the evidence

The police do not *know* the facts; so they cannot tell when a suspect is telling the truth and when not. In such circumstances statements by suspects are not spontaneous; they are assembled by the police or at least under their direction.

Carole Richardson was interrogated for a total of about 20 hours over the course of four days and made four successive statements altogether.

> Carole told her solicitor some weeks later that the statements themselves were dictated to her from a summary of her answers or were dictated to one police officer by another who had been questioning her. 'He would ask me detailed questions and I would answer 'Yes' or 'No'. . . . (The police denied any dictation). (Reprinted with permission from R. Kee, *Trial and Error: The MacGuires, the Guildford Pub Bombings and British Justice*, p. 139. © 1986 Fairrealm Ltd. Reproduced by permission of the author c/o Rogers, Coleridge & White Ltd, 20 Powis Mews, London W11 1JN.)

At the same time the police do not understand the 'answers' they have obtained. So the suspects' statements are not a balanced record of their interrogations; instead, they contain only those elements that are of interest to the police. Once the police have formed a belief of guilt, contrary evidence is reinterpreted or simply ignored (as happened in Cleveland in 1987; see Chapter 12).

Frank Johnson

Frank Johnson was a friend of Carole Richardson's from Newcastle. After hearing about her detention on suspicion of complicity in the Guildford bombings, he realised that he had actually been in her company at the precise time the bombs must have been planted. They had been together at a pop concert given by Jack the Lad, a group from Newcastle, at the South Bank Polytechnic. Frank Johnson was unable to discover which solicitors were representing any of the Guildford Four (indeed, such was the pressure of public outrage, that none of the defending solicitors wished their names to be known). In default of any other course of action, Frank Johnson went to the Newcastle police with his story. He was arrested; he was charged with complicity in the murders, and was compelled to change his story through the medium of a signed statement that was used to discredit him in court, before being released (Kee, 1986, Ch. 12).

Identity parades

Carole Richardson was thought to be one of the 'courting couple' which witnesses had reported in the Horse and Groom – indeed, she had to be for the Crown's case against her to stand. On that basis she attended an identity parade at which a total of 12 witnesses all failed to identify her (McKee and Franey, 1988, pp. 169–73).

> Perhaps the boldest claim was that Armstrong and Richardson were the 'courting couple'. Sir Michael Havers [leading for the prosecution] told the jury that they would be identified from the descriptions given by soldiers in the Horse and Groom. He did not tell the jury that the eight witnesses who had given the fullest descriptions of the 'courting couple' had already failed to pick out Carole Richardson on identity parades and that Patrick Armstrong had never

> been put on parade at all. Nevertheless, Sir Michael said of Private Jonathan Cook that his descriptions were those of Richardson and probably of Armstrong. 'It was a very observant description by Cook. He had seen them leave the pub at about 6.55 pm.'
>
> Private Cook had attended the identity parade. In his two statements to the police . . . he had been insistent that the girl had 'natural blonde' hair. Carole Richarson is a natural brunette. (McKee and Franey, 1988, p. 234)

Withstanding police interrogation

Members of the IRA going on 'active service' are specifically trained to withstand police interrogation without revealing any operational details.

> During previous bombing campaigns in England captured IRA men have resolutely stuck to their training manual and have refused to answer questions put to them by the police. Their counter-interrogation tactic was to fix their eyes on an object in the interrogation room and by concentrating hard could almost make their minds a blank. (Borrell, 1975)

Innocent suspects arrested by mistake, knowing nothing of the crimes for which they have been arrested, behave in a very different manner under interrogation. That innocent, untrained, response was misinterpreted.

> Now that method has been replaced with one that is almost as frustrating for the police. The object is to confuse interrogators by answering with half truths; that is, admitting taking certain actions, and making remarks, which were in fact taken and made by other members of the gang. That cannot then be used in evidence against them or other defendants. (Borrell, 1975).

That argument formed part of the Crown's case at the trial. 'The Crown inferred . . . that there had been advance planning of this counter-information technique' (McKee and Franey, 1988, p. 217). That is a 'Heads I win, tails you lose' argument. As an empirical matter, the behaviour of the Guildford Four under interrogation showed that they had not been trained by the IRA to withstand interrogation. If those interrogations had any evidential value at all, they should have been taken to suggest a lack of involvement on the part of the accused.

The police were under great pressure to find the culprits. The public are anxious and the police cannot be seen to be doing nothing – cannot be seen to be waiting for a 'lucky break'. Parliament hurriedly passed the *Prevention of Terrorism Act*. The bill was introduced in the House on Monday, 25 November 1975. There was an all-night sitting on Thursday, 28 November to debate the bill, and it received the Royal Assent on Friday, 29 November. Among other measures, this bill authorised the police to hold suspected terrorists for up to seven days incommunicado, without access to anyone.

So, once an 'informer' had named the wrong man, it was virtually certain that innocent people – if not these four, then some other four – would be arraigned on a charge of murder, solely on the basis of confessions obtained whilst in police custody. Interrogation is not a search after truth, but after self-incrimination. The only real evidence was the original tip provided by the informer. But that was not produced in court.

The arrests in Balcombe Street

The suspects arrested by the police were mostly Irish, many living in squats around Kilburn, relying on drink and drugs to pass the time and often engaged in petty crime. That pattern of arrests was set by what Paul Hill said under interrogation. But IRA members on 'active service' always rent accommodation, they never drink heavily, they never use drugs, they do not draw attention to themselves and are not picked up as possible suspects. They can only be identified when they are actually caught 'on the job' (as in Balcombe Street on 8–14 December 1975). So 'starting from the other end' is most unlikely to work in the search for an IRA unit on 'active service'. The best strategy is, in fact, to wait for a 'lucky break'.

When that break came, *after* the trial and conviction of the Four, it was misinterpreted. On 6 December 1975, the police discovered an IRA unit actually on the job. They were chased to Balcombe Street, Marylebone, where they surrendered after a six-day siege. Their arrests led to the Guildford Four's appeal based on startling new evidence from Brendan Dowd (who had been arrested in Liverpool on 10 July 1975) and from Joseph O'Connell, Eddie Butler and Harry Duggan (arrested in Balcombe Street, 12 December 1975). These four admitted both the Guildford and Woolwich bombings. They established their presence at both crimes by providing unpublished details, hitherto known only to the police. They asserted that the Guildford Four were innocent, that they had not even heard of the Guildford Four until they read of their arrest in the newspapers.

But this is what Lord Justice Roskill said in his Appeal Court judgment about this new and authoritative evidence:

> As to this we need only say that so far as the new evidence is concerned we reject it in all relevant respects. That evidence therefore gives rise to no lurking doubts whatever in our minds. We are sure that there has been a cunning and skilful attempt to deceive the Court by putting forward false evidence. O'Connell, Duggan and Butler had ample opportunity whilst awaiting trial to work out how the attempt should be made. Doing so was well within the intellectual capacity of O'Connell. The difficulty lay in finding a substitute for Hill. Dowd was brought in for this purpose. Providing him with his lines could not have been easy as he was not, at any material time, in the same prison as the others. He did not, or could not, learn his lines properly. That was the reason why the conspiracy failed. (Regina v. Patrick Armstrong, Carole Margaret Richardson, Paul Michael Hill and Gerard Patrick Conlon, 1977, p. 43C–E. London: Court of Appeal, Criminal Division, 28 October 1977. Crown copyright. Reprinted with permission.)

While Lord Justice Roskill's statement is a judgment in the legal sense, it is also a judgment in the sense of this book – a conclusion reached intuitively.

According to Lord Justice Roskill's judgment, certain parts of the new witnesses statements were lies (Regina v. Patrick Armstrong *et al.*, 1977, pp. 36, 40), on the grounds of certain disagreements between their four statements; so the remainder is set aside. This is the exact contrary of the critique applied to the various statements from the Guildford Four, where the police had great difficulty assembling statements from the Four that the court might find sufficiently consistent with each other.

> . . . it is, in our view, a characteristic of all this evidence both in the statements and during the interrogations, and in the evidence to which we have listened over several days in this Court that the partially true is intermingled with the deliberately false so that false trails may be followed and the ascertainment of the real truth certainly delayed and hopefully made impossible of achievement. (Regina v. Patrick Armstrong, Carole Margaret Richardson, Paul Michael Hill and Gerard Patrick Conlon, 1977, p. 39A–B. London: Court of Appeal, Criminal Division, 28 October 1977. Crown copyright. Reprinted with permission.)

Now, suppose the Balcombe Street gang had been arrested *before* the Guildford Four's trial!

Evaluating the evidence

The Guildford Four were convicted *solely* on the basis of statements they had signed whilst in police custody. But note that a confession entirely by itself is not sufficient. There are people who repeatedly confess to high-profile crimes in which they could not possibly have any complicity. Over 200 people confessed to the kidnapping of the two-year-old son of Charles Lindbergh in 1932 (Jenkins, 1990b). That is well-known to the police, who often keep some detail of a serious crime secret in order to weed out such people. So a confession entirely by itself is not sufficient.

If you walk into a police station and say you were responsible for last week's murder in Northern Ireland – even if you say it in a Belfast accent – you will be told: 'Go away and stop wasting police time!'

> Scotland Yard admitted yesterday that police turned away a suspected IRA terrorist who was trying to give himself up because they did not believe his story.
>
> A spokeswoman said that the man, aged 29, walked into Rochester Row police station, south-west London, early on Monday seeking an interview with detectives. When he tried to confess he was sent away.
>
> The man then telephoned the Royal Ulster Constabulary to vouch for him and when he returned he was arrested. (*Times*, 1988).

Prior suspicion is also needed, however that might be acquired, to interpret your confession as 'true'. Then, but only then, can your confession be cited as evidence in court and used to convict you. That prior suspicion is a bias and is extraneous to your confession, and the origin of that prior suspicion may be a matter of pure chance.

The quashing of their convictions

The convictions of the Guildford Four were quashed on 19 October 1989 on the grounds that 'notes and records relating to crucial interviews with Mr Armstrong and Hill had been rewritten, altered and suppressed and that detectives misled the trial' (Brown *et al.*, 1989). That is the legal pretext.

Now let us look at the real reason. During his interrogation Gerry Conlon mentioned the MacGuire family (Annie MacGuire was his aunt), and that mention led to their arrest and subsequent trial and conviction on a charge of possessing explosives. One of the seven people arrested at the MacGuire home was Gerry Conlon's own father, Guiseppe, who had just arrived from Belfast that very afternoon to stay with his sister and to see if he could help his son, then newly arrested. Guiseppe Conlon suffered from tuberculosis and died in prison in 1980. During his illness he was visited by several people prominent in public life, in particular, by Cardinal Hume.

> My concern in this matter arose first from my contact with Patrick Joseph ['Guiseppe'] Conlon, whom I visited on a number of occasions in Wormwood Scrubs before his death in 1980. I became absolutely convinced of his innocence and because of that developed profound doubts about the justice of the MacGuire convictions. (Hume, 1986)

Cardinal Hume added his personal weight to pressure by solicitors for the Guildford Four and by their families, to three television programmes (Yorkshire Television's *First Tuesday*; McKee, 1984, 1986, 1987), to an Early Day Motion in the House of Commons, January 1986, to Robert Kee's book *Trial and Error*, and joined a very prestigious delegation (Lord Devlin, Lord Scarman [both former Law Lords], Merlyn Rees and Lord Jenkins [both former Home Secretaries]) to the then Home Secretary. That pressure led to a reopening of the case and to the Guildford Four's second appeal.

The pressure of public opinion

A criminal jury is composed of lay men and women. Lay jurors have no experience of police interrogation; they are quite unable to imagine the pressure that can be exerted by experienced police interrogators. In addition, they are aware of public anxieties and are likely to be swayed in their verdict by public pressure. That public pressure got to the Appeal Court as well. It can be seen in Lord Justice Roskill's judgment cited above.

That public sentiment was still evident in 1980. Guiseppe Conlon died in prison of tuberculosis on 23 January 1980 and his body was flown home to Belfast for burial. But even five years after the explosions 'British Airways workers refused to handle his body for repatriation to Belfast' (McKee and Franey, 1988, p. 424).

With public pressure of that magnitude there is serious danger of a miscarriage of justice, and the court ought to be especially sure of the case before convicting. But the public do not know who committed the crime. They merely assume that the police would not have brought anyone to trial without good reason. The public do not realise that the 'good reason' is not itself evidence against the accused, but is, instead, a response to the public's own pressure. The public are not to know if the wrong people are convicted; they merely require someone to be 'done for it'. Such pressure gets to the police, the jurors, the judge and the Appeal Court alike.

But, by October 1989, the pressure of public opinion which secured the convictions in the first place was replaced by a contrary public concern over the justice of those convictions.

The role of chance (again)

Now suppose that military intelligence in Northern Ireland had suggested some name other than that of Paul Hill.

Suppose that military intelligence's other suspect did not know of Gerry Conlon and therefore could not mention him in the course of interrogation.

Suppose that, as a result, some other four had been convicted of the Guildford bombings.

Suppose that there had been no-one in an advanced stage of tuberculosis, associated with those other four, sent to prison.

Then, that other hypothetical Guildford Four might well still be in prison!

Their families and friends would, of course, try to overturn their convictions. But without the support of Cardinal Hume and those other people prominent in public life, there might well have been insufficient influence to get the case reopened a second time.

The case of the Guildford Four has led to a profound change in public concern about the justice of convictions that rely on confession evidence. The Birmingham Six and others wrongly convicted could still be in prison. There would have been no Royal Commission on Criminal Justice.

'Tall oaks from little acorns grow.' Since the initial chance event and its consequential effects could never have been foreseen, neither could the change that resulted. That is why the future of our society is unpredictable.

References

Alberge, D. (1989). Master forger's paintings to go on sale at Bonhams. *Independent*, 3 November, p. 2.

Alberge, D. (1991a). Begged, borrowed or stolen. *Independent*, 5 November, p. 17.

Alberge, D. (1991b). Buyer's market. *Independent*, 15 October, p. 19.

Alberge, D. (2001a). Familiar rubbish on Turner shortlist. *The Times*, 31 May, p. 3.

Alberge, D. (2001b). Turner Prize judges see the lights. and Throwaway art critics lose on paper. *The Times*, 10 December, pp. 1, 3.

Alexander, C. N. Jr, Zucker, L. G., and Brody, C. L. (1970). Experimental expectations and autokinetic experiences: Consistency theories and judgmental convergence. *Sociometry*, 33, 108–22.

Alley, R. (ed). (1981). *Catalogue of the Tate Gallery's Collection of Modern Art, other than works by British Artists*. London: Tate Gallery in association with Sotheby Parke Bernet.

Anon. (1748). *An authentick Narrative of the original, establishment, and progress of the Inquisition in Italy, Spain, and Portugal*. London.

Appleyard, B. (1993). A brick is a brick is a brick. Or what? *Independent*, 8 May, p. 27.

Asch, S. E. (1952). *Social Psychology*. New York: Prentice-Hall.

AudioQuest (1992). *Cable Design; Theory versus Empirical Reality*. Cambridge: AudioQuest.

A-Z of UK Brands. (1990). 2nd edn. London: Euromonitor.

Bachem, A. (1954). Time factors in relative and absolute pitch determination. *Journal of the Acoustical Society of America*, 26, 751–3.

Bailey, E. (1991). Bubble trouble. *Daily Telegraph*, 7 December, *Weekend*, p. I.

Baird, J. C., Green, D. M. and Luce, R. D. (1980). Variability and sequential effects in cross-modality matching of area and loudness. *Journal of Experimental Psychology: Human Perception and Performance*, 6, 277–89.

Baird, J. C., Lewis, C. and Romer, D. (1970). Relative frequencies of numerical responses in ratio estimation. *Perception & Psychophysics*, 8, 358–62.

Baird, J.C., Romer, D. and Stein, T. (1970). Test of a cognitive theory of psychophysics: Size discrimination. *Perceptual and Motor Skills*, 30, 495–501.

Banks, C. (1979). Review of *Flowers in the Attic*. *Washington Post*, 4 November, *Book World*, p. 14.

Barber, D. and Gordon, G. (1976). *'Members of the Jury . . .'*. London: Wildwood House.

Barbour, J. B. (1985). Letter: A question of grades. *The Times*, 21 October, p. 13.

Bardell, G. S. Forrest, G. M. and Shoesmith, D. J. (1978). *Comparability in GCE*. Manchester: Joint Matriculation Board.

Barnes, C. (1986). Atkinson's antics are side-splitting but so very nasty! *The New York Post*, 15 October, p. 25.

Bartoshuk, L.M. (1968). Water taste in man. *Perception & Psychophysics*, 3, 69–72.

Barwick, S. (1991). Birdwood: guilty and not alone. *Independent*, 19 October, p. 15.

Bedini, S. A. (1972). *The Life of Benjamin Banneker*. New York: Scribners.

Bee, M. and Dolton, P. (1985). Degree class and pass rates: An inter-university comparison. *Higher Education Review, 17(2)*, 45–52.

Beebe-Center, J. G., Rogers, M. S. and O'Connell, D. N. (1955). Transmission of information about sucrose and saline solutions through the sense of taste. *Journal of Psychology*, 39, 157–60.

Beeston, N. and Anon. (1990). Heath flies out of Iraq with 33 British hostages. *The Times*, 24 October, p. 1.

Bellamy, C. (1990). Saddam digs in and keeps the world guessing. *Independent*, 10 August, p. 10.

Bellamy, C. (1991). Gulf war body count drops to 1,500 Iraqis. *Independent*, 11 March, p. 1.

Bennett, W. (1991). Champagne fraud that misses out on sparkle. *Independent*, 3 January 1991, p. 3.

Berger, C. and Cockburn, P. (1990). 100 000 Iraqi troops near Kuwait border. *Independent*, 1 August, p. 11.

Berliner, W. (1995). It's more difficult than 1, 2, 3. *Independent*, 9 November, *Section Two*, p. 14.

Berry, A. (1993). Longer days as the moon flies away. *Daily Telegraph*, 26 March, p. 6.

Bien, P. (1988). Blasphemy and bigotry. *The Times*, 27 August, p. 8.

Blake-Coleman, B. C. and Yorke, R. (1993). Letter: Cable con trick cut by Occam's razor. *Electronics World + Wireless World*, May, pp. 391–2.

Blanchard, T. (1995). The cut-price clingy cossie conflict. *Independent*, 19 July, *Section Two*, p. 4.

Blofeld, H. (1989). Pakistan criticise umpiring. *Independent*, 17 February, p. 32.

Blom-Cooper, L., Harding, J. and Milton, E. McC. (1987). *A Child in Mind: Protection of Children in a Responsible Society*. London: London Borough of Greenwich and Greenwich Health Authority.

Bone, J. (1999). Kennedy 'minutes of terror'. *The Times*, 21 July, p. 17.

Borrell, C. (1975). IRA informer got £350 for vital clue that led to bombers. *The Times*, 23 October, p. 5.

Botsford, K. (1990). They loved their child; they also loved God. *Independent*, 30 May, p. 18.

Bovard, E. W. Jr (1951). Group structure and perception. *Journal of Abnormal and Social Psychology*, *46*, 398–405.

Bradberry, G. (1999). The power of posh paint. *The Times*, 9 April, p. 20.

Braid, M. (1992). 'Spitting' Jesus brings down Church's wrath. *Independent*, 12 October, p. 3.

Bremner, C. and Farrell, S. (1997). Paparazzi were 'only doing their job'. *The Times*, 4 September, p. 4.

Brown, C., Helm, S., Kirby, T., O'Sullivan, J. and Reeves, P. (1989). Judicial inquiry ordered over Guildford Four. *Independent*, 20 October, p. 1.

Brown, M. (1992). Royal story produces newspaper sales boom. *Independent*, 10 June, p. 3.

Bruner, J.S. and Postman, L. (1949). On the perception of incongruity: a paradigm. *Journal of Personality*, 18, 206–23.

Buckhout, R. (1980). Nearly 2,000 witnesses can be wrong. *Bulletin of the Psychonomic Society*, 16, 307–10.

Bull, R. and Clifford, B. R. (1984). Earwitness voice recognition accuracy. In G. L. Wells and E. F. Loftus (eds), *Eyewitness Testimony*. Cambridge: Cambridge University Press. Pp. 92–123.

Bulloch, J. (1991). How Bush lost the Gulf war. *Independent on Sunday*, 8 December, *Review*, pp. 10–13.

Bullock, A. (chair) (1975). *The Tate Gallery, 1972–1974. Biennial report and illustrated catalogue of acquisitions*. London: The Tate Gallery.

Burgess, D. A. (1991). Letter: Reform of the A-level. *Independent*, 24 May, p. 22.

Burman, E. (1984). *The Inquisition: The Hammer of Heresy*. Wellingborough: Acquarian.

Burr, G. L. (1914). *Narratives of the Witchcraft Cases, 1648–1706*. New York: Scribner's Sons. Reprinted 1975, New York: Barnes & Noble.

Campbell, N. (1994). *Swan*. London: Heinemann.

Carr, J. W. (1933). Letter, Tonsillectomy. *The Lancet*, 16 December, p. 1394.

Carroll, L. (1872). *Through the Looking-glass, and What Alice Found There*. London: Macmillan.

Chance, J., Goldstein, A. G. and McBride, L. (1975). Differential experience and recognition memory for faces. *Journal of Social Psychology*, 97, 243–53.

Chandler, R. (1987). PTL seeks help under bankruptcy law. *Los Angeles Times*, 13 June, p. I:33.

Chapanis, A. and Halsey, R. M. (1956). Absolute judgments of spectrum colors. *Journal of Psychology*, 42, 99–103.

Chapman, K. (1994). Variability of degree results in geography in United Kingdom Universities 1973–1990: Preliminary results and policy implications. *Studies in Higher Education, 19*, 89–102.

Checkland, S. J. (1987a). £418,000 for painting which cost £170 in June. *The Times*, 12 December, p. 3.
Checkland, S. J. (1987b). Experts fooled by a master. *The Times*, 7 December, p. 3.
Checkland, S. J. (1987c). Painting valued at £400 goes for £847 000. *The Times*, 9 December, p. 1.
Cherry, J. R. (1990). Letter: The life of a child. *Independent*, 1 June, p. 18.
Chittenden, M. and Collcutt, D. (2000). Store links 'taint' wine critics' taste. *Sunday Times*, 26 November, p. A:3.
Chittenden, M. and Welsh, E. (1989). Customers misled in scramble for bargains. *Sunday Times*, 24 December, p. A:8.
Cleeve, L. (1988). *Crimewatch File: The Murder of Police Sergeant Speed*. BBC1, 12 October.
Clifford, B. R. and Fleming, W. (Unpbl.) Face and voice identification in a field setting. Unpublished manuscript.
Clifford, B. R. (1983). Memory for voices: the feasibility and quality of earwitness evidence. In S. M. A. Lloyd-Bostock and B. R. Clifford, *Evaluating Witness Evidence*. Chichester: Wiley. Pp. 189–218.
Clough, P. (1986). Polka-dot Princess starts fad. *The Times*, 10 June, p. 3.
Clyde, J. J. (1992). *The Report of the Inquiry into the Removal of Children from Orkney in February 1991*. Edinburgh: HMSO.
Cockburn, A. (1987). Profits of salvation. *Sunday Times Magazine*, 18 October, pp. 48–57.
Cockburn, P. (1990a). Earthquake in the Gulf. *Independent*, 3 August, p. 17.
Cockburn, P. (1990b). Iraqis calculate benefits of letting hostages leave. *Independent*, 7 December, p. 10.
Cockburn, P. (1993). US Gulf war air success shot down. *Independent on Sunday*, 30 May, p. 13.
Cockroft, J. (1988). The day an unwary Fish was caught in the eye of a hurricane. *Cambridge Evening News*, 14 October, pp. 30–1.
Connolly, K. J. and Smith, P.K. (1986). What makes a 'good' degree: variations between different departments. *Bulletin of the British Psychological Society*, 39, 48–51.
Connon, H. (1994). Sainsbury gives in to Coke. *Independent*, 11 May, p. 27.
Coombs, C. H., Dawes, R. M. and Tversky, A. (1970). *Mathematical Psychology*. Englewood Cliffs, NJ: Prentice-Hall.
Cooper, G. (1995). Frightened women in search of answers. *Independent*, 21 October, p. 2.
Corliss, R. (1993). Trashomon. *Time*, 11 January, p. 47.
Cornsweet, T.N. (1970). *Visual Perception*. New York: Academic Press.
Counsell, G. (1989). Est agnt hs gt wy wth wds. *Independent*, 2 September, p. 36.
Cox, R. (1967). Examinations and higher education: A survey of the literature. *Universities Quarterly*, 21, 292–340.
Crequer, N. (1991). School test results put councils at odds. and Pupils find maths testing. *Independent*, 20 December, pp. 1, 8.
Crossley-Holland, K. (1980). *The Norse Myths*. London: Deutsch.
Crovitz, H. F. (1976). Perceived length and the Craik–O'Brien illusion. *Vision Research*, 16, 435.
Csikszentmihalyi, M. and Bennett, S. (1971). An exploratory model of play. *American Anthropologist*, 73, 45–58.
Curnock, N. (ed.). (1909). *The Journal of the Rev. John Wesley*, A.M., vol. III. London: Charles H. Kelly.
Curtis, T. (1987). '£40,000' painting is just a fake. *Cambridge Evening News*, 24 October, p. 1.
Cusick, J. (1991a). Child sex abuse inquiry isolates Orkney islanders. *Independent*, 8 September, p. 6.
Cusick, J. (1991b). Community where ancient traditions live on. *Independent*, 1 April, p. 5.
Cusick, J. (1991c). Orkney family begins to pick up the pieces. *Independent*, 6 April, p. 4.
Cusick, J. (1991d). Thriller name plot thickens. *Independent*, 29 September, p. 3.
Dart, J. (1987a). Bakker scandal could be a jolt to TV ministries. *Los Angeles Times*, 21 March, pp. II:1, 3.
Dart, J. (1987b). Issued warning about Bakker, Swaggart says. *Los Angeles Times*, 25 March 1987, pp. I:1, 20.
Darwish, A. (1990). US ambassador 'misread Iraqi invasion signs'. *Independent* 12 September, p. 9.
Davies, J. (1991). Innocent until seen sitting in the dock. *Independent*, 18 October, p. 19.
Dawe, T., Wood, N. and Matthews, R. (1987). Wasted warnings of the storm. *The Times*, 17 October, pp. 1, 24.

Dawes, R. M. (1979). The robust beauty of improper linear models in decison making. *American Psychologist, 34*, 571–82. Reprinted in D. Kahneman, P. Slovic and A.Tversky (eds), *Judgment Under Uncertainty: Heuristics and Biases*. Cambridge: Cambridge University Press, 1982. Pp. 391–407.

Dawes, R.M. and Corrigan, B. (1974). Linear models in decision making. *Psychological Bulletin*, 81, 95–106.

del Olmo, J. (1680). *Relación Histórica del Auto General de Fe, que se celebró en Madrid este año de 1680*. Madrid: R. Rico de Miranda.

Denton, G. G. (1980). The influence of visual pattern on perceived speed. *Perception*, 9, 393–402.

Devlin, Lord P. (chair) (1976). *Report to the Secretary of State for the Home Department of the Departmental Committee on Evidence of Identification in Criminal Cases*. HC 338. London: HMSO.

Dickens, C. (1861). *Great Expectations*. London: Chapman and Hall.

Ditchburn, R. W. (1973) *Eye-movements and Visual Perception*. Oxford: Oxford University Press.

Dobson, R. (1996). Why do we have to turn a scare into a crisis? *Independent*, 16 April, *Section Two*, pp. 6–7.

Doughty, W. L. (1955). *John Wesley, Preacher*. London: Epworth Press.

Dowden, R. (1990). Hostage release fails to improve Saddam's image. *Independent*, 3 September, p. 5.

Doyle, L. (1991). Bush call for coup angers US allies. *Independent*, 16 February, p. 3.

Eddy, M. B. (1875). *Science and Health*. Boston: Christian Scientist Publishing Co.

Eddy, P. and Lightfoot, L. (1995). Playing safe. *Sunday Times*, 22 October, p. 1:13.

Edridge, O. (1990). *Heart of the Matter: In God We Trust*. BBC1, 14 October.

Egan, D., Pittner, M. and Goldstein, A. G. (1977). Eyewitness identification. Photographs vs. live models. *Law and Human Behavior*, 1, 199–206.

Eichler, U. (1984). *Doris Lessing's Voices*. Channel Four, 23 September.

Einhorn, H. J. (1972). Expert measurement and mechanical combination. *Organizational Behaviour and Human Performance*, 7, 86–106.

Elliott, K. (1991). No flies on J R Hartley. *Independent on Sunday*, 17 November, p. 26.

Ellis, H. D., Davies, G. M. and Shepherd, J. W. (1978). A critical examination of the Photofit system for recalling faces. *Ergonomics*, 21, 297–307.

Ellis, H. D., Shepherd, J. W. and Davies, G.M. (1975). An investigation of the use of the Photo-fit technique for recalling faces. *British Journal of Psychology*, 66, 29–37.

Encyclopaedia Britannica. (1989a). Indulgence. 15th edn, 6, 301.

Encyclopaedia Britannica. (1989b). Ninety-five theses. 15th edn, 8, 716–7.

Engen, T. and Pfaffman, C. (1959). Absolute judgments of odor intensity. *Journal of Experimental Psychology*, 58, 23–6.

Epstein, R. A. (1967). *The Theory of Gambling and Statistical Logic*. New York: Academic Press.

Eriksen, C. W. and Hake, H. W. (1955a) Absolute judgments as a function of stimulus range and number of stimulus and response categories. *Journal of Experimental Psychology*, 49, 323–32.

Eriksen, C. W. and Hake, H. W. (1955b) Multidimensional stimulus differences and accuracy of discrimination. *Journal of Experimental Psychology*, 50, 153–60.

Fisk, R. (1982). Iranian quest for martyrdom. *The Times*, 7 April, p. 8.

Fisk, R. (1986a). Doomed children on parade for communion of toffees. *The Times*, 7 March, p. 12.

Fisk, R. (1986b). Khomeini's intimations of mortality. *The Times*, 10 November, p. 7.

Fisk, R. (1987). Nation with a death wish. *The Times*, 31 January, p. 7.

Fisk, R. (1990). The fine line between war and peace in the Gulf. *Independent*, 30 July, p. 10.

Ford, R. (2001). More than 28% of all suspected robbers are black. *The Times*, 19 January, p. 12.

Forrest, G. M. and Shoesmith, D. J. (1985). *A Second Review of GCE Comparability Studies*. Manchester: Joint Matriculation Board.

Foster, J. (1992). Scientific approach yields £2m pools win. *Independent*, 20 February, p. 1.

Freedman, L. (1991). Textbooks not much help in trying to make sense of Saddam's strategy. *Independent*, 1 February, p. 3.

Furmston, M. P. and Higgins, P. (1989). *Tribunal Report on the Case of Mr Francis Foecke*. University of Bristol.

Garner, W. R. (1953) An informational analysis of absolute judgments of loudness. *Journal of Experimental Psychology*, 46, 373–80.
Garner, W. R. (1954). Context effects and the validity of loudness scales. *Journal of Experimental Psychology*, 48, 218–24.
Garner, W. R. (1959). The development of context effects in half-loudness judgments. *Journal of Experimental Psychology*, 58, 212–19.
Garrett, S. K. and Wood, R. (1980). *Report of a GCE Inter-board Cross-moderation Exercise in History at Ordinary Level, 1978*. London: University of London, University Entrance and School Examinations Council.
Gayford, M. (1992). Has the rot set in? *Daily Telegraph*, 4 November, p. 18.
Gelb, N. (1986). *The Berlin Wall*. London: Michael Joseph.
Gillie, O. (1990). Self-delusion keeps the chips going down. *Independent*, 9 July, p. 4.
Gledhill, R. (1988). DPP may move against cleared Christ film. *The Times*, 27 August, p. 1.
Green, D. M. and Swets, J. A. (1966). *Signal Detection Theory and Psychophysics*. New York: Wiley.
Gregory, R. L. (1990). *Eye and Brain*, 4th edn. London: Weidenfeld and Nicolson.
Greig, G. (1989). Art experts in a lather over foreigner's £2.2m 'bargain'. *Sunday Times*, 2 July, p. A:4.
Gulliksen, H. (1950). *Theory of Mental Tests*. New York: Wiley. Republished Hillsdale, NJ: Erlbaum, 1987.
Guttridge, P. (1994). Making improper advances. *Independent*, 21 June, p. 22.
Habgood, J. (1991a). Going to Hell. *SeeN*, June, p. 3.
Habgood, J. (1991b). This is not Hell. *Independent*, 15 July, p. 19.
Hackmann, W. (1984). *Seek and Strike*. London: HMSO.
Harris, A. (1988). A sleuth in the Louisiana holy war. *Los Angeles Times*, 22 May, pp. VI: 4–5, 7.
Harrison, T. (1991). Diana, cover girl to the world. *Daily Mail*, 23 November, p. 3.
Hartog, P., Rhodes, E. C. and Burt, C. (1936). *The Marks of Examiners*. London: Macmillan.
Hawkes, G. R. and Warm, J. S. (1960). Maximum I_t for absolute identification of cutaneous electrical intensity level. *Journal of Psychology*, 49, 279–88.
Hawkes, N. (1997). Human error causes 90% of accidents. *The Times*, 8 December, p. 5.
Helliar-Symons, R. D. and Butler, N. R. (1995). M1 chevron trial – Accident study. Project Report 118, Transport Research Laboratory, Crowthorne, Berkshire.
Helm, S. (1989). Guildford inquiry 'may have ignored evidence'. *Independent*, 6 November, p. 4.
Helm, S. (1989). Weight of evidence that tipped the scales of justice. *Independent*, 18 October, p. 3.
Helm, S. (1990). Saddam's hostage TV show. *Independent*, 24 August, p. 1.
Helm, S. (1991). Bush invokes God's will in allied crusade. *Independent*, 29 January, p. 2.
Hildebrandt, R. (1987). Rund 1000 Menschen in den Westen geschleust. (Obituary of Albert Schütz. *Der Tagesspiegel*, 12 July, p. 3.
Hill, G. (1988). The night that toppled Britain. *The Times*, 8 October, Review, pp. 3: 1–2.
Hilton, I. (1991). Fear and loathing in St Margaret's Hope. *Independent*, 15 April, p. 18.
Hipkin, B. (1992). Letter: Decisions that should not be entrusted to bankers. *Independent*, 7 December, p. 16.
Hitchcock, A. (1956). *The Wrong Man*. Burbank, CA: Warner Bros. Pictures, Inc.
Hollingworth, H. L. (1909). The inaccuracy of movement. *Archives of Psychology*, 13.
Honigsbaum, M. (1992). The cautious confessions of a card counter. *Independent*, 20 February, p. 16.
Hood, W. R. and Sherif, M. (1962). Verbal report and judgment of an unstructured stimulus. *Journal of Psychology*, 54, 121–30.
Horsnell, M. (1988). Student 'cheat' in a battle for his honour. *The Times*, 25 February, p. 5.
Horsnell, M. (2002). Burglar captured by victim's sketch. *The Times*, 11 June, p. 5.
Howson, A. G., Barnard, A. D., Crighton, D. G., Davies, N., Gardiner, A. D., Jagger, J. M., Morris, D., Robson, J. C. and Steele, N. C. (1995). *Tackling the Mathematics Problem*. London: The London Mathematical Society.
Hughes, C. and Morris, H. (1990). West failed to read the signs of invasion. *Independent*, 4 August, p. 1.
Hume, B. (1986). Letter: Anxieties over Maguire case. *The Times*, 13 October, p. 15.
Hume, M. (1993). When fashion is no excuse at all. *Independent*, 26 May, p. 22.
Hurvich, L. M. (1981). *Color Vision*. Sunderland, MA: Sinauer.

Independent (1991a). Allah be praised. 9 April, p. 10.
Independent (1991b). Mother was offered blood transfusion. 23 March, p. 2.
Independent (1991c). Publisher fined over 'misleading' thrillers. 28 September, p. 2.
Independent (1991d). Student who gambled loans killed himself. 16 November, p. 9.
Independent (1993). Ancient tablets show days getting longer. 26 March, p.3.
Independent on Sunday. (1993). Opinions. 30 May, p. 22.
James, M. (1991). *Without Walls: Upholding the Bricks*. Channel Four, 2 April.
James, S. (1984). *The Princess of Wales Fashion Handbook*. London: Orbis.
Jeffress, L. A. (1975). Masking of tone by tone as a function of duration. *Journal of the Acoustical Society of America*, 58, 399–403.
Jenkins, J. (1990a). I *think* it was that man there. *Independent*, 24 August, p. 21.
Jenkins, J. (1990b). Innocents who can't help confessing. *Independent*, 19 January, p. 19.
Jenkins, L. (1998). Friend relives horror of night Lawrence died. *The Times*, 16 May, p. 10.
Johnston, B. (1990). Brian Johnston on Bud Flanagan. *Independent Magazine*, 29 April, p. 46.
Jones, J. (1991). A little girl caught between cow-parsley and the climate of our times. *Independent on Sunday*, 8 September, p. 1.
Jones, R. E., Milton, J. L. and Fitts, P. M. (1947). An investigation of errors made by pilots in judging the attitude of an aircraft without the aid of vision. AAF Memorandum Report TSEAA–694–13.
Judd, J. (1984). Where A-levels can be unfair. *The Observer*, 19 August, p. 8.
Judd, J. (1991a). So you think you should have done better? *Independent*, 15 August, p. 19.
Judd, J. (1991b). These results still don't tell us what the real score is. *Independent*, 19 December, p. 19.
Judd, J. (1992). Teachers praised for record increase in GCSE pass rate. *Independent*, 27 August, p. 4.
Judd, J. (1995). Muddle + indifference = a nation that can't add up. *Independent on Sunday*, 5 November, p. 17.
Justice. (1990). Petition: Regina -v- Sammy Martin Davis. London: Justice, 95a Chancery Lane.
Kahneman, D. and Tversky, A. (1979). Prospect theory: an analysis of decision under risk. *Econometrica*, 47, 263–91.
Kamen, H. (1965). *The Spanish Inquisition*. London: Wiedenfeld and Nicolson.
Kasterine, C. (1993). Under-exposure. *Vogue*, June, pp. 144–51.
Katme, A. M. (1992). Letter, 'Blasphemy' in broadcasting. *Independent*, 13 October, p. 20.
Kaye, A. (1990). *Everyman: There but for the Grace of God*. BBC1, 22 April.
Keating, T. (1976a). Letter: Samuel Palmer inquiry. *The Times*, 29 September, p. 17.
Keating, T. (1976b). Letter: Samuel Palmer's works. *The Times*, 20 August, p. 13.
Kee, R. (1986). *Trial and Error: The MacGuires, the Guildford Pub Bombings and British Justice*. London: Hamish Hamilton.
Kelsey, T. (1990). Parents tell of trial by social worker. *Independent on Sunday*, 16 December, p. 1.
Kennedy, D. (1998). Owen's battle to make his mark. *The Times*, 15 August, p. 8.
Kennedy, D. (2000). Rival critics round on cheap wine champion. *The Times*, 2 December, p. 7.
Kennedy, J. M. (1987a). Roberts reaps cash, scolding for predicting his death. *Los Angeles Times*, 16 January, p. I:20.
Kennedy, J. M. (1987b). Roberts' earthly empire grows; so does overhead. *Los Angeles Times*, 24 January, pp. I:1, 26.
Keren, G. and Wagenaar, W. A. (1985). On the psychology of playing blackjack: Normative and descriptive considerations with implications for decision theory. *Journal of Experimental Psychology: General*, 114, 133–58.
King, G. (1978). Hi-fi reviewing. *Hi-Fi News & Record Review*. May, pp. 77, 79.
King-Hamilton, A. (1988). Letter, 'Last Temptation'. *The Times*, 26 August, p. 13.
Kirby, T. (1990). Recovery of baby is priority, police say. *Independent*, 15 January, p. 3.
Kirby, T. (1992). Rail links to Slater kidnapper reinforced. *Independent*, 5 February, p. 7.
Kosinski, J. (1968). *Steps*. New York: Random House.
Kulikowski, J. J. (1976). Effective contrast constancy and linearity of contrast sensation. *Vision Research*, 16, 1419–31.
Labib, K. (1990). Letter: Saddam Hussein's shrewd strategy to mix the issues. *Independent*, 16 August, p. 22.

Lacey, H. (1995). Do celebrity ads work? *Independent on Sunday*, 27 August, *Real Life*, p. 11.
Laming, D. (1986). *Sensory Analysis*. London: Academic Press.
Laming, D. (1988). Précis of *Sensory Analysis*. *Behavioral and Brain Sciences*, vol. 11, 275–96.
Laming, D. (1990). The reliability of a certain university examination compared with the precision of absolute judgments. *Quarterly Journal of Experimental Psychology*, 42A, 239–54.
Laming, D. (1994). Psychophysics. In A. M. Colman (ed.), *Companion Encyclopedia of Psychology*, vol. 1. London: Routledge. Pp. 251–77.
Laming, D. (1997). *The Measurement of Sensation*. Oxford: Oxford University Press.
Laming, D. (1999). Prior expectations in cross-modality matching. *Mathematical Social Sciences*, 38, 343–59.
Laming, D. (2004). *Understanding Human Motivation: What Makes People Tick?* Cambridge, MA: Blackwells.
Lamont, N. (1993). Proposal for an independent central bank. Channel Four News, 26 November.
Land, E. H. (1959). Experiments in color vision. *Scientific American*, 200, May, pp. 84–99.
Land, E. H. (1974). Smitty Stevens' test of retinex theory. In *Sensation and Measurement* (ed. H. R. Moskowitz, B. Scharf and J. C. Stevens), pp. 363–8. Dordrecht: Reidel.
Lang, K. (1998). US critic blamed for French wine scams. *Sunday Times*, 21 June, p. 19.
Laurence, J. (1995). Three pill studies showed increased risk of blood clots. *The Times*, 21 October, p. 7.
Laws, K. (2002). *Physics and the art of dance*. New York: Oxford University Press.
Lawson, J. (1960). *Classical Ballet, Its Style and Technique*. London: Adam & Charles Black.
Lawson, M. (1991). Ghost writer. *Independent Magazine*, 16 February, pp. 38–41.
Leathley, A. (1998). Crash pilot may have tried to do too much. *The Times*, 26 February, p. 8.
Letts, Q. (1996). $3 million victory for Joan Collins. *The Times*, 14 February, p. 1.
Lewis, C. (1988). *Antiques Roadshow*, BBC1, 31 January. (Recorded 9 July 1987).
Lichtenstein, S and Slovic, P. (1973). Response-induced reversals of preference in gambling. An extended replication in Las Vegas. *Journal of Experimental Psychology*, 101, 16–20.
Lister, D. (1990). Paperback edition urged as sales exceed 1 million. *Independent*, 5 February, p. 3.
Lister, S. and Norfolk, A. (2002). Kournikova loses match but still wins money game. *The Times*, 25 June, p. 7.
Locke, J. (1690). *An Essay Concerning Humane Understanding*. London: Printed by E. Holt, for T. Basset.
Loudon, H. (1990). When the wrong face fitted. *Independent*, 31 January, p. 13.
Lucas, E. (1991). Catholics block college plan. *Independent*, 19 October, p. 8.
Lynn, M. (1991a) *The Billion Dollar Battle: Merck v Glaxo*. London: Heinemann.
Lynn, M. (1991b). Prudence and the pill pusher. *Independent on Sunday*, 3 November, *Business*, p. 14.
Lyon, G. (1988). Claim for neutral umpires boosted by statistics. *The Times*, 2 November, p. 46.
Macdonald, M. (1995). Government lawyer sells off biography of Fred West. *Independent*, 19 October, p. 1.
Macintyre, D. (1992). Time for labour to talk tactics. *Independent on Sunday*, 18 October, p. 18.
MacGibbon, R. and Hornblad, C. (2002). *Swan Lake*. BBC2, December 25.
MacKinnon, I. (1990). Kidnapper may have taken baby to Australia. *Independent*, 24 January, p. 1.
MacLeod, D. (1992). GCSE examiners blamed for 'erosion of standards'. *Independent*, 4 September, p. 3.
MacQuitty, J. (1983). The fizzical versus pot luck. *The Times*, 3 December, pp. 9, 13.
MacQuitty, J. (1987). 'Wine writers hedged for decades and wouldn't take a position. I do' *The Times*, 5 December, p. 11.
MacQuitty, J. (ed.) (1982). *Which? Wine Guide 1983*. London: Consumer's Association and Hodder & Stoughton.
Maitland-Jones, A. G. (1934). Some disorders of the upper respiratory tract in the infant and young child. *The Lancet*, 3 November, p. 1003–4.
Malpass, R. S. and Devine, P. G. (1981). Eyewitness identification: Lineup instructions and the absence of the offender. *Journal of Applied Psychology*, 66, 482–89.
Malpass, R. S., Devine, P. G. and Bergen, G. T. (Unpbl.). Eyewitness identification: Realism *vs* the laboratory. Unpublished manuscript.

Mann, J. (1993). Gates tells why US let Saddam alone. *The Guardian*, 9 January, p. 11.

Marshall, A. (1992). Dutch cut their losses on the subsidised art mountain. *Independent*, 16 September, p. 10.

Mates, M. (chair) (1991). Preliminary lessons of Operation Granby. 10th report of the Defence Committee. HC287/I. London: HMSO.

Mausner, B. (1953). Studies in social interaction: III. Effect of variation in one partner's prestige on the interaction of observer pairs. *Journal of Applied Psychology*, 37, 391–93.

Mausner, B. (1954a). The effect of one partner's success in a relevant task on the interaction of observer pairs. *Journal of Abnormal and Social Psychology, 49*, 557–60.

Mausner, B. (1954b). The effect of prior reinforcement on the interaction of observer pairs. *Journal of Abnormal and Social Psychology, 49*, 65–8.

Maxwell, S. (1982). *The Princess of Wales*. London: Queen Anne Press.

May, L. (1989). Bakker gets 45 years in prison. *Los Angeles Times*, 25 October, p. A:1.

McCord, F. (1948). The formation of group norms in waking suggestion. *Journal of Social Psychology, 27*, 3-15.

McFarland, R. A. (1953). *Human Factors in Air Transportation.* New York: McGraw-Hill.

McGehee, F. (1937). The reliability of the identification of the human voice. *Journal of General Psychology*, 17, 249–71.

McGehee, F. (1944). An experimental study of voice recognition. *Journal of General Psychology*, 31, 53–65.

McGirk, T. (1985). Fake Dalis flood the market. *Sunday Times*, 17 November, p. 19.

McGirk, T. (1991). Saved from prostitution in a Hindu temple. *Independent*, 6 February, p. 10.

McGrory, D. (1997). Polar icecaps lured skydivers to deaths. *The Times*, 8 December, p. 5.

McKee, G. (1984). *First Tuesday: Aunt Annie's Bomb Factory.* Yorkshire Television, 6 March.

McKee, G. (1986). *First Tuesday: Guildford Time Bomb.* Yorkshire Television, 1 July 1986.

McKee, G. (1987). *First Tuesday: A Case That Won't Go Away.* Yorkshire Television, 3 March.

McKee, G. and Franey, R. (1988). *Time Bomb: The Guildford Four*. London: Bloomsbury.

Meier, N. C. (1928). A measure of art talent. In W. R. Miles and D. Starch (eds), *University of Iowa Studies in Psychology*, No. XII, pp. 184–99. *Psychological Monographs*, 39, Whole no. 178.

Meier, N. C. (1942). *The Meier art tests. I, Art judgment. Examiner's manual.* Iowa City: State University of Iowa.

Mercer, D. (1978). Editorial. *Sunday Times Magazine*, 26 November, p. 24.

Midgley, S. (1994). Dowager gets suspended sentence for racist leaflet. *Independent*, 16 April, p. 7.

Miller, G. A. (1947). Sensitivity to changes in the intensity of white noise and its relation to masking and loudness. *Journal of the Acoustical Society of America*, 19, 609–19.

Miller, R. (1988a). Did Francis Foecke cheat at maths? *Sunday Times Magazine*, 5 June, pp. 20–6.

Miller, R. (1988b). Torn apart in Cleveland. *Sunday Times Magazine*, 29 May, pp. 20–34.

Milligan, S. (1988). Bible belt sex scandal. *Sunday Times*, 21 February, p. 1.

Mills, H. (1988). Long fuse before the explosion. *Independent*, 18 February, p. 1.

Moon, I.A. (1962). *Signposts Aloft*. Whittier, California: Moody Institute of Science.

Moore, T. and St John, J. (1987). Auction houses call a halt to Dali print sales. *Sunday Times*, 12 July, p. 4.

Morgan, A. (1988). Christ film can run uncut. *The Times*, 26 August, p. 1.

Morris, H., Lister, D. and Haeri, S. (1989). Khomeini orders Rushdie's murder. *Independent*, 15 February, p. 1.

Morrot, G., Brochet, F. and Dubourdieu, D. (2001). The color of odors. *Brain and Language, 79*, 309–20.

Murphy, R. J. L. (1978). Reliability of marking in eight GCE examinations. *British Journal of Educational Psychology*, 48, 196–200.

Murphy, R. J. L. (1979). Removing the marks from examination scripts before re-marking them: does it make any difference? *British Journal of Educational Psychology*, 49, 73–8.

Murphy, R. J. L. (1982). A further report of investigations into the reliability of marking of GCE examinations. *British Journal of Educational Psychology*, 52, 58–63.

Murray, D. M. and Wells, G. L. (1982). Does knowledge that a crime was staged affect eyewitness performance? *Journal of Applied Social Psychology*, 12, 42–53.

Nelson, M. (1998). *Cutting Edge: Casino*. Channel Four, 15 February.
News at Ten. (1991a). 16 January.
News at Ten. (1991b). 5 April.
Nisse, J. (1993). High-priced warranties keeping Dixons in profit. *Independent on Sunday*, 17 January, *Business*, p. 1.
Norman, G. (1976). A question of art: Are thirteen Samuel Palmer drawings brilliant modern forgeries? *The Times*, 16 July, p. 12.
Norman, G. (1987). Records tumble at charity sale. *The Times*, 3 July, p. 18.
Norman, G. (1989). Tom Keating fans spend £165 000. *Independent*, 20 December, p. 2.
Norman, G. (1991). Portrait sold to Getty in £4m coup. *Independent*, 30 October, p. 6.
Norman, G. and Lucie-Smith, E. (1990). The good, the bad and the Pollocks. *Independent*, 4 August, p. 44.
Nuki, P. and Corbishley, C. (1998). Shop warranties cost more than goods covered. *Sunday Times*, 8 November, p. 1:4.
Ogley, B. (1987). *In the Wake of the Hurricane*. Westerham: Froglets.
Owen, R. (1998). Vatican doubts visions of Mary at Bosnia shrine. *The Times*, 25 September, p. 22.
Owen, R. (2002). Expert attacks latest tests on Turin Shroud. *The Times*, 21 August, p. 11.
Oxford Dictionary of Quotations (Knowles, E., ed.), (1999). 5th edn. Oxford: Oxford University Press.
Pacheco, J. F. (ed.) (1983). *The Legacy of George Mason*. Cranbury, NJ: Associated University Presses.
Parker, R. (1987). *The Wine Buyer's Guide*. London: Dorling Kindersley.
Peek, L. (2001). Hingis sues over shoes that 'hurt feet'. *The Times*, 13 June, p. 9.
Pelikan, J. J. (1989). Roman Catholicism (part). *Encyclopaedia Britannica*, 15th edn, vol. 26, pp. 931–9.
Perpetual (1994). *Monthly Savings Plan*. Henley-on-Thames: Perpetual Unit Trust Management Ltd.
Peterson, W. W., Birdsall, T. G., and Fox, W. C. (1954). The theory of signal detectability. *Transactions of the IRE Professional Group on Information Theory*, PGIT2-4, 171–212.
Pettifer, J. and Bradley, R. (1990). *Missionaries*. London: BBC Books.
Pfaffmann, C., Bartoshuk, L. M. and McBurney, D. H. (1971). Taste psychophysics. In L. M. Beidler (ed.), *Handbook of Sensory Physiology*, vol. IV. *Chemical Senses*, Part 2, *Taste*. Berlin: Springer-Verlag. Pp. 75–101.
PHS (1984). Diary: Meritocratic. *The Times*, 3 October, p. 14.
Piaget, J. and Inhelder, B. (1956). *The Child's Conception of Space*. Trans. F .J. Langdon and J. L. Lunzer. London: Routledge & Kegan Paul.
Piaget, J. and Inhelder, B. (1969). *The Psychology of the Child*. Trans. H. Weaver. London: Routledge & Kegan Paul.
Pierce, A. (2002). Paint firm sees red over Dulux copying. *The Times*, 24 April, p. 7.
Pile, S. (1988). *The Return of Heroic Failures*. London: Secker and Warburg.
Pollack, I. (1952). The information of elementary auditory displays. *Journal of the Acoustical Society of America*, 24, 745–9.
Pollack, I. (1953). The information of elementary auditory displays. II. *Journal of the Acoustical Society of America*, 25, 765–9.
Porteous, T. (1991). 'Infidel' sheep anger Algerians. *Independent*, 17 June, p. 12.
Poulton, E.C. (1989). *Bias in Quantifying Judgments*. Hove, UK: Erlbaum.
Qualifications and Curriculum Authority (2001). Report on monitoring enquiries and appeals upon results. Website (www.qca.org.uk/rs/statistics/enq_appeals.asp), 27 March.
Randolph, E. (1936). The revolutionary history of Virginia, 1774–1782. *The Virginia Magazine of History and Biography*, XLIV, January, p. 45.
Rayment, T., Davison, J. and Hodgkinson, N. (1987). Sent away for life. *Sunday Times*, 12 April, p. 25.
Regina v. Patrick Armstrong, Carole Margaret Richardson, Paul Michael Hill, and Gerard Patrick Conlon. (1977). London: Court of Appeal, Criminal Division, 28 October.
Regina v. The Accused. (1987). Birmingham: The Crown Court, 5 March.
Rendall, J. (1990). Daddy's girl and the cool millions. *Independent on Sunday*, 4 March, p. 23.
Renton, A. (1991). Dead author in court-room thriller. *Independent*, 24 September, p. 1.
Reynolds, G. S. and Stevens, S. S. (1960). Binaural summation of loudness. *Journal of the Acoustical Society of America*, 32, 1337–44.

Rich, F. (1986). Stage: 'Atkinson at the Atkinson'. *The New York Times*, 15 October, p. C19.
Risset, J. C. (1969). Pitch control and pitch paradoxes demonstrated with computer-synthesised sounds. *Journal of the Acoustical Society of America*, 46, 88.
Rizi, F. (1683). *Auto de fe de 1680*. Madrid: Museo del Prado.
Robinson, D. (1988). Son of Man. (Review of *The Last Temptation of Christ*). *The Times*, 8 September, p. 16.
Robinson, J. (1986). A nose for a winner. *Sunday Times Magazine*, 10 August, p.42–3.
Rogers, S., Kaufman, E. L., Reese, T. W. and Volkmann, J. (1947). Accuracy, variability and speed of adjusting an indicator to a required bearing. South Hadley, MA: Mount Holyoke College.
Ronay, E. (1987). De-canting the tasters' dogma. *Sunday Times*, 13 December, p. 48.
Rose, A. (1989). The bubbly bottles are close to bursting. *Independent*, 2 September, p. 33.
Rose, A. (1991). Let them drink sparkling wine. *Independent*, 7 December, p. 37.
Rosenhan, D. L. (1973). On being sane in insane places. *Science*, 179, 250–58.
Ross, C. (1979). Rejected. *New West*, 12 February, pp. 39–43.
Ross, C. (1980). Editor's choice: none of the above. *Los Angeles Times*, 17 February, *The Book Review*, p. 3.
Rowley, R. R. and Studebaker, G. A. (1969). Monaural loudness-intensity relationships for a 1000-Hz tone. *Journal of the Acoustical Society of America*, 45, 1186–92.
Roy, A. (1988). Snap decisions earn a pretty export penny. *Sunday Times*, 6 March, p. A:14.
Roy, A. and Fernand, D. (1989). Satanic curses. *Sunday Times*, 19 February, pp. A:15–17.
Ruddock, M. (1987). Personal submission to the Kimberley Carlile inquiry. Unpublished.
Ruddock, M. (1998). Yes, and but, and then again, maybe. In R. Davies (ed.), *Stress in Social Work*. London: Jessica Kingsley. Pp. 93–100.
Rushdie, S. (1988). *The Satanic Verses*. London: Viking.
Sargent, A. (1992). Letter, 'Blasphemy' in broadcasting. *Independent*, 13 October, p. 20.
Sauvageot, F. and Chapon, M. (1983). La couleur d'un vin (blanc ou rouge) peut-elle être identifée sans l'aide de l'oeil? *Les Cahiers de l'ENS. BANA*, 4, 107–15.
Scott, G. R. (1940). *The History of Torture throughout the Ages*. London: T. Werner Laurie.
Segrave, B. (1971). *The Most Powerful Briton in America*. ATV, 25 May.
Sellars, J. (1974). *Samuel Palmer*. London: Academy Editions.
Seton, C. (1987). Judge attacks rape trial 'system'. *The Times*, 7 March, p. 3.
Shepard, R. N. (1964). Circularity in judgments of relative pitch. *Journal of the Acoustical Society of America*, 36, 2346-53.
Sherif, M. (1935). A study of some social factors in perception. *Archives of Psychology*, 187.
Sherif, M. (1936). *The Psychology of Social Norms*. New York: Harper.
Sherif, M. (1937). An experimental approach to the study of attitudes. *Sociometry*, 1, 90–8.
Shulman, A. (1993). Letter, Controversy in Vogue. *Independent*, 27 May, p. 27.
Simpson, C. (1976). The Tate drops a costly brick. *Sunday Times*, 15 February, p. 53.
Sinha, D. (1952). An experimental study of a social factor in perception: The influence of an arbitrary group-standard. *Patna University Journal*, Jan–Apr, pp. 7–16.
Sobel, D. (1995). *Longitude*. New York: Walker.
Sox, D. H. (1988). How an age of mystery ended. *The Times*, 15 October, p. 36.
Spencer, J. (1989). A case of prosecution by Christians only. *Independent*, 14 April, p. 15.
Starkey, M. L. (1952). *The Devil in Massachusetts*. London: Robert Hale.
Stevens, S. S. (1956). The direct estimation of sensory magnitudes – loudness. *American Journal of Psychology*, 69, 1–25.
Stevens, S. S. (1975). *Psychophysics: Introduction to its Perceptual, Neural, and Social Prospects*, (ed. G. Stevens). New York: Wiley.
Stevens, S. S. and Greenbaum, H. B. (1966). Regression effect in psychophysical judgment. *Perception & Psychophysics*, 1, 439–46.
Stevens, S. S. and Guirao, M. (1962). Loudness, reciprocality, and partition scales. *Journal of the Acoustical Society of America*, 34, 1466–71.
Strafford, P. (1976). Putting the critic in his place. *The Times*, 11 October, p. 14.
Sullivan, K. (1991). Rushdie translator stabbed to death. *The Guardian*, 13 July, p. 10.

Index

(Substantive subjects are in roman type, illustrative examples in italics. Page numbers in bold refer to figures or tables, italic numbers to the reference list)